AMERICAN DREAMERS

Charmian and Jack London

CLARICE STASZ

ST. MARTIN'S PRESS ♦ NEW YORK

AMERICAN DREAMERS: CHARMIAN AND JACK LONDON. Copyright © 1988 by Clarice Stasz. All rights reserved. Printed in the United States of America. No part of this book may be used or reproduced in any manner whatsoever without written permission except in the case of brief quotations embodied in critical articles or reviews. For information, address St. Martin's Press, 175 Fifth Avenue, New York, N.Y. 10010

Design by Glen M. Edelstein

Library of Congress Cataloging-in-Publication Data

Stasz, Clarice.
  American dreamers : the story of Charmian and Jack London /
Clarice Stasz.
    p. cm.
  ISBN 0-312-02160-7
  1. London, Jack, 1876-1916—Biography—Marriage..2. London, Charmian—Marriage. 3. Novelists, American—20th century—Biography—Marriage. 4. Wives—United States—Biography.
  I. Title.
PS3523.O46Z89 1988
818′.5209—dc19   88-11494
[B]   CIP

First Edition
10 9 8 7 6 5 4 3 2 1

To Kendra

CONTENTS

PART III.
FROM WILDERNESS
TO REDEMPTION

PREFACE

It was Charmian who first drew my attention.

I had moved to northern California from Baltimore, to a house looking out toward Sonoma Mountain, a mud volcano forming the western ridge of the Valley of the Moon. There, a two-mile narrow drive from the hamlet of Glen Ellen, sat the Jack London State Historic Park, which consisted then of the House of Happy Walls, Charmian's widowhood home turned museum, Jack's grave, and the ruins of Wolf House, their dream home destroyed by fire.

My visit was inspired by a discussion with a friend about Nancy Milford's extraordinary biography of Zelda Fitzgerald. This was the early seventies, when the heat of the women's movement propelled us to seek women lost to history. *Zelda* touched us, for it laid out so neatly what we had known to be true, that women's talents often suffered in the service of their spouses' creativity. We wondered how many other gifted women married to artistic men had submerged their needs for self-expression in self-destructive ways. My friend urged me to visit the park and look at the pictures of the author's wife, who had written *A Woman among the Headhunters*.

All I knew about Jack London was that he had written a famous dog story, *The Call of the Wild*, which I had never read. On the basis of no information, I had classified him with certain other boorish male literary personalities and suspected he had been a horrible husband. This nasty theory sent me rushing to the state park. Upon approaching the House of Happy Walls, shrouded in the gnarled branches of madrona and oak, I sensed a mystery lay inside. The interior, with its bare wood floors and touches of aquamarine paint, was much lighter in feeling than the dark and rough volcanic rock of the exterior. The ranger pointed out a hidden staircase and a secret viewing door. The owner of the home clearly had not had a simple and accessible personality.

The exhibits surprised me further. I had been unaware of London's activities in socialism and agriculture, his war correspondence, as well as the prolific literary output of fifty-three books. What most caught my attention, however, was a glass case at the top of a stairwell, an exhibit easy to miss in passing from the first floor to the second. In it was a photograph of Charmian, dressed in a muslin pants outfit and floppy cloth hat, surrounded by a group of naked Solomon Island women. A small pistol perched upon her left hip; the same pistol lay near the photograph in the case. I was to find out later that this photograph disturbs many viewers. (Indeed, in 1911 Jack had great difficulty convincing the Macmillan Publishing Company to override its typesetters, who wished it cut from his *Cruise of the Snark.*)

For me, here was a promise of a Spouse of a Famous Man who maintained her integrity, a story different from those we were used to reading.

I learned that Charmian had written not one, but two journals of their venture through the South Seas, and I immediately read both. The journals convinced me of my initial impressions. When I began reading the biographies of Jack, however, I was confronted with a very different woman. Irving Stone, author of the most famous of these books, *Sailor on Horseback,* called Charmian "petulant" and "childish," a burden to Jack. This picture was not consistent with the woman who wrote the journals I had just read, the only female crew member on the Pacific crossing, who charmed both the upper-class Hawaiians and Tahitian natives with ease, and who refused to disguise herself as a man in order to see a prizefight in Australia.

The more I explored Jack's personality as expressed in his literary work, the more puzzled I was over his treatment by both critics and biographers. It seemed that only certain facets of his personality were explored—his alcoholism, his attraction to brutality, his manic activities—all those characteristics that shape the image of the macho American writer. Worse, these commentators coldly suggested he deserved the terrible tragedies that befell him, tragedies that were beyond his control. Yet his letters and stories revealed to me a man of sweeping sensitivities: to the common people, to language, to nature. He was a captive of beauty, with an extraordinary sense of the infinite romance and mystery of life. He was also madly in love with Charmian.

Analogies to the Fitzgeralds grew stronger. Like Zelda, Charmian was an aspiring writer. Like Scott, Jack struggled with an addiction to alcohol and borrowed from his wife's life for his novels. Jack also shared Scott's desire to rise in social class, to chase the American dream as far as he could. Charmian shared Zelda's ostentation, rebelliousness, and ability to enchant people who expected to dislike her.

At that point I approached Irving Shepard, London's grandnephew and executor of the literary estate, for permission to prepare a biography of Charmian. He granted me access to all materials, a privilege few other scholars had been granted, in part because of the irresponsibility of some of the early writers. It was a sign of Mr. Shepard's cautiousness, though, that he held back telling me of the existence of her forty years' worth of unpublished diaries until I was well into the work!

It is good I was so naive about the Londons, for I would never have attempted the project. Like the Fitzgeralds, the pair were inveterate self-historians. They kept elephantine scrapbooks of clippings, typed letters in multiple copies, requested handwritten letters be returned, and filed all letters received. An adept photographer, Charmian kept a running pictorial documentary of their wanderings, along with her daily diary entries. Both left notes for autobiographical novels. Eventually I completed a manuscript on Charmian's life, which I entitled *Mate-Woman,* one of Jack's favorite names for her. My story lacked a focus, however, and subsequent attempts to improve it failed. One course remained—to abandon the work.

I went on to write a book on the underside of the American dream, a study of contemporary America, and found that it oddly tied in with my research on the Londons. That work illuminated how the Londons fit into the social history of their time, how they responded to the culture and self-consciously used their celebrity to shape that culture.

Now the differences from the Fitzgeralds really stood out.

While both couples saw themselves as having a place in history, only Scott and Zelda accomplished that goal in the United States. But the irony is how much more of a real impact the Londons made in shaping our culture. In the final analysis, Scott Fitzgerald left a few elegant writings and, with Zelda, fed a later generation's nostalgic longings for a brief period in our history when American expatriates were able to brew enrapturing tales. As children of the middle class, they followed a path that is still appealing to those from the urban eastern shores, a return to a European Eden, which is ultimately a step back into an illusion.

Yet the Londons, who left permanent marks on American attitudes and values, have little recognition today. Children of pioneers, their search for the American dream was more wide-ranging, directed not toward returning to the past but toward exploring the frontier, whether it be South Sea isles, ecological ranching methods in the west, or the movies made in Hollywood. They were always pushing into new territories and broadcasting their ventures in the process, sharing their dreams through newspapers and books read around the country. Jack London was one of the most popular men of his time, noted for much more than his writings, because he so exemplified the self-made American man and offered hope to others who had similar aspirations.

Their explorations included human relations as well as physical feats. Quite against the norms of the day, they conceived of marriage as a partnership of "dearest mates." They impressed observers with this rare blend and inspired others to reexamine the old models. Achieving their ideal was a different matter, but their attempts and determination are still inspiring now, almost a century later.

Indeed, the Londons were so venturesome that it is difficult to limn a single portrait of the pair. Their fostering of invented lives, to borrow James Mellow's term for the Fitzgeralds, makes a search for truth an elusive process. Charmian and Jack were skillful actors who knew how to please an audience. It was no problem for Jack to write one man that he did not like to hunt and then just days later write another about how hunting was one of his three favorite breaks from writing. Charmian could tell a reporter she did not mind Jack's smoking and then wail in her diary over his blasted cigarettes. They held up mirrors to the world, enchanting others while hiding their private selves.

This feigning and pretending had its conscious, manipulative side, particularly in the marketing of London's books. But it was often innocently presented, like a child playing a role to please an honored guest or feared teacher. Indeed, a hallmark of the Londons was their youthful exuberance as they traveled on their various journeys. They were not afraid to be beginners and maintained this openness in spite of tragic consequences and warnings of danger. Jack called Charmian "the kid who never grew up," meaning it as a compliment, an admirable quality reflecting his own boyishness.

Buoyant and hopeful, they sought a perfect existence in many different settings. When one path led to failure, they took up another. The theme of their lives was like that of many of us today, innocents seeking paradise.

It is easy to uphold the Londons as an example of the American dream gone wrong. What is difficult to understand is why this man and woman so desperately grasped the dream, where their hunger came from, and just how their journey changed them. Sorting out the truths of their lives from the myths reveals that they found the journey worth the price they were forced to pay. They discovered that the pursuit of material desires led to greater treasure, maturity, and self-understanding. Among the last of the great nineteenth-century Romantic adventurers, the lives of Charmian and Jack London force us to reflect upon our own pursuit of the dream almost a century later.

PART I
AN
ELUSIVE
EDEN

If I could joy in aught, sweet
   interchange
Of hill and valley, rivers, woods and
   plains,
Now land, now sea, and shores with
   forest crowned,
Rocks, dens, and caves; but I in none
   of these
Find place or refuge; and the more I
   see
Pleasures about me, so much more I
   feel
Torment within me, as from the
   hateful siege
Of contraries

John Milton
Paradise Lost

PROLOGUE

On the evening of Saturday, November 19, 1905, the country's best-known young writer stood quietly in the shadows of a chilly railway platform in downtown Chicago. Though barely five foot seven, the man's broad chest helped give the impression of stature and power. The deep laugh lines beside his eyes and down his cheeks suggested a warm and friendly nature. His suit was of well-cut fabric in the latest style, his shoes polished to a high sheen. Just one small discrepancy in his affluent appearance hinted that he was not just another businessman: the soft flannel shirt with its loosely draped collar. That tiny deviation from the fashionable man's attire of the day might cause a viewer to question the propriety of the wearer. A banker or other successful businessman wore stiff

removable collars about his neck, evidence that he was har-
nessed to his work.

Jack London needed no such proof. The frequent attachment of his name to stories in such diverse magazines as *The
Atlantic Monthly, The Youth's Companion, Cosmopolitan,* and *Frank
Leslie's Popular Monthly* demonstrated his commitment to the
turn-of-the-century demand that a man must "Work, work
whether you want to or not."[1] Furthermore, his adventures as
seaman on a sealer, railroad tramp, Yukon gold seeker, and war
correspondent in Korea marked him as the ideal man. As
Theodore Roosevelt extolled to the country, the most laudable
male "does not shrink from danger, from hardship, or from
bitter toil."[2]

Though his unstarched shirt marked him as unconventional,
even bohemian, tonight Jack London was preparing for that
most bourgeois of acts, marriage. He was going to do right by
the woman he had lived with for eight months to protect her
reputation. Indeed, he was so driven to follow the precepts of
respectable society that he had canceled his original plans to
marry his awaiting lover, Charmian Kittredge, in Iowa at the
end of the month. Instead, when he learned that his divorce
was final, he had wired her to catch the next train for a wedding
in Illinois.

Weary from his own three-hundred-mile journey, Jack found
himself with a long wait; Charmian's train was three hours
behind schedule. An impatient man, with only cigarettes to
occupy him, he could have felt nothing but relief and joy when
the light of the approaching engine washed over the station.
Charmian, the woman who had made this most materialist of
men believe in love, would soon be in his arms.

Though exhausted from the sudden and unexpected journey, the tiny woman descended from the stairs to her waiting
lover's arms with a light and perky step. It was her nature to
overlook discomfort and present the world with a cheerful,
vibrant demeanor.

She too was dressed with style and taste, in a dark gabardine
traveling suit, custom tailored to show off her Gibson-girl figure. Though petite, even fragile in appearance, her exemplary
posture and chestnut tan hinted that she enjoyed physical activity. Although her hat was fussy, her undergarments silk and

belaced by her own meticulous handwork, she was not a typical gentle lady of the day. Bonds with conventional women, Jack London had sorely learned, fit him like the starched collars he detested. Charmian had been quick to obey his command that she appear in Chicago, but both knew she had come out of choice, not submission. She was his Mate-woman, his "twin brother," his comrade in hardship and adventure, not a domestic and matronly caretaker.

Her late arrival left them no time for a lingering reunion. They needed a special license to marry on Sunday, and London was in no mood to wait a day until the city offices were open. As a favorite of the powerful publisher, William Randolph Hearst, he was able to call upon the *Chicago American* city editor to rout a clerk from bed to meet them at city hall near midnight to write out the official permit. An elevated train took them to the offices of Notary Public J. J. Grant, who married them using Charmian's late mother's wedding ring as the symbol of their vows.

Arriving at last at their honeymoon hotel, the Victoria, Charmian slipped upstairs while Jack scrawled "Mrs. Jack London" below his own name on the register. Before he could obtain his key, three newspapermen waylaid him with questions about his lecture tour and books. While responding, Jack eyed a fourth reporter looking over the register and made a quick escape to his room to join his bride.

The subsequent hours were a fitting introduction to the life Charmian would share with her celebrity husband. Reporters banged on the door, besieging the couple for interviews. Notes, cards, and telegrams slid under the door and flew over the transom. Phone calls added to the din. London resisted all entreaties and remained faithful to his promise to give the Hearst papers the scoop. Charmian noted in her diary that the night had been made "hideous by reporters," yet added "Jack adorable—my perfect bridegroom and lover at last."

As they always will, the reporters had the final word. Lacking facts, they made them up. The stories were littered with untruths: Charmian was blond, both were twenty-seven, she had traveled two thousand miles to meet him, he had met her after divorcing his first wife. In fact, Charmian had brown hair, was five years older than her twenty-nine-year-old husband, and had been his mistress for two years. The national press seemed more interested in using the Londons as the latest exemplars of true love than in telling the messy truth.

In fact, this cosmetic version of events was shocking enough to many readers because of its reference to the divorce. Earlier in the month club women of Bible Belt Kansas had canceled lecture dates with London "because of his violation of the sanctity of the marriage vow."[3] The Buffalo press concurred: "Home ties are too sacred a thing to be so lightly broken as they were in the case of the Western novelist."[4] Following the wedding, the provinces even more hotly condemned the couple. One called Charmian as "ugly as a mud fence" and Jack a "vile wretch," who, if he fell overboard from his boat, would present no loss.[5]

Moral commentary was fueled further by a journalistic twist to the facts that produced front-page headlines for several days. This invention was perpetrated by reporters jealous of Jack's loyalty to Hearst. Competing papers shouted "Jack London Marriage Invalid" on the basis of a recent Illinois law forbidding remarriage less than a year after the granting of a divorce decree. The claim was not a serious one, because legal authorities quickly pronounced the marriage valid. Still, libraries in Pennsylvania and Connecticut ordered London's books off the shelves, and ministers warned their congregations about the "socialist apostle of immorality."

Jack and Charmian could not be more delighted. They clipped and saved the stories and made jokes about them. As a writer trained in journalism, London understood its value was not in telling the truth but in purveying images to the public. He was also wise enough about human nature to know that those same women in the Bible Belt would be even more anxious to read his stories as a result of the public censure. His response was to give the reporters more material to use on the front page yet another day. "If my marriage is not legal in Illinois, I shall remarry my wife in every state in the Union!" he valiantly proclaimed.

While the impulsive marriage was not designed as a publicity stunt, Jack London knew an opportunity when he saw one. Even though he would agree with his critics about the sanctity of marriage, he allowed himself to be used as a focus for moral commentary. London did not care that he was being held up to the world as a scoundrel; he and Charmian were so convinced of their having a great and unique love that they believed themselves to be above the masses, indeed, that they had a duty to show the masses what a man-woman relationship should be.

The wonder is they were not very wrong in their conviction: they *were* a special couple.

I

BORN TO
SORROW

Alone, by night, a little child,
In place so silent and so wild—
Has he no friend, no loving mother
    man?

—*Samuel Taylor Coleridge*

The real significance of weddings is not for the bride and groom, who have already made a commitment to one another through their courtship, but for the relatives. Marriage binds two lines of strangers, the ceremony providing a bridge for all the new relationships that result. Interestingly, Charmian and Jack excluded their families from their wedding. (Their witnesses were the city editor from the *Chicago American* and Manyoungi, Jack's Korean valet.)

Charmian's parents were both dead, but she had a populous array of relations in Maine and California. Jack's mother lived in Oakland, as did two of his stepsisters. Yet each had grown up feeling alone in the world, unconnected to their relatives. It was this sense of isolation that permitted each to ignore differences in age, education, and social class and reach out to the other. It was this feeling of solitary individuality that hinted at a similarity more profound than shared hobbies or interests, that of a childhood of emotional starvation.

The mistreatment in their early years led them as adults to disguise their histories. Early in his career, Jack developed a set of stories designed to present his youth to others as he wished it to be known. These tales were told so often that he came to believe them and, in turn, convincingly distracted later researchers from examining the core of his past. Charmian simply avoided speaking of her youth, except for a few brief references to her cavalry officer father and sweet poet mother.

The heart of their distortion was denial. No child wants to believe he or she is unloved, yet that was the horrible secret Charmian and Jack each hid within.

Thanks to her mother, Dayelle Wiley, the record of Charmian's neglect is readily apparent in the spidery hand of the journals and letters she wrote before and during her marriage to Willard Kittredge. Daisy, as she preferred to be called, was born in a log cabin with a twin brother on September 9, 1847, on a farm near Oshkosh, Wisconsin. As the oldest girl, she was sent to school with the expectation that she in turn would teach the four sisters and brothers who followed her in the family.

Judging by Daisy's earliest surviving notebooks from her early adolescence, the education was a success. She grew enamored of poetic forms and wrote sentimental verse about the soldiers in the Civil War battles she read of in the papers. She also composed long stories and novellas that centered on beautiful young women, dashing cavaliers, mansions and servants, duels and dances. The settings reflected an earlier Europe, if not a European fantasy. Appropriately, some were written in French or German.

Unfortunately, Daisy was unable to distinguish her romantic imaginings from the realities of life in pioneer America. During the war the Wiley family had profited by selling its farm and running a boardinghouse in Racine. A month after Daisy recorded the taking of Richmond, a night made resplendent with "bonfires brightly burning, starry banners floating, and cannons booming," the Wiley family packed its household goods into wagons and joined a train of fellow pioneers on a trek through the Platte River valley to Salt Lake City. There, Daisy's illusions brought her tragedy.

Salt Lake City was a Mormon settlement, and Daisy and her younger sister Tissie immediately set out to start the first "Gentile" school in the region. Her interest in teaching did not last long, however, nor did the family feel welcome in the community. Less than a year later, on October 6, 1866, Daisy married Captain Willard Kittredge, provost marshall with the local cavalry, and said farewell to her beloved family, who left immediately after the ceremony for the more receptive lands of southern California.

Few facts come from Willard Kittredge himself, only a black pocket diary used as a notebook during his last four years of life. There he recorded his birth in 1829, which made him thirty-seven to Daisy's nineteen years of age at the time of marriage. He also penciled in his service dates, noting that he had been with the 41st Infantry in Oregon until 1859 and soon after joined the First California Volunteers, which sent him to Salt Lake. Nothing he left explains why this young man left a prosperous and close-knit clan on the shores of Maine to spend his life fighting in the western wilderness.

If Kitt, as he called himself, remains an enigma, Daisy made permanent an unbecoming portrait of her husband.

It is easy to see why they would be attracted to one another. She was a pert, bright, sociable woman blessed with one of the most alluring physical characteristics of the day, lush, long, curly black hair. (In later years Charmian hinted of a Spanish sea captain in Daisy's family tree.) In his officer's dress—for surely they met at a military dance—Kitt must have resembled the dream lovers of her romances.

The honeymoon was brief. Daisy whined continually in letters to her sister Netta.[1] Her husband was crude in language, using the word "thar." He was a "Careless Dog"; he wearied her with the need to remind him constantly to comb his hair and neaten himself. He was a "home-dog" who would not go out without her. He was "blind as a bat." His greatest sin was planning to go out in public with a torn glove. Please, she requested of her relatives, direct her mail to "Daisy Wylie Kittredge" and "leave off the Mrs. I won't let any friends call me 'Mrs. Kittredge' that I can help." She also proceeded to starve herself and enjoyed worrying him with her shrinking figure.

Her reports were not all negative. At times she would tease Netta about how handsome Kitt was, how Netta would fall for him too. And in December she confessed that "Captain Kittredge is almost as much of a lover as ever, Nettie, with the exception of the 'blissful sighs' of pain which are by no means as frequent as formerly."[2]

Netta and the rest of the Wileys were not surprised by Daisy's attitude—they had wondered if she were even capable of loving a man. Her idealism and reserve gave her aristocratic airs; the vulgar and commonplace were not part of her world. Others admired her intelligence and ethics, yet recognized that she was in a real sense disconnected from life around her, a separation that left her dark and somber in mood. They would have understood her writing on her twentieth birthday:

> I have just been making an anxious inspection of my physiognomy in the glass for the purpose of discovering any incipient crowsfeet. . . . There is a family tradition that I was once a tolerably good-looking baby, but there is no evidence of it extent. . . . Perhaps it is this beauty of decay that makes it sadder to contemplate; we feel such an indescribable loneliness creep over us when the trees and flowers put on their loveliest robes to die.[3]

Daisy's maudlin tone and preoccupation with death echoed sentiments frequently expressed in the diaries of other pioneer women like herself. The move west freed men from the restraints of civilization and provided immediate challenges to test their bravery, strength, and other masculine virtues. For women, it burdened their yokes, in that it was their duty to secure domesticity in a rough and difficult environment. Sensitive and perceptive women raised to be more genteel were imprisoned by the cruel demands of the new homesteads.

Understandably, the relationship foundered. Kitt mustered out of the service and irritated Daisy further by not seeking employment as quickly as she wished. They separated, and Daisy went alone on the rough Western wagon route, one of the last pioneers to travel this way, across the deserts and over the Sierras through Truckee, finally down the central valleys to her family in Ventura County, California. There, Daisy moved into the tent compound on a ranch the family owned in San Buenaventura, where she settled in to study German and other courses to qualify herself as a schoolteacher.

In late 1867, Kitt arrived from Oregon in a tattered state. In spite of her family's urgings, Daisy refused to join him. Instead, she and sister Tissie took positions with schools in the Los Angeles area. Both soon suffered nervous collapses. On her twenty-first birthday, Daisy pulled seven gray hairs from her head. On her twenty-second, she stood "on the edge of my departing girlhood" to face "the bleak, stern realities of my condition."[4]

Though too depressed to return to teaching, Daisy continued to educate her younger siblings and enjoy a full round of entertainment. Her journals increasingly resembled her early stories, with their detailed descriptions of encounters and conversations between young men and women; this time, however, she was always the heroine. Popular magazines of the day, such as *Godey's Lady's Book*, welcomed her poetry, for it fit the national ideal of womanhood so well.

By 1871 she had reunited with Kitt, who was owner of a hotel serving railroad workers. One would not guess from her writings then that she was pregnant. Her first letter following Clara Charmian's birth on November 27, 1871 complained of Kitt's incessant pipe smoking and avoidance of her. This behavior, she said "proves how uncalled for and superfluous it is for a girl to suffer a pang of unhappiness for any lover who professes to be dying for her. As a wife she will find out when she has been deceived it is then, only, that her duty compels her to bear all patiently." She wrote nothing about her new child, who was soon put in the care of Daisy's sister Netta.

Kitt went to Northern California to continue managing a hotel, and when Charmian was one-and-a-half Daisy was well enough to bring her to San Francisco. There they lived in a home dubbed the "House of Pleasure," but for Daisy dreams had "banished, leaving neither despair nor happiness, only a quiet apathy."[5]

When Charmian was two, the family had a brief glimpse of happiness. They moved to Petaluma, a town forty miles north of San Francisco, where they leased the best hotel in town, the

American. The local paper predicted success for the venture, praising Kitt as "one of the few good men who knows how to keep a hotel."[6] While Kitt ran the bar and billiard room, Daisy oversaw the housekeeping. Although aided by servants, she felt she had the worse end of the venture and begrudged his more convivial work. For the most part, though, she enjoyed dressing the family up to show themselves off to the town and found comfort in the Congregationalist services. She was stable enough emotionally to take into the household her sister Tissie, who had suffered another nervous collapse.

Significantly, few of Daisy's numerous letters mentioned Charmian. Kitt had become "the most affectionate of papas," and Charmian responded in kind, begging to crawl into bed with him in the morning and covering him with hugs and kisses. Daisy most frequently described Charmian as a "little mischief."

On a bright Sunday morning in June, one J. Wyatt, a local "hoodlum," dashed Daisy's happiness when he maliciously struck a match to the hay bails at the American Stables down the street from the hotel.[7] Flames fanned by the strong west winds common during that time of year whipped through adjoining establishments. It was the biggest fire Petaluma had seen in years. While the volunteer fire company, 172 strong at the time, worked with speed, lack of water and defective hoses hampered their efforts to quell the blaze. When it became apparent that the landmark hotel could not be saved, local merchants and townspeople stripped the interior of its furnishings and decor. Charmian, sick at the time, was carried out in someone's arms.

Kitt's loss was not beyond repair. The hotel owner was fully insured and planned immediate reconstruction. The furnishings were also insured. His out-of-pocket loss, most likely in liquor, food, and miscellany, was no more than one thousand dollars. Daisy had five hundred dollars of her own money that she kept to herself rather than offer toward restocking the business, so the household must have been solvent. Characteristically, she thought only of the great inconvenience forced upon her by having to move to what she considered a backwater town, Santa Rosa, and then dug in her heels when Kitt suggested they resettle there.

Kitt's refusal to stay in Petaluma, the first place where Daisy felt at home since leaving Wisconsin, sent her into emotional collapse. Netta once again took care of the child, until her own marriage in 1876 to Roscoe Eames. Kitt returned to San Fernando to build and run hotels, but the family was seldom together. After Daisy contracted "quick consumption," she grew preoccupied with the Bible and addicted to the legal narcotic drugs of the day. Charmian was passed from one family member to another. On October 27, 1877, just short of Charmian's sixth birthday, Kitt wired Roscoe Eames, newly settled in Oakland with Netta: "Daisy died at eight o'clock last evening."

Charmian was sent back to live with her father at his current hotel. One evening her aunt Tissie arrived to find her sitting on the bar surrounded by laughing, rough men. That news led the Wiley clan to pressure Kitt to allow the child to live with Netta. One of Charmian's most vivid memories was of traveling alone by train, dressed in a black ruffled cashmere morning dress, her long hair crimped in black ribbons. She was led to her own room that night and felt for the first time the security of being in a permanent home.

One would think that, after all the instability she had endured, Charmian would find solace in life with an aunt who had been a frequent caretaker since birth. It was not to be.

Netta Wiley Eames possessed most of the traits that had left Daisy incapable of intimacy, the most notable being an unrelenting self-centeredness. Netta too was a striking woman, with brilliant violet eyes, oval face, and porcelain complexion, and she used her charms for her favorite activity, flirting with men. She seemed to enjoy the chase more than the commitment and had broken off her engagement to Eames several times before finally marrying him. Even after the marriage, she remained aligned with Victoria Woodhull, the heralder of free love. Whereas Daisy grew obsessed at times with various versions of patriotism and Christianity, Netta became a true believer in the practices of spiritualism and vegetarianism sweeping the region. Emotionally stronger than her deceased sister, she was self-confident and commanding. She used her great intelligence with cunning and was always able to twist logic to support her point of view. In a rare moment of perceptive self-analysis, she once said, "I would have made a good Inquisitionist. I cannot let go. I must convince people of what I see they ought to do for the good of their souls, for their salvation here and hereafter. I know I am fanatical. But I cannot help it."[8]

Charmian became enthralled.

The seduction was subtle, and as is in the case with many families in which parental bewitchment occurs, much appeared normal, even admirable, on the surface. The young girl had her own well-furnished room in a comfortable house in a respectable neighborhood of Oakland, then the commercial center of California. She was given books and art supplies, taught to play the organ and the piano, dressed fashionably, and fed well. Physically, Charmian's life with Netta was a vast improvement over hotel life, where the main source of entertainment had been a rough wooden cellar door treated as a slide, and dollhouse furniture formed from playing cards.

The child welcomed these benefits and appreciated her aunt and uncle's largesse. The advantages did not come without trade-offs, however, and what Charmian lacked haunted her throughout her life. Into her seventies, when she was still making notes for her never-published autobiography, her copious remarks on her childhood remained skewed, with large blanks where an adult with a normal childhood would have favorite reminiscences.[9] To the end of her life, she seemed puzzled and even guilty over her early years.

Most notable is the total absence of reference to playmates; Netta kept Charmian a virtual prisoner in the house. Instead of sending her to one of the area's many private schools, which contributed to the city's reputation as the Athens of the Pacific, she taught the girl at home, as she herself had been taught by Daisy. During the day, she gave lessons in literature, drawing, and geography, subjects the Wiley family knew best. In the evenings, Netta would play music or invite friends over, perhaps for seances, which frightened the youngster, who had some of her mother's nervousness.

She did participate in the usual children's social activities, yet no names appear in her reminiscences, no stories of secrets shared and enjoyed with one girl or another. There was not one special friend.

Also missing from Charmian's notes is reference to Roscoe Eames, whom one would have expected to play the role of foster father. Her only notable comment was that his whiskers reeked of tobacco and she could not stand to have him kiss her. Roscoe was a clever, if eccentric man, a graduate of San Jose State Normal School who invented a shorthand system and taught secretarial courses, as well as captained a commuting ferry. His absence from her childhood reminiscences remains a mystery. He may have often been absent (a real possibility, given the periods of adultery stemming from the couple's belief in free love); his influence may have been overwhelmed by the magnificent impression left by Netta on the girl.

Cut off from peers, missing a strong adult male influence, Charmian had only Netta for security and direction. Early in the relationship, a battle of wills left Netta the victor. The aunt asked Charmian to get her an apron, to which the child very composedly replied, "Papa says I am to mind only him. I am *his* little girl and not yours." Netta reminded her that he had sent her to Netta, and added, "You must always obey Auntie or Auntie will be very unhappy." When Charmian still balked, she was locked in her room. Several hours later, Netta heard a weak little voice say, "I'll be good, Auntie—I'll be good." After that, Charmian recalled being absolutely obedient.

Another consequence of this isolation was the development of a rich imagination. Significantly, young Charmian personified the objects around her, giving tables and teapots human attributes. Making copies of old masters' paintings and etchings, she fell into states of reverie in which she saw "processions of people my physical eyes have never seen—troops, myriads, familiar to me, or not familiar—faces, gestures, colors, robes of the past." Charmian experienced these "beatitudes," as she called them, throughout her life; without warning they would envelop her in bodily ecstacies of indescribable joy. She thought these "powers of child observation the only 'heaven,' so-called, one ever gets."

Her imagination also fed her fears. She was a fitful sleeper and fretted away the early morning hours. Instead of comforting the girl's dreads, Netta disturbed her even more by intimidating her into silence. "Those thin houses were a horror to the sleepless, for it was almost like occupying one room," Netta wrote years later in explaining why she would not put up with Charmian's nighttime wakefulness.[10]

Netta's badgering extended to naming. Throughout her life, even when both were elderly women, Netta called Charmian "Childie" or "Old Lady," both terms suggesting helplessness and dependence. She belittled Charmian's abilities and denied her good sense. In doing so, of course, Netta kept the armor around her own malicious narcissism.

As children often do when faced with such a restrictive, dominating caregiver, Charmian worshipped her enslaver, believing Netta could do no wrong. Netta's convictions became her own (save, it seems, spiritualism). Her thoughts of Netta were "like birds circling about a tower of light. If the child dashed herself against this tower rather hard from time to time—what matter: she was a real lover. Even when the crash came the truth did not leak out of the child's brain to the others. The aunt was still perfect." The imagery here is telling. The aunt is powerful, the tower a fatal attraction. The birds fly not free, but toward the destructive light. The child is not one creature with a clear identity, but a collection of separate creatures both worshipful and self-destructive.

In truth, Charmian was alone in the tower. The most consistent theme in her childhood recall is that of solitariness: "Quiet house where I was seldom disturbed at my work or play or study, or reading as omnivorous as I was supposed to be able to absorb and classify." The result: "MUST BE ALONE where many persons are concerned."

She was not unhappy in these moments. But through her dealings with Netta, which were so tantalizing and dangerous, she came to fear unpleasantness in her dealings with others. She held back, learned to pose, and by early adulthood developed a captivating and gracious social manner that disguised the insecurities and rich fantasy life inside her. She had the soul of an artist.

*   *   *   *

While the Wiley family mourned Daisy's death, the adults of another family in San Francisco were fretting in their kitchen over money. The father, a thin, kindly looking man with a long beard and gentle eyes was despairing over his inability to sell sewing machines. The competition was getting harder as the sluggish economy closed workers out of factories and forced them to find other ways of paying the rent. His wife, almost child-sized, bewigged, with an odd scar creasing her forehead, bemoaned the need to move once more. Playing nearby were two little girls, the oldest about seven, and a toddler, a boy of one-and-a-half, scurrying unconcernedly about the rough soft-wood floor.

The Londons were never a family that onlookers would envy. Indeed, seldom would they have the leisure to appear alto-gether on the streets, and if they did so, would merge indistin-guishably among the other working-class families of the city— dour, clean, but a bit haggard.

Though Yankee in origin, they were not the sort of people with whom the Wileys would have associated. It was not be-cause of their rough-clothed appearance, but the scandal of the family's very formation.

During the years Daisy Kittredge had weeped and pined for a better husband, Flora Wellman had longed to meet a hard-working, business-minded man like Kitt. Flora had reached San Francisco at age thirty-one, following a childhood of comfort as the daughter of a leading citizen of Massillon, Ohio. Her paternal grandfather had been a college president, her mater-nal grandfather the noted Welsh circuit rider "Priest" Jones, her father a canal builder, financier, and inventor of a popular stove. Petted and spoiled by her father, especially after her mother died, Flora was given private tutors who developed her natural talents in elocution and music.

Hot-tempered and willful, Flora seemed destined to become the pampered wife of some wealthy beau. When she was thir-teen, misfortune arrived in the form of a long fever that stunted her growth, damaged her hair, and ruined her eyesight. When she was fifteen, her father lost his wealth in the panic of 1858. A year later she ran away from home to live with one married sister, then another, eventually making her way to the Bay Area, where she supported herself as a piano teacher and seam-stress.

Independent and scornful of traditional customs, she was quick to adopt spiritualism, social reform, women's suffrage, astrology, and other free-thinking attitudes. In San Francisco, she was not looked upon askance as a single woman, and if the living was harsher than in Ohio, it was softened by the vitality of the city with its quaint hillside cottages, colorful sidewalk entertainers, political torchlight meetings, and bell-laden horsedrawn wagons.

Soon after her arrival to the city, Flora met a short, stocky, egotistical man of fifty-three, "Doctor" William Chaney. He was formerly a farmer in Maine, then became a self-taught attorney, and finally found happiness when he discovered astrology (then a little-known practice in the United States). Chaney became a prophet for following the stars, wrote and published primers, and traveled the country selling the method as a most valuable tool for improving mankind. Optimistic and enthusiastic, he easily attracted crowds wherever he traveled, and they would grab his pamphlets and books. By the time he met Flora in June 1874, he had left his third wife of six.

Chaney was convinced that astrology offered the obvious solution to mate selection, as well as the timing and rearing of a superior child. His theories met their crucial test in 1875, when, after a year of living without benefit of marriage, Flora announced joyfully that she was pregnant. Chaney urged abortion. As he later explained, "There was a time when I had very tender affection for Flora; but there came a time when I hated her with all the intensity of my intense nature and even thought of killing her and myself."

The next morning, despite Flora's pleadings, Chaney announced he could never consider her his wife, sold the furnishings, and left. She went to a neighbor's house, obtained a pistol, and shot herself in the forehead, fortunately producing only a flesh wound. A mob of over a hundred gathered, swearing to hang Chaney from the nearest lamppost.

The *San Francisco Chronicle,* which in those days made domestic news front-page headlines, ran a you-are-there version of the event, "Driven from Home for Refusing to Destroy Her Unborn Infant—A Chapter of Heartlessness and Domestic Misery." The story followed how the couple had become "the center of a little band of extreme Spiritualists, most of whom professed, even if they did not practice, the offensive free-love doctrines of the licentious Woodhull. To do Mr. Chaney justice, he has persistently denied the holding of such broad tenets." The reporter likened Flora's attraction to Chaney as "that which drew Desdemona toward the sooty Moor," and drew her sympathetically as the woman who had assisted "in the details of business, darned his hose, drudged at the wash-tub, and took care of other people's children for hire, and generously gave him whatever money she earned."

Chaney fled up the coast to Oregon, only to face further scornful diatribes from suffragette Abigail Scott Duniway, editor of *The New Northwest*. He never communicated with Flora again.

The babe was of course Jack, then called John, who was born in his normal time on January 12, 1876, listed as the son of Mrs. W. H. Chaney. When he was twenty-one, he somehow discovered these news articles and hunted Chaney down to ask him about the paternity. Chaney sent two lengthy responses. In one, he noted that he and Flora had never actually married and, furthermore, that he could not be Jack's father because he was impotent at the time. In both he described Flora's involvements with other men and included names of others who could have been witnesses to her activities. He added that a detective who had investigated the case reported that Flora's pistol had in fact not been discharged.[11]

Many have accepted Chaney as Jack's biological father; Jack's daughter Joan worked on a biography to redeem the reputation of the man she believed to be her grandfather.[12] Yet the circumstantial evidence speaks against this possibility as much as for it. There is neither a striking resemblance nor lack of one in the two men's faces. Although Chaney had been a ladies' man who had had six legal wives, he had failed to impregnate any woman before or after Flora. (He may well have meant sterility when he claimed impotence.) Flora's later actions mark her as a manipulator who lacked the cunning and finesse to be very successful. Generally she just exasperated people with her transparent schemes.

Unless one holds that paternal genes are dominant in establishing personality (as some London biographers actually have assumed), it is less important to know who Jack's real father was than to know that Flora was left to carry and bear the child without a mate. Her spiritualist friends did not desert her, and she supported herself well enough by sewing and teaching piano. Still, the loss of Chaney was devastating, and she projected her anger onto her unborn son.

Weakened by the delivery, Flora quickly took her doctor's advice and sent the child to Virginia Daphne Prentiss, who had recently lost her baby in childbirth. An ex-slave married to Alonzo, a white carpenter, Virginia Prentiss believed the black race was the superior race. Jack stayed with Mammy Jenny, as she had him call her, for eight months; the bond she established with him was so strong that she was to be kin for the rest of his life, the only adult female providing love in his youth. His mother provided no such support. As Virginia Prentiss later recalled, Flora "was on the go from morning till night, teaching and sewing and seeing people. She seemed to be sad and angry at the same time, and all the time, but her angriness would not let her just be sad for a while and get over it, but kept driving her and driving her. I took care of her baby, but she was so busy that she couldn't even come to see him very often."[13]

One of Alonzo's friends was John London, a widower who had recently come from the prairies with his two youngest children, Eliza and Ida, whom he had placed in the Protestant Orphan Asylum while he sought to establish a home for them. One day he noticed the fine sewing on Alonzo's shirt and asked to meet the seamstress. That meeting with Flora led to their marriage on September 7, 1876.

John saw this spunky woman, so adept at domestic arts, and expected he was getting a choice mother for his girls. Flora looked at this hard-working man toughened by pioneer life, a man skilled with his hands and eyes in many crafts, and thought she was securing her financial future. Both would soon find their dreams frustrated, but the primary victims of their disenchantment would be the children in the family.

In his later reconstruction of his childhood for friends and the public, Jack's major themes were poverty and hunger. In *John Barleycorn* he wrote, "I had been born poor. Poor I had lived. I had gone hungry on occasion. I had never had toys nor playthings like other children." The truth was otherwise. His best chum, Frank Atherton, knew real poverty. Frank's family taught him to wash the dirt off his body with dried corncobs in order to save the expense of water and pulled him out of grammar school to work in a basket factory in the Sacramento valley, where he made fifty cents a day and lived in a shed. He always enjoyed his visits to the London household for their dinners of thick pan-fried steaks and potatoes.

More likely, Jack sensed Flora's own feeling of impoverishment, the knowledge that she would never again enjoy the wealth of her girlhood days. John London was an industrious man, who attempted various ventures, including a truck garden, potato patch, chicken ranch, bee farm, and grocery before settling in Oakland as a night watchman. Flora continued her sewing and lessons and took people in as roomers when the current dwelling provided space. As a result, the family was certainly better off than the typical working-class household of the day (one need only read London's later descriptions of workers' lives to glean the difference), though not members of the respectable middle class to which Flora had once belonged.

Jack's hunger was not for food but for security and recognition. In notes for a never-published autobiography, he jotted a picture of being alone at age three, "while they are beating carpets in the yard—twilight coming on—& then they disappear from yard & I am wholly alone—the primitive fear in me."[14]

Flora has often been blamed for Jack's sense of desperate loss, and it is hard to exonerate her. He was her only natural child, yet she would not show him affection or provide reassurance. It was their common tragedy that he perceived her influence as totally negative.

When older, he had three stories he would repeat to others to explain his distance from her. In one he told of being frightened by her seances, where she communicated through Plume, an Indian chief. Like Charmian, overheard spiritualistic practices filled his lively imagination with dread. He also carried throughout his life a grudge against his mother for the time she had insisted that John London spank the boy when his stepfather did not want to. Significantly, Jack never disclosed what he had done to earn the punishment. Finally, he would speak of his mother's hysterical temper tantrums, which led him to seek women who would hold their tongues.

But just as he denied the presence of meat on his childhood table, he may also have blocked signs of Flora's caring. Certainly she made every effort to provide for the family's physical needs. The girl who had grown up with maids did not shirk preparing tasty, healthful meals nor sewing sturdy clothes. She also insisted that Jack receive the best education and harangued the principal of his elementary school in Oakland because his teacher was not giving her son sufficient attention.

When Jack was a young man feeling defeated by the numerous failures in his life, Flora at times provided the sole encouragement that kept him at his writing.

If Jack had little good to remember about his mother, his favorite words for John London were "kind, always kind." He enjoyed recounting how he would follow his stepfather about the fields or go fishing with him on San Francisco Bay on the family boat (another sign they were not impoverished). Frank Atherton joined some of these bay excursions, where John London taught the boys about bait and lines and tides.

Yet Frank's stories, which are told with the naive eye of a youngster, hint at another truth. His account of his first meeting with the family is especially telling.[15]

After school one day, Frank joined the family for dinner. As they approached the house, Flora looked out, chided Jack for being late, and ordered him to bring the wood and coal into the house for the evening. Jack introduced Frank to his parents before performing his chores. The contrast between the Londons struck the visitor: "He was so tall and stalwart, while she was so short and stout. They reminded me of a dwarf and a giant I had once seen in a sideshow."

Before the meal John London did most of the talking, telling Frank stories of his experiences in the Civil War and the two years afterward living in a prairie schooner with his children amid the Pawnee tribe. During the meal John and Jack teased Flora about the household poverty. Jack told Frank that they were so poor, Flora used a newspaper for a tablecloth, turning it over when dirty to use the other side. To indicate this remark was a joke, John London winked at Frank. Flora grew so upset that she went to a closet to pull out "several nice linen table cloths, exhibiting them proudly," which Jack then called bed sheets. Though Flora eventually laughed with her tormenters, she continued to protest that the family was not destitute.

This small scene reveals the difficulty men of that time faced in their efforts to assert their masculinity. Stories of war and frontier, long gone, must be retold with reverence. Flora and her domesticity must be mocked. Upon leaving for his night watchman job, John London must leave an impression of courage upon the family. (Frank's imagination conjured up images of the man being struck from behind or shot by a thug lurking in a dark place.) John London clearly chose the past, the vision of the frontiersman, over the civilized world of urban Oakland.

It is hard not to side with the boys and men in Frank's stories. They are relaxed and charming. They tell tall tales and jokes. They pull pranks and tease. They resist women's small-minded concern with a full coal bucket and fine linen. It takes some reconsideration to sympathize with Flora's position.

The fact is that John London, whose behavior left later researchers to conclude he had been victim of a tiny henpecking wife, was a drinker, and he was probably not "kind, always kind." The signs are all too clear. One of Jack's earliest memories was of the farm in San Mateo, where he took his stepfather buckets of beer to the field. On one such day his father did not notice that his seven-year-old son had become drunk from sips of the bucket and almost ran over him with the horse and plow, an accident suggesting the father was not too sober either. When Frank visited the family in Oakland several years later, he observed that Jack's father had "indulged in a few drinks, for he talked almost incessantly, relating numerous stories, which Jack told me afterward he had heard many times," and then almost always fell asleep in an alcoholic stupor. As part of their outings on the bay, he took the boys to the saloons, where he would have three or four whiskeys.

"The homes of America," proclaimed one Women's Christian Temperance Union pamphlet of the day, "have no enemy so relentless as the American saloon." In truth, only a small minority of men then were alcoholics like John London, but their illness played predictable havoc with their families. Each time John floundered and failed, his solution was to escape to a new town and a new business, forcing his family to readjust to new houses and new kinds of chores. By the time Jack was nine, the family had jumped around the bay from San Francisco to Emeryville to Alameda (an island adjoining Oakland), then back across to the San Mateo coastline, over again to the Livermore Valley, finally to settle in Oakland for good, though changes of home would follow in that city. Frequent moves cut them off from the possible support of friends and community, increasing the feeling in each that only by individual, self-reliant action could one survive.

Moreover, compared with the Irish, Italian, and Central European immigrant neighbors they despised, the Yankee Londons were at a further disadvantage in coping with a competitive urban culture. They could not enjoy the benefits of ethnic loyalty and solidarity to see them through hard times. Nor did they have that superb social service institution for such newcomers, the Catholic Church, to provide an anchor.

Frequently wives of alcoholics apply all their talents to compensate for the failings of the drinker. They take control, exhibiting competence with a brightness that illuminates all the more their husbands' failings, and thus become the objects of resentment to the children, who wonder why such capable people cannot change their fathers' behavior. Hence, young Jack could not see that Flora's seances brought in additional income, nor could he understand the physical and emotional toll being married to John London took upon her. The principal of one of Jack's Oakland grammar schools admired her for her spunk and felt she was married to a poor provider. Jack's first wife later told her daughter, "You remember how bent Grandma's shoulders were. Her poor little hands all out of shape. Even that didn't begin to compare with his terrible children [John's older sons from his earlier marriage who came to visit the family.] They almost killed Daddy [Jack] twice."[16]

With the adults preoccupied by their own troubles and conflicts, the children were left to fend for themselves. At age four Jack went to school with ten-year-old stepsister Eliza because there was no one at home to look after him. She read to him while he dried the dishes and helped him with his homework once he started school. He had dreams of owning a grand house that she would share with him; one room in this house would contain nothing but books.

The children were deserted by their parents for weeks at a time—just where they went is unclear.[17] As an adult Eliza would not speak of her family and once confessed to Charmian that the happiest time of her childhood had been her days in the orphan asylum. When Eliza was sixteen, one Captain James H. Shepard, a middle-aged widower, wrote to Flora asking if she could board his motherless children in her country home. Through some misunderstanding, he appeared at the ranch when Flora and John were off on one of their mysterious trips. Eliza welcomed the unexpected guests and three months later eloped with Shepard. (Jack's stepsister Ida, for whom he had little fondness, later made a similar escape.) Jack was desolate when Eliza left, but the family soon moved to Oakland in a neighborhood close to both Eliza and Virginia Prentiss, each of whom would cater to the boy during his adolescence.

Jack London's character was significantly shaped by growing up in a family in which one of the parents was an alcoholic. His personality took on typical and classic dimensions that have been recognized only recently by scholars of dysfunctional families. Externally, he "wanted to be good; not to swear, not to do this, not to do that"[18]—not to add to the disruption of an already disturbed family. He developed a high sense of responsibility and motivation. He delivered papers, helped on an ice wagon, set up pins in a bowling alley, and swept out saloons on Sundays, turning much of his money over to Flora. (She was more concerned that he work less and do his school-work, but he always proudly believed that he was the savior of the family, a deception necessary to his hard drive.)

His part-time jobs may have been a good excuse to avoid others. He had been intimidated by the leaders of youthful gangs and had no buddies other than Frank Atherton, who himself was a loner. He used part of his earnings to add to his picture card collection, finding in this hobby one means to compete successfully with other boys. Otherwise he hid in the public library or in his room with his books. When riding the trolleys with Frank, he read rather than passing the time with his friend. He recalled being "essentially lovable, needed love, and did not get it," and "hardened himself in the process."[19]

He valued his drive and even his solitariness. "How loneli-ness made him observant and perceptive," he reflected on himself. These traits would enable him to write over fifty books in less than twenty years, to perform his daily chore of writing one thousand words regardless of grief and pain and illness.

Isolation also brought him deep personal insight at a young age. "I early learned that there were two natures to me. This caused a great deal of trouble, till I worked out a philosophy of life and struck a compromise between the flesh and the spirit. Too great an ascendancy of either was to be abnormal, and since normality is almost a fetish of mine, I finally suc-ceeded in balancing both natures." In truth, he never found that balance, and only in his last months learned to transcend this conflict so common to the American character. Indeed, his life was to be marked by highly dramatic contradictions as he sought the leveling point.

2

DIFFERENT, YET THE SAME

The Youth, who daily farther from the
   East
Must travel, still is Nature's Priest,
And by his vision splendid
Is on his way attended.

—*William Wordsworth*

Charmian and Jack each matured in Oakland, a small city on the eastern shore of San Francisco Bay. To San Franciscans, it was a dull bedchamber community on the Contra Costa, the "other side," the wrong side. Yet those who chose to live there, even those who commuted almost an hour to San Francisco by steam ferry every day, had many reasons to laugh at their neighbors' pretentions.

San Francisco had been the gold rush boom town, a man's city, misruled by graft and corruption, in so much disarray that citizen vigilante committees had been necessary at times to provide social order the government could not secure. It was a city of Barbary coast honky-tonks and dives in which working men sought refuge from unpredictable employment. Block-sized stone mansions emerged from the steep and barren hill-sides, a too-visible sign of the vulgarities of wealth to the strug-gling families in shanties below. While it is not certain that Mark Twain said, "The coldest winter I have ever spent was a summer in San Francisco," he did observe, "The wind blows there a good deal in the summer months, but then you can go over to Oakland, . . . it does not blow there."[1]

In contrast, Oakland had started as a logging town, the base for the stripping of the majestic redwood forests that covered the Piedmont hillsides. Its founders foresaw a flow of gold for themselves in the development of this land of abundant sun-shine and huge live oaks, its sunny meadows of wildflowers and golden poppies. Quail, deer, rabbits, and even grizzlies abounded; oysters, clams, and fish were plentiful. Though the developers were no less scoundrels than those in San Fran-cisco, they nonetheless ensured that the town grew through thoughtful planning. They understood that their fortunes de-pended upon providing good transportation, utilities, schools, and culture.

Oakland's biggest coup over San Francisco was in becoming the terminus for the transcontinental railroad completed in 1869. Throughout the 1870s the city prospered from the re-sulting boom in jobs and housing, while San Francisco ex-perienced "the discontented decade," a time of labor revolts related to frequent spells of joblessness. Thus, both Charmian and Jack's families cast their lots well with the "city beautiful," as it came to be called. It proved the better choice, and each youngster found in its bounty numerous pleasures, though not of the same sort.

An incident from their youths hints at the different Oakland each knew.

One evening Charmian listened in rapture as her aunt and others discussed their attendance at the Tivoli Opera House, then featuring the operetta *Satanella*. "A magical performance it was of inexplicable appearing and vanishings of sulphorous deities, with all the glamour of intermixed Fairyland and Heaven arranged against black-and-red but enchanting sin."[2] Then twelve, Charmian was considered too young to observe such "forbidden treasures."

While Netta thought the show unseemly for a child, seven-year-old Jack London faced no such restriction. Not only did he see the spectacle, he sought to replicate it in his backyard. There, with a friend, he built a little hell of his own with a bonfire under the apple tree by his house. His reign as the satanic majesty ended abruptly when his vice-devil accidentally smashed a spade on Jack's nose. The evening ended with blood and tears shed on sympathetic Eliza's pinafore.

This incident demonstrates the two realities shaping Charmian's and Jack's differing experiences of city life: class and sex. Jack had a freedom Charmian would not know until she married him. As a middle-class girl, she could not roam the streets alone at night, hunt with a slingshot for mud hens down at the estuary, or hang around the waterfront saloons to listen to the sailors' stories. On the other hand, she had advantages Jack later envied. As a working-class lad, he had no one at home with whom to share the books he was reading, no leisure to draw or play music, none of the self-assurance that comes with learning manners and mores at social teas and dances. (Although at times Flora taught piano, there is no evidence she thought to pass her training on to her children.)

Still, neither was typical of their sort. The sense of solitariness and separateness they felt in their families would be made stronger by circumstances outside the home as they grew up. Charmian's enjoyment of athletics and sex would mark her as an unusual young woman, not quite the girl a man would want to take home to meet his mother. Jack's travel and self-education would help him rise above his working-class background, only to find the gentry considered him more of an amusement, a pet, than a full member of their society.

* * * *

While Netta certainly crippled Charmian's self-esteem, she nonetheless provided well for the girl in practical ways. She gave the child an abundance of books, art supplies, and music sheets to nourish her curiosity. She encouraged her to ask questions and disagree with opinions (a skill later put to good use against Netta herself). She valued education at a time when half the children in Oakland were receiving no schooling at all and most of the rest were permitted to attend just long enough to learn the three Rs.

One of Netta's most self-serving moves gave Charmian the

key to design her own life. From the first, she and Roscoe impressed upon the girl the sacrifices they were making to support her. They made Charmian believe she owed them for their benevolence and that it was her duty to become self-sufficient as soon as possible, not only to pay for her own support, but to provide for her aunt and uncle in their later years. To that end, Roscoe taught her his shorthand method and gave her typing lessons. This training was unusual—most secretaries, or clerks as they were more commonly known, were men. The office was considered an unladylike place, the typewriter a machine unfit for woman's touch.

Charmian quickly learned the tasks; indeed, she proved to be a virtuoso. Her manual dexterity had a genius all its own. She could type at the stiff, clumsy Royals of the day at the speed of dictation without error. Moreover, she enjoyed the activity as much as she did working her fingers on a Chopin étude or the seam of a blouse. It was as if she connected to the world through her hands and was content only when they were busy.

Typing may well have been even more satisfying to her than her music. Of her piano playing, she held a low opinion:

> Despite my flair for music, for line, for color, for living life, I have come to believe that I lack or have not developed intelligently what I might term . . . *cosmic rhythm.* I can go just so far—quite far at times—in musical interpretation, enough to get my teachers excited. Then I hear others play Beethoven and I see that I miss somewhere in the long run. Miss a rhythmic something.[3]

Typing was the one arena in which her chronic self-doubt could not win: she could not deny the physical presence of pages of perfect type. She had a basis for self-pride that neither she nor anyone else, especially Netta, could deny her.

At fourteen she was assisting Roscoe in teaching his methods to his students. At sixteen she was able to support her way for two years at Mills Seminary and College by working as private secretary to Susan Mills, principal and business manager of the school.

Mills was then the preeminent western institution for young women, with the college curriculum patterned after that of eastern men's colleges. Admission requirements for the Bachelor of Arts program required knowledge of virtually all the writings of Cicero, Virgil, Xenophon, and Homer (in the original Latin and Greek) and well-known commentaries on the works. The Bachelor of Letters requirements replaced Greek with French or German but also included mathematics. Charmian took a nondegree program for those studying the arts, with courses in drawing, piano, rhetoric and literature, and art history.

In her early days at Mills, Charmian came upon a motto posted on a wall that left a greater impression on her life than anything else in her experiences at the school:

WORK, as if you were to live forever;
LIVE, as if you were to die to-morrow.

She took the message to heart, determined to spend every minute for some useful purpose, to seek new adventures fearlessly. As a consequence, she self-consciously adopted a lifestyle centered around organization, hard work, and self-discipline. She became a record keeper, noting the number of books read, miles walked, or hours practiced. These accounts were proof to herself that she was not leading a wasteful life. Her Yankee forebears would have approved.

Social life was carefully supervised by Susan Mills. Students could not send or receive letters without her permission. Sunday visitors were forbidden lest their presence make "unfit the pupil for the duties of the week." Nor could the girls attend balls or parties or leave the grounds "unless accompanied by guardians or teachers, or receive calls from gentlemen who have not been introduced by parents to the principal." Mills girls could, however, in a body attend events at the University of California, and through these gatherings, Charmian probably made the contacts among faculty and students on that campus that formed the basis for her social life throughout her twenties. With her quick laugh, lyrical voice, and sensuous figure, she became "the most popular girl in Berkeley" of her day, the "best dancer . . . and with more fraternity pins than anyone."[4]

In one area, physical fitness, Susan Mills agreed with the

latest reformist ideas, believing that exercise was not debilitating to the female sex. A daily walk in the fresh air of at least one mile (thought then to be a great exertion for a young woman) was compulsory. In the gymnasium, students in blue woolen exercise suits worked out with Indian clubs, dumbbells, and wands.

This regimen suited Charmian's temperament well. She designed a set of daily calisthenics that she performed religiously into her seventies, and she walked far more than the required mile. She also became a strong swimmer, who attracted attention at the municipal baths and parks with her daring high dives from thirty-foot perches.

Of all her physical activities, however, one became a passion —horseback riding. Her interest began early, during her toddler days in Petaluma, where she shifted the window blinds at the sound of horse hooves to watch the passing riders. Noticing her fascination, someone designed a piece of worsted on a lath for her to play-ride. "There was a horrid difficulty in simulating a side-seat effect on a lath," she quipped. Later, while reading *Ben Hur,* she felt herself grow excited for the reins. An Oakland neighbor owned pure white Percherons, French draft horses, and "to meet one of those superb equine forms pacing in grandeur, yard-long manes, sweeping tails of snow, crimped by expert hands, was to me the very investiture of triumphant Greek sculpture with life." She drew horses in her art booklets, even during Congregationalist services. But her commitment to riding was cemented by tragedy.

The story survives via Willard Kittredge's small pocket diary, begun in 1883 as an account book for his frequent travels and expenses. In the fall of that year, when Charmian was twelve, he began a journey eastward to his hometown in Maine. His shaky hand belied poor health, although his precise ailments went unrecorded. During 1884 and 1885, his entries repeated themes of "health better," then "very sick," then "took morphine." Finding odd jobs, he worked his way to Oakland, arriving in March 1886, when he moved into the Eames household to be nursed through what were clearly his dying days by Netta and Charmian.

Concerned one evening that Kitt immediately receive a new drug, the doctor ordered fourteen-year-old Charmian to take his own phaeton and rush to the druggist. Though she had ridden old mares during country visits to relatives' ranches, the prospect of driving a cunning street horse through city traffic terrified her. The reins trembling in her hands, overcome as well by the imminent death of her father, she experienced one of her beatitudes. As the horse did her bidding, she felt the grief drift away. She thought, "My own brave cavalry dad's own daughter, oh, at last! A regular Kittredge, by heaven. Like Sir Richard Kittredge, in 1593." So the horse became a symbol for the father she had lost, and her sense of power from controlling the animal endowed her with the means for overcoming pain and distress.

When Charmian left Mills, her first financial goal was to earn enough money to buy her own horse and board it. Her riding was both out of step and ahead of the times. It was outmoded in that the typical female city resident wishing to cover long distances on her own would take to a bicycle, matter-of-factly pedaling ten or twenty miles without benefit of labor-saving gears. But Charmian chose to ride her horse astride, not side-saddle, and was considered scandalous.

She made quite an impression on onlookers. Eight-year-old Raine Edward Bennett first glimpsed her on a bright windy morning in Berkeley when she galloped past on a white horse. Startled, the youngster watched her disappear down the road in a cloud of dust, for he had never seen a woman on horseback before. "That brazen creature! She's riding to perdition," sniffed a woman nearby. "Ladies use sidesaddles. Only hussies ride bareback."[5]

Charmian thought it strange that so many people who looked without disapproval upon a female bicyclist would object to her bestride a horse. She became an outspoken advocate of cross-saddle riding, eventually publishing an article in its defense in *Out West* magazine:

> It does seem incredible that for some five hundred years intelligent women have been twisting their bodies into the one-sided position on horseback, and it may be that if the origin of the side-saddle were more generally known, there would be less delay about discarding it as an out-of-date nuisance. According to the records, Richard the Sec-

ond of England took to wife Anne of Bohemia, who, unluckily for herself and especially for posterity of her sex,
suffered from hip disease. The royal lady, unluckily again
for all concerned, cherished a fondness for riding, and
some contrivance had to be devised to meet her peculiar
needs. Thus the side-saddle came into existence, and it is
more than probable that the first cavalcade of mounted
cripples—for of course the court ladies were not to be
outdone by their royal mistress—called forth many stares
of wonder and smiles of amusement for spectators of both
sexes.[6]

Vogue, she concluded, thereafter triumphed over judgment
and sense.

Charmian attacked the belief that "a woman should ride only
a perfectly safe horse, anyway; and a side-saddle is all right on
such an animal." Through careful reasoning she concluded
that women had no choice but "safe horses" because good
horsemanship was so difficult on such a saddle, which was hard
physically on, even dangerous to, both the rider and the animal. And if most riding instructors pushed the sidesaddle on
women, she suggested it was not because they were right so
much as they could earn so much more money in the lengthy
instruction required to master using one.

If Charmian believed the sidesaddle deserved "even a worse
fate than French heels, hoopskirts, and bustles," she was not
so reformist as to join the "bloomerites," women who wore
pants. She felt a stylish divided skirt was "equally comfortable,
and off the saddle look[ed] just like any other skirt." This
compromise was an important one. Women then were having
a difficult enough time convincing others that an athlete could
be "a specimen of true womanhood." Cross-saddles gave
women independence to ride alone (for no one was needed to
help them mount or dismount) and to ride quickly and long in
comfort and safety. No wonder they were called "brazen."

Yet Charmian made an even more defiant attack on the concept of the lady—she accepted Netta's unconventional views of
sexuality. She had grown up in a household where the adults
freely and openly sought sexual relationships with others. She
knew that Roscoe's absences from the household had been to

live with other women. She watched as Roscoe accepted
Netta's "protégés" into the family. She had been instructed
carefully by Netta in the use of sexual wiles and contraception.

Jack London disclosed some of Netta's philosophy in his
novel *The Valley of the Moon.* In it, the heroine, Saxon Roberts,
consults with Mercedes Higgins, an "old, burnt-faced woman,"
on the ways of men. Bragging on her hold over men not only
as a young woman, but even in her current witchlike state, Mrs.
Higgins tells Saxon the magic is:

> Variety! Without it in a wife, the man is a Turk; with it, he
> is her slave, and faithful. A wife must be many wives
> . . . a garden of flowers, ever fresh, ever different. . . .
> Never let the last veil be drawn. . . . Each veil must seem
> the only one between you and your hungry lover who will
> have nothing less than all of you. Each time he must seem
> to get all. . . . It must not be so.[7]

It is "man's queerness," she explains, that woman must "remain a flower almost plucked, yet never plucked."

Women who used their wiles successfully, Netta/Mrs. Higgins argued, knew when to lure a man with wine, when with
dress, when with song. They needed no beauty, for their wisdom was the greater attractant. "The greatest of all arts is the
conquering of men." And she gave these arts "glimmerings of
profounds inexpressible and unthinkable that hinted connota-
tions lawless and terrible." Saxon admits to being frightened,
"and I know so little, that I had never dreamed of . . . *that.*"

Charmian may not have been as frightened as Saxon was.
With her first kiss, she was taken that "the effect was so exquisite, that it could not be entirely sensual. . . . The result was too
spiritual—the heightened brightness of everything to the
MIND. The body could not be brightened, benefited, without
the message of the brain to fix the fact. Therefore . . . the body
was mind, in order to sense the ecstasy."[8]

She was pleased when a professor called her attention to
Robert Browning's verse "There's nothing low in love, when
love the lowest." She questioned what Netta had taught her,
that one form of sexual passion was better, higher "than that
of lower types of humans, or of the animals." She decided

instead that passion and sex were creative urges, the sources of everything in life; hence they could not be considered low unless used for wrong purposes. The peak life experience was reached through this creative sexual ecstacy, and then in the fruit of that ecstacy.

In short, Charmian decided that sexual indulgence was normal and healthy. That her men friends agreed was the final proof. She talked with them about others with cold wives and noted how such husbands became unfaithful "or else they withered, and became anti-social in their habits." She promised never to be accused of frigidity. She took as her philosophy of life, "Love dangerously."

Although she was ready to give in to passion and saw it as a healthy means of self-expression, she was careful not to equate such submission with loss of power. She would bed her lovers willingly, but that would not give them the right to rule her life. One day on a new job the manager, while showing her around, said, "Of course, you understand there will be no unnecessary conversation with the clerks." Charmian was startled, for it seemed so obvious a point. She then realized that if there were to be any flicker of flirtation in the office it would come from the manager himself. She found herself drawn to his fine black eyes, good mouth, small mustache, then shook herself back with the thought, "Am I a dog, that I should desire a master to make me fear?"[9] Throughout her life, whenever a lover pushed too far—threatened to dampen her independence—she would withdraw her affection until she felt he was ready to accept her autonomy.

Just when Charmian lost her virginity is unknown. Although she had early taken up Daisy's habit of journal keeping, she destroyed her youthful diaries in 1937 after discovering that Irving Stone, then writing a biography of Jack, had broken into the locked cabinet where she had put the few private papers she wished him to omit. He claimed later that they showed her to be preoccupied with men, jealous of other women, and unable to hold any man's attention for long. But this portrayal is not supported by the single pre-Jack diary that does survive, so it is hard to accept his summary as valid. All we can be sure of is that she was not a virgin when she first made love to Jack— but she was in her thirties then.

Still, however much she rebelled against certain societal precepts, Charmian remained ensnared by Netta. After two successful years at Mills, the aunt felt "compelled to remove" her from the school and bring her home again.[10] Very likely she wanted Charmian's wages to go to the household, so the young woman found herself joining the commuters on the Key Route rail cars to the ferry, where she crossed over to the San Francisco waterfront. There too she defied convention by working as a secretary for a shipping firm. (Middle-class women by definition did not work, unless they were spinsters teaching in schools or nursing in hospitals.)

By young womanhood, then, Charmian Kittredge was an enigma to others. She was pert and winsome, a favorite partner at dances, a charming conversationalist, a pianist sought out by singers for concerts. But she insisted on working at what was still considered a man's job in San Francisco, on charging on her horse alone through the Piedmont hills, and on finding sexual satisfaction without benefit of marriage. None of the long skirts, ruffled blouses, or silk underdainties could disguise the fact that she was not considered the perfect specimen of womanhood in 1889, but a threat to the very idea. She did not understand the seriousness of her challenge and was instead puzzled that, however popular, she did not quite fit into society.

*   *   *   *

While Charmian Kittredge's adolescence and early adulthood can be presented fairly in several pages, Jack London's could fill a half-dozen books (and indeed he did so, describing his experiences). Between 1891 and 1900, he completed the eighth grade, worked in a cannery, became an oyster pirate (a form of juvenile delinquency then), reversed himself to serve the law as a member of the Fish Patrol, sailed to Japan on a three-masted sealer, worked in a jute mill, shoveled coal at a power plant, tramped across the country, went to prison, attended Oakland High School while working as its janitor, became known as the Bay Area's "boy socialist," tried the University of California at Berkeley, and traveled to the Yukon. He also became a writer. What matters here is less what he did on a particular day than how his basic character was established by these actions.

The most striking features of his life during his adolescence were impulsiveness and wanderlust, perhaps legacies of his family, who had moved nineteen times in the first thirteen years of his life. During this time the quiet, obedient boy who had avoided the rougher play of his classmates rebelled, sought to be one of them. His experiences on the Oakland waterfront, at sea, in factories, and on the road tested his body, sometimes cruelly. As a result of these explorations, he would enter adulthood determined to break away from his neighborhood and the limitations it presented.

Although his adventures were not unusual for a young man of his class, they were atypical for their variety and number. The other boys and men he met did not have such disjointed life stories. They became outlaws or sailors or tramps or factory workers, while he moved from one endeavor to another. Where most boys of modest means sought apprenticeship (Frank Atherton took up taxidermy) and ways to avoid the treacherous lot of casual labor, there is no indication that Jack ever thought about what he wanted to be. He had grown up in a family where plans seldom materialized, where wishes turned into pipe dreams, and he acted as though life was a series of accidental encounters.

Jack was ill prepared for adult work. True, he had held numerous jobs as a child, even imagined, as children of alcoholics do, that his contributions were saving the family from destitution. He had developed an overgrown sense of duty that would drive him the rest of his life. Still, he lacked the guidance and stability to direct his life. His stepfather proved a poignant model of how not to succeed. And for all his rejection of Flora, young Jack could not help but adopt her ache for an easier life. In their attempts to make up for his parents' disregard, both Virginia Prentiss and Eliza encouraged in the youngster a belief that he was deserving of the best from life, that he was special, set apart from the average lad.

He did not quite believe the world owed him a living. The books of the day, however, did promise rewards to those who worked hard to improve themselves. Like many youngsters, he read the Horatio Alger stories, in which homeless boys find success through honesty and industry. Alger's stories, in which the heroes are presented as orphans, imply that the boys create themselves and owe their achievements to no one else. Jack embraced this philosophy throughout his life. He would seldom give credit to the others who played a role in his accomplishments, nor would he much consider that social and economic forces in California then circumscribed his life choices and opportunities.

But the book that most influenced his values was one he read at a much earlier age, when he was eight, living on the ranch in Livermore. There he came across a tattered copy of Ouida's *Signa,* with its last forty pages missing. As he explained in his essay "Eight Great Factors of Literary Success": "The story begins: 'It was only a little lad.' The little lad was an Italian mountain peasant. He became an artist, with all Italy at his feet. When I read it, I was a little peasant on a poor California ranch. Reading the story, my narrow hill-horizon was pushed back, and all the world made possible if I would dare it. I dared."

As with the Alger stories, the youth has mysterious origins, hence is thrust into the world without heredity or history. Unlike the Alger stories, which were based on the realism of the new urban America and taught boys the values of that world, *Signa* was a melodramatic romance, (splashed with sugar-coated eroticism young Jack likely missed) that saluted the ideals of beauty and adventure. Most significantly, the hero becomes not a man of business but an artist, a violinist, who fights for his music and is buoyed up by the rich cultural sea in which he struggles. It is good that the last forty pages were missing, for there the hero sacrifices his art and kills himself in despair when he discovers the woman of his dreams is the mistress of his father! Deprived of the story's tragic end, Jack saw only the gilt and roses of Renaissance life contrasted with the dust and plainness of the ranch.

Three other books during this time also affected his values. William Makepeace's *From Log-Cabin to White House,* a tremendously popular boy's book of the time, was a life of James Garfield, who had lost his father as an infant, worked hard on the family farm, read every book he could find, and pulled himself up from a canal hand to president.

Washington Irving's *Alhambra,* lent to him by a perceptive

schoolteacher, set in his mind a permanent dream of a fantastic house. From the bricks of a fallen chimney on the Livermore ranch, he laid out his vision of the building, its terraces, towers, and arcades labeled in chalk. When a guest dressed stylishly in well-polished boots, smart hat, and fine clothes appeared one day, Jack mistook him for a sophisticate and showed off his proud castle. The stranger sneered and, later in the day, hid *Alhambra* deep in the cellar crawl space of the London ranch house and laughed tormentingly while the frightened boy dove into the dark spidery cave to retrieve his treasure. (That John and Flora would have such a vindictive friend is a further hint of their dealings.)

One of Paul Du Chaillu's books, probably *Explorations and Adventures in Equatorial Africa,* stirred a desire to explore hidden river valleys with their dangerous cannibal tribes. Frank Atherton recalled Jack recounting these stories and expressing the hope of becoming an adventurer, of being the first white man to walk through these secret places. His confidence in such a dream again indicates how different he was from the boys around him, who thrilled over the same tales, yet could not place themselves in the explorer's boots. The imagination that stood him so well as a writer shows itself in his easy identification with these men.

Because his family life was so confusing and unsupportive, these and other stories were more important in shaping Jack's character than they were for other boys who read them. Indeed, it was books, not people, that gave some direction to his life. He was proud of their influence and loved to tell how, at the age of ten, his family settled permanently, and he escaped the tawdry life around him:

And then came the city of Oakland, and on the shelves of that free-library I discovered all the great world beyond the skyline. Here were thousands of books as good as my four wonder-books, and some were even better. . . . I read everything, but principally history and adventure, and all the old travels and voyages. I read mornings, afternoons, and nights. I read in bed, I read at table, I read as I walked to and from school, and I read at recess while other boys were playing.[11]

He read so much that his parents encouraged him to get odd jobs, not so much for the money, but to stop what they believed was "St. Vitus's dance" caused from lack of exercise.

The isolation from other boys that resulted from his reading prevented Jack from preparing fully for manhood. Not being a member of a gang, he missed out on gossip of older lads who had gone to the factories, married, and started families. He also failed to learn cooperation and teamwork, the value of calling on others when in trouble. The Alger stories and the travel books ignored completely the day-to-day demands on adult men in the urban work place and as husbands and fathers. They neglected too to remind readers that money must be found to support art or explore distant lands.

Graduation from grammar school in 1891, which marked Jack's passage into manhood, resulted in a tremendous shock. John London was out of work, and when Jack was asked as class historian to deliver the graduation address, he declined for lack of a decent suit, and did not even show up for the exercises. The family's lot became worse when John was struck by a train and seriously hurt. High school was now out of the question.

Jack immediately took a job at Hickmott's cannery, of which he later wrote, "Month in and month out, the shortest day I ever worked was ten hours. . . . I asked myself if this was the meaning of life—to be a work-beast. I knew no horse in the city of Oakland that worked the hours that I worked."[12] Neither his family nor his reading had prepared him for the wretched labor conditions during this time, when no laws prevented child labor or work-place hazards.

Still, Jack was fifteen, considered an adult in those days, and worked only a summer, not "month in and month out." Missing is any sense of the camaraderie that brought some solace to workers of the time. This was one of the most intense periods of widespread and well-publicized labor organizing in Bay Area history, yet Jack seemed ignorant of its presence. He was then a loner who, instead of seeking to join with others to solve common problems, solved the problem only for himself by fleeing from it. As he later observed, "though I had never even heard of a school called 'Individualism,' I sang the paean of the strong with all my heart."[13]

Furthermore, his natural childhood obedience had prepared

him to be a compliant worker. He formulated a gospel of work, a devotion to the dignity of labor. Being young, he was able to keep up with the pace of the machines, proud that he could produce more than others around him. "To shirk or malinger on the man who paid me my wages was a sin, first, against myself, and second, against him. I considered it a crime second only to treason and just about as bad." Had a strike occurred, he was ready to be a strike-breaker and have his head bashed by a militant trade unionist.

However proud he was of his work, he soon searched for easier ways of earning money. This was the final era of the sailing ship, and Jack had grown up among seafarers, bargemen, and bay sailors. Like most Oaklanders he could handle a small craft on the tricky currents of the bay with ease. While spending his meager spare time on his skiff, he observed how other daring youths with swift boats were turning to thievery. Oyster pirates raided the beds controlled by such monopolies as the much despised Southern Pacific Railroad. Although the act was a felony, the public and many police sympathized with the raiders, even encouraged the theft. Jack joined after convincing Virginia Prentiss to lend him the money to buy the sloop *Razzle Dazzle*.

His later accounts of this time are so charming that one wonders why he did not stay with it longer. He claimed to become known as the "Prince of the Oyster Pirates," bringing in more bushels alone than two-man crews, raiding in the light of dawn while others hid. He even claimed to have a consort, Mamie, also known as the "Queen," who shared the boat with him. In later years he would wax romantic about sitting "glass in hand, in warm-glowing camaraderie, with the oyster pirates, adventurers who refused to be slaves to petty routine."[14]

In truth, the pirates were a rowdy crew who would sooner compete with three-week drunks than play cops-and-robbers. Several days skulduggery could bring in fifty dollars, as much as Jack made in a month at the factory. Jack did not have to venture out often to earn his parents' rent and meat, with plenty left over to spend at the bars. At Heinhold's saloon he soon learned to cast off his old values of money or else lose the comradeship of his fellow adventurers, who expected him to share in the buying of rounds. He later explained, "And somehow, from the day I achieved that concept sitting on the stringer-piece of the Oakland City Wharf, I have never cared for money. No one has ever considered me a miser since, while my carelessness of money is a source of anxiety and worry to some that know me."[15]

Yet his deepest feelings were of pain-filled inadequacy:

> All the time I was striving to be a man amongst men, and all the time I nursed secret and shameful desires for candy. But I would have died before I'd let anybody guess it. I used to indulge in lonely debauches, on nights when I knew my crew was going to sleep ashore. I would go up to the Free Library, exchange my books, buy a quarter's worth of all sorts of candy that chewed and lasted, sneaked aboard the *Razzle Dazzle,* lock myself in the cabin, and lie there long hours of bliss.

After rivals destroyed his boat, he quit the game.

Jack's and his fellow pirates' struggle to become men is especially touching because they sought to express an image of manhood that was less and less possible. The West had been won, and the qualities required in that battle served ill in the emerging urban and industrial world. As a young man, John London had supported his wife and seven children on the prairies by farming, hunting, and trapping. As a middle-aged man in a Western city, he had to rent a home, not build his own, and buy the food and clothes for his family. His impressive skills were worth little in a labor market in need of factory workers and dock hands, and he spent his final years as a watchman earning bonuses for every bum he turned in to the authorities. Idolizing his stepfather, Jack could not understand that the frontier ethic was inappropriate for the world he was entering.

Jack's problem was not so much the lack of fitting skills as the belief in frontier values—rebelliousness, self-reliance, determination—that were inappropriate to the industrial work place. Indeed, John London deserves much credit for taking the boy out on the bay, for teaching him about wind, currents, and tides, knots, sails, and winches. Young Jack's problem was not lack of motivation or ability but temperament.

John London's other means of expressing his manhood, saloon life and drinking, made ready sense as a symbol of adulthood to the boy. He saw the saloon as a place where he could win his "manhood's spurs" by following its unwritten rules of behavior. He learned that not buying others drinks or refusing to drink himself would lose friends he found beside him at the bar, but he accepted these expectations. John Barleycorn "devolved upon me as a social duty and a manhood rite," an "escape from the narrowness of women's influence." Drink changed an ordinary, commonplace afternoon into a "gorgeous, purple afternoon" where anything could happen—an enchanting story could be told, a song could be belted out boisterously, a sudden fistfight could explode.

It was a world that could not continue to hold him, however, for he could never fully identify with the men around him. However much he resisted Flora consciously, her world, with its more refined and domestic values, dominated his ideas. In addition, struggling for recognition from within was a creature sensitive to the world around him, a poet searching for a voice.

Always aware of the divisions within himself, Jack thought that alcohol was the means to resolution: "As John Barleycorn heated his way into my brain, thawing my reticence, melting my modesty, talking through me and with me and as me, my adopted twin brother and *alter ego,* I, too, raised my voice to show myself a man and an adventurer."[16] In fact, it brought only the appearance of peace to the warring factions within him, by making it seem the "manly" or physically adventurous, impulsive side was defeating the intuitive, artistic side.

His next two jobs showed him the trickery of John Barleycorn and of his outmoded ideas of manhood.

After quitting the oyster pirates, he accepted an offer of a job from Charley LeGrant of the California Fish Patrol. As deputy, Jack would cover the turbulent waters of the Carquinez Strait, where the fishing village of Benicia was situated. He earned no pay but received half the fines paid by the fishermen he arrested for violating various laws. The switch to a legal occupation changed his life little. What few dollars he made went into the saloon keeper's drawer, even though that meant going without underwear. One night in a drunken stupor he fell into the strait and, while drifting in the cold waters, felt himself giving up, desiring to turn the accident into suicide.

He soon quit the patrol and bummed around the Oakland waterfront, where he had his worst experience with alcohol. When a campaigning politician dispensed free drinks one evening, Jack and his friends took some bottles and drank to the point of senselessness. Poisoned, he felt "my correlations breaking down, my legs tottering under me, my head swimming, my heart pounding, my lungs panting for air." Dragged onto the trolley for home by a friend, he smashed a window to get air, then passed out. He realized the next day he had been lucky to live.

On January 12, 1893, he signed on as a boat puller seaman aboard the *Sophia Sutherland,* a three-masted sealing schooner bound to Japan.

It could not have been easy. A bay sailor on a first ocean voyage, he was a ready target for the mockery of the hardened Scandinavian crew. The demands of this work on his body, with his delicate hands and feet ill suited for line-tugging and seal skinning, must have been crippling at times. Worse, he would have no privacy in the bunk below, no escape to the library and candy store. To avoid ridicule, he designed a small oil lamp that allowed him to read the books he had smuggled aboard under the covers and out of sight of his mocking mates.

He was very much like Humphrey van Weyden, the sensitive aesthete who found himself imprisoned amid madness in *The Sea Wolf.* He found the violence and crudeness of his fellow sailors repulsive and fascinating at the same time, for their actions expressed the dark energies he had sworn as a boy to control. So far his experiences had not provided an escape from the shadow pursuing him.

He did catch sight of the volcanoes of Hawaii, which renewed his thirst for adventure in "primitive" lands. He savored the discipline, the scheduling of work to bells, the efficient and careful use of space below, and followed these practices for the rest of his life.

The captain was a teetotaler, and Jack felt he was free from drink. Then they hit the Bonin Islands, where for ten days he joined the "full-blooded men, lusty, breedy, chesty men, free spirits and anything but niggards in the way they foamed away life." It was "the old story," he later recalled, using John Barleycorn to relieve the monotony of the sail. During the thirty-seven-day return voyage to San Francisco, the men replaced drink with endless stories of how they would spend their wages. Most soon lost them within days of returning home and signed onto another boat much earlier than they would have liked.

Jack returned home on August 26, 1893, to find his parents impoverished. He took a few of his dollars to buy a secondhand hat, some forty-cent shirts, two fifty-cent suits of underclothes, and a secondhand coat and vest. He handed over the rest to pay his family's bills. Like Charmian Kittredge, he felt a duty to his parents, however much they had failed him, and placed duty before his own comforts and preferences. He was now a good young man of the era, hard working and responsible.

3

THE WANDERER

Therefore, from job to job I've moved
    along.
Pay couldn't 'old me when my time
    was done,
For something in my 'ead upset it all.

—*Rudyard Kipling*

No amount of romanticizing can disguise the fact that young Jack had been a wastrel and was lucky not to have landed in jail by this point. Few who knew him could imagine that within a few short years he would become well known as a socialist and a writer, on his way to earning the riches he imagined.[1]

His parents' financial problems echoed the nation's economic chaos. The filing for bankruptcy by the Philadelphia and Reading Railroad earlier in 1893 had started a national crisis. Soon prices of grain, cotton, steel, and timber fell off steadily, while stock market prices fluctuated unpredictably. Other railroads went broke, and many of the great financial trusts collapsed. The deepening depression made work hard to find, and when found, it paid too few coins to keep hungry stomachs filled.

Jack was thus especially fortunate to get a post in a mill setting jute on bobbins ten hours a day for ten cents an hour. The work was more tedious than hard, a job many unemployed in Oakland would envy. For Jack, though, it was a personal affront, an outrage to his inteliect and sense of self-worth. When the manager refused to raise his pay, he quit. Brief though the experience was, he made use of it years later in one of his best stories, "The Apostate," in which Johnny, a young mill worker, is described as "a twisted and stunted and nameless piece of life" as a result of his work in a Southern textile mill, "a sickly ape, stoop-shouldered, narrow-chested, grotesque, and terrible." The fear of this outcome in his life must have been a driving force in fleeing the factory.

Recalling one of his four "wonder-books," the biography of Garfield, he rejected schooling as a means for improvement, rationalizing that, "a canal boy could become president. Any boy who took employment with any firm, could, by thrift, energy, and sobriety learn the business and rise from position to position until he was taken in as a junior partner. After that the senior partnership was only a matter of time."² So assured, he became a car washer, then a coal shoveler for the Oakland, San Leandro, and Hayward Electric Railway, believing his hard work would get him promoted into an electrician's slot. He found instead that he had been hired for thirty dollars a month to do the work previously done by two men at forty dollars a month each. It was a lesson that would make his later acceptance of socialism an easy one.

During this time he made his first attempts at writing for money. Once established, Jack would claim proudly that he alone had been responsible, that he had fought his battles alone. In fact, Flora provided the impetus that set him putting words to paper.

He was sitting at the table one evening, resting from a thirteen-hour day at the jute mill, when his mother pointed out a notice in the *San Francisco Call* offering a twenty-five-dollar prize to the best descriptive article submitted. Jack declined, asserting he had neither time nor topic. She suggested that he rise early in the morning to write of something he had seen at sea. The result, "Typhoon off the Coast of Japan," took first prize, beating students from Stanford and Berkeley. In a few hundred words, this poorly schooled seventeen-year-old boy carried the reader onto the *Sophie Sutherland* on a day a storm threatened the schooner and its crew. London's ear for rhythm and his awareness of the importance of precise description, two qualities that make his best work so compelling, appear even in this early scribble:

> The sun had an angry look. . . . Huge gunies rose slowly, fluttering their wings in the light breeze and striking their webbed feet on the surface of the water for over half a mile before they could leave it. Hardly had the patter, patter died away when a flock of sea quail rose, and with whistling wings flew away to windward, where members of a large band of whales were disporting themselves, their blowings sounding like the exhaust of steam engines. The harsh, discordant cries of a sea-parrot grated unpleasantly on the ear, and set half a dozen on the alert in a small band of seals that were ahead of us. A seagull with slow, deliberate flight and long majestic curves, circled round us, and as a reminder of home, a little English sparrow perched impudently on the fo'castle head, and cocking his head on one side chirped merrily. The boats were soon among the seals, and the bang! bang! of the guns could be heard from down to leeward.

Partway through the description, London introduced the character of a bricklayer dying of consumption. At storm's end his body is being sewn in canvas for sea burial. These references, almost insignificant in light of the entire piece, shift the story from a simple nonfiction description to a sketch foreshadowing the later mythical stories of nature that would be his most poetic creations. It was certainly a piece he could show with pride.

Jack's article and a photograph appeared in the paper on November 12, 1893. Having made as much from that short essay as from working for several weeks at the mill, he promptly submitted another article, which was just as promptly rejected by the *Call* editor as "gush." When his luck with magazines was no better, he grew discouraged about ever being able

to rise above manual labor, to become more than what he came
to call a "work beast."

*　　*　　*　　*

National events provided Jack's real initiation into adulthood.

The winter of 1893 had been unusually bitter, accentuating
the hardships of the unemployed. Over five hundred banks had
failed during the year; strikes and lockouts grew more common
and violent. By the spring of 1894, a number of groups such
as the Nationalists led by Edward Bellamy, author of *Looking
Backward,* Christian Socialists, and Populists organized to protest failing economic conditions. Jacob S. Coxey had tried for
several years to get a good roads bill passed in Congress to
provide public-work jobs for those who needed them. When
that effort failed, he devised the idea of an "industrial army,"
a cadre of able-bodied unemployed to march on Washington
to dramatize the needs of the poor. On March 25, 1894, Coxey
and his men started from Massillon, Ohio.

A similar army, initially of 25,000 men, formed in San Francisco. When on March 27 the mayor of that city refused to
provide them with supplies, they crossed over to Oakland,
where the citizenry, unhappy about this invasion, arranged for
their swift departure by boxcar to Sacramento. This "gift"
provoked anger and violence. Eventually, under the leadership
of a young printing compositor, Charles T. Kelly, a group of
about a thousand men accepted the ride out of town. Thus,
"Kelly's army" was born.[3]

Recalling Milton's "Better to reign in hell than serve in
heaven," Jack left a few days later, on April 6, jumping freights
to catch up with the rear of the contingent days later in the
desert. While jumping a freight on April 9, his coat caught fire,
leaving him unprotected during the snowy nights. On April 13
several brakemen shook him up for a bribe to stay on the train
and left taking a gold ring he had received from a girl friend
and all his money save fifteen cents. By April 17, in the midst
of a furious blizzard, he had caught up with a detachment of
the army in Laramie, Wyoming.

Tramping gave Jack the first opportunity to use his wits to
survive. His powers of concentration and determination

helped him endure the long hours riding the rods, blinds, decks, and even sometimes the cowcatcher. His heightened awareness and cleverness made him the winner in the daily cat-and-mouse game played with the railroad police. His quick way with words brought him success in the "threshing machine," where each man in the car was required to tell a good and new story or else be "threshed about." More important, he acquired confidence in his ability to handle any situation or crisis that he might face. To meet each day without certainty of meal or shelter and end the night having satisfied both was a rare accomplishment, one that, like Charmian Kittredge's typewriting, was a source of pride no one could steal or belittle.

The young man savored the adventure even through great difficulty. He marched through half of Iowa without shoes and at one point was criticized as a shirker by Kelly, who did not understand why such a sturdy lad wanted to ride in a wagon rather than hike. In Des Moines the army built flat boats to paddle down the river to Keokuk. When Jack's outfit got ahead of the main army, they thought little of breaking into the awaiting provisions to feast at the expense of the larger group. Always the individualist, he accepted that "the grub was to the man who got there first," for often enough in his life others had gotten to the grub ahead of him. Kelly understandably felt otherwise, and Jack quit the march.

As so often happened during his adventures, odd moments of relief appeared. He went north to Chicago, where he used four dollars sent from Eliza to buy clothes, go to the theater, and take a fifteen-cent bed at the Salvation Army. After viewing the World Columbian Exposition, he visited for several weeks with his aunt Mary Everhard in St. Joseph, Michigan. Later in the journey he found similar respite in Washington, D.C., where he worked as a stable cleaner. His heart was never in full-time tramping, and he may have taken these breaks to prove to himself that he was really not one of the downtrodden with whom he shared straw beds in the cars.

One experience marked his actual maturity:

On June 19, 1894, one John Lundon, age 18: Single: Father & Mother Living, Occupation—Sailor; Religion—Atheist;—was received at the Erie County Penitentiary,

for a term of 30 days, charge of Tramp, sentence by Police
Justice Charles Piper—Niagara Falls, New York; and was
released on July 29, 1894.

Jack had slept the night outside the city, and at dawn decided
to find the falls. On the way a policeman arrested him when he
was unable to name the hotel where he was staying.

His trial and subsequent imprisonment were Jack's first experience with the ways the powerful can exercise justice. The
trial was hardly that, merely a judge, acting also as clerk, announcing the sentence of thirty days, without any opportunity
for defense or rejoinder. Jack's ire rose: "When I asked for a
lawyer I was laughed at. I'd show them. I knew something
about the law and my own rights, and I'd expose their malad-
ministration of justice. Visions of damage suits and sensational
newspaper headlines were dancing before my eyes."[4] Instead,
he faced the humiliation of being marched in a chain gang
before the eyes of the disapproving tourists, then put on a train
for the Erie penitentiary. There he was bathed, strip-searched,
barbered until his head was "smooth as a billiard-ball just
sprouting a crop of bristles," and given striped prison clothes.
When he asked to write a letter to his family, he was refused.[5]

In prison he saw things "unbelievable and monstrous." As
continues in today's jails, an elaborate black market existed,
used to buy and sell cigarettes, coffee, or in Jack's case, notes
written for illiterate fellow prisoners. Long-term inmates dominated new arrivals with tauntings and beatings and were allowed certain freedoms from the guards in exchange for their
control of the halls. In *The Road,* Jack claims to have become
one of these hall-men, who peddled the bread they were supposed to give out just as "outside the walls on a larger scale
. . . the captains of industry" did the same.

Jack's acceptance into the gang of thirteen who ruled the five
hundred others is doubtful. Young blond newcomers with soft
blue eyes were more likely to be raped or victimized in other
ways than be handed a share of control. Though Jack attributed
his success to convincing one particular tough that he would
help him commit crimes once both were out of the prison, it
is more likely the tough conned or overpowered him, and Jack,
like so many victims, identified with his oppressor enough to

adopt the role convincingly as his own in his later writings. It is the kind of deception at which he became brilliant, so persuasive that he fooled his readers. London understood that his middle-class readers were attracted to power, and London was always quick to give it to them, even if it meant portraying himself as a brute.

London's published account of jail ignored more than the sexual exploitation; it omitted how his exposure to the brutality awakened his perception of racism and class difference in society. After watching blacks and mulattoes suffer harsher abuse than whites, and hall-men rule over the mass of prisoners, he concluded prison to be a microcosm of society at large. He was humbled that such a system could make him, a healthy and intelligent man, helpless to prevent the inhumanity brought on by those in power. He left with a fervent wish to change the society that would allow such conditions, and in later years wrote brilliant, bitter indictments that stirred public outcry.

Throughout all of his tramping, he unwittingly behaved like a professional writer, keeping a diary in which he recorded jottings of what he saw and did, the slang and hobo argot he heard, jokes and lyrics of popular songs he learned, and quotations from books and notably poetry he read en route. That he was able to preserve this diary through his months of difficulties shows his reverence for the material. Moreover, wherever he went he visited the public libraries, widely available thanks to the philanthropy of Andrew Carnegie, and spent his days in their quiet shelter filling his mind while fellow tramps merely warmed their bodies.

In Baltimore he discovered that knowledge could fit into a system, that the various books he read and the experiences he had had in recent months could be connected. There he came across a group of well-educated professional hoboes who exploited the sylvan setting of Druid Hill Park to discuss philosophy, science, sociology, economics, and revolution. It may have been from them that he first heard the names Kant, Spencer, and Marx. These discussions inspired him to seek further education and gave him his first notions of class consciousness. He developed a crude understanding of how social forces of the time were affecting his choices. "I was scared into thinking.

. . . All things were commodities, all people bought and sold. The one commodity that labor had to sell was muscle." But unlike the capitalist's stock of shoes, which could be replenished, the laborer's stock diminished with each day of effort. By the age of forty-five or fifty, he would be worked out, "and nothing remained to him but to go down into the cellar of society and perish miserably."[6]

Years later, in *The War of the Classes,* he confessed that the vision of these men terrorized him, that he swore a great oath: "All my days I have worked hard with my body, and according to the number of days I have worked, by just that amount am I nearer the bottom of the Pit. I shall climb out of the Pit, but not by the muscles of my body shall I climb out. I shall do no more hard work." His desire to be of the middle class in fact drove him to work much harder with his mind than he had thought possible in these formative years. Like others of the working class, he mistakenly believed work of the mind to be effortless and easy, not "real work." But seeing only the result of study in these intellectuals, not the years each spent suffering from eyestrain, headache, and fatigue over books, Jack thought their way of life softer and more materially rewarding. He would become one of them, even though that meant returning to school.

*　　*　　*　　*

Returning to Oakland in 1895, Jack moved in again with his parents, who supported his desire to attend high school. He was an odd sight in Oakland High's class of 1897, rough and uncouth, older than the others, dressed in ill-fitting wrinkled shirts and the long baggy trousers favored by street hoodlums. The teachers were distressed by his inaudible recitations and slumping in his seat, signs to them of contempt. He chewed tobacco (to soothe the pain in his cavity-riddled teeth) and was observed sauntering into saloons on nearby Broadway. His classmates mistook his nervousness and shyness for rudeness; few saw how the rawness cloaked a quick and avid mind, one richly garbed by years of wide-ranging reading and travel.

Georgia Loring, daughter of a prominent Oakland family, took his slovenliness to be less a reflection of his poverty than an attitude of "don't care," a determination to do what he wished, even to the point of being dirty and unkempt. She felt sorry for him, thought he needed "sympathy and care . . . or perhaps, it was 'Home and Mother.' " Despite his "awful conceit" and frequent expression of resentfulness toward the wealthier students, she found appeal in his "understanding smile and expression of lovableness of character" that contradicted his behavior. She also sensed his unusual intellectual drive, "almost a mental ruthlessness for pursuing his ideas."[7]

Rejecting others' snobbishness, he bulldozed into school activities. In the high school literary magazine, the *Aegis*, he published descriptive pieces of his adventures on the *Sophia Sutherland* and stories of the Frisco Kid, a teenage tramp who steals the clothes off a dead boy and corrupts another boy by giving him chewing tobacco. The Kid's ungrammatical talk and rebelliousness tantalized Jack's fellow students, who developed a grudging respect for his knowledge of life beyond their orderly and respectable homes.

He also joined the Henry Clay Debating Society, a youth group favored by the well-to-do in town. His peers thought him conceited, with good reason. Their hostility only challenged him to prove that shabby roughnecks could be quick-witted. He discovered his delight in rousing argument and learned to get attention by taking radical positions, which he would back up with facts from his exceptional memory.

Still, his major intellectual and emotional growth occurred outside of school. During a visit to the Oakland Library, he attracted the attention of Frederick Irons Bamford, recently hired to develop the long-neglected reference department. A Canadian by birth, a genteel traditionalist in style, he was nevertheless a committed Christian Socialist who urged upon Jack not only Marx, but Ruskin, Carlyle, Arnold, and Morris. Jack's articles for the *Aegis* took on a more political tone. He shocked Mr. McChesney, the principal, with an article attacking "the powers that be" for creating a program of "long hours, sweating systems, and steadily decreasing wages."

Beside the city hall in Oakland was a tiny triangular park with crisscrossing paths, benches, and frequent band concerts that attracted many townsfolk. The members of the newly formed Socialist Labor party saw this setting as the perfect place for soapboxing. Passing by the park on the way to the library, Jack became acquainted with the activists, who included Max Schwind, a forceful debater, Frank Strawn-Hamilton, a brilliant philosopher tramp, and Herman "Jim" Whitaker, an Englishman who ran the local socialist cooperative grocery.

In time Jack was touting socialism at the Henry Clay club as well as on the bandstand at the park. His public role was established with a *San Francisco Examiner* article on Christmas morning of 1895, which gave almost a full page to a cartoon drawing of London, a brief biography, and his article "What Socialism Is—The Boy Socialist Describes the Meaning and Intent of the New Philosophy." There London disputed the familiar association of socialism with anarchy, depicting it as a form of pure democracy. In fact, his ideas were muddled, and would send any orthodox Marxist running. Socialism to him then was really a way to protest the social injustices he had seen in his brief life, combined with anticapitalism, an attack on the trusts he thought responsible for the inequities. It was a stance appealing to many listeners during those turbulent days.

The Oakland socialists did not find his view of the movement unusual. Conspicuously absent from their ranks were laborers. They were instead well educated—ministers, lawyers, teachers, college students—who were utopian and reformist rather than radical. For example, a major theme in their platform was municipal ownership of water supplies. Their reading lists did not even include the writings of Karl Marx and Friedrich Engels. As such they offered Jack a different model of work: the man who uses his brains, not his muscles, and earns much more as a result. The intellectual hoboes he had encountered during his tramping days in Baltimore had excited him with the adventures of the mind, while the intellectual socialists of Oakland proved such adventures could fulfil his childhood dream of a large house with a roomful of books.

Another set of friends introduced him to middle-class manners and mores. Through the library he became acquainted with Fred Jacobs, a slightly built, studious boy preparing for entry into the University of California. Fred had helped Jack with some of his English assignments and admired his determination to improve himself.

He introduced Jack to friends who were curious to meet this young phenomenon. Bess Maddern, a slender and athletic woman, had, like Charmian Kittredge, broken with tradition to

support herself, as a mathematics tutor. Her family, who opposed education as a waste of time and considered housekeeping to be the only suitable job for women, did not object to
taking her money for room and board, however. Ted Applegarth and his sister Mabel were from a cultured English family
that overlooked Jack's unrefined manners. Though neither the
Madderns nor Applegarths were wealthy, they were able to live
in an elegant, late-Victorian style, in which the women dominated both the tastes of the household and the conversation.
Unlike Jack's family, where expressions of kindness were few,
the Applegarths were openly warm and loving with one another.

Jack fell in love with Mabel, a delicate, golden-haired, blue-
eyed dainty. Her mother had shaped her into the epitome of
the late-Victorian lady, adorned with lace and long-flowing
skirts, beguiling with her upper-class British accent, quick to
state unoriginal opinions on a smattering of topics, skillful at
shaping the mood of a gathering with a bit of poetry or a light
contra-danse on the piano. She was also typically set in repose
on a sofa and required rest after the briefest exertion. This lack
of vitality was not trained: she was slowly losing her life to
consumption.

Mabel was just as taken by Jack's vitality and earnestness, his
desire to acquire the ways of parlor society. Her family welcomed him, inviting him for dinners, literary discussions, musicales, picnics, bicycle trips, sailing, and even a summer vacation
in Yosemite. Their influence was so strong that, according to
his later account, he did not drink during this period.

Later, in his brilliant quasi-autobiographical novel about upward mobility, _Martin Eden_, Jack was to dissect the turmoil and
trauma of this time on his psyche. Martin, a sailor and aspiring
writer, encounters a family like the Applegarths. The result is
not an easy passage into a different social class, but the beginning of profound splits in personality. Everything the Applegarths offered counterbalanced Jack's previous years:
polish/uncouthness, sobriety/drunkenness, good woman/bad
woman, repressed sexuality/impulsive sexuality, sensitivity/
brutishness, companionship/loneliness, satiation/hunger. It
was not just their lack of material want that attracted him;
more, it was their validation of the sensitive, aesthetic side of
him, which had been ignored until this point. Nevertheless, he

was not comfortable: however much he modified his speech or learned the subtleties of bourgeois courtship, he considered himself a street-corner tough playing a role, a fake.

Frantic to find peace, Jack grew impatient with his schooling. Convinced he could do better on his own, he quit high school to prepare for the university entrance exams on his own. Bess Maddern, now engaged to Fred Jacobs, tutored him in algebra. When he learned that Jacobs and Ted Applegarth had enrolled at the University Academy in Alameda, a cramming school, he convinced Eliza to lend him the money to join them. His stay was short. His explanation in later years was that they expelled him for accomplishing too much work in too short a time, thus compromising their program. Jack suspected the real reason was the threat that he, a threadbare socialist, presented to the wealthy clientele of the school.

Upon his dismissal in April 1896, he immediately signed up with the Socialist Labor party in Oakland. He also began cramming for the entrance exams on his own. Studying virtually every waking hour for twelve weeks straight, he hoped to learn enough geometry, chemistry, history, literature, and classics to be accepted as a special student. On August 10, 1896, he rode his bicycle to the campus for a three-day marathon of tests, which he passed, enabling him to join the boisterous class of "Naughty-Naughts." In spite of his claims that he achieved this success alone, he owed much to the support of Flora and Eliza, Fred and Bess, the Applegarths, and his fellow socialists, who had provided food, shelter, and encouragement.

Jack's aim was not to be graduated, but to take sufficient courses in composition, philosophy, and history to become a working writer. Aside from attending a few dances with Bess and Mabel, he did not participate in campus activities. Another aspiring writer, Jimmy Hopper, found him crossing the campus one day, cradling over a dozen books. Hopper was struck by Jack's boyish, frank joy, made more lovable by the lack of two front teeth. Hopper captured Jack's great thirst for understanding, describing his brain as:

a dry sponge—impossible of saturation in its many folds. He was never satisfied by the instruction he received and rushed to the library to read and study more about the idea. He was full of gigantic plans. He was going to take all the courses in English, all of them, nothing less. Also, of course, he meant to take most of the courses in the natural sciences, many in history, and bite a respectable chunk out of the humanities.[8]

With such unattainable goals, Jack designed for himself a self-defeating agenda. He left after one semester, with a good record and for unknown reasons, bitter feelings about professors —"boneheads" became a favorite epithet for them throughout his life.

He next tried another unsuccessful turn at writing, spending his time scrawling ponderous essays, humorous fillers, sonnets, triolets, juvenalia, and short stories. Nothing sold. Ten years later, while composing *Martin Eden,* he documented the rejection he received in return for his determination and self-discipline:

> In one of the great juvenile periodicals he noted whole columns of incident and anecdote. Here was a chance. His paragraphs were returned, and, though he tried repeatedly, he never succeeded in placing one. Later on, when it no longer mattered, he learned the associate editors and sub-editors augmented their salaries by supplying those paragraphs themselves. The comic weeklies returned his jokes and humorous verse. . . . Managing to obtain the addresses of two newspaper syndicates, he deluged them with storyettes. When he had written twenty, and failed to place one of them, he ceased. And yet, from day to day he read storyettes in the dailies and weeklies—scores and scores of storyettes—not one of which would compare with his. In his despondency, he concluded that he had no judgment whatever, that he was hypnotized by what he wrote, and that he was a self-deluded pretender.[9]

He began to envision an "inhuman editorial machine" with no live, warm editors at the other end.

He did see his letters to the editor on socialism appear regularly in Bay Area papers and, on February 10, 1897, made news by being arrested for violating a new law by speaking in public without the mayor's permission. Defending himself with florid argument in support of free speech, only one juror held for conviction. In March he received 546 votes in an unsuccessful bid for a seat on the Oakland Board of Education.

Distraught by failure in his chosen profession, through Eliza's influence Jack was given a job in the laundry at the Belmont Academy, where for several months he sweated all day sorting, washing, starching, and ironing the clothes of professors and their wives. (His one self-satisfying rebellion was in starching the underwear.) Somehow a confidence in his writing ability took hold, for he decided he would persist at these grim tasks whenever necessary to buy free time to labor at his desk. Thus, while an observer might think he had made little progress in the six years after his graduation from grammar school, in his own mind he had forged the rough shape of a mature identity.

* * * *

On July 14, 1897 the S.S. *Excelsior* tied up in San Francisco with a cargo of worn but happy men, their pockets filled with Yukon gold. Jack caught a severe case of gold fever, but he had no money to stake his way. As usual, Eliza came to the rescue. She mortgaged her house to outfit Jack, asking only that he bring along her husband, who had a weak heart. The idea was a mad one, but like so many people along the Pacific coast, the Shepards gladly went into debt to buy four thousand pounds of food, tents, and warm clothes, a year's worth of supplies for the two men. Only eleven days after the first news of the gold strike, they waved farewell to friends and family from the deck of the S.S. *Umatilla*.

Jack sent Mabel a precise description of the trials of the famed Chillikoot Pass, an account that also shows how he used calculation to make sense of the world: "I have 1000 pounds in my outfit. I have to divide it into 10 to 15 loads according to the trail. I take a load and come back empty. That makes two miles. 10 loads means 19 miles, for I do not have to come back after the 11th load if there is one. If I have 15 loads it means 29 miles."[10] Shepard soon turned back and returned home. Jack continued the hard march, adding a month in a boat over a lake and wild river before reaching the claims area of Henderson Creek. On October 15 Jack went to Dawson to file a claim,

but spent several weeks in the saloons before getting to that
essential piece of business.

In his reminiscence of the Klondike, grub staker Edward
Morgan said of Jack's behavior:

> I believe that he had staked a claim, . . . but I never saw
> him working one, never met him on the trail, and do not
> remember ever having seen him except in some Dawson
> bar. . . . I remember him as a muscular youth of little more
> than average stature, with a weather-beaten countenance
> in which a healthy colour showed, and a shock of yellow
> hair, customarily unkempt and in keeping with his usual
> slovenly appearance. It seemed to me that whenever I saw
> him at the bar he was always in conversation with some
> veteran sourdough or noted character in the life of Daw-
> son. And how he did talk.[11]

Another acquaintance remembered him sitting on the edge of
his bunk, gesticulating with hands stained by tobacco, trying to
persuade a companion that there was no scientific proof of the
existence of God.

In fact, Jack spent much of the winter confined to the Yukon
cabin he shared with several others. ("Forty days in a refrigera-
tor," he later quipped.) Among the books he read those days
of eternal darkness were Charles Darwin's *On the Origin of Species,* John Milton's *Paradise Lost,* Herbert Spencer's *The Philosophy of Style,* Karl Marx's *Das Kapital,* and Ernst Haeckel's *The
Riddle of the Universe.* Like many self-taught individuals, he developed a curious, often contradictory philosophy of life that
included belief in evolution and dissolution, survival of the
fittest, superiority of the white race, atheism, determinism, and
individualism.

His experiences in the Yukon particularly consolidated his
racial beliefs. When Jack was growing up, the majority of whites
in Oakland were foreign-born. Yankee Californians, like many
Americans of the time everywhere, felt threatened by these
people, who spoke broken English, dressed oddly, and often
practiced that most distrusted of religions, Catholicism. (The
"white man" in the vernacular of the day thus referred only to
Caucasians of English and Northern European origin; Italians,

Jews, Hungarians, and such were considered separate races.)

The great influx of Chinese in the Bay Area contributed to the pioneers' hatred of other races. In Jack's own household, Flora was outspoken in her prejudice, and as a boy he thought nothing of playing malicious tricks on Chinese people.[12]

Seeing what he was raised to see, in the Yukon Jack was impressed by the adaptability and power of the Anglo-Saxon, the settlers' resourcefulness in mining the earth despite unrelenting obstacles. He was not racist in the usual sense, for unlike most of his companions, he admired the survival practices of the native Americans he encountered. This attitude went beyond a simple, romantic Noble Savage stereotype. Indeed, he was genuinely sympathetic to the suffering of the native Aleuts, under the brutal domination of the invading settlers. Their situation was sad, he observed, because they were victims of an inexorable process of nature to which they must succumb.

Furthermore, Jack differed from other Social Darwinists in refusing to accept evolution as an excuse for cruelty and exploitation of "inferior peoples." The process would of itself ensure their extinction, he argued, so it was immoral for the Anglo-Saxon to abuse these members of the human species for personal gain.

His consideration of women was tempered as well. As his later stories showed, he lost none of his sense of mystery and wonder for women as a group, but he greatly broadened his view of the roles they could play. Frontier life forced the wives and daughters of Dawson businessmen to shed the false modesty, coyness, and artificial helplessness of parlor society. Jack saw for the first time what women could achieve if they were treated equally in society, and he preferred that outcome. Accordingly, he admired the prostitutes' strength of character and noted their general similarity to "respectable" women. And he mourned the harsh fate of the many Indian women who suffered abuse in marriage to prospectors.

It was in the Klondike too that Jack became fully a "man among men." There, where the struggle for survival stripped all social pretenses, he acquired an appreciation for camaraderie, for joining with others in mutual effort and celebration. His generous friendship, a quality that struck those who would meet him throughout his life, blossomed in that frigid setting.

Another trait he developed was what Buddhists would call a "beginner's mind." Klondiker Emil Jensen, who spent most of the winter with London, best captured this quality:

> To him, there was in all things something new, something alluring, something worth while, be it a game of whist, an argument, or the sun at noonday glowing cold and brilliant above the hills to the south. He was ever on tiptoe with expectancy, whether silent with wondering awe, as on a night when we saw the snows aflame beneath a weird, bewildering sky or in the throes of a frenzied excitement while we watched a mighty river at flood-tide. I never tired of his companionship.[13]

His naive, childlike wonder thrilled harder men and compensated for his lack of physical strength. His intellectual wit exhilarated them as much as a good fight, and they appreciated him for forcing them to apply their minds, for most people viewed them only as brutes.

Jack was loved as well for his tolerance and humor. Although he would fight a point very hard and never accept an easy answer, he would not become angry at his opponent nor force his point by bullying. He was especially skillful at getting others to contradict themselves and then baring their illogicality with a simple, underisive laugh that charmed both victim and listener alike.

Yet the qualities most Klondikers recalled were those of good friendship. The youngest of the group, he was praised for his winning smile and a generosity several described as "irrational," so selflessly was it offered. He seemed to recognize others' needs before they were aware of them and then set about satisfying them, whether that involved searching other cabins for new reading matter, making a two-day hike for tobacco, or lending a hand at the woodpile. When a fellow striker grew seriously ill, he helped the doctor break an eighty-mile trail to bring in moose meat. And, toward the end of his stay, he gave up the one bottle of whisky he had been saving all winter to sedate a man undergoing an operation.

Like many of his fellow adventurers, by springtime Jack had

come down with scurvy, the result of a diet limited to hardtack, bread, and beans. His gums swelled and bled, his breath stank, and his joints ached and puffed up so badly that he could do only the most necessary physical labor. The doctor urged him to leave immediately, for he was in a race with time for survival.

In July 1898, when Jack disembarked from the steamer that returned him from the Yukon, he learned his stepfather had died the previous October, leaving Flora to support herself and Ida's son Johnny Miller. The rent was due on the tiny cottage in which they lived, and there was little for food.

Sick and indebted to the Shepards, Jack faced a worse situation than the one he had left. His only trades were sailoring, which was unacceptable because it would take him away from home, and laundryman, for which no openings existed. Though he accepted any odd job that came along, he was still forced to pawn his personal effects: the silver watch Captain Shepard had given him for the Klondike, the bicycle from Eliza, and a raincoat inherited from John London. During August he joined a stampede to the California gold country, where false news of a strike led many hapless men like himself to waste their few resources.

After pursuing that worthless venture, he finally made a decision about his life: he would follow his previous impulse and become a writer—only this time he would succeed. He was listening to his intuition, and its message was a good one. The fact is that, had Jack London been born of the class of the Madderns or Applegarths, he would already have been well established as a journalist or writer. Throughout grammar school he had shown a talent with language, so much so that the principal excused the tone-deaf boy from singing class, provided he use the time to compose essays. Had he come from an educated and prosperous family, he would have been graduated from a university and perhaps working on a local paper.

But it was his working-class background that gave him an education in language that the university could not provide. His stepfather and the men he met in the bars, on the rail cars, and on the *Sophia Sutherland* were storytellers who acquainted him with the power of the well-shaped plot, the surprise ending, the interesting character. He had grown up in an oral culture that sustained and enriched language and provided him with a voice that stood out from the other writers of his day. This background, combined with his passion for reading, gave him a foundation for success; he needed only to acquire the practices of the professional. And that is what he set to do.

On September 17, he wrote the editor of the *San Francisco Bulletin* that "I have returned from a year's residence in the Clondyke [sic], entering the country by way of Dyea and Chilcoot Pass." The letter was returned with a note in pencil at the bottom: "Interest in Alaska has subsided to an amazing degree. Then, again, so much has been written, that I do not think it would pay us to buy your story." As Jack would prove, the editor was wrong.

For once, instead of fleeing failure, Jack entered a rare period of keen self-criticism. Somehow he understood that, however much Flora, Eliza, and his friends encouraged his writing, they were ignorant of modern trends in style and subject that were heralding in the approaching new century. The Applegarths and his college teachers had shown him masterpieces from the past, but it was obvious the magazine and book publishers were not looking for masterpieces in 1898. To solve his problem, he invented a method recommended even today to aspiring writers: he studied the market.

There is no question that, in becoming a professional writer, Jack London was a self-made man. His compulsiveness and overwork finally paid off. Whenever he was not mowing a lawn or painting a fence, he was at the Oakland library ransacking the shelves for the latest short stories, which he analyzed for style, plot, and subject matter. The more he read, the more surprised he was by the superficial cleverness of the works, the stock variations on old themes. He even developed tables for plot creation, whereby a potboiler could be created like a Chinese dinner, by combining different elements from different columns. He was not the first writer to understand that, in order to have the time to create a masterpiece, one must serve as a hack to buy the time.

To improve his style, he chose Rudyard Kipling as a model. The critics measured the work of other writers against the vigor and economy of Kipling's. Determined to adopt Kipling's style, he copied story after story until he felt Kipling's rhythm and voice become part of his own.

To increase his vocabulary, he started collecting lists of words from his readings and the speeches of socialist comrades. The words and their definitions were pinned to his mirror or strung on wires over his bed so he could review them first thing in the morning and last at night. As old slips were mastered, new ones replaced them, and he acquired a strong and supple control over language and diction.

One of his most insightful inventions was a special book-keeping system designed to fit his perception of writing as a business like any other. It allowed him to know where a manuscript had been sent and what editor held it currently. By calculating its potential net profit (after deducting the cost of stamps), he knew whether it was worth making an additional stamp outlay. Because he had a plan for each manuscript, the method also saved him useless anxiety over rejection. Over the ensuing months, his ledger books were filled with hundreds of entries as he sent his products to market.

Yet his most important observation was more theoretical. Jack recognized that realism was the genre to pursue, that the public was losing interest in the notorious purple prose of the late-Victorian era. On the other hand, he understood that his middle-class readers, while rejecting old fashions of speech, were nostalgic for traditional values and settings. Just a few years earlier, historian Frederick Turner had upset the country with his proclamation that the American frontier was closed. Jack would keep it alive in their memory through his choice of subjects, which early in his career meant the Yukon but would expand later to include the South Seas, socialist movements, and Eden-like ranches. More than anything, his recognition that this was a time of rapid change and transition secured his acceptance with readers, who were excited by the modernity of his tone and inspired by his depiction of new frontiers but reassured by his emphasis on old-fashioned values and relationships.

Rewards were few. He won two ten-dollar prizes for submissions to a Republican Club essay contest, yet had to threaten court action to get the money. He sped through a 21,000-word serial for *Youth's Companion,* which took months to notify him of rejection.

Were it not for changes in his social life, he might have

eventually followed his old pattern and given up. Of Jack's old Oakland friends, only Bess remained. Her fiancé, Fred Jacobs, who had enlisted in the Spanish-American War, died of fever en route to Manila. The Applegarths had moved to College Park, an area of San José forty miles away, a long trip on an old bicycle. Besides, he had lost his love for Mabel in the Yukon, where he saw women, both native and white, who displayed strength, courage, and hardiness. He found he preferred this kind of woman to the daintier ladies of genteel society. Bess Maddern was closer to his new ideal, but she escaped the tragic loss of her fiancé with work and did not see Jack often. Although Jack still had his socialist colleagues, they were generally older men, mentors, not intimates in whom he could confide.

The socialists eliminated any possibility of an amorous reunion with Mabel. Their philosophy gave him a reason to understand his growing disillusionment with her kind. "As a brain merchant I was a success. Society opened its portals to me. . . . The women were gowned beautifully, I admit; but to my naive surprise I discovered that they were of the same clay as all the rest of the women I had known down below in the cellar." Only these women were worse, because "the life they lived was materialistic. And they were so sentimentally selfish!" Similarly, he found the preachers, politicians, businessmen, professors, and editors he met through households such as the Applegarths when "not alive with rottenness [were] like well-preserved mummies." He despised that all these people failed to understand that "the beautiful clothes they wore were bought out of dividends stained with the blood of child labor."[14]

While distraught over the loss of Jack's romantic affections, Mabel served graciously as a comforting friend. He tested her hard. When she pressed him to give up writing and take a job in the post office to meet his duty to his family, he complained that he had danced to the tune of duty all his life. He recited to her a powerful litany of sacrifices he had made for his family —his childhood jobs, his returning from sea to give his wages over to pay off his parents' debts, his father coming to collect money from him at the high school where he was janitor. "If only someone had said, 'I understand,' " he cried.

Someone did understand. When Jack passed the civil service test with a score high enough to guarantee a job, Flora told him to forget the mail carrier's job and stick to his writing—they would survive somehow. She reminded him of his few successes: his contest prizes and the recent acceptance of his Yukon story "To the Man on Trail" by the *Overland Monthly*. For once he did not mock her advice.

4

THE
TAMING

And the mists had all solemnly risen
now, and the world lay spread before
me.

—Charles Dickens

While young Jack London was pursuing adventure, Charmian Kittredge was widening her connections in East Bay society. She was thought a stylish and high-toned addition to any social event: gracious with strangers, witty in conversation, well opinioned on the arts. Still, she maintained her wild side, her daring rides astride alone in the hills and her familiarity with writers thought to be of questionable morals such as Thomas Hardy and Henrik Ibsen. As she moved through her twenties, she continued to attract ardent suitors, even became engaged, but never walked down the aisle. One fiancé had bought an expensive Australian saddle to add to her comfort on her rides. Another admirer was always on the verge of leaving his wife for her but never did.

In the early 1890s, while Jack was playing street tough and sailor, Charmian led a humdrum life:

> . . . six days of the week spent in the office journeying back and forth on the ferry; the hours stolen before bedtime for snatches at the piano, for doing special laundering, for sewing and mending and casting up meager accounts; the two evenings a week of social diversion she permitted herself, and on the seventh day, Sunday, her day of solace, out among the blessed hills. But it was lonely, this solitary riding. Nobody of her acquaintance rode. . . . After years of it, one did get tired of this eternal riding alone.[1]

Later in life, when reminiscing, she seldom mentioned this period. Indeed, one could conclude she felt herself then within a chrysalis, emerging to full beauty only upon meeting Jack London.

Small inheritances from her father and then a Kittredge uncle in Maine bought her freedom from work. She used the money to invest in a rental property in Berkeley, which, it was understood, was to be available later on to secure Netta's old age. Still, the income from it enabled her to turn several rooms in the Eames household into a suite for herself and to hire a Swedish maid. Living amid such comforts, however, was not thought proper for a middle-class woman, who was to receive them through the benevolence of a father or husband, not by her own labor.

In the late 1890s, Roscoe became business manager for the *Overland Monthly,* the noted journal of Western literature and commentary started years before by Bret Harte. Netta took on editorial duties, and Charmian signed on too, probably as a volunteer, as "assistant sub-scissors." In addition to helping with clerical chores, she wrote book reviews, which were unsigned. Thus, she was among the first to read the Yukon stories of Jack London.

The *Overland* promised only five dollars for Jack's four-thousand-word story "To the Man on Trail" and, in spite of his repeated requests, did not pay even that small amount. When he finally went in person to collect his money, head editor James Howard Bridge assured Jack that, while his "White Si-

lence," the next piece they had accepted, was "the most powerful thing that has appeared in the magazine for a year, . . . he
was afraid it was a fluke and perhaps it would be impossible for
me to repay it."[2] Bridge explained the undercapitalized state
of the *Overland,* its inability to match the national magazines'
rates, but made an offer tantalizing to Jack nonetheless: if Jack
could sustain in later stories the quality of writing in "The
White Silence," Bridge would give his work a prominent place
in the magazine and see that the newspapers and reviews
puffed London's name before the public. During the year Jack
produced a series of Yukon stories, several of which formed his
first book, *The Son of the Wolf,* and Bridge kept his promise to
attract publicity.

By early 1900 Jack would see the benefits of his trading
income for recognition, but throughout 1899 he must have
doubted the wisdom of his decision. During this year he made
140 trips to the post office to mail 287 manuscripts. Of these,
266 were rejected. He averaged thirty dollars a month income,
less than he would have made in the post office, but at less cost
to his body. While the *Overland* paid him only seven dollars and
fifty cents for some of the best stories he was to write, the *Black
Cat* gave him forty dollars for a forgettable science fiction yarn.

Yet 1899 may have been the happiest year of his life. Freed
from manual labor, as he grew secure with his system of writing
he found time for pleasure as well. His contentedness shines
through his frequent letters to Cloudesley Johns, postmaster at
a small desert post office, aspiring writer, and socialist who had
written Jack a fan letter following the appearance of "To the
Man on Trail" in the *Overland.* Jack wrote encouragingly to the
stranger, and soon the two were exchanging philosophies of
life, books and news clippings, literary commentary, and criticism of one another's writings. Cloudesley's mother, a successful magazine writer, also joined in the correspondence, and his
grandmother, Rebecca Spring, once a friend of Emerson,
Holmes, and Longfellow, gave Jack a feeling of personal connection to those great thinkers.

The letters show a man frequently delighted by his self-
discoveries, with little of the bombastic self-display of later
years. He marvels at the writers he encounters: Ivan Turgenev,
Robert Louis Stevenson, Rudyard Kipling, Ambrose Bierce,

Edith Wharton, Edwin Markham, Frank Norris, Montesquieu, Diderot, Rousseau, Herbert Spencer, Charles Darwin. He is lighthearted about rejections and the need to dun the *Overland* to collect his payments. He is frank about his two great weaknesses as a writer—his refusal to rewrite and his inability to create plots. (He was never ashamed of borrowing themes from others and rightly saw his talent as being able to elaborate on old stories in new and compelling ways.) He explores the publishing world with Cloudesley: who is having a writing contest, which publishers pay what amount, whether sending a certain editor a particular story is worthwhile. Cloudesley and his mother were the first people Jack knew who understood the publishing game and could give him practical direction he trusted.

Although he continued his heavy regimen of study, Jack did not put in long hours at his profession. He chided Cloudesley for working seventeen hours a day at his typewriter, arguing that four, maybe six hours at the most, were the maximum a writer could spend productively. Characteristically, he established a rule he was to follow to his dying day, whether sick or well, penniless or wealthy, in a jungle shack or in his den:

> Am now doing a thousand words per day, six days per week. Last week I finished 1100 words ahead of the required amount. Today (Tuesday), I am 172 ahead of my stint. I have made it a rule to make up next day what I fall behind; but when I run ahead, to not permit it to count on the following day. I am sure a man can turn out more, and much better in the long run working this way, than if he works by fits and starts.[3]

(In experiments eighty years later, psychologists would prove London's rule for productivity.)

As he gained confidence in himself as a writer, he came into his own socially. He accepted that his odd dress—a sweater when fashion dictated a jacket, or a wrinkled bicycle suit—was often out of place, but no longer felt the need to copy society in order to be accepted by it. Friends from the past, from sailing and tramping days, as well as new ones, socialists and fellow artists, would clamber up the stairs to the bedroom-den in his mother's cottage to pull him away for a game of chess, a fencing match, or hours of debate. "I have the fatal gift of making friends without exertion," he correctly observed. He was always ready to lend some money he knew would not be repaid or help a woman friend through some emotional turmoil over a lover. Yet he remained ignorant of his generosity and kindness. "The strangest part is, that while considering myself blessed above all with the best of friends, I know I have never done anything to deserve them or to hold them."[4]

Of women, save for bicycle trips with Bess Maddern, he made little mention. To Cloudesley he explained, "We agree as to aversion to getting married; but not so as to women as one might link oneself for life. . . . As passionate as you, with probably less curb, I think I must have been created for some polygamous country. While I have a strong will, I deliberately withhold it when it happens to clash with desire. I simply refuse to draw the curb."[5] Sensing Cloudesley to be a man of sensitivity, Jack gave no more details of his activities with women. With friend Frank Atherton, however, who was more used to the seamier side of city life, he went to the Barbary Coast, where in the "dives and dens of iniquity," a peroxide blond, almost entirely devoid of clothing, screamed the song "Take Back Your Gold" without managing to be on key once throughout the entire number. In the balconies, "lewd females leered boldly at the men," luring them to buy spiked drinks and be robbed. While Frank was simply disgusted by the sight, Jack's reaction was more complex, both amused by the scene and intellectually challenged at the same time. If you want to get rid of this corruption, he advised Frank, then remove the profit motive. That he knew his way around the brothels so well suggests he was using them as his "polygamous country," but there were other ladies as well, such as the nameless benefactress who got his bicycle out of hock.

Not until eighteen months after his return from the Yukon, the fall of 1899, did Jack join wholeheartedly again with his socialist friends. Indeed, many of his comments to Cloudesley before this return show him struggling with his attempt to reconcile his belief in Anglo-Saxon superiority with utopian socialist ideals. In a discussion of altruism, he observed:

Nursing the inferior whites, segregating the hopelessly vicious and idiotic so that they may not breed, and developing those that are not so, draws its own line. To-day, the very opposite prevails as regards the lower classes; that is no reason it should always be so. Mind you, we must come to understand that nature has no sentiment, no charity, no mercy; we are blind puppets at the play of great, unreasoning forces.[6]

The lower classes he wished contained were of course the European immigrants, those whites he believed were not as blessed as the Anglo-Saxons. Until the influence of Spencer and Darwin weakened, as it must have by late 1899, Jack had a difficult time reconciling his admittedly inconsistent beliefs with those of his friends organizing the workers.

For readers almost a century later, it is virtually impossible to grasp the preoccupation with purity that prevailed at the turn of the century. When Jack received a likeness of Cloudesley and expressed distress over the weak chin that struck him as effeminate, he was upset not by taint of homosexuality, but that his friend, who had conveyed an image of masculinity, did not have the face to go with that persona. Since Cloudesley looked less than purely male, Jack hastily concluded the likeness surely was not an accurate one. They were both, after all, pure members of the Anglo-Saxon race and had a heavy responsibility. Purity was a gift of nature, a bounty of talent, and with it came an obligation to lead the human race ever higher on the steps of evolution. The Chinese, the Indian, the Slav could not advance, and ultimately owed their comfort in life to the wise actions of the white man. In a way, this social Darwinism was similar to Puritanism: like the wealthy colonists in Massachusetts, those of Anglo-Saxon blood were predestined to succeed and bore the responsibility for tending to those less blessed in their community.

It was one of Jack's newer socialist friends, Austin Lewis, who saw the subtle change in Jack's thinking and understood how the young philosopher was a short step away from the road to more destructive principles. An Englishman by birth and education, Lewis was an attorney devoted to the socialist cause. In his spare time he translated the works of Karl Marx and Friedrich Engels to make them available to those who could not read German. Jack correctly saw Lewis to be a perceptive stylist and valued his criticism. Lewis, however, was worried about his admirer, and later noted:

> In 1899, Jack London was young, vigorous, with a sure sense of emotional values and a mind which was beginning to show marks of cultivation and development. One would have predicted for him a wholesome, beautiful existence. But even then there were other concepts and theories of life attracting him, seducing him, destroying him, really. . . . Jack stood with one foot planted in the soil of social democracy, but the other foot was already being clogged in the morasses of the philosophical teachings from which have sprung fascism.[7]

Lewis's fears proved unfounded. Though in later years London often portrayed characters with fascist leanings, most notably Wolf Larsen, he was not often sympathetic toward them. Still, he struggled with the conflict between racial superiority and social altruism until his last work, an unfinished novel about interracial love.

Jack's major contribution to the party at this time was as a speaker. One frequent talk was "The Question of the Maximum," in which he discussed the theory that there is a limit to any human endeavor, and once that limit is achieved, one falls backward or changes the character of the advance. Of the rise of the common man through the centuries, he concluded, "That he has done this, only in the end to pass into the perpetual slavery of the economic oligarchy is something at which his whole past cries protest. The common man is either worthy of a better future, or else is not worthy of his past."[8] While Jack had doubts about the ability of workers to rise up against the capitalist machine, his talks attracted those workers and piqued their interest in the party.

If the Socialist party failed to shape Jack's beliefs into a more orthodox package, it did introduce him to two women of a type he had never known. About ten years older than Jack, Jane Roulston was a Wellesley graduate with all the composure of a proper Bostonian spinster. He was later to use her as the model for the Red Virgin in *The People of the Abyss,* a fascinating, maternal woman all men desired, whose devotion to the cause was so all-encompassing that she denied herself intimacy. If women in the Yukon had shown him physical courage, Jane was the first in his life to show that a woman could build her life around moral commitment and intellectual mastery.

The other woman, Anna Strunsky, was a Stanford student known already for her outstanding skill in debate. She first met Jack in the fall of 1899 at a lecture by Austin Lewis. When introduced to this new comrade, she felt "as if I were meeting in their youth, Lasalle, Karl Marx, or Byron, so instantly did I feel that I was in the presence of a historical character."[9]

With the high cheekbones and healthful dark coloring of her Russian Jewish parentage, she struck Jack as a beautiful genius. A rebellious woman (who had once been suspended from Stanford for receiving a male in her room instead of the parlor), she identified with Jack's vitality, intellectual curiosity, and convention-breaking inclinations. She admired his ability to take over a roomful of petty-minded intellectuals, who watched in shock as this tousle-haired, smiling, casually dressed youth demolished their arguments. The Strunsky family offered a convivial meeting place for artists and political activists; it was there that Jack first met Emma Goldman, whose beliefs in feminism and anarchy marked her as "the most dangerous woman in America." The Strunsky household's passion and fervor made the Applegarths look like pale, vacuous mannequins.

Anna was not blinded by Jack's charisma and also recognized the dangerous trends in his thinking. Almost immediately she noted his use of stereotypes in a Jewish character, Jaky, a man who haggled and bargained.[10] She upset him by insisting on addressing him as "Mr. London" for months—he was not used to women so resisting his charm. She distrusted his attitude toward women, noting that his outspoken vocal support of feminism was contradicted by his sexual prowling. Just as repugnant to her was his desire to "beat the capitalist at his own game" by becoming wealthy and successful, for she believed anyone trying to attain such goals would necessarily become a capitalist in the process.

Anna was used to the attentions of men—later she blamed her allure for never fulfilling her promise in the larger world

—and controlled their relationship. If she had wished, she could have convinced him to abandon his ethnic prejudice and marry her, but she never so wished.

*   *   *   *

The new year rang in a new century. Politically, it was a time when America was being called upon to bear the white man's burden. Many voices matched those of William Allen White, who claimed, "It is the Anglo-Saxon's manifest destiny to go forth as a world conqueror. He will take possession of the islands of the sea. . . . This is what fate holds for the chosen people." The country maintained an army of 60,000 in the Phillipines, brought 1,280 Cuban school teachers to Harvard for an education, sent 5,000 tons of corn to a famished India, and planted similar real and symbolic flags around the globe.

For Jack, the sound of the bells was less a call to action than a melodic promise of fame. International affairs mattered less to him than the state of the economy, which was booming. This meant more money in people's hands to spend on such extras as the 5,100 magazines that had emerged during the nineties. Now that the depression was a mere unhappy memory, readers were less interested in stories of business success through effort and hard work than tales in which the heroes were men of courage, stamina, and vitality, men unafraid to master others or the environment, men for whom money was less important than the execution of will. Yet such a man had to have a social conscience as well. Few were better suited to express these contradictory values than the vigorous young London.

Fame's door cracked open when the acceptance of "An Odyssey of the North" by the *Atlantic Monthly* caught the interest of Houghton Mifflin, which offered a contract for Jack's collection of Yukon stories, *The Son of the Wolf.* Then *McClure's Magazine* accepted "The Grit of Women" on the condition that he "change the opening and eliminate the profanity."[11] *Youth's Companion* took "Dutch Courage," the first of a number of children's stories he would write for that publication. He was now a nationally known writer.

For Charmian, the new year brought only a reminder of time's swift passing. Now twenty-nine, she had spent half her life at the typewriter. She was too old for college boys, and all her women friends had married. Still ensnared by Netta, she even spent her summer vacation as a chaperone in Yosemite for her aunt and her aunt's latest lover, a painter.[12]

Lacking much sense of her own value, Charmian's relationships with suitors took on a destructive pattern: she fell passionately for whoever came along, often inappropriate men, such as Herbert Dugan, an affluent and married San Francisco store owner. They would get her in bed with verbal hints and promises of commitment but fail to meet her emotional needs. As it was, having been raised by two philandering adults, she was ignorant of a day-to-day intimate relationship based on honesty, trust, and self-integrity. Her independence was further stifled by Netta's double messages, pushing Charmian into relationships with one hand while grasping for her own selfish motives with the other. When the inevitable collapse of the latest romance came, Netta had new ammunition to fault her "Childie."

Understandably, Charmian saw no particular reason for cheer one January morning when Netta insisted that she give up her precious solitary lunch to meet Jack London.[13] For one, she was tired of Netta's meddling in her life, particularly when it came to men. She was also repulsed by her brief glimpse of Jack on an earlier evening, when he appeared to discuss some *Overland* matter dressed in shabby trousers, dark gray woolen shirt, and torn cap. His grinning greeting showed dark gapes where teeth should have been. "So *that's* your wonderful Jack London!" she later sniffed. "He is not the only genius among your friends, but certainly none of them ever came to our house looking like this one."

Sullenly entering Young's restaurant in San Francisco the next day, she encountered a beguiling figure. Now the rogue appeared in a suit (a cheap one, she noted), with appropriate shirt, tie, and shoes. (It was the first and last time she was to see Jack in a starched collar.) His wide-set large gray eyes met hers directly, melting her prejudice against the hoodlum, sailor, and unsuccessful Yukon adventurer. "Looking for something he has never known," she thought, and she eased into conversation, aided by his calm attentiveness, his curiosity about her.

She told him about her work, her pride in being able to

support herself through her quick and deft fingers and her investments. She admitted she too was a socialist, and they discussed local people in the movement. During a general discussion of books, they found they were both fond of Kipling.

Netta interrupted the conversation to suggest that Charmian be the reviewer for *The Son of the Wolf,* which Jack had provided in galley form. He agreed, asserting that this well-read woman was just the person for the job, and pressed Charmian when she hesitated.

Several days later he appeared at the house to introduce Netta to fellow socialist Jim Whitaker. While Netta and Jim talked, Jack drifted into the parlor, where Charmian sat at the piano playing Chopin. At his request she switched to popular tunes of the day, and soon both were singing along together. He then asked to see her library. As she handed him Hardy's *Tess of the D'Urbervilles* to borrow, she caught him staring, seeming to want to know her better. Shyly he commented, "I have a conscience about books. Please know I'll take care of this as though it were my own."

Reflecting over these meetings later, Charmian laughed at herself. Netta had been right after all—the boy was delightful. But he was just that, twenty-four to her twenty-nine, not at all like the mature men she courted, from established families, educated at the university. Anyway, her great need was for another, one with whom matrimony at last seemed certain.

Jack searched for her whenever he stopped by to see Netta, whose solicitous ways were attractive to the mother-hungry man. Netta saw her opportunity to latch onto a rising star and called him her "boy," a title he was happy to accept. She eventually became his "Mother Mine." To Cloudesley he wrote, "Have made the acquaintance of Charmian Kittredge, a charming girl who writes book reviews, and who possesses a pretty little library wherein I have found all the late books which the public libraries are afraid to circulate."[14]

When Charmian came in one evening to find the galley proofs of *The Son of the Wolf* on her boudoir table and began to read, she was so mesmerized by Jack's haunting imagery and honest portrayal of the harshness of nature that she read the proofs straight through, glancing up at the mirror afterward to grow embarrassed by the sight of the sailor hat that remained half-pinned to her hair. Running downstairs, she protested to Netta that she lacked the intellectual wherewithal to prepare a thoughtful review. Netta argued and won, so Charmian sat down to compose her review.

Though generally praising the stories, Charmian was quick to notice "certain inadvertencies—false syntax and flagrant misuse of an occasional word—which are the result of inexperience or carelessness." Her concluding comments included reference to their shared belief in the popular race theories of the day: "Jack London has the avowed belief in an ultimate democracy to be achieved by all peoples whose institutions, ideals, and traditions are technologically Anglo-Saxon. 'Not that God has given the earth to the Anglo-Saxon, but that the Anglo-Saxon is going to take the earth for himself,' he declares convincingly."[15] Hence, Charmian became Jack's first reviewer, although only he knew that fact, because Netta took the material and incorporated it into a biographical sketch of London written under her own name.

One day Jack suggested a Saturday date to Charmian, a ride in the hills together, she on horseback, he on his bike. They laughed over the stir that comical sight might cause, and she agreed. Several days later she found a note from him, canceling the date for reasons "my letter to your aunt will explain." The letter announced his plans to marry Bess Maddern on Saturday. The idea had come to him suddenly, he admitted, but he would "be steadied" by the marriage, be "a cleaner, wholesome man because of a restraint laid upon me in place of being free to drift wheresoever I listed." Jack's language echoed the popular notion that man, a base creature tending toward immorality, benefited and matured by yoking himself to the nobler character of woman.

Charmian thought he was deluding himself. She knew he had been convinced after reading Max Nordau's essay "The Natural History of Love" that the emotion was nothing but a physiological phantasm. A materialist who believed that when one died, it was as final as when a mosquito is swatted flat, Jack outspokenly condemned romance.

The idea of marriage had come impulsively while preparing to move his mother and Johnny Miller into a larger house. Bess Maddern had come by to hang curtains, and glancing up at her on the ladder, he realized he was already tied to supporting a family, so he may as well tie himself down to a family of his own choosing. He was fond of Bess and admired her orderliness, which he shared. He saw her too as an emotional shield between himself and his mother, who imposed herself upon his frequent social gatherings (and perhaps too often stole the show from him with her dramatic renditions of Cleopatra). He may have hoped Bess would take over as dominant woman in the house and lessen his mother's intrusions.

Bess accepted his offer knowing he did not love her. Like many in his circle, she too subscribed to an antiromantic philosophy. She agreed that good friendship was more important and that, as strong descendants of the British Isles, they would bring forth the best of children. (Jack had a terror of less than perfect offspring.) Bess's spirit had been broken by her family when her aunt Minnie Maddern Fiske, the greatest American actress of the age, failed to convince them to let her bring Bess onto the stage. Jack probably misread her few signs of rebelliousness—her determination to be well educated and her daring to wear bloomers when cycling (an attire that drew as many insults on the streets of Oakland as Charmian received on her horse). She was in fact resigned to domesticity and, seeing how Jack had accepted the responsibility of his mother and stepnephew, took him to be a dependable, reliable man.

Pleased with himself, Jack took out his pen to explain his decision to Anna, a woman closer to him in many ways than Bess. "For a thousand reasons I feel justified in making this marriage. It will not, however, interfere with my old life or my life as I had planned it for the future." Anna would know he meant that mating restricted the inferior female, in this case Bess, so that the man could go on with his work more easily. Jack rested with pride now that science had paved a smooth path for him.

* * * *

Jack and Bess were joined in a simple ceremony at her family home on April 7, 1900. Their honeymoon was similarly modest, a cycling trip to Santa Cruz, a beach resort, for a brief stay.

Jack immediately encountered hints that science might not be perfect after all. To his surprise, Bess's discomfort in the water and clumsiness at swimming demonstrated that her athletic prowess was not as extensive as he had expected. This boded poorly for a woman selected to bring forth "seven Saxon sons and seven Saxon daughters." The sex may have been uncongenial, for Netta reported that Jack brought Bess to her for some education in the marital act.

Once home, Jack faced a greater problem: his mother, who in protest had not even attended the wedding, and Bess were incompatible. Flora was an exceptional housekeeper, whereas Bess had been reared to direct servants to actually clean. Flora believed in the world of spirits and occult, of chance and luck, whereas Bess was literal, earthbound, and believed the force of her personality could shape events. Their dispositions shared two characteristics: obstinacy and unreined temper. Johnny Miller, a spoiled and surly child, added further dissension. In later years Bess described to her daughter Joan the incident that caused the final break. At dinner one night Flora dropped into a trance, and Bess responded by throwing a glass of water in her face. Jack roared with laughter, then quickly found another house nearby for his mother and nephew, which gave him the new financial burden of two separate households to support.[16]

Once the women were under separate roofs, they crafted a congenial relationship. Flora would appear at the door and spend the day with Bess, talking, sharing recipes and other domestic details. By then worn down by life, Flora never smiled or showed affection and had poor opinions of most people. Her daughter-in-law became her one solace in the years to come.

Yet even without these initial difficulties, the marriage had a poor prognosis. For most of Jack's life, he had sought strength and security by escape, whether through adventure, drink, or obsessive work. Through these highly distracting, tension-generating activities, he sought to avoid his own despair over the warring factions within himself. He used involvement in risky endeavors to avoid feeling pain and helplessness at having been emotionally abandoned by his parents. While claiming not to be deluded by romantic love, Jack was just as deceived by his scientific model, which idealized Bess as a redeeming angel of mercy who would keep him on the straight and narrow.

At least the mating was a success—Bess was soon pregnant.

If Jack was quick to be disillusioned about his hopes for a happy marriage, his life outside the family made up for the deficits. *The Son of the Wolf* was published on the day of his marriage and sold quickly, becoming one of Houghton Mifflin's top five sellers in 1900, a year of considerable publishing activity. Jack's clipping bureau sent him dozens of praise-filled reviews from all over the nation. Topeka, Salt Lake, and Boston all agreed that this boyish Californian with a checkered past promised to join the greats of literature. His success was all the more phenomenal given the predilection of eastern publishers and most readers to turn toward Europe for the standards, as well as the actual settings, of literature.

What the rest of the country had failed to recognize before Jack's appearance was the degree of literacy and culture in California. Richard Harding Davis, a well-traveled journalist, concluded from his visit that Californians read books with more care and held more thoughtful opinions than those living in New York or Europe. Miners and ranchers several days' travel from a railroad spur sought a steady supply of books from their friends in the Bay Area cities. In the Yukon, Jack found many men with whom to trade books, his Milton for the six volumes of Gibbon's *Decline and Fall of the Roman Empire* or a Kipling.

Above all, California was the most cosmopolitan area of the country, for it included not only European influences, particularly Spanish, but Mexican and Asian culture as well. Jack perceived this complex dance of ethnic groups, races, and social classes better than other writers then (and perhaps even since). In *The Son of the Wolf* he condensed this interplay by examining the Anglo-Saxon and Indian in the terrible Arctic cold. Those familiar with these stories know they explore more elemental human issues—confrontation with one's fallibility and one's death—but what struck readers then was his redemption of both the white race and masculinity. "His style is strong and vigorous, and the book produces in the reader a deeper faith in the manly virtue of our [white] race," approved the *Atlantic Monthly*. The wolf, explained Anna Strunsky in her published review of the book, *is* the white man.

The wolf was also London, wily and solitary in a world fraught with terror. The best stories, like the best of all his

work, were therapeutic, allowing him to express in disguised
form his feelings of helplessness and abandonment, his self-
destructiveness. In response to newspaper reporters, he offered his idealized persona, that of the son of a pioneer trapper
who had followed his father's footsteps to conquer the wilderness.

Law, order, and restraint extended further into his daily life.
Voltaire's dictum for happiness, "The body of an athlete and
the soul of a sage," inspired him to join the many other health-
conscious Californians of the day and take up Indian clubs,
fencing, and swimming on a regular basis. He limited sleep to
five-and-a-half hours a day, awakening in the early morning
darkness when the household was cold and quiet, to study the
books piled about his bed. Leisure time was apportioned to
Wednesday and Sunday afternoons, when he hosted boisterous spaghetti feeds for his odd assortment of friends and hangers-on.

Seemingly proving that his philosophies were correct, other
signs of good fortune appeared. The publishers were offering
ten to twenty times his first payments for work previously
turned down many times over. Young gadfly publisher William
Randolph Hearst grabbed him for the first of many boxing
stories. After he won a two-hundred-dollar prize for his essay
"What Communities Lose by the Competitive System," *Cosmopolitan* offered him a full-time job as an editorial advisor and
writer on special topics. He gladly turned it down, having already accepted a contract from S. S. McClure at one hundred
twenty-five dollars a month for five months as an advance
against royalties from a first novel. When his 1900 accounts
closed, he found he had earned over twenty-five hundred dollars for twenty-six manuscripts and collected only 108 rejections, compared to 266 for the previous year.

Flush with success, he advised the youthful readers of the
Junior Munsey on "First Aid to Rising Authors." There he argued only two worthy motives for literature, the need to deliver
a message to the world and the need to make money. He
classified himself as motivated by the latter: "It's too bad, we
know, that we are not to be satisfied with a crust of bread and
a beggar's garb; but then, you see, we are only clay born. Our
sins be upon the heads of our progenitors, or whosoever had
the shaping of us. We are the ones who suffer from the belly

need."[17] His list of "healthy wants" filled lines, including good air, right food, saddle horses, cameras, and canoes. Money provided the chance to go places and see for himself, instead of pore over atlases and dim photographs. It was to include marriage and "multiplication." And it was to allow him to provide help "when India starves, or the town needs a library, or the poor man in our neighborhood loses his one horse and falls sick." Little did he know that he would one day quickly and easily remedy these hungers, and even less did he suspect that their satiation would not satisfy.

It is telling that his two major writings during this time concerned the roles of men and women, and that he argued so differently in each that they seem written by two different men.

For McClure he worked up a Yukon romantic yarn, *A Daughter of the Snows.* Here he introduced Frona Welse, a strikingly different figure from the typical soft-spoken Eastern heroines with their hopes of marrying into European royalty. Frona Welse is a dynamic woman of a type rare in American fiction. In the first chapter she proudly brags how she can swing clubs, box, fence, swim, do high dives, and walk on her hands. Returning from college to her wealthy father in Alaska, she is indomitable on the inland trek to Dawson while men drop injured and dead around her. Once ensconced in her father's home, she becomes the Lady, entertaining guests, playing piano, and performing as Nora in an amateur production of *The Doll's House.* Yet she wears short (ankle-length) skirts and befriends a town prostitute. Though independent in some ways, she puts aside her athletic antics and increasingly pursues a domestic life.

The competition of admirers for Frona is implicitly a debate concerning masculinity. Vance Corliss is an effete Yale man who hesitantly, though successfully, proves he has the mettle for frontier life. He has difficulty accepting Frona because she is knowledgeable about sex and is at ease with her sexual feelings. She also traps Vance with her logical repartees. When he is angry over her visiting with the prostitute Lucile, Frona notes that he can hardly be spotless:

"But I am—"
"A man of course. Very good. Because you are a man,

you may court contamination. Because I am a woman, I may not. Contamination contaminates, does it not? Then you, what do you here with me?"[18]

So much for the double standard.

Gregory St. Vincent is more blatantly masculine, making claims, later disproven, to brave adventures. Hints throughout the novel that he is a coward build to the climax in which he violates the frontier "faith of food and blanket" in a series of melodramatic encounters. Thus, London suggests that appearances of manliness do not make a man, for actions and character are what matter. The "real man" in the story proves to be the softer-appearing Vance.

Critics attacked London for portraying so "unrealistic" a heroine. Such women do not exist, they argued. But they did exist, and Yukon history is rich with stories of women matching Frona's accomplishments. More to the point, their attack was an oblique criticism of the so-called New Woman being touted in the media of the day—an athletic, outspoken, cigarette-smoking female who dared to show her ankles in public. Thus, while to modern readers *A Daughter of the Snows* reads as a soppy melodrama, it was in fact a radical critique of sex roles, cleverly disguised as a boiler-plate romance.

The story also showed that Jack believed the benefits of being an Anglo-Saxon extended to women as well as men and that the critical hierarchy of society was based on race rather than sex. In this regard he broke from the social Darwinists, especially Herbert Spencer, who strongly contended that evolution was the scientific basis for the traditional superiority of the male.

On the other hand, in collaboration with Anna Strunsky, he prepared *The Kempton-Wace Letters*. Anna had been struggling with her materialist convictions, which maintained that love was a disorder of the mind and body, and her idealistic feelings, which valued romance as the awakening of a personality to beauty and higher virtues. To settle the argument, Jack proposed a book in which he took the role of a pure materialist and she the position of an idealist. She argued the reality of love as a basis for intimacy and marriage. He called it a "prenuptial madness" that interfered with the mating process and thus confounded the survival of the best of the race. For society's good, man should choose for marriage not the woman who attracts on the basis of lust, but the Mother Woman, "made preeminently to know the lip clasp of a child." A sensible marriage is based "upon reason and service and healthy sacrifice," averred Jack.

No spunky Frona Welse for me, he seemed to say: her athleticism is fine but she is too sexual and not maternal. A domestic woman like Bess is the ideal, an intelligent, talented woman who can produce good breeding stock but be content in the home. In truth, his argument was a rationalization for his current unhappy situation, an attempt to convince himself more than the reader that his scientific marriage had been a good decision. As the book progressed, his true feelings emerged, and in a striking concession allowed Anna's defense of romance to win in the end.

Alas for Bess, on January 15, 1901, she delivered not a sturdy Saxon son but a girl, Joan. She was too ill afterward to care for the baby, so Virginia Prentiss moved into the household as nurse. Jack had expected a boy, "no whining puny breed." But at nine-and-a-half pounds, the "damn fine, healthy youngster" soon won his heart, if not renewed affection for her mother.

5

THE
ETERNAL SEARCH

The Poet, gentle creature that he is,
Hath like the Lover, his unruly times.

—*William Wordsworth*

While Jack was finding his marriage less sweet than he had anticipated, Charmian was trying to untangle various romantic knots. Perhaps it was at this time that Will Minstrel broke off their engagement by sending his new lover around with a note of rejection. Or, "the problem," as she referred to it cryptically in her diary, may have involved other lovers, for we know the troubles caused a rift between her and Netta, and that years later she wrote to her aunt: "I want to refer to the subject of LOVE—say your love toward me: Auntie, Auntie, bless you—you know, and I know, that never have you really and truly and warmly loved me since the days, so long and long ago, of the mix-up about Harry, and Edward, and Herbert. Life was never the same again, to either of us, you and me."[1] Herbert was likely Herbert Dugan, whom Charmian continued to love although he failed to leave his wife for her. Harry could have been painter Harry Culmer; and Edward, Netta's new amour, Edward Payne, a retired minister. Charmian's later autobiographical notes did little more than hint that a commotion had occurred.[2]

Whatever, the resulting argument with Netta so beleaguered Charmian in the fall of 1900 that she went to visit her father's extensive kin in Maine. The trip marked the first time since her two years at Mills that she had been separated from her aunt, as well as the start of a rite of passage into an adult identity of her own.

Like Jack, Charmian was not inclined toward self-analysis during times of trouble. True, she kept a daily log of her feelings, but through her entire life showed little awareness that a study of these entries could help her identify troublesome patterns and avoid them in the future. She hadn't the temperament to set her own goals and had become accustomed to accepting the goals society (find a husband) and Netta (keep the money coming in) dictated. Lacking strong expectations about life freed her to face adventure fearlessly, so she stepped up into the train that was to carry her for a week cross-country with a mind open to new possibilities.

A prosperous and well-educated group, the Kittredges were scattered about Searsport, West Eden, Bangor, and Bar Harbor. They were so warm and welcoming to Charmian that one evening she fled to her room to cry in joy over their attentiveness. And in New England she found that to be unwed at twenty-nine was to have much company, for spinsterhood was a respectable and common outcome for women in that man-short region. Nevertheless, she found suitors enough to take her for moonlit sleigh rides and to clam bakes and country dances.

Content on the surface, at night private unrest reared up. "Slept poorly. Disgusted," she noted with her distinctive backhand in her diary. Insomnia led to blue spells and headaches.

Part of the stress was caused by her drive. She pushed herself to be productive as though using a scientific system similar to the one Jack devised: so many hours a day of physical exercise, of piano, of bending over the tiny stitches of a silk blouse or chemise, of puzzling over copy sketches of Gibson girls. She hated being lazy or unproductive and berated herself on those days when she did not meet her expected quota. Some of her unhappiness, too, was due to her being severely restricted by the Maine winter, unable to earn her keep by her own labor, dash on a horse through the countryside, or sail. However hospitable the Kittredges, however grateful Charmian, she could not help but feel that their conventionality emphasized her feelings of separateness. As a vegetarian socialist she was a stranger amid these meat-and-potatoes Republicans.

Relief came when the sale of one of her Berkeley properties netted her fifteen hundred dollars for travel. In February 1901 she went to Boston to enjoy the art museums and the latest plays, such as *Sweet Nell of Old Drury* and *Sherlock Holmes.* There she met a New Hampshire politician who accompanied her and her girl friends about frequently. Of a train ride to Manchester, New Hampshire, she wrote ecstatically, noting the "delightful trip" with his company "*all night!*" Several days later he asked her permission to visit her in Maine and, when she departed for further travel in Philadelphia and Washington, sent her off at the station with a bag of candy. During her visits in those cities she was beset by one Robin Blackman, who persisted in showing up where she was "in spite of the fact that I wouldn't see him."

Still, men played a minor role in her diary. More common were references to specific artistic experiences: seeing the much-awaited Sarah Bernhardt in *L'Aiglon,* being mesmerized by Rosa Bonheur's magnificent and controversial painting *Horse Fair,* deploring the state of theater in Philadelphia. She showed strong and well-formed opinions, an eye for discerning the value in works that more conventional society disdained.

In May, she accompanied a young couple on a month-long tour of England, France, Germany, Belgium, and Holland, that rush through the continent required of better-class Americans at the time. During the stormy North Atlantic crossing, other passengers lay moaning below, seasick in their bunks, but Charmian spent long hours walking the deck with the officers, asking questions about the ship and nautical life. "Just now I feel like I want to travel the rest of my life," she exclaimed to her companions. She kept a separate travel diary to have room for more extensive commentary on the architecture and art works. The trip was like a forced march, requiring great endurance, which she maintained in spite of a nasty cold. She would keep up; she would not be an unpleasant companion.

Her summer in Maine began inauspiciously with a case of mumps. After that, she longed to return home. The suitors continued their quest, but she felt a promising relationship would stand the test of distance.

It was not until the winter of 1901 that she returned to Oakland and her old job, leaving only a hint of her future amid her address listings, "London Jack, Bayo Vista Avenue, Piedmont."

*   *   *   *

1901 had been as much a transition year for Jack as for Charmian. He ran into unexpected difficulties with his writing career, became more isolated from his fellow socialists, moved more into artistic circles, and drifted further from Bess.

His writing plans were brought up short when S. S. McClure pronounced *A Daughter of the Snows* an inferior book and sold the manuscript to Lippincott for publication. McClure anticipated the later critical complaints about the female lead, Frona, whose assertiveness and physical feats seemed to him outlandish. McClure found little to admire in the spirit of those pioneer women who left the claustrophobic drawing rooms of the east for the harsh yet invigorating frontier.

London's collected Yukon stories, *The God of His Fathers,* received good critical response, but it was a second book on the same theme as the first and so did not command as much publicity. Worse, it brought no income, for McClure applied the royalties to the previous advance payments he had made on the rejected novel. In a rare moment of objective review, even Jack admitted the stories did not equal the earlier ones.

In spite of his growing reputation as a feature writer for Hearst's *San Francisco Examiner,* London grew disconsolate. He felt himself mired in "hack" work, forced to produce forgettable stories such as those concerning "Delightful memories suggested and recalled by the visit of Julius Beeker to the Bunderfest shooting hall."[3] A local columnist wondered whether Jack "had resolved to wear the purple and fine linen of yellow journalism and dine daily on mock turtle and the fatted calf à la prodigal."⁴

Jack's presence split the Oakland socialists, some of whom questioned his understanding of the cause and disapproved of his Anglo-Saxon jingoism. The pragmatists prevailed, however, and convinced their comrades to support Jack in a run for mayor of Oakland. In accepting the nomination, he noted, "It is we, the Socialists, working as a leaven throughout society, who are responsible for the great and growing belief in municipal ownership."⁵ The party platform appears strangely conventional to modern readers used to identifying the movement with revolution. It called for an eight-hour work day, public trade schools, public control of street-car lines and utilities, and social services for disabled and aged workers. The demands were milder than Jack, with his more anticapitalist views, would have made.

Word of his candidacy in January 1901 gave local columnists the chance to jibe: "I don't know what a Social Democrat is, but if it is anything like Jack London's stories, it must be awful."⁶ Another quip asked whether the name of the city would change to London or Jacktown. Significantly, he did not campaign, nor did he find it odd to declare fervent commitment to the cause but pay it only lip service. The *Oakland Enquirer* claimed he failed to canvass because the socialists feared having a popular idol as leader, for he could easily turn into a party boss.⁷ This may well be true, for it is hard to imagine him voluntarily giving up an opportunity to be in charge. His hope, that his name would give socialism prominence in the campaign, was met; reporters hungry for copy created supportive stories without direct help from Jack. As expected, he lost the election, garnering only 246 votes to John L. Davie's 2,548.

Fellow socialists saw his growing celebrity as a boost to their cause, and they did not have to convince him to take to the rostrum of large meeting halls. He went willingly to speak before literary clubs, women's groups, and gatherings of academics as well as the Ruskin Club and Socialist Labor party.

Even if the speeches were not scheduled to be about socialism, Jack simply took advantage of the podium to change the topic. Invited to address the Women's Press Association of San Francisco on Rudyard Kipling, he calmly announced that he had selected a different topic, "The Tramp." Tramps, he argued, were part of the surplus labor of society, recruited when production needs are high and disowned when economic crises or technological improvements occur. Thus tramps were those who chose the freedom of the road over slavery. In a satirical conclusion, he attacked society for believing it unethical to kill the tramps off, while at the same time allowing them to starve to death. London so inflamed the well-dressed listeners that the chairperson had to adjourn the meeting to avoid pandemonium.[8]

Often his talks had little to do with the socialism his colleagues advocated, but he spoke with such evangelistic fervor that his message was conveyed by its delivery, not its content. Working-class people would be transported by his descriptions of personal experiences in factories; middle-class people were captivated by his brilliant rhetoric and obvious literacy. Few recalled him as having a powerful voice, but all agreed he had a commanding presence that made up for vocal weakness. "It wasn't the logical Germans, Swedes, and English that kept the party going," recalled socialist Jim Whitaker's daughter Elsie, "it was Jack London. . . . He dealt with the facts of life and poverty—he was graphic. He knew. He had a real love of humanity."[9]

Jack found these presentations invigorating. Sincere and fervent in his beliefs, he wanted to convince factory and sweatshop workers to take control of their lives as he was doing. He enjoyed shocking and belittling those listeners he held in contempt. He was the center of attention, and he grabbed the spotlight as much as he could—and deserved it.

During this time he used his speeches to shape a number of articles, including "The Scab," "How I Became a Socialist," and "The Class Struggle." He knew such work was unlikely to pay much money, yet he gave it even more care than his fiction, writing revisions after consulting with other readers, a practice he followed with few of his manuscripts. Still, on the private level, socialism was his opiate against the pain of conflicting drives, against the recognition that his life plans were not bringing the reward he had expected. He told Jim Whitaker of walking down Market Street in San Francisco, looking at the window displays, and remembering how he had looked in those same windows as a boy and yearned for things. Now that he had money, he did not want a thing that he saw—so he cried.[10] Socialism gave him personal recognition no paycheck from an editor could provide, and he felt much more vigorous and alive while debating at the Ruskin Club or harassing a university gathering than putting out his thousand words. The wonder is that he did not give up writing altogether.

More revealing signs of Jack's inner turmoil are conveyed by his treatment of his family. In eleven months he moved them five times.

When spring rains turned the basement of the Fifteenth Street home into a pond, Jack accepted an offer from sculptor Felix Peano to share his ornate pseudo-Italian villa, La Capricciosa, in exchange for board at the Londons' table. Given the lack of a steady monthly income, Jack hoped the arrangement would reduce his financial pressures. But Bess was distressed in this odd house with its tiny rooms, tight, winding staircases, and curious sculptures. She saw a housekeeping horror while Jack found simple joy in the lunacy of the design.[11]

Bess had a respite in June when Jack took his family to spend a month at Camp Reverie in Forestville, a redwood-laden community along the Russian River north of San Francisco. The camp was based on a popular model of the day, where families would gather to hear lectures on philosophy, history, and literature and participate in various arts. Netta Eames's lover, Edward Payne, was president of the association and invited Jack to be a featured speaker. The gathering included socialist Jim Whitaker and his family, as well as some of the Strunskys.

In addition to lecturing, Jack played the role of "irresistible villain" in a camp play, while Bess took on the "deserted, but admiring wife." None, including the actors, guessed they would one day be playing these roles in real life.

After returning to La Capricciosa, the writer and sculptor had a falling out. In spite of his lack of money, Jack moved his family not to East Oakland, which he could afford, but to the lower foothills of Oakland (the Bayo Vista address Charmian noted in her diary), a fashionable new district for more prosperous people.

In February 1902 he had Bess pack the family up one more time, to the first shingle bungalow built in northern California.

For thirty-five dollars a month (to him a bargain), Jack held sway over five acres in the poppy-covered Piedmont hills and a sprawling home with more space than the family needed. The large and sunny rooms were finished in redwood, providing the informal warm and inviting interior he was to favor the rest of his life. From the broad, cool porch he had a view that took in all of San Francisco Bay for a sweep of forty miles. At that time the hills were cattle country, overseen by cowboys in brilliant Mexican dress. Flora and Johnny Miller were given a cottage on the property, and Jack imagined "chicken houses and yards for 500 chickens, barn for a dozen horses, big pigeon houses, laundry, creamery, etc."[12] Bess, however, found that she was even more isolated than ever, far from the grocery and her child's doctor.

This move marked a significant watershed in Jack's life. Until recently Jack had been urging Cloudesley Johns to leave the desert and move into a city; he defined himself as the gregarious sort who needed the frequent stimulation of friends and urban bustle. Now, though but a scant half-hour trolley ride from Oakland and the ferry slip to San Francisco, he seldom went to the city. He was establishing roots in an area very like the ranch of his youth where he claimed in his various autobiographical statements to have spent his unhappiest years. In fact, as Charmian later observed, orchards and animals had been a delightful childhood setting for a boy with Jack's temperament. It was not ranch life that he deplored, but the fact his father had failed to keep the land. New-found success gave him the opportunity to make up for his parents' failure and enabled him to banish the images of humiliation and incompetence his parents represented. He could now prove himself their betters.

His flight from the city also reflected a change in friends that had been on-going throughout 1901. Like many Americans, Jack liked to believe he was making his choices autonomously, when in fact his actions were much shaped by those about him. Among sailors, he drank; at home, he did not. Among socialists, he argued intellectual ideas; among artists, he organized bubble-blowing and kite-flying contests.

During 1901 the socialists held less sway in his life as a new group of Bay Area bohemians, known among themselves and eventually in the press as the Crowd, captured his interest. Joaquin Miller, the bearded "poet of the Sierras," played daredevil westerner and guru to the group. James Hopper, a winsome, witty journalist, composed Kiplingesque magazine fiction based on his earlier experiences as a schoolteacher in the Phillipines. Jim Whitaker, the only crossover from the socialists, had become an income-earning writer as a result of Jack's support of his family for three months while Jim worked full-time trying to break into print—and succeeded, much to his sponsor's pride. Xavier Martinez, the most colorful figure of the group, a painter trained in Paris, briefly disturbed the Crowd's equilibrium when he married a teenager half his age, Jim Whitaker's daughter Elsie. Blanche Partington reviewed drama and opera for the *San Francisco Call.* Her brother, Richard, was a portrait painter, and her sister, under the stage name of Frances Peralta, was a successful opera singer. Only one member of the group would achieve lasting fame with Jack, Arnold Genthe, a wandering German student who became a popular portrait photographer.

The most significant member of the Crowd, and the one who convinced Jack to move to the country, was poet George Sterling.[13] When friends first introduced the two at a restaurant in 1901, Jack virtually ignored the lanky figure with his distinctive Roman-nosed profile and whiny voice. His lack of interest in the older man was predictable. With fellow Californian novelist Frank Norris, Jack was a progenitor of the age of realism in American literature; Sterling was last heir to a decaying era of lyrical expression. A transplanted easterner from a family of comfortable means, George had attended private schools, including a seminary. When hard times forced his family to move west, he became assistant to his maternal uncle, Frank C. Havens, an Oakland real-estate magnate who represented to Jack the worst kind of capitalist. George was married to Carrie Rand, a statuesque beauty whose interest in art was limited to self- and interior decoration. Her sister Lila was Havens's wife, and others thought Carrie hoped George would move up in the firm to afford her the comforts her sister enjoyed.

George also had a literary protector, Ambrose Bierce, the grand Mikado of the Bay Area literary scene who chopped off heads and awarded sinecures with equal ease. An oddly prim and cantankerous character, Bierce encouraged the excesses in George's old-fashioned but meticulously crafted odes. Bierce demanded utter loyalty from his protégés, and George gladly complied. An irreversible anglophile and snob, Bierce was known for such satirical writings as *The Devil's Dictionary,* as well as a preoccupation with horror, mystery, and death, especially by suicide. He strongly influenced the development of George's own noted brand of cynicism and moodiness.

In time, the two met again and discovered to their mutual pleasure that they shared many common interests behind their surface differences. Both were avid readers and talkers, dedicated to their writing. Full of passion and fun, they shared an enthusiasm for an occasional rowdy adventure on the Barbary Coast. They liked being outdoors, whether swimming, fishing, or boxing with a friend. Often emerging from behind their bombastic veneers were the sweetness and gentleness of their kindly temperaments. Both were known for their generosity and loyalty to friends and soon became most generous and loyal to one another.

The London-Sterling relationship has been described as latently homosexual and overly masculine, as if to belittle the quality of their friendship. Such characterizations only display an ignorance of the social world of the time, when same-sex relationships, not heterosexual ties, were the primary bonds. Letters from man to man or woman to woman regularly expressed an affection denied those of a post-Freudian period. ("I wrap you in love. Then I kiss you full on the lips, and say farewell," wrote Anna Strunsky to Charmian.)[14] If Jack accepted from George the nickname of "Wolf," and George in return that of "Greek," they did so as women once would exchange rings, as a sign of commitment to their friendship. They maintained that commitment, and during much of their long relationship were in contact only by frequent letters.

Perhaps some see homosexual ties because of the intensity of emotion that was felt. Although Jack had admired Ambrose Bierce's work and recommended it to Cloudesley Johns, once he met George he changed his tune, pounding his friend about Bierce's inadequacies like a jealous lover.[15] Accustomed from childhood to being the center of attention, he could not tolerate George's devotion to the father figure who claimed, "You shall be the poet of the skies, the prophet of the suns." George would not be swayed, however, and had his own fits of jealousy over Jack's female interests. Needless to say, Jack was not swayed by his best friend's objections in these cases either.

An important value they shared was lack of support for monogamy. Each was accused by friends of corrupting the other in this matter, when the evidence suggests they were both faithless before their meeting. Although Jack liked to brag about his familiarity with scarlet women, his easy talk suggests less activity than claimed. On the other hand, as was befitting a skillful Don Juan, George let his well-bred demeanor fool observers. Throughout his life George was never able to resist any woman who said a kind word about poetry, and he gladly fulfilled their Byronic projections. In the men's early times together, however, they certainly shared some joint carousing, much to the displeasure of their wives.

The great tie between them remained literary. Jack envied George's extraordinary control over poetic craft. Poetry was Jack's favorite form of literature, and he had been greatly disappointed when, after months of copying and mimicking, he had to admit having no talent. He saw in George the embodiment of the nineteenth-century Romantics he admired most and sought out the poet's advice on his own prose. Fortunately, George's classical education made him a masterful editor who over the years corrected Jack's word choices, grammar, punctuation, and style. Unfortunately, Jack often had sent the manuscript off for publication before the thoughtful criticisms arrived.

In turn, George wrote many of his poems with Jack in mind. In later years, as the poet realized his star would never rise, he grew more dependent upon his famous friend's reassurances. He even asked Jack to claim to be the author of a play he had written so that it would be taken more seriously by readers. And, when in financial straits, he would sell Jack a plot, a convenience that allowed the receipt of money without embarrassment to either. (Jack would also buy plots for similar reasons from Sinclair Lewis during that young author's involvement with the Crowd several years later.)

A similarity in temperament also united the two. Both men suffered from severe splits and conflicts in their personalities that kept them from feeling comfortable in any setting. George, a noted sybarite, had never reconciled his split with the church, and often abhorred the womanizer and drinker in himself. Elsie Martinez watched him skulk off alone for hours at a time from raucous parties, as though to appease the hungry spiritual side of himself. Jack ricocheted between a heady, willful, hungry egoism and a sincere, surging compassion for others in need. Sometimes he was bitter that his desires were being stifled by duty, but more commonly he felt torn between the two as legitimate and warring claims and never, however great his personal debts, restricted his kindness to family and begging strangers. But seeing the two as inimical drives, he seldom felt full satisfaction when he took care of others, for his starving childhood self was there to complain. Life was very complicated for these two, and each found comfort in discovering another soul caught up in similar conundrums.

When George decided he wished Jack to move closer to his own home in the country, Jack was readily amenable. Throughout the fall of 1901, his letters to both Cloudesley and Anna showed a marked emotional instability. To Cloudesley he complained, "I am rotting here in town. Really, I can feel the bourgeois fear crawling up and up and twining around me. If I don't get out soon I shall be emasculated. The city folk are a poor folk anyway. To hell with them."[16]

The "bourgeois fear" and "emasculation" had to do with his marriage and financial responsibilities, not only to his immediate family, but his mother, nephew, and Virginia Prentiss. Bess's matter-of-fact and literal nature had seemed stabilizing when he was poor and unknown but failed to please his more successful self. He inscribed her copy of his Yukon stories with the following: "The first book of mine, 'all of your own,' you said. But what matters? Am I not your own, your Daddy-boy?" He called her Mommy-girl, at first in praise of her devotion to Joan. Later he chafed at her refusal to be separated even overnight from the youngster.[17]

A tug of war developed. One raging argument concerned whether tomatoes should be cut latitudinally or longitudinally. Neither would give in or admit to the silliness of the dispute.

He wanted much more than a Mommy-girl for a spouse. He encouraged her to buy fineries, to dress as befit the wife of a more successful man. She refused. She did accept household help but would not play the role of charming hostess, for she was not comfortable among large numbers of people. Her refusals sent him out with Sterling for brief sexual adventures. These all-night prowls left her with a fear common to women then, that he would infect her with venereal disease.

He became more outspoken in his unhappiness with her, telling male companions of her sexual coldness, of her preoccupation with gossip. He called her thinking, once appealing for its precision and detail, "microscopic" and "shallow." Bess's inclination was to withhold and control her feelings, while Jack had a flair for exaggerated expression. Her own favorite daughter Joan would one day write, "Bess neither praised nor flattered. Lifelong she retained her belief that if someone did something well there was no reason he could not do it better." This attitude was hardly agreeable to a man as desperate for continual praise and reassurance as Jack was. Even so, in early 1902 friends did not believe he would leave her, for he talked hopefully about having a son, and indeed Bess was soon pregnant.

To Anna, Jack expressed more than his dark moods. She had been coming to his home regularly to work on *The Kempton-Wace Letters,* and the two engaged in a rich correspondence when apart. As Jack grew discontented with his family life and writing difficulties, he turned to Anna for succor, stirring Bess's suspicions. He told of recalling at a Champagne-and-terrapin New Year's dinner "the sordid orgies and carouses of my youth," of pulling "out of the slime," and then thinking of Anna. In January 1902, he must have made some verbal overtures to her, which were rejected, for he wrote a lengthy apology that explained why he felt no shame even though "my manhood to your womanhood may be all wrong."[18] She resisted his advances.

*　　*　　*　　*

It was about this time that Charmian became reacquainted with Jack and joined in the Crowd's social functions. She went to the Wednesday gatherings at Jack's place, where jollity and sport passed at a frenetic pace with clattering din. The grand architect of all that occurred, Jack transformed play into a fine art. There were card games of pedro, whist, poker, and black-jack, where people avoided sharing a table with George Sterling because he grew so violent upon losing. Then a call to the piano, Charmian likely at the keys, to sing in harmony. Next might be a berry- and mud-tossing fight in the meadow. Following dinner, while the sun set, all would gather on the porch to hear George read his latest poetry or Jack recite Symons, Rosetti, Swinburne, or his favorite, Browning.

Jack especially sported with the young women guests, who could tell he was not the most loyal of husbands. Exuberant tricks were commonly played to attract attention. When Jack lay in his hammock napping one afternoon, several women sewed him up in it and lit a fire underneath. He seemed to accept that a joke had been turned on him for once, but days later, when the prank had been forgotten, he took the salad he was tossing and poured it over the troublemakers.

Any newcomer would have to face Jack at least once with boxing gloves or foils—and this included women, for he sanctioned no cowardliness and wanted only equally audacious friends around him. Charmian had no trouble giving him a good fight with fists or foils. Joseph Noel, a journalist and member of the Crowd, watched her fence one evening with foils, steel mask, padded breastplate, and a short tailored skirt "that fitted tightly over as neat a pair of hips as one might find anywhere." After Jack was beaten handily, he grabbed her and kissed her, leading Noel to conclude that "the eternal search was on again."[19]

Jack may indeed have been interested. He urged Anna, who avoided the Crowd's gatherings, to attend because among other reasons, "Charmian Kittredge, charmingly different from the average kind is here."[20] Anna did take a liking to Charmian, as did Bess, but not so other members of the Crowd, especially the Sterlings. When Noel suggested to the clique that Charmian be invited to the more intimate Sunday get-togethers as well, George strongly objected, claiming she threatened the security of people's homes. But Jack was in charge, and oblivious to the backbiting, Charmian continued to join the group.

If Jack was attracted to Charmian, he did not pursue her, for Anna was foremost in his mind, and as spring passed, she warmed to him. Like many unfaithful men, he shared with Anna his unhappiness with Bess, and intimated he was no longer having sexual relations with her. By June he was "sick with love" for her and signed himself "The Sahib."[21] Anna idealized Jack then and was unaware of his reputation for seeking out a partner of the evening among the young women flirting with him at his parties. She even went out in public with him, and no longer stifled his proclamations of love. Still, she would not give herself physically. "How unsatisfactory it is to meet you out among people," he complained. "How you slip away from me."[22]

Also during this time, Charmian was considering a return to the east coast. Since her departure from Maine, she had been pursued by a college professor there who wanted to marry her.[23] She declined, saying they needed more time to be with each other to determine whether they were suited. His work kept him from being free to visit until the spring of 1903, but Charmian was willing to be faithful to him in the meantime. She was enjoying her first real independence—Netta, Roscoe, and Edward Payne had moved their menage à trois to Glen Ellen, a hamlet in the Sonoma Valley. There they built Wake Robin, a lodge surrounded by rental cabins for families coming to enjoy activities similar to those at Camp Reverie. Charmian lived in Berkeley with the affectionate family of her uncle Harley Wiley, whose daughter Beth became like a sister to her. Now when she returned home in the evenings from her clerical job, she was free from the intrusions of her guardians.

One break did come to Jack during this troubled period. George Brett, president of the Macmillan Company, sought London out for a possible book. He accepted *Children of the Frost,* a series of tales in which the reader viewed the Northland through the Indian's point of view. The stories demonstrate London's complex view of social Darwinism. The Indians are portrayed sympathetically, as people of courage, dignity, and communal strength, able to survive the worst natural disasters. There is social criticism of whites who marry Indian women and force Indian women to do "squaw work," thus breaking the unity of the tribe. The theme of loss involves more than the account of Indian cultures falling before the inevitable white supremacists; it extends to the world itself, depicted as a place of savagery and terror. The dark forces of northern wilderness symbolized the pessimism growing in Jack.

By midsummer of 1902 he was three thousand dollars in debt, writing twelve to eighteen hours a day, and sorely in need of diversion from his withholding lover and troublesome wife. Release came in the form of an offer from the American Press Association to cover the end of the Boer War in South Africa. Upon reaching New York, he received a cable canceling the trip. To make use of the travel, he convinced George Brett to sign him for a book of photographs and text based upon slum life in London, where Edward VII was about to be crowned.

In England he disguised himself as a down-and-out merchant sailor to join the poor in the workhouse, the infirmary, at night on the street, and hop-picking in the country. Combining these observations with research at the British Museum, he managed in seven short weeks to produce his masterwork of nonfiction, *The People of the Abyss,* the book that was to remain his favorite. That he wrote the book clearly indicates Jack was not totally consumed by the drive to make big money: both he and Brett were surprised when it made a profit, for it had been thought too unpalatable by middle-class magazines to be picked up as a serial.

In fact, London's account, a precursor of the "new journalism" to come sixty years later, proved a compelling mixture of sociology, narrative, and autobiography that sweeps the reader into the lives of the East-enders. He leaves one wondering about the fates of the men of Frying Pan Alley, the starving couple on the bench Coronation Day, Bert the hop picker, and the Sea Wife. His clever logic continually surprises the reader, as when he suggests that poor Aleut natives are better off than most civilized persons. The chapter entitled "Property versus Person" summarizes without comment a series of court cases, allowing the reader to draw the obvious conclusion that stealing food is punished more severely than an act of violence against a fellow slum dweller. He found the conditions worse than any he had seen while tramping the States, and was sickened by sights he had to look at "a second time in order to convince myself that it was really so."[24]

While in England, he grew distressed over Anna's failure to write. He heard nothing for six weeks, then returned to his room one afternoon to find two letters. Exhausted from spending thirty-six sleepless hours among the homeless, he sat down to read, overjoyed at the bounty. The first letter was a pleasure. The second, written later, struck him hard. In it Anna announced she was moving to New York to work for radical causes. Somehow she had learned that Jack had been having sexual relations with Bess all through the recent months and accused him of lying to her. (Very likely the source, if indirectly, was Bess herself, who was known to discuss their sex life with others.)

Jack wrote back in fury, denying he had lied, saying she should know that "long, long after a child is conceived, a man may know his wife." He called her "the cruelest woman I have ever known . . . who can wound others in degree equal only to her own capacity to be wounded." He could have been speaking of himself. He grew ironic, self-pitying. "You beg my pardon for your impetuousness worming that 'I love you' from me. Then I do not love you, and I have spent months building up a wonderful tissue of lies. Wasted months, and years, for, not loving you, the thing is purposeless."[25]

With no reason to return, Jack wandered about the Continent retracing many of the routes Charmian had taken two years earlier. A curious blank exists in his life with regard to this trip. A most autobiographical writer who found time to record even the most trivial daily knowledge (such as the names of relatives or the shape of a friend's sculpture), he omitted Europe from his creative hoard. Nor did he send descriptions of his experiences to his correspondents. Perhaps he was too absorbed by his problems—his rage at Anna, his enchainment to Bess—to attend to the cities and civilizations through which he wandered.

Upon learning in early November that Bess had given birth to a second daughter, named Bess after herself (and later called Becky), Jack unhappily boarded a ship home. On the cross-country train he wrote Brett, "I learn that Miss Anna Strunsky is now on her way to New York. She is my collaborator in *The Kempton-Wace Letters.* She will come and see you, for she wishes to . . . do some general revising. I am sure you will find her charming."[26] Brett did and signed on their book even though he expected it would not sell well.

Anna arrived in New York just after his departure, so he did not see her again. She found a position with Gaylord Wilshire, a leading socialist publisher. Following several months of convivial notes, Jack suddenly lashed out at her. He accused her of being a child, "one who will always titillate . . . and who enjoys more in anticipation than do others who grasp and satisfy and feel the pangs of hunger that is sated and yet can never be sated."[27] In spite of his nasty attack, Anna remained friends with Jack. She soon had another romance, with William Walling, a millionaire socialist she did not criticize, as she had Jack, for selling out because he was a success at the capitalist's game.

At the same time, Jack lost one of his closest friends, Jim Whitaker, over a disagreement concerning socialist strategy.[28] Observing the incomprehensible misery of London's East End slums had pushed Jack into a more revolutionary stance. Where before he thought socialism would come naturally as society evolved, now he believed it deserved an unnatural shove. Like most of the other Oakland socialists, Whitaker was a Fabian and so desired change to come gradually by peaceful means. When the party was discussing a new pamphlet, Jack suggested it be headlined "Let the capitalists tremble" in bold print. Whitaker protested that this herald was misleading, for the tone of the statements within were not inflammatory. Jack pushed for a vote and won. Feeling rejected, Whitaker abandoned both the party and the good friend who had given him the resources to become a writer. Failing to see how his own obstinacy had forced the issue, Jack felt it was Whitaker who rejected him. Their many mutual friends were forced to choose between them, and most opted for the more famous of the two.

It was during that winter of unhappiness and self-doubt that Jack wrote his great classic *The Call of the Wild.* Because his three previous books with Macmillan had not been best-sellers, Brett asked to buy all rights for two thousand dollars outright, with the promise that the company would do extensive advertising, which would also promote demand for London's future works. Jack agreed, and never regretted losing the royalties on what proved to be his most popular book. In a time when the average man worked in a factory or a dark office, the lure of the struggle with nature, so ineluctably drawn by London, satisfied vicariously the need to escape the growing crowds and technology of the cities.

Yet perceptive readers would find another level of meaning in the story of Buck. Within this mythic fable London presented philosophical beliefs of the day tempered by romanticism. The story of Buck's initiation from spoiled house pet to Ghost Dog, leader of a pack in the Alaskan wilderness, artistically expressed such ideas as racial memory, the belief that people inherited the memories of their ancestors; the survival of the fittest through violence; and the role of hierarchy as the basic organizational principle in the world. Surviving trials thrust upon him by both men and other animals, Buck finds love in submitting to the kindly discipline of Thornton. As in London's own life, even love proves a phantasm, for Thornton is killed, and Buck left to pursue the call of the forest, "mysteriously thrilling and luring."

Buck's ordeals mirrored the initiation experiences of London's own life, with one exception: he had no John Thornton, no loving master to guide the final and crucial step of transformation that results in personal unity. For the time being he had to divert the "pangs of hunger that is sated and yet never can be sated" with his art, which provided him with spiritual fulfillment:

> There is an ecstasy that marks the summit of life, beyond which life cannot rise. And such is the paradox of living, this ecstasy comes when one is most alive, and it comes as a complete forgetfulness that one is alive. This ecstasy, this forgetfulness of living, comes to the artist, caught up and out of himself in a sheet of flame. . . . [Buck] was sounding the deeps of his nature that were deeper than he, going back into the womb of Time. He was mastered by the sheer surging of life, the tidal wave of being, the perfect joy of each separate muscle, joint, and sinew in that it was everything that was not death, that it was aglow and rampant, expressing itself in movement, flying exultantly under the stars and over the face of dead matter that did not move.[29]

With this passage London demonstrated an awareness of how to transcend the contradictory ideas and conflicting desires within himself, but he had a long journey of initiation ahead before he could apply this resolution to his own psyche.

PART II
A GARDEN ON EARTH

All these were theirs, for they were
  children still,
And children they should have ever
  been.

Lord Byron
Don Juan

6

GOD'S OWN
MAD LOVER

Your kisses, and the way you curl,
Delicious and distracting girl,
Into one's arms

—*Arthur Symons*

If judged by his acts, rather than his words, Jack London was a doting and loving father. Anglo-Saxon rhetoric and preference for a boy flew out the window at the sight of his sweet daughters. Joan, who resembled her dark, slim mother, grew up to become a fiery social activist, who in 1938 wrote a critical yet sympathetic book about her father's socialist beliefs and psychological makeup and in old age worked on a manuscript honoring his place in her childhood. Becky, a towheaded copy of Jack, even in her eighties lit up with delight when recalling visits from her "Daddy," and never minded that it was the fifth time that day that someone had asked her the same question. Few men separated by divorce and for long periods from their children receive such guileless recognition. He clearly touched them where it mattered and left them with a sense of self-esteem that had been missing in his own life.

Whatever his feelings for Bess, Jack seemed determined to do well by his daughters. Upon returning from England, he had foregone the company of the Crowd, and apart from a few public talks on his experiences, devoted himself to his writing and his family. Bess felt more secure about the marriage and settled in for the winter with relief that he was happy at work and that Wednesdays would no longer mean an invasion of the bohemians. To Cloudesley he wrote, "By the way, I think your long-deferred congratulations upon my marriage are about due. So fire away. Or, come and take a look at us, and at the kids, and then congratulate."[1]

Charmian came often to visit Bess and the girls and found Jack's stance toward her "always friendly, if a trifle imper-sonal." He gave her a copy of *The Cruise of the Dazzler,* a juvenile novel he had serialized in the magazine *St. Nicholas,* inscribing it "In memory of the *Jessie E.* and the run before the wind," a reference to a sailing afternoon they had shared with friends. He also impressed her with his "almost superhuman struggle" to shake himself free from magazine hack work and devote his talents to more literary creations and socialist essays.

With creditors banging on the door and insulting him in public settings, his commitment to nobler goals flew in the face of practicality, but it paid off. In late winter *The Call of the Wild,* which had been serialized in the *Saturday Evening Post,* sold out its ten thousand copies in one day. Comparing him to Rudyard Kipling, Bret Harte, and Stephen Crane, critics vindicated London's great promise that had not shone since his first book.

Flush again, Jack hired two servants, brought up Virginia Prentiss (whose own two children had died before adulthood) to watch both girls, and bought the thirty-foot sloop *Spray* for sailing on San Francisco Bay. When Frank Atherton came to visit with his wife and new baby, Jack talked them into moving rent-free to a cottage on the property. He opened his house again for visitors, who this time included not only the Crowd, but many hangers-on from both socialist and artistic circles. While he needed their praise and attention, he was no longer innocent of their motives. Elsie Martinez saw his contemptuous side, how he would make a sycophantic guest get down on all fours and push a peanut across the floor on his nose, then wham the victim on the rear end. He grew cynical as he heard more proof that many of his fellow socialists were less interested in serving the working class than ruling it.

Observing her family's fragile stability collapse, Bess lost her usual unrelenting self-control. Until then known as a patient hostess, at times she became less than gracious when company was around and lashed out when Jack spent the night away. So when he decided to rent a cabin for the summer of 1903 at Wake Robin, Netta's small resort in Glen Ellen, she felt relieved. There she would have more limited and manageable household duties, while Jack would be isolated from the influence of his pernicious city friends. She hoped that, like Camp Reverie two summers before, it would be a healing place.

Jack had other plans. He took his family to the cabin in June, then left, saying he needed the quiet of the *Spray* to begin writing his new book, *The Sea Wolf.* That spring Charmian, in an article for *Sunset* magazine, had written, "Lusty yachtsmen skimming the familiar waters of San Francisco Bay may listen for the industrious click-clicking of a typewriter mingling with the singing of ropes and the swish of blown spray, as Jack London sails his boat and weaves romance." Jack was thinking less of clicking at the typewriter than having "a hell of a time with any woman I could get hold of," and considered, then rejected, Charmian as a possible choice because he knew from Bess that she was involved with another.[2]

Before going out on his boat, Jack spent a weekend with the Sterlings. In a buggy ride down to the Oakland waterfront, a wheel broke and the crippled carriage tossed both men badly. Jack suffered a badly injured knee. Still in Glen Ellen, Bess called Charmian and asked her to pick up some things and take them to Jack, who had decided to postpone his cruise and return to his family until he was healed. Frank Atherton was packing Jack's trunks for him when Charmian arrived, surprised to find him bedridden. Jack started a conversation about various philosophical matters, and told her "some of the things in her that I didn't like." As she was about to leave, he grabbed her and kissed her, hoping to convince her to join him later on his trip.

Jack went up to Glen Ellen, while Charmian remained in

Berkeley. From there, he wrote her that he had recognized that her "lips were reluctant. They knew the wrong they did. It was the heart that spoke true."[3] He went down to see her, but made a date with another woman for the sailing trip. Charmian was holding back, insisting he visit her at her uncle's if he wanted to see her. He returned to Glen Ellen more desirous than ever of having her as his mistress.

In reality, like a line from one of his favorite poems, it was Jack who became "God's own mad lover dying on a kiss." The man who three scant years before had considered love a worthless quirk of physiology became intoxicated by a woman his friends considered a plain, show-offy spinster. The man burned by the only two women he had ever truly loved—Mabel and Anna—threw all caution aside and pronounced his ardent devotion in letters gushing with a self-disclosure never displayed before or after.[4] Certainly Charmian had never received such frank and immediate attention from an admirer before.

Jack later claimed he was the more interested party than she, and while her letters were destroyed, his give a strong impression of a hard pursuit, an effort to convince her and cajole her hand. She *will* come to him, he observes, because "it is inevitable. The hour is already too big to become anything less than the biggest."[5]

It did not take her long to come to him, amid a redwood grove while on an outing. Following their first sexual encounter, he praised her: "Had you been coy and flattering, giving the lie to what you had always appeared to be by manifesting the slightest prudery or false fastidiousness, I really think I should have been utterly disgusted. It would have been to me a terrible belittling of you. But you were not! . . . You are more kind to me than any woman I have ever known."[6]

Although Jack's original intention had been to make Charmian his mistress, he found himself so drawn to her that he wanted to possess her more fully. What appeared to be a contradictory nature to others delighted Jack. He was tantalized by her mixture of propriety and rebellion. Finding that the prim and genteel lady was lustful and sexually vigorous in private was like discovering a secret treasure. He wrote of "the bowl of her—its very exquisiteness defeating passion except in its best (purest, grandest) manifestation."[7]

Though dainty in size, she was in fact very strong and well coordinated, much like his first heroine, Frona Welse. "Clasp her rounded arm," he observed, and what seemed "a soft, satin-smooth yielding thing" would soon "spring into an alert marble hardness, that bore life and coursing energy in its firmness." Yet his favorite part of her was her legs, "firmly muscled like a boy who has spent his early years swimming."

Jack also was impressed that, while Charmian knew the domestic arts, she refused to domesticate her mind and was better read than most of his friends. He liked the way she handled herself with others, her "boyish camaraderie" with men, her easy way with women. He was attracted to her vibrant way of talking, her use of her strong hands to emphasize points. He considered her an artist in life, who molded herself to the self she desired to be. Such self-direction was congenial with his own.

Most important, he felt safe with her, believing that for the first time in his life he had someone he could speak to honestly about his most private thoughts and feelings. On June 18 he wrote her of his passionate desire for frankness, but his need to "shrink from the pain of the intimacies which bring the greater frankness forth." He had wanted to turn his eyes away from her, "to go on with my superficial self, talking," yet he could not, in spite of memories of old pain and incoherent hurts. He exposed himself to her as "a rough, savage fellow, who likes prizefights and brutalities, who has a clever turn of the pen, a charlatan's smattering of art, and the inevitable deficiencies of the untrained, unrefined, self-made man which he strives with a fair measure of success to hide." By early July he had determined they would "live life together," but he was not completely committed. As often happens with uncertain spouses, he led Bess to believe he would start a new life with her. He spoke of moving to the desert in southern California, where they could enjoy their family apart from the pressures of the Crowd and the city. It was an odd plan, and characteristically Bess agreed on the proviso that they be in a location where her household needs could be served easily.

His decision to quit the marriage is conveyed on July 11 in a letter to Cloudesley, himself a newlywed. "I laugh when I think of what a hypocrite I was when, at the Bungalow, I demanded from you long-deferred congratulations for my marriage but, believe me, I was a hypocrite grinning on a grid. . . . It's all right for a man sometimes to marry philosophically, but remember it's damned hard on the woman."[8]

To his biographers years later, Bess portrayed herself as the innocent victim caught totally unaware. She recounted how one afternoon she had seen Jack and Charmian on the hammock and had been unconcerned because she had often seen the two talking during the past year. Also, she claimed to have felt too sorry for Charmian to think of her as a possible rival. After several hours with Charmian, Jack went over to Bess and said he was leaving her. "Why, Daddy, what do you mean? You've just been talking about Southern California," she replied. Jack simply repeated over and over that he was leaving for good and gave no reason.

In fact, before he actually announced he was leaving, Bess had been enraged with jealousy and suspicion. On one day she had insisted on reading a telegram he had received, which turned out to be a message from another woman about their sailing plans. On another day she had retrieved from a wastebasket the torn-up scraps of a letter Charmian had sent to Jack, but since it was typed and unsigned, Bess could not identify the sender. (She took it to Netta, who told Charmian, who told Jack.)[9] Thus, the final break on July 24 could hardly have been so unexpected.

One fact is sure: Bess never suspected Charmian. Worse, on Jack's prompting both she and Netta continued to act as Bess's friends and comforters after he left. Charmian was not happy with the deceit, but she knew to do otherwise would be to jeopardize a divorce. That left Bess certain she knew who had stolen her husband—Anna Strunsky.

After leaving Bess, Jack returned to Piedmont, cleared his belongings from the bungalow, and set up joint housekeeping with Frank Atherton and his family in a six-room flat in Oakland. (As usual, Flora and Johnny Miller were moved nearby.) Like the rest of the Crowd, Frank was unaware of the real reason for the breakup. Jack fooled him and the others by spending frequent nights carousing with George. (One evening they tried hashish, and Jack explained to a puritanical

Frank that it was necessary to experience things directly in order to write about them intelligently.)

Only three people knew about the affair: Netta, Roscoe, and Edward Payne. In one of her crueler moments late in life, Netta told Irving Stone she had had no knowledge of the affair and in no way sanctioned it when she found out. But as early as August 3, 1903, Edward wrote the couple:

> I have not the least idea that you *need* the love of anybody else on earth—since you are pouring out the whole of yourselves in the worship of one another. But even if you have no sense of need you cannot help yourself; for you are not only a loving, but a very loveable pair. . . . Indeed, I am looking to you two to be the fulfillment of a very dear and high ideal that I have always borne in the heart of me —a man and a woman all human and actually meet and beautiful to one another, and in their united strength and beauty, very beautiful to those who are near to and know them.[10]

Secrecy enabled them to build an uncommonly strong base. With few to speak to about the relationship, let alone appear before, they could define their union free of others' beliefs. Forced to communicate primarily by letter, they could reflect at leisure on what they meant to one another, how their united strength and beauty would be defined.

From the start Jack defined the relationship physically as well as spiritually: "We are so alike in so much, that, as you have remarked, perhaps we are too alike for each other. But there is a great difference between us, which in connection with our likeness, makes us preeminently for each other. . . . You are, when all is said and done, of women the most womanly; and I, I hope, am somewhat of a man."[11] He praised their "wonderful physiological affinity, that makes the feel of our flesh good and a joy," noting that without it, their life together would mean nothing "but irk and irritation and hatred." Unlike Mabel, Anna, and Bess, Charmian did not deny him.

Jack did not mean to cast Charmian in the role of his loyal handmaiden; rather, he wanted to work with her to define a relationship superior to that of their friends. While this was a time when romanticism bloomed in fiction and news stories, the notion of a married couple committing themselves exclusively as friends was thought strange. Once wed, women and men were to move into separate worlds—the woman at home, the man outside. This was the marriage of the Sterlings, the Martinezes, the Hoppers. Jack offered a manifesto for a new and unique way of loving.

He began by telling her how he had loved many, though all the time there was something greater he yearned after. Once, after making love, he had told a woman of this dream. To his puzzlement, it angered her. He then realized how pale and weak the dream made her seem. The dream was for a "great Man-Comrade," a man with whom there could never be misunderstanding, who honored both the spirit and the flesh, who encompassed both fact and fancy. He was to be both "practical in the mechanics of life" and "fanciful, sentimental where the thrill of life is concerned. He should be delicate and tender, brave and game; sensitive as he pleased in the soul of him and unfearing and unwitting of pain." Such a man would face life frankly, perhaps sin greatly, but would just as greatly forgive.

The Man-Comrade was a stunning projection of the wholeness he lacked, a grasping for recognition of the artistic, feminine side of himself along with his more visible, conventionally masculine side. Typical of lovers, he cast this projection onto Charmian:

> There was a loneliness about you that appealed to me. This, perhaps, by some unconscious celebration, may have given rise to my vision of you in the grass . . . The wonder of it is that in a woman I should find, not only the comradeship and kinship I had sought in men alone, but the great woman-love as well.[12]

Rejecting the popular idea of the day, the two agreed that comradeship, not obedience of woman to man, forged the strongest love. Their pet names of Mate-Man and Mate-Woman became an affirmation of the equal sharing and respect they held for one another. If Jack did at times in their relationship haul out his rights as an Anglo-Saxon patriarch, he could count on being called down by his love, and even himself.

Headaches and depression grabbed Charmian when she slipped too much into acquiescence, and their occurrence shook her out of passivity. Their declaration of mutual dependence was a working document, its principles guiding—not always successfully—the day-to-day acts of their union.

Charmian was captivated by his impassioned document. A man she loved had finally come up to her deepest longings, that she be allowed full expression of her needs, that she be complementary and equal to someone. Later, people sniped that her attraction to Jack was to his success, a claim that does not ring true. The men who courted her in New England promised affluence, comfort, and a good reputation in their communities. She had tried that life in Maine and found it stifling. It was the life Jack had offered Bess and that Jack himself found lacking—Charmian knew he would give her something else. He represented thrill and danger, like the willful black stallion she had ridden on her father's dying day.

More, where Bess had begrudged Jack's celebrity, Charmian was game. She had watched Netta dabble with young artists over the years and encourage their careers. Honest about the limits of her own artistic talents, Charmian got vicarious pleasure out of boosting those with greater gifts. She could now join with Netta and become part of his creative efforts. She understood that their union incorporated a potential rival, his work, and quickly made peace with it.

Separation increased his own entrancement. He began a theme that echoed throughout the years of their time together. "As I tell you repeatedly, you cannot possibly know what you mean to me. The days I do not see you are merely so many obstacles to be got over before I see you."[13] Casting her as an ideal version of the man he would be made fearful demands on her, but she was up to meeting them. Her actions did in many ways match those of his dream figure, but more important, she accepted the ideal as an alluring challenge. She *would* be what he wanted, because it seemed so wise a choice for her.

Also, Charmian was used to being drawn by another's personality. Even now, in her thirties, in spite of her rebellious streak, she was tangled in parts of Netta's web. She had always been fearful of yielding to anyone as a result, but found that yielding to Jack, who made her feel gifted and special, was "sweet." Indeed, his frenzied ardor made it seem *he* was doing all the yielding, making all the sacrifices, even though he acknowledged that "it is the woman that gives and the man that takes, and you have given me yourself and all that means. Yours the risk, yours the terrible penalty that woman always pays if the world comes to know; mine is no risk, no penalty at all. . . . I would willingly cut off a hand,—anything, in order to meet you halfway."[14]

In October he suggested that they not wait a year to marry, but instead find some place in Hawaii, Nevada, or California to have a ceremony, if only to show that they meant well "according to Mrs. Grundy's dictates," and have the full legal ceremony again in a year. "We will respect the world, but the world's way can never make us one into more to each other or one into more married than we are now." She refused his plan, and it would be many months before their affair was known even to his friends. He also took out an insurance policy and named her as beneficiary, warning her to prepare for the scandal if he did die.

During this long second half of 1903, their respective work continued, Charmian again at the shipping office, Jack at his writing. Since both were well known in the East Bay, their meetings were few and stealthful. Even a brief return to his family when Joan came down with typhus did not shake his resolve to divorce.

In late December Jack completed *The Sea Wolf.* This superb tale concerns the conflict between Humphrey Van Weyden, a humanistic intellectual saved from shipwreck by the crew of the *Ghost,* and Wolf Larsen, the brutal, individualistic captain of the ship.

The only female character, Maude Brewster, another shipwreck victim, makes a clumsy entrance midway into the plot. Maude is an odd mixture of ethereal Victorian womanhood with the physical courage, wit, and assertiveness of what was being called the New Woman in the press. Jack inserted her into the story at the time he fell in love with Charmian, and her presence reflects the hold Charmian took on him. From then on she would serve as the model for the heroine of his novels that had elements of romance. There was no other woman in his mind.

*   *   *   *

The Sea Wolf completed, Jack found his financial situation in shambles. *The Call of the Wild* was now in print and selling very well, but for Macmillan's gain, not his. Too, Bess had gone to the press charging Anna Strunsky with stealing her husband and announced she would never divorce. Given growing debts and the continual battles with Bess, he sought the old solution to his troubles, travel. He gratefully accepted a contract from William Randolph Hearst to report in both words and photographs on the Japanese-Russian War.

When Jack arrived in Yokohama in late January of 1904, he found the Japanese were using every pretext to detain leading world journalists (such as Richard Harding Davis) in Japan. Guessing correctly that the Japanese were planning a surprise attack in Korea, Jack attempted to sneak off to that country in a crowded steamer. When authorities turned that ship around, he chartered a junk, which survived the storm-battered eight-day crossing. For several months Jack wandered around the countryside, usually on horseback, but never got close to the front. Though separated from the action, Jack sent Hearst nineteen stories with accompanying photographs on the backdrop of the war, while other journalists remained frustrated in Tokyo.

Before departing, Jack had determined that Charmian and George Sterling should handle the final editing and proofs of *The Sea Wolf,* and also ordered Macmillan to send her part of his usual royalty payments for her work. In order to keep in touch with her, he arranged for a *San Francisco Examiner* editor to serve as intermediary and forward their mail to each other. Because Jack wanted Charmian's name out of the divorce negotiations, she left her job and went in February to stay with friends in Newton, Iowa.

A mix-up at the newspaper almost destroyed their plans. The editor taken into their confidence had become ill, and his replacement both unwittingly forwarded Charmian's letters to Bess and failed to send Jack's to Charmian. Jack grew angry with his lover's apparent coldness, and she went out dancing with an old suitor from previous Iowa visits. In April Jack discovered the blunder and tried to correct it; Charmian soon received a bundle of his letters.

Surprisingly, Bess had not identified the writer as Charmian, perhaps because she typed the missives and signed with a code name. Jack confided in his sister Eliza, who had been ignorant of the affair, and asked her to intercede and calm Bess down. Bess responded with what she had been resisting all along: an agreement to dissolve the marriage. She had her lawyer place attachments on all of Jack's property, including his literary holdings at various publishers.

The foul-up was not good for the relationship, and Jack's subsequent letters treated Charmian more like his editorial assistant than lover. Worse, Netta intervened and pressured Charmian not to return to California in time for Jack's June return. Given the delicacy of the situation, it was wise advice, but its consequences were further detrimental to the couple. Thus, when Jack wired "Coming" to Charmian on May 31, she packed to go to the St. Louis World's Fair on assignment for an Iowa newspaper. Upon her return she found a series of telegrams from George Sterling. One said ominously, "Bess sues for divorce, accuses Anna Strunsky." Another reported Jack's expected arrival date. She held back.

London's very literary reputation was at stake, for a man could commit no worse sin, outside of murder, than leaving a wife and young children for another woman, and Bess was using the press to broadcast her accusations. He was very conscious of the moral position of his readers and pandered more to their traditional ethics than he personally preferred. Thus, in the second half of *The Sea Wolf,* Humphrey Van Weyden and Maude Humphries, stranded alone on an island, treat one another with the delicacy of the drawing room. London knew in fact two such personalities would have sexual relations but could not even hint at such to the readers of the day and had to reassure his editors of his attention to "prudery."

Those dearest to him defended him to reporters. When Bess claimed she had once come upon Anna sitting in Jack's lap, Anna told New York reporters how that was "absurd. . . . the silly little stories about the lovemaking that went on before Mrs. London's eyes. His behavior was most circumspect toward me and always has been. . . . He was blindly in love with his wife." Flora told the *San Francisco Chronicle* that her son had "never said an unkind word" about Bess, that he was "loving, affectionate, and generous to a fault."

Imagining he would return to the arms of his lover, Jack was distraught to find her absent, his good friend's reputation besmirched by Bess, and legal papers awaiting him at the pier. In them he read Bess's charge that he had contracted a venereal disease and infected her (a common and often true accusation then). Having been pressed before a year of separation had passed, Bess's suit prevented a simple case of desertion and quick freedom. Moreover, when confronted by him, she said she intended to tie up his funds and would never give him his freedom. Despondent, he detailed these circumstances to Charmian, concluding, "I see no reason why you should not return to California, for my troubles with Bess are bound to continue for a weary long while. You may crop up in the midst of it, you may never be mentioned. But elect to do as you see fit. If you remain away till divorce is granted, you may remain away for years, you may die and be buried away."[15] On the same day he had a rail ticket sent to her.

Still Charmian did not return. Jack's pressures could not overpower the force of Netta, who convinced him to move in with her at Glen Ellen and get to work. He did, beginning collections of stories, *The Faith of Men,* and of revolutionary essays, *War of the Classes.*

A strange drama unfolded. The communications among the three were efficient and businesslike when concerning manuscripts, while at the same time conflicting and frantic when about the couple's personal plans. Eventually, recognizing that Jack's work was the most important matter and that he needed Charmian for that work as well as personally, Netta relented. Charmian cabled "Coming" on July 27, and they were reunited in early August. Several years later, when discussing this time with a friend, she wrote "I don't think he's ever quite forgiven me. He had to fight it out alone."[16]

* * * *

Charmian found a different man awaiting her at the station. He was angry but did not express it. They spent several days of passion in Glen Ellen, but then he left to live again in Oakland. They agreed that she would give up her job for good to become his regular editorial assistant and secretary. As pay, she would keep all his original handwritten manuscripts, a promise he honored despite many tempting offers from others over the years. They proved to be a valuable insurance policy after his death.

Reacquainting himself with the Crowd and the Bay Area, he had the better of the deal. Her diary became a repetition of her time in Maine: so many hours of piano practice, the length of daily hikes, a listing of books read. While she grew attached to the physicality of rural life, she longed for urban pleasures— plays, concerts, and convivial conversation at good restaurants. His letters were filled with descriptions of parties and fun she missed.

On one Crowd outing, a trip on the *Spray* in September, Jack responded to the attentions of Blanche Partington and soon began an affair with her. Charmian detected a coolness in his letters, but he dissembled: "No dear, I have no particular trouble bothering me now. I think, most probably, that you and I are in a very trying stage just now. The ardor and heat and ecstasy of new-discovered love has been tempered by time, on the one hand; and on the other hand, we are denied a growing comradeship which should be ours right now."[17] Reassured, she continued to type his manuscripts.

Jack was not the only one lying to her. During her few visits to Oakland, Charmian often met with members of the Crowd, especially Carrie Sterling and Ida Brooks. Now aware she was the reason for Jack's marital breakup, they humored and placated her, all the while knowing Jack was taking Blanche to concerts, parties, and bed. They thought Charmian should be punished for deceiving Bess and deserved to lose Jack to the drama critic. The Sterlings invited her to George's birthday party in December and even gave her a place to sleep during her trips to Oakland; Charmian was completely unaware of their true feelings.

By winter, Charmian was wise enough to know that something was wrong. It was not just his compulsive behavior that worried her—his reports of writing dozens of letters a day, of spending every solitary moment (and there were many) driven to write beyond his thousand words and read even more books. She reflected on the change that had come over him since the yachting trip with the Crowd and correctly concluded he had been seeing Blanche. In time, she realized there were other women as well. Accepting herself to be a jealous woman, she "had to be *absolutely satisfied* that I was the one woman in the world to him, at the time I married him."[18]

One December afternoon in Glen Ellen, as the light faded with the early sunset, Charmian told Jack he could go, that she could no longer keep him bound to her. He looked at her, his face disclosing no feeling, and without a word rose and left the room. Scarcely a minute later, he rushed back to say, "You were never so dear to me as you are this minute." She realized then that she had found "an unselfish use for myself in the world—he needed me—and I loved him." Several days later she again offered him his freedom, which he again refused. (Much later Charmian learned that Jack had taken her offer of freedom to mean she would kill herself to set him free. That presumed offer of sacrifice could only seem endearing to a man so fond of nineteenth-century Romantic poetry.)[19]

Charmian returned to spend two months in the East Bay, where she was checking the construction of a house on one of her Berkeley lots. She was very happy, not only at the renewed interest from Jack, but the frequent hospitality of the Sterlings. Jack too was buoyed by a new project, a play he was writing with the advice of actress Blanche Bates. So when Charmian read the headline "Reported Blanche Bates Will Wed Jack London," she was not concerned. As usual the papers exaggerated the truth, claiming Jack had been seen in the front row of the actress's performances for three nights running, and creating a great deal of attention "by reason of his peculiar dress of which he has become noted." The story was a convenient ploy to keep the public from knowing the true details of Jack's life, as well as to fill empty seats in the theater.

Jack was writing the play for Minnie Maddern Fiske, but when Bess found out, she started a row throughout the Maddern clan. Mrs. Fiske withdrew her interest in the work, forcing Jack to seek another actress. Ethel Barrymore told reporters she was willing to do it, but later decided its western heroine to be too out of character for eastern tastes.

It was probably during this period that Jack stopped seeing Blanche Partington, for in February, when Charmian returned to Glen Ellen, Jack spent several weeks with some of the Crowd cruising the Sacramento delta, and Blanche was conspicuously absent. Her departure from his life did not settle unresolved tension in his relationship with Charmian. Even though he knew she was in great pain because of ear infections that had resulted from too many twenty-two-foot dives into chilly waters, he wrote only businesslike letters. She should correct the proof sheets for his essay "The Class Struggle," send out copies of his play, and write a cheery note to George, who was unhappy. One day she wrote an uncharacteristic "Hell!" in her diary.

He appeared in Glen Ellen in March, very depressed, and she realized his cool, erratic behavior had little to do with her. He later called this the time of "Nietzsche's 'long sickness'," when the loveliness of the world meant nothing to him. Eventually he admitted, to her alarm, that certain bowel problems indicated cancer (though the real dread was possibly of syphilis). Death seemed an unsatisfying prospect, not that he feared it, but because his growing success, with its fame, comforts, and financial reward, would be meaningless. He was close to attaining the goals he had always desired and discovered his hands could just as well be empty.

Both Netta and Charmian urged him to consider the recuperative powers of the quiet and beauty of Glen Ellen. He refused, and she saddled the horses that would take them over the canyons toward his boat mooring in Napa. The ride was momentous: Jack would later write a story, "Planchette," based partially on it, and Charmian gave it much space in her biography of Jack.

Riding through canyons dark with damp sword ferns and fields of dew-glistened flowers, Charmian felt Jack slipping away from her for good. Suddenly his posture changed, and he began to talk enthusiastically about life at Wake Robin. His possible feelings at the time can be seen in "Planchette," where he captured the erotic attraction between the couple:

All things tended to key them to an exquisite pitch—the movement of their bodies, at one with the moving bodies of the animals beneath them; the gently stimulated blood caressing the flesh through and through with the soft vigors of health; the warm air fanning their faces, flowing over the skin with balmy and tonic touch, permeating them and bathing them, subtly, with faint, sensuous delight; and the beauty of the world, more subtly still, flowing upon them and bathing them in the delight that is of the spirit and is personal and holy, that is inexpressible yet communicable by the flash of an eye and the dissolving of the veils of the soul.[20]

To Charmian, "he had come over and out, by some sweet miracle, I cared not what, from his valley of the shadow."[21] At that moment he sealed his commitment to her, chattered excitedly about moving into a cabin at Wake Robin, bringing his Korean valet Manyoungi to keep his house, sharing books with her.

At the top of the grade he reined in, put his hand on her shoulder, a touch she had felt little of in recent weeks, and thanked her for pulling him out, for seeing his need for rest: "I am all right now—you need not be afraid for me any more."

7

COMRADES
IN ARMS

And what you have called world, that
shall be created only by you: your
image, your reason, your will, your love,
shall thus be realized.

—*Friedrich Nietzsche*

Jack's anxieties over his illness were unfounded: all he
needed was minor surgery to correct some hemorrhoids.
Charmian took horse and steamer to Oakland to be near him
during his stay so they could work together in the hospital. She
noted that "these days are the turning point in the lives of Mate
and me. We are more truly learning each other, our worth to
each other. Mate is secretly occupied with the Crowd concerning me, standing for his own, loyally; but I know nothing of it
until later, at Glen Ellen."

Aggrieved by her rejection, Blanche Partington had no trouble turning the Crowd against Charmian; still friendly with the
Sterlings, Bess added to the fray. Their accusations that Charmian broke up the marriage forced the conventional hand of

Jack, who stood firmly in support of his lover and lambasted the Crowd in return. Charmian may have been the scapegoat for other anger, that Jack was rejecting them, that he was moving north to Glen Ellen, not south to Carmel, where they were planning to establish an artists' colony. Ignorant of the affair, Charmian accepted an invitation to attend the opera with Blanche and wondered why Jack, normally a spirited admirer of the high art, seemed "uncomfortable and preoccupied" throughout the performance.

In May, back in Glen Ellen, Jack confessed the truth about Blanche and the Crowd. In addition, after discussing the stories the Crowd had spread about Charmian's infidelity to him, they compared diaries and reassured one another. Charmian was shaken less by Jack's unfaithfulness than her discovery that "dear friends" were in fact "treacherous and small." He was still welcome among them; she was not. Worse, the brouhaha continued through the fall, leaving Charmian permanently scarred by the viciousness of the attacks. The gregarious side of her personality, which had always been forced, retreated, and she gave in to her solitary nature.

It is a testament to Charmian's character that she would later reach out to Blanche, and the two would become lifelong friends. In 1907 the two women intimately recalled this difficult time and became fond of one another thereafter. Blanche brought Charmian roses, and Charmian forgave her old rival, saying she knew how lovable Jack London was, that she could not dislike a woman for having loved him. In time, the two became like sisters, advising one another on clothes, going to the latest plays together, and exchanging confidences. Jack was never comfortable with this friendship and would take to taunting or teasing Blanche, only to have Charmian put him in his place.

George may have been the only member of the Crowd to rise above the gossip. Better than anyone he understood Jack's infidelity—his own marriage was not very satisfying. He was less hurt by Jack's commitment to Charmian than the decision not to move to Carmel, where George was hoping to resettle. George also failed to appreciate how little money Jack had left after the success of *The Sea Wolf*. Jack explained he had made at least fifteen thousand dollars, once an unbelievable sum to an ex-jute-mill worker, but it had been spent on lawyers, doctors, and the support of his various relatives. But Jack added kindly that George was "the only person in the world I'd take the trouble for," and concluded wistfully, "No, I am afraid the dream was too bright to last—our being near to each other. If you don't understand now, someday sooner or later you may come to understand. It's not through any fault of yours, nor through any fault of mine. The world and people just happen to be so made."[1]

That summer George quit his job, hoping to live in Carmel off the rental of his Piedmont home. It was not a happy summer for Carrie Sterling, who wrote cryptically to Blanche of George's failure to keep his promises.[2]

While Carrie continued to insist she would have nothing to do with Charmian, George went alone to Glen Ellen in September to make his peace. He composed a verse likening Charmian to a violet, "frailest and tenderest" of earth's brood. From that point his acceptance of Charmian was indisputable. Over the years his letters to Jack included frequent messages of warm wishes to Charmian, along with playful asides. He dubbed her "de Chums" and carried on a separate correspondence with her as well. There is little to suggest, as other biographers have, that during the Londons' marriage George Sterling disliked Charmian—quite the contrary.

In celebration of George's peace offering, the trio went down to the city for several days of carousing. Later that month Xavier Martinez invited the couple to his San Francisco studio and painted a portrait of Jack. Upon learning of the impending marriage, Anna Strunsky sent Charmian lilies of the valley. And Jack's oldest socialist mentor, Frederick Bamford, opened his arms to her as well. These gestures, few though they were, brightened Charmian's mood, but the biggest lift was in knowing that Jack's divorce would be final in late November, and they need no longer hide from the public.

*   *   *   *

During the trying times of 1904, Jack found a new source of inspiration and hope.

Contrary to his self-perception, Jack London was a most susceptible man. Whereas personalities could not sway him,

printed words could. One can trace major changes in his behavior to books he was reading—an essay on the uselessness
of romantic love led to his marrying Bess. One can also see him
revise his past in terms of his current reading—after becoming
familiar with socialism, he ascribed political motives to his
youthful wanderings, when in fact he had had no political
awareness during that time. If Spencer, Darwin, and Marx influenced much of his twenties, Nietzsche took hold of his early
thirties.

London first discovered Friedrich Nietzsche's writings in the
fall of 1904, when he was working on *The Sea Wolf.* As was his
habit, he read as many of the philosopher's books as he could
find. When Charmian was troubled in the summer of 1905,
Jack gave her his *Thus Spake Zarathustra* as a tonic, which she
found a great comfort.[3] The therapeutic message both received from *Zarathustra* was the call to re-create themselves, to
pour their passions into joyous creative expressions of power.
London was inspired by Nietzsche's claim that "the world belongs to the strong who are noble, . . . to the noncompromis-
ers." They were given a rationale for nonconformity, a motive
for achievement.

The uninformed often align Nietzsche with racism and ram-
pant individualism and, upon learning that London was attracted to his theories, assume the same of him. The result is
to misinterpret Nietzsche. Whereas Nietzsche accepted the
idea of racial groups inheriting certain traits and talents, he
condemned racism and nationalistic aspirations. He wrote of
"blond beasts," the opposite of the superman, those who acted
on uncontrolled animal passion and hatred. (Nazism proved a
full expression of these unthinking types.) As an Anglo-Saxon
chauvinist, Jack confused the blond beasts with the supermen,
equating them. He imposed Spencer on top of Nietzsche to
support the notion of white cultural superiority.

Significantly, both men believed the superman, the individual who channels his baser instincts into creativity, should not
do so at the cost of others. Only weaklings enjoy the suffering
of others. Jack demonstrated his agreement with this philosophy in the destruction of the selfish individualist Wolf Larsen
in *The Sea Wolf.* More optimistic than Nietzsche, Jack also believed that love was the ultimate value, that survival depended

upon cooperation and adaptability to others as much as on personal strength. Thus in *Martin Eden,* the young writer whose life so closely resembles Jack's commits suicide because he has been unwilling to accept socialism and lost his faith in the redemptive qualities of love.[4]

While Jack often disclaimed his devotion to Nietzsche, the philosopher's emphasis on self-mastery took strong hold. Consequently, Jack would grow more disenchanted with organized socialism, seeking to replace it with a personal vision of cooperation, that of the agrarian dream made real through his self-direction.

Jack's experiences in Japan and Korea had furthered his belief in the superiority of Anglo-Saxons. His letters to Charmian remarked on how Japanese women bathing him noted "my beautiful white skin," on his longing for "a mouthful of white man's speech," and "white man's news," his abhorrence of Koreans, beasts who had no compassion for their animals.[5] As if to provide a tangible example of his superiority, he brought back with him his cook, Manyoungi, who also acted as his valet and personal aide.

Jack had much company in his beliefs. As a boy in Oakland, he learned not only to taunt the Chinese but the numerous white immigrant groups in the town. Americans of British descent were in the minority in the country and clung to their rights as original settlers. During the economic strife of the end of the century, they fought the competitive threat of the dark, ill-educated foreigners. Bay Area papers encouraged prejudice with cartoons depicting stereotypes of the drunken Irish, greedy Jew, and shuffling black. Joke inserts made ethnic slurs. University professors who lectured in support of white superiority were viewed by colleagues as reasonable.

Yet, however much the intellectuals he read supported racism, London's acceptance of white superiority did not include race hatred. For one, the most loving adult figure in his childhood had been a black woman of great and outspoken racial pride. So if Flora London whined about the micks and guineas who spoiled her life, Virginia Prentiss counterpointed with her model of dignity and competence. Furthermore, his familiarity with the tribal peoples of the Yukon instilled an admiration for their cultures and a sadness for their inevitable passing. As years passed, these moderating influences finally dominated the harsher racism he expressed at this time.

Racism was becoming a divisive issue in socialist groups throughout America during 1904–1905, but party leaders were not about to lose London as a spokesperson over it. The nationwide condemnation of his divorce, if anything, only added to his appeal, for the public seemed more drawn to the notorious than to the pure. Jack clutched at their support as one of his two "bribes for living" (the other being Charmian). He did more for the cause in 1905 than any other time.

The impulse for his renewed activity was the public response to his speech "Revolution," delivered to students and faculty of the University of California at Berkeley on January 20.[6] More aptly, it could be called a sermon. Stirred by his memories of the London slums, he argued that the cavemen had a better standard of living than many in modern society. He made points by using hypnotic repetition in his rhetoric:

> Consider the United States, the most prosperous and most enlightened country in the world. In the United States there are ten million people living in poverty. By poverty is meant that condition of life in which, through lack of food and adequate shelter, the mere standard of working efficiency cannot be maintained. In the United States there are ten million people who have not enough to eat. In the United States, because they have not enough to eat, there are ten million people who cannot keep the ordinary measure of strength in their bodies. This means that these ten million people are perishing, are dying, body and soul, slowly, because they have not enough to eat.

He followed this with examples from real life, such as the Chicago garment worker whose average wage for a sixty-hour week was ninety cents, and the New York City woman who out of desperation strangled her two infants, then took poison. After enumerating the sins of capitalism, he called the audience to come forward and repent through revolution. He attributed to revolutionaries the qualities of Nietzsche's superman: vitality, cleanness, nobility, unselfishness, driven by creative energy

toward good. Pointing to the revolutionaries in Russia, he intoned:

> I think of all the assassins in Russia as comrades. Remem-
> ber that when the embattled farmers of Lexington fired
> upon British soldiers, their acts were no worse than what
> assassins and revolutionaries are doing in Russia today. In
> this country ten million are living in poverty. . . . The
> capitalistic class cannot comprehend how near the revolu-
> tion it is. "It will not come" is the prevailing belief. It will
> come in our time.

The speech, which was repeated often that year, caused a
furor among those attending and in the press. "Jack London
Calls Russian Assassins His Brothers," blazed one headline.
When Jack referred to William Lloyd Garrison, the great anti-
slavery leader who said "to hell with the Constitution" for
defending slavery, the papers screamed "Jack London Says To
Hell with the Constitution." His name became synonymous
with wild-eyed threats to convention. His own high school
refused to allow him to speak before its debating society for
fear he would corrupt the young.

Local socialists once again took advantage of his enormous
press and nominated him again for mayor of Oakland. Running on a platform that pledged to work for better health care,
welfare, and education for the working class, Jack garnered 913
votes to Frank K. Mott's 5,545, a considerable improvement
over his earlier attempt.

Jack was soon drawn into the national socialist scene by
Upton Sinclair. After attending the City College of New York
without once hearing of socialism, Sinclair was determined to
find a way to introduce the cause to college students. The
result was the Intercollegiate Socialist Society. The signers for
the group included feminist social scientist Charlotte Perkins
Gilman and lawyer Clarence Darrow. At a meeting in New York
on September 12, 1905, the group unanimously elected the
absent Jack as president of the society. The organizers understood that London's role would not involve administration but
public relations. They expected rightly that his name would
open lecture doors forbidden to more conventional revolu-

tionaries. London accepted the idea of a tour, using the Lyceum Bureau to book him with women's clubs and other groups that would pay him to lecture; he interspersed free lectures at schools between paying engagements. It was during this tour that his marriage to Charmian took place.

Rather than break for a honeymoon rest, the tour wound eastward on rickety and dirty trains. A socialist before she met Jack, Charmian supported the tour wholeheartedly. As she wrote to Frederick Bamford, "Although he is my Jack, I realize how much he belongs to a few others, if not to the world at large indeed. It is a great thing to learn to love thus unselfishly —better than being loved, I might say."[7]

She thrilled when Mother Jones marched up to the rostrum at Harvard University and greeted Jack before the crowd with a kiss on each cheek. She was amused when Yale University officials hemmed and hawed over whether it could handle an appearance of the "socialist-sensation monger." (The poster advertising his appearance showed him in a red turtleneck sweater with a mass of flames in the background; the word REVOLUTION was the sole description of the event.) She was angry when none of the "capitalist publishers," including his own, did anything about the epidemic of library censorship of his works. She felt proud to visit Hull-House with Jack and spend the afternoon listening to him talk with Jane Addams.

If a honeymoon on a socialist lecture tour did not strike Charmian as strange, neither did the accompanying media furor. The precipitate marriage guaranteed the couple would be given extensive, if unreliable, coverage. While the early coverage was devoted to moral outrage, the press quickly shifted to a more interesting subject, Charmian herself, whose winsome ways turned the head of many a reporter. Their appearances brought front-page headlines, and her picture was often set larger or more prominently than Jack's. Some of the more interesting stories were doubtless dropped from Jack's own mouth into that of a hungry reporter. So too he instructed Charmian, who was to become equally adept at public relations, for her first interview, with the *Boston American* in December.[8] What is her hobby? Jack. Her cause? Socialism. Why does she love him? Because he lets her do as she pleases, and shouldn't she let him do the same? What of his cigarettes? She doesn't mind—they're his only recreation. This quick immersion into the world of media madness led to her lifelong advice to others, "Never believe what you read in the newspapers."

As he was to do throughout their life, Jack devised tests for Charmian to prove her mettle.[9] In Boston, when asked if she wished to watch an appendectomy and brain operation, she hesitated, then agreed because: "I roved my adventurously promising career beside the bright comet I had taken for better or worse, emergencies in war or travel by sea or land. I must never fail my man who despised a coward beneath all things under the sun. Here was my chance for a certain kind of preparation. Nerves I confessed in abundance. Had I *nerve* also?" Indeed she had, enough to go into the stockyards and a medical school dissection room as well. These incidents removed any remaining doubts in his mind about her gameness.

In the middle of the lecture tour, the couple did have a real honeymoon, in Jamaica, where they watched the "buxom, broad-smiling, broad-hipped negro wenches" and were unnerved by the primitive music so reminiscent of the "disturbing call of modern 'jazz' orchestration." They visited coffee plantations, blind to the exploitative labor system. Years later Charmian remembered the rosy color of a dress she wore, the pearl-handled fan she carried to dinner in Havana. When Jack was almost arrested for accosting a cabdriver who may have overcharged him, she was smug that he would not "abase his Anglo-Saxon pride before the impudent half-breeds." Most white Americans of the time would have agreed with her.

On the other hand, once back on tour in New York, Jack upset the wealthier members of the movement. It did not help them to read the *New York Times* story that misinterpreted Jack's reference to the "blood-red banner" of revolution as a symbol of war and destruction, rather than the brotherhood of man as he intended. Invited to speak at the Grand Central Palace Hotel before a crowd of four thousand business leaders and their spouses, he was even more provocative in his attacks on capitalism. As he later wrote to Anna Strunsky, he "rattled the dry bones some."

It did not take disgruntled comrades long to find something to attack, namely, his traveling in first-class Pullman cars accompanied by an Oriental valet. Jack saw no inconsistency in wanting working people to be freed of oppression and drudgery while other industrious people acquired more than basic comforts. "Would my giving up a servant put food in the starving mouths of a workingman's family, relieve the sweatshop girl of her torturous labor, or make good-thinking men of selfish capitalists? Any fool could see this logic!" He would not submit to critics who wished him to adopt a working-class life-style when often they themselves were not willing to do so. Unlike his attackers, he knew firsthand the wretchedness of working-class life and saw nothing particularly noble in reducing his pleasures as a symbolic gesture.

His critics made too much of his few comforts. In fact, the frantic pace of the circuit provoked tonsillitis and other infections, the last of which in North Dakota in February caused him to cancel the remainder of the tour. Contrary to the images readers obtain from his adventure stories, Jack London did not have a strong constitution. His hands and feet were small for his stature, his wrists and ankles prone to injury. He did not have a natural stamina for heavy physical work, nor did he develop it. He hated to walk, to the point in later years where he would take a cab to travel a city block rather than go by foot.[10] He had very bad teeth and gums that gave him pain all his life. If, in photographs, he appears strong, it is an illusion caused by his broad chest. Charmian had a much stronger constitution and did not, like him, become seasick on the boat to the Caribbean; she was ill only once with the flu during these hectic months.

Forced by Jack's weakened state to return to Glen Ellen, the couple could look back with gratification over their accomplishments. More than anyone else at the time, he was the college man's idol, and his lectures made many more sympathetic toward the movement, if not always active members of the Intercollegiate Socialist Society. Although the press often misquoted him, in some instances editors requested fact-finding follow-up stories that lent support to Jack's generalizations. Thus, the *Chicago American* documented that many women sweatshop workers in that city supported children on a salary of ninety cents a week. Because his speeches were based upon his thorough and meticulous research, other writers and soapbox orators borrowed freely from them.

As if to memorialize both his love for Charmian and his socialism, Jack began to write *The Iron Heel,* a novel of workers' revolution. The story is written as a historical document discovered seven hundred years in the future. Its author, Avis Everhard, reports on her revolutionary activities during the 1912–32 uprisings against the capitalist oligarchy or Iron Heel.

The daughter of a college professor, Avis joins the underground after falling in love and marrying Ernest Everhard, a self-educated working-class leader of the revolutionaries. Like Charmian had done with Jack, during her first meeting with Ernest, Avis disdains his poorly cut clothes and blunt speech. But as she learns of his ideas about the oppression of workers, she accepts him as her oracle and lover. In one amusing aside, she admits she had worried that his lovemaking would be violent and impetuous, but assures us that "no woman was ever blessed with a gentler, tenderer husband."

As the revolutionaries increase their attacks, the Iron Heel responds by controlling the press, manipulating and buying off unions, and jailing agitators. It also bombs Congress as a pretext for arresting the revolutionary leaders, who include Ernest and Avis. Avis escapes and literally lives underground in a cave on Sonoma Mountain. She and her comrades kidnap and convert the son of an oligarch. Their organization develops so successfully in spite of the political oppression that, in one day, they free prisoners from jails all over the country. Ernest reunites with Avis, and they go to Chicago, where the Iron Heel, alerted to the revolutionaries' plans, fill the streets with regiments that shoot unarmed people. The manuscript ends abruptly, for presumably the pair are caught and executed.

Like so many of London's works, the novel depicts women of courage and initiative. When Ernest is in jail, Avis decisively directs her group's schemes. It was Jack's way of acknowledging Charmian's role in his cause, his confidence in her comradeship with him. The woman who stood by him at the autopsy table without flinching and held herself proud before critics could be counted on to help lead the revolution.

But the revolution ended on paper. If Nietzsche spurred Jack and Charmian to press their energies toward the social good, the philosopher also fed their strong need for adventures that would make them stand out above others. All during 1905 and

1906, while the couple was making significant personal sacrifices for THE PEOPLE, as Jack would call them, they were preparing for unusual personal satisfactions. Content that he had done his share for the cause, Jack turned down requests to write articles on child labor in the south and on the trial of labor leaders William Haywood and others, charged with killing Idaho's governor.

Two drastically different dreams tempted them. Both had come about within days of the other during the summer of 1905, before they had begun the tour. The first was a continuation of Jack's dream of his own ranch, and began with the June 6 purchase of the 129-acre Hill property, a wooded rise up the base of Sonoma Mountain that included a cottage, saddle horse, colt, work horses, furniture, farm implements, and a cat. Draped in Spanish moss that thrived in the fog-laden air, the trees gave a haunting feeling to the property. The blood-red bark and gnarled branches of the manzanita and madrona increased the strange romance of the landscape. Most trees and shrubs were evergreen, their colors shimmering in light breezes with shades of blue-green and gray seldom seen in the deciduous trees of the east. One could walk several yards away from house or road, down into a deep canyon, and feel that one had crossed into a mysterious wilderness, far from any civilization.

Jack wrote George of his plans: "I am really going to throw out an anchor so big and so heavy that all hell could not get it up again."[11] He was speaking of the ranch but would in fact be ordering the foundry to shape a real anchor. As Charmian later recounted, she, Jack, and Roscoe Eames were discussing Joshua Slocum's *Voyage of the Spray* when Jack raised the possibility of their building a forty-five-foot sloop and sailing around the world. When Eames, a lifelong yachtsman and one-time ferryboat captain, said the idea was workable, Jack devised a five-year plan to establish his ranch while building the boat. Later Charmian pressured him into giving the trip higher priority so they could go while they were still young and keen.

The design was Jack's own.[12] He chose a craft he had never in fact seen, a ketch, a compromise between a yawl and a schooner, a two-master with the larger sail forward. She was to be fifty-seven by fifteen feet overall, forty-five feet at the waterline. With his typical hyperbole, he described her as "the strongest boat ever built in San Francisco." She had no house nor hold, so the deck was virtually unbroken, with the cockpit sunk beneath the deck to make the pilot more comfortable in rough weather. Though a sailing vessel, it was to include a seventy-horsepower motor for use in harbors and up rivers. After much argument among his friends, he and Charmian chose *Snark,* from the Lewis Carroll poem, as its name.

Most important, he spared nothing in constructing it, including an iron keel, an engine shipped from New York City, select Puget Sound planking for the deck, and four watertight compartments. He labored lovingly over the plan for the bathroom ("his sacred place," Charmian once confessed) with its ingenious pumps, levers, and sea valves. Local yachtsmen, few of whom had sailed beyond the bay, laughed at the expensive refinements.

They laughed even more at "London's folly" as the boat took form in the San Francisco shipyard of H. P. Anderson. From the start Jack doomed the project by hiring Roscoe to oversee the construction. None of Jack's friends was qualified for such a job, and Roscoe was certainly among the poorer choices. The one-time business manager of a literary magazine could hardly be expected to manage a construction entailing forty-seven different unions and over one hundred different firms. But Jack was deeply loyal to his friends and family and preferred them to strangers for all types of jobs. Too, it must be remembered that Charmian and Jack were living on the Wake Robin property with Netta and Roscoe, with whom they shared meals and social activities.

Caught up in self-importance, Roscoe was an easy prey to the unscrupulous, who must have thought, "He's representing Jack London, isn't he? The man who wrote *The Call of the Wild?* And he doesn't know much about construction materials, does he?" Hence, as London later guessed, every warped board in the lumberyards and every rejected fitting from the metalworks went into that hapless boat. Nothing was delivered on time except the bills, often inflated and misrepresented. The proposed cost was seven thousand dollars; the actual was over thirty.

When it was all over, Jack composed a delightful account of

the "inconceivable and monstrous" course of events surrounding the construction. Making fun of himself, he recounted the times he and Charmian would move to the city in hopes they were about to sail, only to be told at the end of two weeks it would be two weeks more, then four. As the sailing date crept from October 1906 to November, then into April 1907, friends, like a "gang of harpies," began to place bets for the sailing date. "Why, the womenkind among my friends grew so brave that those among them who never bet before began to bet with me. And I paid them too."

The most monstrous interruption occurred at five o'clock on the morning of April 18, 1906 when Charmian awoke to feel the earth "heave as if some great force laid hold of the glove and shook it like a Gargantuan rat." Within half an hour, she and Jack were riding to the top of Sonoma Mountain, from which they could see columns of smoke coming from the direction of the county seat of Santa Rosa, where many lay dying, and from San Francisco far to the south across the Golden Gate straits. Below them, where they expected to see the State Home for the Feebleminded, hovered a large dust cloud.

Tempted by disaster, they took the first available train and ferry to San Francisco, then followed events for two sleepless days and nights so Jack could prepare a story for *Collier's Weekly*. By the time of their arrival, a great fire had broken out, which would be responsible for most of the hundreds of deaths. Undaunted by the danger, they barely escaped being trapped by walls of flame and the explosions set off by dynamiters hoping to stop the fire. Jack's story noted:

> An enumeration of the buildings destroyed would be a directory of San Francisco. An enumeration of the buildings undestroyed would be a line and several addresses. An enumeration of the deeds of heroism would stock a library and bankrupt the Carnegie fund. An enumeration of the dead—will never be made. All vestiges of them were destroyed by the flames. The number of the victims of the earthquake will never be known.[13]

Indeed, even today historians argue the exact count.

Atop Nob Hill they dozed briefly on a doorstep, although the

Fairmont Hotel nearby was already in flames. Noticing them, the house's owner invited them in to show his years of collected treasures, now about to go up in flames. Taking Charmian to the piano, he asked her to play. Jack encouraged her as well, "Do it for him—it's the last time he'll ever hear it." Crying, she played until the man could bear it no longer.

The earthquake provoked one of the more unseemly acts in Jack's life. Building supplies in the city were naturally at a premium, and forbidden to be used for any purpose other than the critical construction of homes and businesses. Back in the comforts of Sonoma mountain, Jack mortgaged the Oakland home where his mother lived and signed on for hack work to pay black market prices for materials to complete the *Snark*.

To be fair, the other members of the Crowd seemed similarly self-centered about the event. George Sterling, who had been attempting to convince the Crowd to move to Carmel, found many joining him, including Arnold Genthe, whose studio had gone up in flames, and Jimmy Hopper. As a result, the noted Bay Area bohemians permanently resettled to start the Carmel art colony.

The *Snark* construction was so protracted that parts of the boat were breaking down and wearing out before the rest was completed. On January 1, 1907, Jack invited dozens of his friends and cronies to celebrate the launching. As the *Snark* slid down the ways, a crunching sound heralded approaching disaster. Onlookers watched helplessly as it munched through the underpinnings to sink its heavy hull into the mud below. Jack muttered about sabotage as he arranged to have the ketch dragged up from its unseemly rest and towed to Oakland for final work, where it was made ready for departure by April.

The composition of the crew fit the comedic character of the venture. Jack decided that he and Charmian would be assisted by Roscoe, who was to serve as navigator, Bert Stolz, a young athletic Stanford student, and most important, Tochigi, the new valet. Needing one more crew member, preferably a cook, they let word out to the public that they were accepting applications. Several thousand people—students, professionals, down-and-outers—volunteered to serve. Baffled by this pile of supplications, Jack one day told Elsie Martinez to pick one, and she selected Martin Johnson, a clerk in his father's jewelry store in Independence, Kansas. Jack wired "Can you cook?" Martin replied, "Sure, try me," and immediately set out for the local restaurant to learn the chemistry of the kitchen. Martin was the only one of the original crew to complete the journey with the couple (not because of his cooking). Of the group, only Jack, Charmian, and Roscoe had any significant experience sailing a small vessel, and most of that had been within the limits of the San Francisco Bay and delta.

* * * *

The Londons were less mad than the press and gossips intimated. The fact remained that in spite of the inconceivable and monstrous obstacles, they succeeded in accomplishing what many have trouble even dreaming of. Their achievement was a reflection of their relationship and their system for working together.

Although early in the union Jack claimed that women should not interfere with the business of life and adventure, he quickly changed his philosophy to include Charmian as a partner in all his activities. Jack and Charmian consciously borrowed the rhetoric of equality—"Mate" from the sailing life, "Comrade" from socialism—as an expression of their commitment. This agreement was greatly at odds not only with conventional Americans, who pushed separate spheres of life for wives and husbands, but with their bohemian friends, who believed women should be muses, mistresses, or very domestic and obedient wives, all for the service of the man's creativity. In time, the Londons' unusual relationship would find praise in the press and women's magazines, but never be fully honored by their artist friends.

Although partnership was the stated model, psychological undercurrents pressed both Jack and Charmian to tug and pull power more in one direction or the other. Jack took pride in describing Charmian as a boy, or the "kid who never grew up." Consciously, he meant this as complimentary, for he valued youthfulness and vigor, and was proud that he was often described as being "boyish." She was a fellow playmate. Still, during periods of unrest in the relationship, it seemed to others he was belittling her adult skills, her mature emotions.

Charmian never lost sight of being older than Jack and often seemed driven less by a lover's concern than by a maternal love that verged on spoiling. He was her "infant," for whom she wanted "to create and hold for him and with him all the joyous things" he had missed in his childhood. "So I try to provide for him the things he did not have." To that service she would become his protector as well as companion, and advise those around him how to behave, as well as guard his privacy.

The union was not seamless. However much they felt like equals psychologically, they were to have periods of struggle for control. On the surface, Jack was the usual provocateur, whose outlandish act of one form or another would send Charmian into withdrawal and self-pity before equilibrium was reestablished. It is easy to conclude from these blatant assertions of dominance that he was really in charge. Yet in quieter ways and more persistently, Charmian would get what she most wanted from him, and was able to draw from him ardent love claims, the kind one would expect of a new romance, years into the marriage. Charmian truly suffered at times, but she was not helpless and knew how to turn the tables on Jack in more subtle ways.

Their first summer together taught them that the philosophy of partnership would not be easy to practice. One of the first disputes was over finances. Accustomed to financial independence, Charmian thought she would retain some money of her own, mostly from her real-estate investments in Berkeley, and control their account. Jack insisted otherwise. "Any other arrangement was frowned upon—at the suggestion a frost seemed to spread over his face. And, seeing that it was he, I found the bondage sweet."[14]

Similarly, he preferred seeing her in lace, silk, and furs, and often bought her jewels. Aware of Bess's mistake in preferring sober clothes, she took on the fanciful style, aware that others whispered behind her back that she was vain and superficial. More correctly, she made self-decoration an art form and sought unique fabrics to take to the best seamstresses to construct striking gowns of costumelike fantasy. (For the *Snark* voyage she designed comfortable muslim pants outfits to protect her from the sun and heat of the tropics.)

Although Jack did reshape Charmian's life in some ways, patriarchy was not the rule. If someone pointed out her acquiescence to him on some matter, she would as quickly point out his submission to her on another. Most important to her was having a room, including bed, of her own. Partly this was for practical purposes: still subject to insomnia, she wanted no distractions to awaken her. Inclined to squirming, chatter, and late-night work sessions, Jack London was not an easy man to share a bed with. He conceded with no difficulty; he preferred a space of his own, so why should not she?

Separate beds were no reflection of their sexual habits. A person whose senses were her primary tie to the world, Charmian puzzled over the frigid stances of other married women she knew. Doubtless Jack's friends, married to such women, failed to comprehend how her physical frankness attracted and satisfied him, for it meant he need no longer separate women into the two categories of mother and mistress. They had sex with great pleasure; Charmian confided in her diary that Jack "nearly loved me to death" or that they had a "grand lolly" with almost blushing frequency through much of the marriage.

Though they were able to agree upon the basic structure of their living arrangements, their daily habits were not as compatible. Each held distinctive world views, and such different outlooks brought surprise and novelty to the other.

A casual glance at Jack's den proved he was an organizer. It was an office designed around files, cubbyholes, and sorting slots. In time the barns would store well-annotated books and boxes of sorted news clippings alongside the hay and ranch implements. He was a man of schedules, and he kept them.

Moreover, in spite of his frequent disparagement of academics ("boneheads"), he was the most academic of men in outlook: he believed unquestioningly he need only read all he could about an activity in order to do it. This faith explains much of his seeming enterprise and versatility. Books taught him to pull teeth, to breed pigs, to repair his sloop. There are more books on more activities than could fill a thousand lifetimes, and he was driven to learn as many of them as possible.

Because she was more secure and self-satisfied than Jack, Charmian had less need to conquer the world and control it. From early childhood her stance toward life was one of embrace and welcome, not struggle. In Jack's eyes she was the more fearless of the two for her willingness to walk into situations he would spend days reading in preparation for. She recalled him telling her:

> You don't know at all how you do things. You just do them. And sometimes fall down and cannot do them again. I'm too practical—that's why I'm a good teacher. Now you, my dear, make a rotten teacher! For instance, that riding lesson today. You ride as if you had ridden into the world in the first place; but I'm damned if you can show me how to "post" on a trot as you do.

And he was correct. She just absorbed things, whereas he had to plan everything ahead of time. Consequently she was more patient and helped him see the long view of things, particularly during the frustrating wait for the *Snark*.

On the other hand, both agreed his mind had superior training. Like his fictional characters, Jack often spoke as though he were captain of a star debate team. He would argue a point for the thrill of the battle, caring not at all if he seemed a bully, so long as the resulting ideas were rich. Charmian was not the first woman to respond to his parrying with tears, and when she did, he scolded her firmly, saying that he had known enough hysterics as a young child and could not bear "all the bestiality and uncontrol of the phenomenon" as an adult. She did not resent the lecture but instead tried to benefit from the experience and decided to accept it as an education of "an inestimable treasure."

Her education limited to the arts and humanities, Charmian often adopted Jack's attitudes toward social and political issues. The change was evident in her position on socialism. Before Jack, she was a member of the party, though not active. With his encouragement she became a founder of the first Women's Socialist Society in Oakland. When asked to speak at its first meeting, she said, "I have never made a speech in my life, but I decided that if I were a martyr, I would be a martyr to socialism," and proceeded to argue the importance of good salaries for women. She also wrote short articles for *Wilshire's*, the leading socialist paper.

Her bending to Jack on the matter of religion was easier. Raised to no faith, committed to materialist philosophy, he denied the existence of any supreme being beyond the inexora-

ble force of evolution. Charmian, however, was a Congregationalist and attended services up to the time of their affair. She
went more for the music and ritual than out of conviction,
however, and showed no signs later in life of deep religious
feeling. She did not even exhibit the same fascination Jack did
for Christ, nor his admiration for the Bible as literature.

Their great bond, though, was the work of Jack London,
including his writings, his ranch and boat plans, and very important, the publicity surrounding them all. Charmian felt
greatly honored to be Jack's secretary and editorial assistant,
and in no way saw such work as demeaning or detracting from
her abilities. If anything, she felt blessed to be married to
someone who could use her greatest talents. She was earning
her keep, and it was a much richer keep than she would be
earning alone at the shipping firm.

Their days followed a strict ritual. Jack would arise early—
Charmian often just drifting into her first sleep near sunrise—
and read. Following breakfast together, he would write his
thousand words while she typed the previous day's work. A late
lunch might include friends staying in the Wake Robin guest
cottages. The afternoon was given over to swimming, riding,
and outdoor play. Late afternoon was when they most commonly had sex. The evenings would be spent at cards, music,
or reading aloud.

One San Francisco reporter visiting the ranch found that
Charmian

> . . . drives with the speed of a little hurricane. You ought
> to see her fixing things. She arranges whole cords of
> manuscripts for publication, gets the pages in order, reads
> pages of proof, typewrites all his letters, by hundreds,
> turns round and round like a top, and when Jack runs shy
> of ideas she says just one word, and the tracery of a contin-
> uous thread of gold thought is renewed with intense activ-
> ity.[15]

Edgar Larkin, a guest at the ranch, saw Charmian break up a
breakfast conversation by simply walking into a room and looking Jack in the eye. No words were necessary—all knew that
8:30 was work time.[16]

The orderliness paid off. From the time of Jack's move to

Glen Ellen in 1905 until the *Snark* departure in 1907, Jack completed *White Fang, Moon Face, Before Adam, The Iron Heel, The Road,* and *Love of Life,* along with book reviews and newspaper articles. To fund the *Snark* he sought and obtained contracts with both *Cosmopolitan* and *Collier's* for stories on the voyage. Those serializing his longer works often insisted on changes, deletions, and additions to the original manuscripts. The output was planned like a military campaign. Jack wrote Frederick Bamford that, "having got half-way through a book, Charmian and I decided to take a vacation. For twelve days we were away through the mountains on horseback, continuously riding. These twelve days are equivalent to the Sundays of three months, and by working Sundays for the next three months, we will have earned this vacation."[17]

They had certainly earned more, and grew fretful as the *Snark* plans were delayed month after month. One blessing came in the form of a full reunion with the Crowd. Thinking the Londons were about to depart, in the fall of 1906 George convinced Carrie to break her silence of one-and-a-half years and make peace with Charmian. The two couples met for dinner in Oakland, during which Charmian noted a strain in the Sterlings' relationship. Carrie asked them to come to Carmel; they went in November.

There was no town at Carmel then, little more than a few farms and woods adjoining the spectacular coastline with its wild beaches and dunes. Such land was cheap. As much an outdoors person as Jack, George delighted in the rich harvest of impressions a simple excursion to dig mussels, pry up abalone, collect birds' eggs, or chop firewood could bring.

George was a bit peeved by Jack's preference for life on his mountain slopes, but George had no trouble bringing down to this perfect rural atmosphere virtually all of Bay Area bohemia, many of them permanently. As drama critic for the *San Francisco Call,* Blanche Partington was out of a job temporarily now that the theaters were dark. Her brother Richard had watched his "School of Magazine and Newspaper Illustrations" literally collapse, and temporarily moved his family to Carmel for its abundant and free fish and game. Jimmy Hopper, who had given up law to write, was already on his way to becoming one of the most effective and popular journalists of his time. (London admired him greatly; he thought Hopper's account of the great earthquake much better than his own.) Arnold Genthe, who found that his own photographs of the earthquake brought him fresh fame, had no trouble continuing his business from the seaside colony.

All of these people were well acquainted as members of the Coppa's restaurant artists' group. They were relaxed among one another and accepted the heightened eccentricities common to creative personalities. An important addition to the group was Mary Austin, who had originally been refused a place at the exclusive dining table. Austin had since left her husband and child and moved to Carmel in January 1906, so was well settled by the time the quake refugees arrived. Her *Land of Little Rain* had brought her both fame and the independent income to build a house near George, including a treehouse, "the Wickiup," she mounted each morning to work. She and George shared a fascination with drama, and delighted in sharing fantasies with one another.

Austin did not take the news of Jack's arrival well at first. She had observed him during his separation from Bess, when Charmian too was away in Glen Ellen. "Jack London thought . . . that the [sexual] assault that men of genius yielded to, or withstood according to their capacity, was the biological necessity of women to mate up, ascendingly, preferring, he thought, the tenth share in a man of distinction to the whole of an average man. Women flung themselves at Jack, lay in wait for him."[18] Austin found it hard to excuse women who would "come into what they themselves call inspirational relations with men of creative capacity." Austin thought women should find the artist within themselves, not serve as muses.

Believing social revolution and intellectual debate more important than whims of fantasy, Jack was not disposed to admire Austin either.

Austin credited Charmian for bringing the two together to the point of "Platonic exchanges," and found herself fascinated by Jack's social Darwinism and endless intellectual curiosity. She found him "sagging a little with the surfeit of success, obtained through idleness, making him prefer the lounging pitchwood fire or the blazing hearth" to Sterling and Hopper's energetic hikes over the landscape.

Although the Carmel artists were serious workers who agreed no social contact could take place until the morning's private attempt at creative work was done, Jack and Charmian's arrival marked a break, a party that lasted for several days. Arnold Genthe drew a memorable portrait of a beach picnic:

> George Sterling, who was proud of his classic contours, had climbed to the top of the cliff in his bathing trunks. Somewhere or other he had procured a trident and he was standing silhouetted against the sky while Jimmy Hopper was taking his picture. This was too frivolous for Mary (dressed in the beaded leather costume and long braids of an Indian princess) who was gazing at the setting sun. Standing on the beach with outspread arms, she began something which sounded like a quotation from Browning. " 'Tis a Cyclopean blacksmith," chanted Mary, "striking frenzied sparks from the anvil of the horizon." London was standing with a fork in hand, having just disposed of an abalone steak. Taking a look around which included both Mary and the horizon, he exclaimed, "Hell! I say this sunset has guts!"[19]

By the time Jack left, Austin was won over by his generosity, and admired the literary relationship he had forged with George. Any fears she felt that Jack would interfere with her own ties to George had vanished.

Tales of the parties and amateur dramatics put on by the Crowd quickly reached the press over the next few years, and Jack was often included as a main participant. For example, several years later disputes arose among the group concerning a production of a play. A clever reporter told the public two factions were the cause: the nonrespectable element, imbibers headed by George and Jack, and the eminently respectable teetotalers, headed by photographer Arnold Genthe and Charmian. Debate set in over the costumes for the Greek drama, namely to wear lingerie or not. The underclothes wearers won.

Temperament was supposed to be highly valued. Fond of raw duck, Jack was accused of exterminating the local population. Mary Austin was said to spend her days wandering the woods in reverie. But the chief temperamental asset was hair. "Art is long, why not hair?" the reporter was advised.[20]

Such stories, accepted as truth by some historians, were fraught with hyperbole and error. Once settled in Carmel, George realized it took more than quiet surroundings to encourage his poetic flow and entered long periods of abstinence from alcohol. Though eccentric, Mary Austin was the preeminent professional at her craft, and continued to work daily despite an occurrence of breast cancer in 1907. Jack and Charmian actually visited Carmel only three times, for stays of only several days. Thus, the local duck population had little to fear. As for the Crowd, its members had to trek to Glen Ellen to visit the Londons, who thus protected their precious work schedule.

The innocent fun the Londons experienced in Carmel that winter was soon disrupted. In the summer of 1907, George achieved unexpected notoriety when his mentor, Ambrose Bierce, published *The Testimony of the Suns* in *Cosmopolitan*, prefaced by claims that Sterling was the greatest poet this side of the Atlantic. Curiosity seekers swarmed about Carmel, even stealing woodchips from George's chopping block. Worse, several months later Nora May French, a stunning but disturbed golden-haired poet George had brought to Carmel, took cyanide in despondency over a lover. Following this, the Carmel group began to talk obsessively about her death, which they venerated as the only way a poet or hedonist could die. Members of the group agreed to carry vials of cyanide with them, with a pledge to use when the time came that life was too meaningless. Both Carrie and George were to carry out that oath.

As the launch day of the *Snark* finally neared, Charmian directed the loading of the vessel, and the workmen were impressed with her knowledge of stevedoring, which she likely picked up from years on the waterfront. Dray loads of wood, coal, vegetables, blankets, tinned food, and books crowded the boat. Photographic equipment was specially packaged for the tropical heat and moisture. The men packed clothing, fishing tackle, guns, harpoons, and hundreds of reams of paper, paper for typewriting, paper for Jack's pencil scrawls, paper for Charmian's letters. So much loading postponed the departure date by two days.

On April 20, as they packed the remaining goods into crevices under the eyes of reporters, sightseers, and well-wishers, the crew was greeted by a U.S. marshall, who pasted a five-by-seven piece of paper onto a mast. A ship chandler named Sellers had attached the boat for a two-hundred-fifty-dollar debt, one of many Jack had to settle that day. Since it was a weekend, it was impossible to lift the embargo.

On April 23 daylight broke over a crowd of thousands on the wharves of the Oakland estuary. Photographers and newsmen came to write of what they believed to be the last sight ever of the Londons and their crew. Along with curiosity seekers came members of the Bohemian Club of San Francisco, the Oakland Elks, writers, artists, and most of the Crowd, who strung Jimmy Hopper's blue-and-gold varsity sweater on the masthead. The farewells said, the *Snark* broke dock and turned toward the narrow Golden Gate straits.

Several months before, on New Year's Eve, Charmian had summed up the previous year with feelings that must also have been true on this morning:

Today closes the happiest year of my life—my first year of wedlock. I'm so much happier than I ever hoped to be and Jack London, my husband, says the same of himself. It seems too good to be true, but true it is, if anything is true. Our life is ideal for both of us. And now we have before us the real *adventure* of our lives. Soon we'll be sailing on high seas for the South Sea Islands, and it is not too much to expect, to believe our happiness will go with us.

8

HAWAIIAN FANTASY

A sense of marvel drifts to me—
Of morning on a purple sea,
And fragrant islands far away.

—*George Sterling*

Although they had sailed off into the sunset, the Londons were not having a very romantic time. Once through the Gate, the spunky boat was rocked by ocean swells for days. "I'd like to see Tochigi make even a feeble attempt to be something other than a corpse," Charmian dolefully noted. The overcast weather depressed their spirits further. Being least sick of all, Charmian spent these first days cleaning up the filth, grease, and litter in the engine room, bathroom, two staterooms, and cabins, scrubbing furiously with ammonia and a small amount of water. Of the crew only she and Jack seemed to care about the dirt, but afterward she "felt more like a white woman."[1]

On the fourth day, Charmian collapsed as well. "This has been a very exciting day. Listen: Jack shaved, and I washed my face and hands."[2] The crew members' noble attempts to perform their chores alternated with scurrying dives to the rail to give up their latest food. Because any rapid movement resulted in vomiting, Charmian logged four hours for the manicure of her nails—she would look good whatever the cost to her energy.

Declared by Jack the tightest ship afloat, the *Snark* was a sieve. The sides leaked, the bottom leaked, the self-bailing cockpit flooded. The gasoline in supposedly nonleakable tanks behind a supposedly airtight bunkhead filtered out to contaminate the foodstuffs and turn the craft into a floating bomb. The dynamo refused to deliver power to the lights. In the bathroom, Jack's special pride, the pipes burst the first day out, ruining all hopes of modern hygiene.

On the third day, a gale struck, carrying away the jib and staysail. The flooding increased; the engine remained silent. The boat rode the trough of the wave, so that to look upward would be to see a hundred tons of water in a massive snarling curl. In such weather, a vessel the size of the *Snark* should have been headed into the wind, using a maneuver known as "heaving to," which would allow it to steer itself with all hands in safety below deck. The *Snark* refused to heave to. In desperation Jack first threw out an unusually fancy sea anchor, which promptly collapsed, then a large makeshift timber float, which merely dragged behind.

While the seasick men struggled with these many problems, Charmian kept the wheel. It was quickly apparent that her seaworthiness and grit were a factor in their survival. Distressed several days later that the others seemed to consider the trip a "mere picnic on the breast of an unruffled lake," she shirked no duty, indeed took up the others' slack, and without ceremony rose to first-mate position.

Like most sailors, Charmian quickly grew to dislike the sea but love the boat:

> It is beautiful, the sea, always beautiful in one way or another; but it is cruel, and unmindful of the life that is in it and upon it. It was cruel last evening, in the lucid sunset that made it glow dully, to the cold, mocking, ragged sunrise that made it look like death. The waves posi-

tively beckoned when they rose and pitched toward our bit boat laboring in the trough. And all night long it seemed to me that I heard voices through the planking, talking, talking, endlessly, monotonously, querulously; and I couldn't make out whether it was the ocean calling from the outside or the ship herself muttering gropingly, finding herself. If the voices are the voices of the ship, they will soon cease, for she must find herself. But if they are the voices of the sea, they must be sad sirens that cry, restless, questioning, unsatisfied—quaint homeless little sirens.[3]

When Jack grew despondent over the ship's failure to heave to, she convinced him to stick by it. He grew even more enamored of her cheerful temperament through the crises, and called her "the Crackerjack" or "skipper's sweetheart" before the others, endearing names he knew meant a lot to her.

Jack was generally disgusted by the other men. Even after his gentle lecture on seamanship and discipline, they were unwilling to perform the continual chores required to maintain a floating home. The only one proving to have any use at all was Martin Johnson, who handled the ordeal of cooking from a store of spoiled provisions but was otherwise not as helpful as Jack had hoped. Bert Stolz might have been an engineer with a Stanford degree, but he had no practical knowledge of how real machines worked. Not surprisingly, poor Tochigi, when not actually ill, was too terrified to be of any use. The worst crew member turned out to be Roscoe Eames, the official navigator.

When the journey had been in its planning stages, Jack knew that Roscoe lacked ocean-sailing experience but admired his intelligence and was convinced by Roscoe's claims that he could learn navigation. The early days out seemed to reward Jack's confidence: Roscoe went through periodic rituals on deck with a sextant, disappeared to the books below, then reappeared "with cabalistic signs on paper" to announce a string of numbers. Two weeks out, however, Charmian wrote her correspondents, "You may not have heard: but Roscoe is making voyage on the inside of the earth's crust, while the rest of us (barring Bert, who is on the cosmographical fence) have a strong belief we are progressing on the outer surface of the globe, with an ascertained astronomical system surrounding us. Either Roscoe will have to find a hole through which to climb into our stratum, or we shall be obliged to crawl through to his warm kernel."[4] At first they were amused by his theory, perhaps because his magical act with sextant and compass were so convincing. When asked about their location, he would play with the gadgets, dip into his cabin, and return with a cipher code, such as "31-15-47 north, 133-5-30 west." Feeling intimidated by his performance, the others would nod and go on with their duties. One day Jack paid closer attention and realized Roscoe was making no sense.

Wanting to prove to Charmian that "she was a most fortunate woman to have a man like me," Jack promptly grabbed the navigation books from their library and taught himself the instruments and charts.[5] (Later he mocked his pride, informing his readers that his experience proved any young man could learn celestial navigation.) On May 17, as predicted hours before by Jack, the crew joined together on deck to watch the merest bit of Mauna Kea, the snow-hooded volcano on the island of Hawaii, creep above the horizon at the precise point he indicated. On May 21, after twenty-six days of ceaseless tossing, they slid into the port of Honolulu, much to the surprise of those on shore, who had read in the papers that the Londons were lost and presumed drowned.

In 1907 Hawaii was a land of contradictions. The white haoles who had deposed Queen Liliuokalani in a bloodless coup the previous decade now ruled as an oligarchy. Miscegenation between Polynesians and whites was widespread; its acceptance, however, depended upon whether the Polynesian blood was royal, *alii*. While the ruling class ruthlessly exploited land and labor, its Congregationalist religious scruples supported racial equality and universal education. But equal education was a long way off in fact, and the islands lacked much of a middle class. There was the ruling white and royal Polynesian elite, with the masses of various Oriental and Polynesian workers far below.

As noted socialists, one might expect Jack and Charmian to study this unusual culture and report disappointingly to comrades and the public on the subjugation of workers. They did not. Indeed, Charmian's travel book began, "Come tread with me to a little space of Paradise."

Elysium was what they chose to see for the most part, and considering the circumstances, it is understandable why. There was no way they could study the land in anonymity, as Jack had while tramping in the United States and Britain. They were celebrities, hosted by the social and business leaders of the islands. For the first time, they mixed with capitalists for extended periods of time, and they liked what they found. The Hawaiian ruling class was well educated (Yale was a favorite for the sons), handsome and healthy looking (from both the climate and the influx of Polynesian genes), and in defiance of their puritanical forebears, playful. No better proof of the Anglo-Saxon creed, of the Nietzschean dictum, could be found than this gracious, skillful group.

Jack and Charmian looked forward to bringing socialism to these business leaders, but failed to anticipate that the business leaders would convert them in return. The couple's own housekeeping was modest—a small rustic bungalow on the shores of Pearl Harbor, merely a breezy bedroom with tiny veranda and kitchen. Much of the time, however, they were guests at town homes, mountain homes, and ranches where the wealthy ruled. Though they too were used to having a servant around, they were not accustomed to the scale and level of opulence these Hawaiian families took for granted. That they were so generously treated in these households convinced Jack and Charmian that they were equals and deserved the same level of comfort.

Hawaii also brought out Charmian's belief in white superiority. On her first visit to Honolulu proper, she was disappointed to discover a bustling Japanese city rather than a tropical Polynesian town. Only in the business district did she find "her own kin" or native Hawaiians in their floral-print clothes and leis. Another day, while walking dreamily beside a row of shops, she found herself face to face with a "bristle-headed, impudent-eyed Japanese coolie . . . I know that I, as a white woman, should rather have died than step around this coolie Asiatic. In his country, perhaps; in mine or any other than his, decidedly no." Experienced from her years of boxing, she put up her fists, and the astonished young man quickly slipped aside, no doubt wondering at this mad haole woman. When she described this encounter to Jack at lunch, he clucked, "Why the poor kid! She is learning the world."[6]

After traveling through various plantations, Charmian sent an article to their socialist comrades at *Wilshire's*. Believing the rhetoric about Hawaiian workers fed her by the plantation owners, she painted a congenial portrait of life for them. She noted how all the various immigrants had been induced to come with promises of "little homes and bits of land, schools and kindergartens." Child labor, a problem in the United States at the time, did not exist. "The native Hawaiian element is happy-go-lucky, and real poverty is a stranger to it. The upper-class Hawaiian has plenty and the lower-class is content with little, and there is always work for him to do, when he wants it."[7] That *Wilshire's* would publish such comments indicates the extent to which social Darwinism was acceptable in the movement, Eugene Debs's and other socialists' fighting of racism to the contrary.

As with Jack, her racist leanings were not inspired by hatred. Their first exposure to Hawaiian society was a party for a group of congressmen on a junket, hosted by Prince Jonah Kalanianaole, better known as Prince Cupid, and his resplendent wife Elizabeth. Off to the side sat Queen Liliuokalani, her eyes glaring in cold hatred of the Americans. Charmian sympathized with her: "Imagine her emotions, she who received special favor from Queen Victoria at the Jubilee in London; she who then had the present Kaiser for right-hand courtier at royal banquets, and the escort of Duke This and Earl That upon public occasions, now sitting uncrowned, receiving her conquerors." When Charmian extended her hand, the queen gingerly touched it "as if she preferred to slap it." Charmian's heart reached out toward the woman, and she was saddened at the cruelty the "survival of the fittest" brought upon such persons.[8]

London's later descriptions of their experiences contained similarly mixed attitudes. The introduction to his story "Goodby, Jack" twists an ironic knife into the romantic conception of the Hawaiian elite:

Hawaii is a queer place, everything socially is what I may call topsy-turvy. . . . The most exclusive set there is the "Missionary Crowd." It comes with rather a shock to learn that in Hawaii the obscure, martyrdom-seeking missionary sits at the head of the table of the moneyed aristocracy. But it is true. The humble New Englanders who came out in the third decade of the nineteenth century came for the lofty purpose of teaching the Kanakas the true religion, the worship of the one only genuine and undeniable God. So well did they succeed in this, and also in civilizing the Kanaka, that by the second or third generation he was practically extinct. This being the fruit of the seed of the Gospel, the fruit of the seed of the missionaries (the sons and the grandsons) was the possession of the islands themselves—of the land, the ports, the town sites, and the sugar plantations. The missionary who came to give the bread of life remained to gobble up the whole heathen feast.

The remainder of the story concerns a member of the "missionary crowd," an Apollo of a man who discovers (through an O'Henry twist of plot) that his lover is a leper. The rich and beautiful, London reminds us, are not exempt from the laws of nature, even though social Darwinism, the "survival of the fittest," gives them an edge.[9]

The story "Aloha Oe" was clearly inspired by the congressional junket. There he portrays Senator Jeremy Slambrooke, who sees, not the blossom-bedecked Hawaiian countryside, but only "the labor power, the factories, the railroads, and the plantations." His fifteen-year-old daughter Dorothy stands beside him on the steamer that is about to pull out for the States. She searches for Steve, the man she loves; aware of the young age at which girls marry on the islands, she wonders why he did not propose. Then she recalls a tea where some of the women had spoken ill of a girl who had married a *hapa-haole,* a half-caste. Though Steve's Polynesian blood is but a quarter-strain, it is enough to make him unacceptable to the senator. As the boat pulls away, the strains of "My love be with you till we meet again" burn Dorothy's heart like acid because of their irony. London's sympathies are fully with the girl, implying that he values romantic love more than caste notions.

Similarly, in "The House of Pride," London unfavorably portrays another man of the missionary crowd who has racial purity foremost in his mind. Percival Ford discovers one night that his righteous and proud father had sired an illegitimate son with a Hawaiian woman. Rather than extend himself to his half-brother, as a friend encourages, he bribes the man to leave the islands forever.

Other Hawaiian tales refer to the extraordinary beauty of those of white and Polynesian background.[10] This is a tremendous shift away from the pure social Darwinism of London's earlier writings, which suggested that the races should stay separate, that the white race would dominate the world because of its inevitable superiority. London showed no awareness that these observations contradicted his philosophy.

Very likely his new-found commitment to racial mixing came from Luther Burbank. Upon moving to Glen Ellen in 1905, London made acquaintance with Burbank, by then internationally known for his successes in plant breeding. Burbank had of course been as influenced by Darwin as London, more so in that he applied the principles in his daily work. Burbank was convinced that planned interbreeding was the basis for social progress. In his *Training of the Human Plant,* written at the time of London's visit, he observed:

> I have come to find in the crossing of species and in selection, wisely directed, a great and powerful instrument for the transformation of the vegetable kingdom along lines that lead constantly upward. The crossing of species is to me paramount. . . . The mere crossing of species, unaccompanied by selection, wise supervision, intelligent care, and the utmost patience, is not likely to result in marked good, and may result in vast harm.
> . . . let me lay emphasis on the opportunity now presented in the United States for observing and, if we are wise, aiding in what I think it fair to say is the grandest opportunity ever presented of developing the finest race the world has ever known out of the vast mingling of races brought here by immigration.[11]

Burbank was convinced the blending of the races of the "North, powerful, virile, aggressive," with the "luxurious, ease-loving, more impetuous South" would result in "a magnificent race, far superior to any preceding it."[12]

London's attraction to this theory was more than scientific. As we have already seen, before any exposure to the work of Carl Jung (whose works were not yet available in English), he had contrived a theory of personality based upon a unity of opposites. The perfect comrade would combine the feminine and masculine elements; so too, it would follow, would the perfect race be a mixture of the best of all.

Burbank also argued the importance of environment in the development of good stock. Heredity is only the sum of the effects of the environment on previous generations; environment is the architect of heredity. No one is predestined to a particular character or fate. The proper environment can strengthen the weak, as well as ensure that the strong express their virtues. For London, capitalism with its exploitation of labor was the most destructive feature of the United States environment.

Thus, in "Chun Ah Chun" the hero is a Chinese version of the man who molds his own magnificent destiny. As a coolie in a sugar field, Ah Chun studies the management of the plantation and realizes that "men did not become rich from the labor of their own hands." Having saved most of his meager earnings, he goes into partnership with a friend in an import business. Soon he is on his own, importing thousands of Cantonese coolies to Hawaii. He marries a woman of Polynesian, Italian, Portuguese, English, and American blood. The blend of the races in his fifteen offspring "was excellent, . . . healthy and without blemish." The story relates Ah Chun's cleverness in marrying his twelve daughters off to wealthy white men. In the end he flees to Macao, where he lives his final days in peace, free from the family fighting caused by the corrupting influence of the money his crafty capitalism had earned.

Indeed, however much Jack enjoyed the company of the Hawaiian elite, and he did heartily, his stories clearly show he did not fully admire them. A frequent companion was Lorrin A. Thurston, a lawyer and newspaper editor, who had been the leading conspirator in the revolutionary overthrow of the royalty. He had also been a major force behind the creation of a government that denied full civil rights to the Hawaiian people and Oriental immigrants. When the U.S. Congress insisted that Hawaiians be allowed to vote, Thurston cleverly convinced Prince Kalanianaole to join the Republican party and run for Congress. The prince was a great favorite both on the islands and in Washington, but he was never able to garner the power he desired for his people from the white oligarchy.

Perhaps to humor Jack, Thurston invited him to be guest speaker at a private social club. Jack chose his most incendiary speech, "Revolution," and delighted in telling his wealthy listeners their lives were not secure. Charmian reported on the event to *Wilshire's:* "The average gathering of capitalists to hear such a reading is anything but courteous, and too resentful and too fearful to be intelligently attentive," but this group was polite. Even the press was not its "usual vicious self," and when Thurston himself asked Jack to order him some books on socialism, the couple took the gesture to mean "the seed is planted."[13] They were, of course, wrong.

Members of the elite like Thurston clearly had a motive other than conviviality in extending themselves to London. Hawaii was then little known in the States, and they counted on his publicizing the island's wonders, hoping to attract tourists. London obliged, though not always as they wished.

One story did please them.

It started one day when Jack was watching the magnificent surf of Waikiki—its waves "bull-mouthed monsters, and they weigh a thousand tons."[14] His ego shrank in awe at the power, when suddenly, from the crest of a foaming, tumbling wave, arose a young Polynesian man, erect and poised on the edge of a board. London compared him to a brown Mercury, heels winged by the swiftness of the sea. Challenged to participate with the Kanaka in his royal sport, Jack found a surfboard and joined some children in a class.

Enter Alexander Hume Ford. A natural promoter, he had decided to make the island pastime "one of the most popular on earth," meaning, that is, to make it respectable for whites. Although Ford advised her to wait until Jack tried the sport first, Charmian refused and plunged with them into the deep surf.

Their first time out was spent primarily underwater. Coming up for air, they "were able to compare size and number of stars.

Of course, his were the bigger—because my power of speech was not equal to his." During those "laughing, strenuous, half-drowned hours," she wished she were a boy, so she could be larger and comparatively stronger than her five-foot-two frame allowed.[15]

Soon afterward Jack published a rousing account of these events in *Woman's Home Companion.* [16] Aware his readers would doubt that a full-grown man could balance on several feet of wood, London devoted a large section of the article to the physics of the activity. His description of surfing itself is so laden with sensation that the reader easily joins him in the dangerous ride. As with so much of his nonfiction, however, he simplified to convey a more spare and powerful message. Nowhere did he mention that Charmian was beside him the whole time, and he thus gave his women readers the impression that the sport was beyond their ken.

With his modest self-mockery, he did include the anticlimactic consequences. While Charmian and Jack proved whites could surf, they forgot the inherent weakness of the race. Following several long days in the surf, Jack became "a sun-burned, sun-peeling Mercury": lips swollen, eyes puffed shut, joints so burnt he could not bend them, shoulders cruelly grilled. Another curious malady, a hivelike disorder, splotched several large areas of his body on top of the sunburn. For several days he could only waddle naked on palms and heels.

Another set of stories earned much criticism from Hawaiians after they appeared. These started with a steamer trip on June 29, 1907, for which Jack and Charmian were the only passengers with round-trip tickets. While boat departures on the islands were usually grounds for frolicking celebrations, this was instead "a funeral in which the dead themselves walked," for this was the boat to the leper colony of Molokai.[17]

Situated on a small peninsula cut off from the rest of the island by precipitous cliffs several thousand feet high, the settlement then had a self-sufficient population of eight hundred. Patients kept all money earned. Those who could not work were cared for by the board of health. The community ran farms, dairies, and cattle ranches. It had six churches, a YWCA, several assembly halls, a bandstand, a racetrack, baseball fields, an athletic club, glee clubs, and fishing boats.

Once ashore Charmian and Jack struggled to overcome their disgust at the hideous deformities around them, concerned how their response would affect the afflicted. A crack shot with pistol or rifle, Charmian was relieved to be asked to join a group at a target range. Upset by her failure to make a bull's eye once during the practice, she blamed the "heavy and un-familiar gun" along with "the audience of curious men whose personal characteristics were far from quieting to *malahini wahini* nerves."

Her nerves were not helped by Jack's desire to learn as much as he could about the medical facts of leprosy during their few days in the community. Consequently, she joined him for sev-eral days watching minor operations and treatments, sights she felt too gruesome to describe to her correspondents.

The Fourth of July festivities, which she reported in detail, were most fantastic:

> This morning we were shocked from dream by noises so strange as to make us wonder if we were not struggling in nightmare—unearthly cackling mirth and guttural shout-ings and half-animal cries that hurried us into kimonos and sandals. . . . In the eery whispering dawn there gam-boled a score or so "horribles," men and women already horrible enough, God wot, and but thinly disguised in all manner of extravagant costumings. They wore masks of home manufacture, in which the makers had unwittingly imitated the lamentable grotesquerie of the accustomed features of their companions—the lopping mouth; knobby or effaced noses, flapping ears; while equally cor-rect in similitude, the hue of these false-true visages was invariably an unpleasant, pestilent yellow. Great heaven! —do our normal countenances appear abnormal to them?[18]

Some rode on horseback; a clown perched on a donkey; others danced alone. All mimicked and joked as they moved toward the site of the day's activities.

There then appeared, in the silver, dewy light, a cavalcade of women riders, wild draperies of brilliant-colored long skirts flowing behind them. All morning this cavalry trooped about singing and calling to various segments of the village. Like so many American towns on this day, the afternoon was a time for races and contests, the evening for a talent show. "No one, listening outside to the unrestrained merrymaking, could have guessed the band of abbreviated human wrecks, their distorted shadows monstrous in the flickering lamplight, performing, unconcernedly for once, their Dance of Death."[19]

Though composed in public, Charmian had difficulty dealing with her uneasy feelings. The worst was the day a group of young girls were summoned to entertain her: "Clustered around a piano, one played with hands that were not hands—for where were the fingers? But play she did, and weep I did, in a corner, in sheer uncontrol of heartache at the girlish voices gone shrill and sexless and tinny like the old French piano, and the written mouths that tried to frame sweet words carolled in happier days."[20] Her heart went out to all the women patients, for the disease seemed to do more extensive damage to females, and the recognition of their loss of beauty showed in their eyes.

These and similarly detailed descriptions of life on Molokai appeared in print after Jack's death in Charmian's book *Our Hawaii.* By then she was a revered guest, and her frank commentary on the leper colony sparked no controversy. Jack's publications, however, over the next few years brought great scolding in the Hawaiian press even if they simply mentioned the disease.

London's most thoughtful and reasoned essay on the lepers of Molokai appeared in two popular magazines, *Woman's Home Companion* and *Contemporary Review.* It was a successful attempt to represent both the truth behind the disease—its very low contagion—as well as the humanity of the afflicted. "Just tell the world how we are in here," they begged him, and he did.

Leprosy also appears in his Hawaiian stories, typically as a metaphor for a fate similar to that symbolized by the ominous white silence in his Arctic tales. It spares no caste or class. Importantly, its victims are heroic figures. In "Koolau the Leper," which is based upon a true account, the hero leads a rebel band of the afflicted to the Kalalau valley. In his determination to stay with his family, the real Koolau had murdered Bert Stolz's father, then a deputy sheriff in the valley, to avoid being sent to Molokai. London's story depicts the final days of the leper band's stand against authorities with poignancy and sympathy for their fight.

Immediately following the Londons' departure from the islands, several reporters told stories of their passing bad checks. The reports were probably untrue, provoked by several businesspeople who had tried to fleece them for repairs of the *Snark.* Having been a reporter himself, Jack was able to ignore this kind of attack.

His reaction was different, however, when Thurston permitted biting criticisms of London to be printed in the *Hawaiian Advertiser's* pseudonymous "Bystander" column, which said among other things that London had abused the Hawaiians by writing "sensational and untrue stories about Molokai after visiting the island as their guest."[21] The attack was not mild: the article called Jack a "dirty little sneak" and an "ungrateful and untruthful bounder." Jack responded that he had paid his own way for the trip to the colony and that he was determined to tell the truth of what he saw there. He attacked the newspaperman for his provincialism, his willingness to exploit "the weaknesses and afflictions of other lands" while seeking to bury Hawaii's particular problems. "Of what use is a Promotion Committee, and of public broad-minded citizens, when they allow a set of mediocre reporters to set their ethical newspaper pace for them?"

When Jack and Charmian returned to the islands five years later, the criticism was forgotten. Their publicizing of the whole truth, as they saw it, had sparked great interest on the mainland, and they were distressed to see how much tourism had encroached on the once peaceful shores they loved. It was a despoiling they had unwittingly helped along.

If Molokai stirred the Londons' admiration for the grace with which the afflicted suffered, Maui aroused all their senses with its "incessant atmosphere of wonder and expectation," a landscape rich with gulches, palisades, needled peaks, tropical trees and vines, mossed cliffsides, resounding waterfalls, and swift-rolling clouds. No spot on the trip was more impressive than the Haleakala ranch, eight thousand feet up its namesake crater.[22]

The wiry, handsome Louis von Tempski managed the sixty-thousand-acre spread, where his young family spent a most isolated life in a rambling old house furnished with a good library, a piano, and a commodious guest wing. From the well-tended garden could be viewed "terrace upon terrace of hills, champaigns of green speckled with little rosy craters like buds turned up to sun and shower; and off in the blue vault of sea and sky, other islands, dim and palpitating like mirages."

As a cattle ranch, it was well equipped for horses, and noting Charmian's skill, Louis allotted her the best of the lot. For days they rode the land, up and across the extinct blow hole of a volcano, shambled over frozen lava beds and down lush meadows to the sea, and then over to the Ditch country with its rich foresting.

Soon to follow was a visit to the one-hundred-and-fifty -thousand-acre Parker spread, the largest of all Hawaiian estates, and the live Moana Loa volcano. While there one day, Jack suffered a fall from a "perfectly safe" stolid-looking children's horse, which bucked him as soon as he was seated. Landing on his shoulder and head, Jack sprang up and gathered himself to continue riding. That evening, his head ached maddeningly, and in spite of Charmian's cold compresses, he passed into a delirium, his face scarlet, his tongue babbling nonsense. In despair, Charmian reversed the treatment, applying heat to the base of his skull, and relief quickly followed. This was the first of several times that Charmian's coolness and wherewithal would save Jack's life.

*   *   *   *

While their public remarks on Hawaii emphasized the beauty of its land, the hospitality of its people, and its tragic blemish of leprosy, their private notes told another story. To readers it would appear they spent their five months on the islands attending balls with noted socialites, lolling on the beach and in the surf, or riding horseback through the wild landscapes of the 150,000-acre Parker ranch. All this occurred, but not at the expense of work.

Their first activity wherever they settled was to turn their lodgings into an office. Jack would find a table or desk, which would soon be littered with scraps of notes, manuscript pages, and the stack of pencils Tochigi sharpened every morning. Charmian would set her faithful Remington on a table alongside their beloved "Victor" record player. Both preferred to work to music and had brought over three hundred disks with them, including sets of language lessons the crew could study in preparation for their stops in non-English-speaking colonies.

On their first day in Hawaii, Jack opened the mail to find a rejection of *The Iron Heel.* He simply turned around and, in that warm semitropical splendor, began "To Build a Fire," his masterwork about a man who freezes to death in the Yukon. During the crossing, he had kept Charmian busy typing *Martin Eden,* which they worked on for the next nine months. Despite their many activities in the islands, Jack handed Charmian at least nine other articles and stories to prepare for publication.

As journeys do, the demands of travel brought new insights into and demands upon their relationship. Jack's observations of Charmian overcoming challenges increased his ardor. In his inscription in her copy of *The Road* he wrote:

Dearest My Woman:—

Whose efficient hands I love—hands that have worked for me long hours and many, swiftly and deftly, and beautifully in the making of music; the hands that have steered the Snark through wild passages and rough seas, that do not tremble on a trigger, that are sure and strong on the reins of a thoroughbred or of an untamed Marquesan stallion; the hands that are sweet with love as they pass through my hair, firm with comradeship as they grip mine, and that soothe as only they of all hands in the world can soothe.

Your man and Lover,
Jack London

Always a romantic man, he delighted in taking her to a jeweler to purchase yet more proof of his affection.

Indeed, he was so proud of her that he determined to see her develop her own fame as a writer. She had published a variety of articles before their marriage, and through her work on the *Overland* was familiar with editorial procedures, so it was not an unreasonable idea on his part. Before starting the journey, they had decided to save time by having Charmian keep a long diary that would be sent to Netta, then passed round-robin among their friends. Jack quickly saw book possibilities in the material and encouraged her to edit it into a book appropriate for the general public. What began as a minor chore soon became a major duty; on top of Jack's monumental demands for note taking, typing, and transcribing, she now had her own manuscript to attend to.[23]

The pace could be fearsome for both. As Jack explained to George Sterling: "Arrived at five this A.M. Read mail for three hours. Have dictated letters to Charmian the whole day long; have not even glanced at a newspaper; Charmian has a stack of my letters turned over to her to answer when she finds time. It is not nearly ten P.M. and I am still writing letters. Not a line of my own work today, and I have only knocked off for meals."[24] There was plenty of reason for this effort: the unexpected bills for the repair of the *Snark,* the costs of the ranch property, and the household expenses for Bess and his children, his mother and Johnny Miller, and Virginia Prentiss. Also, Netta, who had been given control of his business affairs, was doing a good job of siphoning money into her own Wake Robin, informing Jack he should be happy to contribute in gratitude for her efforts.

While Jack continued to produce great quantities of work despite the pressure, his addictive behavior returned, leaving Charmian to face its unhappy consequences. She was able to accept part of his illness, his cigarettes, but like most spouses of addictive personalities, denied his drinking. The consequences of her denial forced her into coping in ways that increased her unhappiness and unwittingly helped Jack to avoid recognizing his disease.

Always sensible about her own health habits, Charmian had never approved of cigarettes; seldom wise about his body, Jack had been a chain smoker since early adolescence. The inevitable conflict is displayed in the humorous banter in a letter written to Frederick Bamford in 1906:

Just wait until you and I get together again, and I'll lay down how my philosophy makes room for my cigarettes. And after that I'll turn you over to Charmian to have her add a clincher. (Just watch me, I'll fix him!—C.K.) I am sorry you are not feeling well. Believe me, it is my firm conviction that cigarettes in the country are not so harmful to a man, as the city and no cigarettes. (But think what the country would be without them!—C.K.) Don't forget I shall have to make room in my philosophy for my cigarettes. (I wonder if I shall in mine!—C.K.)[25]

By the time the *Snark* was ready to sail, Charmian had made known that her philosophy had little room for the burning weed, and Jack agreed to quit his seventeen-year habit. "For love of life?" she asked. "No, for love of wife," he replied.

He endured the four-week crossing to Hawaii without a puff, but upon reaching land soon indulged again. Charmian grew so cross at the "damned tobacco irritabilities" that she considered smoking herself to inoculate herself from the noxious effects. To Netta she complained with some insight, "Jack has gone back to smoking, and it's almost more than I can face. It's a form of hysteria, isn't it? A neurotic streak. It's partly this hotel life—people smoke and drink so much—one round of cocktails after another. He and I are so close that what affects his nerves affects mine. I wish I liked to smoke."[26] Several years later she did try a puff now and then, but doing so was beyond her imagination at this point.

Displacing some anger at Jack onto herself and her own writing, she wrote in her diary, "Mate criticizes diary [the *Snark* manuscript]; misunderstanding my attitude, and I shed many tears. My eternal loneliness. I mold myself insofar as I can to him, but I cannot stand irritability—nor will I mold myself so far—the cursed smoke! I am hardly myself half the time." During much of July and August, she suffered from insomnia and tension headaches. (These were partly provoked by their having to share a bed at various houses, so that Jack's restless slumber habits disturbed her more.) One especially frustrating day she noted, "Too old to go into hysterics, too young to go crazy."

While his smoking was only a personal annoyance to her, his drinking affected others. One evening in September before a dinner party, Jack went out ahead of time for some drinks. He returned drunk, spilled coffee all over himself at the meal, upbraided Charmian publicly for phantom wrongs, and then left without saying good night.

Such behavior was not typical of Jack, but it did occur at times. He was never an alcoholic that drank constantly, day in and day out. Rather, his imbibing was always tied to situations and circumstances. If he was in a city with restaurants and bars, he would drink. If he was on a boat on the Sacramento delta or the Pacific, he could abstain completely. He had grown up associating alcohol with male conviviality, and the pattern persisted. Prior to this episode in Hawaii, Charmian had only a few brief hints of this aspect of his character. Before he moved in with her in Glen Ellen, they had too few and scattered meetings for her to notice. Once in the country, he restricted his alcohol consumption to a drink or two in the evening.

Her first encounters with his nemesis were on their honeymoon trip, both in Jamaica, when he lingered in the bars to compensate for the months of socialist lecturing, and in New York, where the demands from revolutionaries and publishers pressed more than at any other point on their journey. It was easy for her to excuse his excesses then. It was less easy in the late winter of 1907, when, in anticipation of the *Snark* departure, they had moved down to Oakland. There it was hard for him to give up habits learned in childhood, and harder still for Charmian to understand his habits.

In Hawaii she finally confronted him over her unhappiness, her shielding and lying to excuse him. They had their first hard quarrel, which drove them apart for a day. During those hours something happened that left Charmian utterly secure that Jack did love her faithfully in spite of his recent coolness, and she moved to a quick reconciliation. When he returned battered from a bar fight two weeks later, she was miserable at first, then readjusted. "I *am* a sympathetic woman; and if I am sometimes vain, I think I understand my vanity. And without it where would I be anyhow?"

With these small acts, she moved closer to cooperating with his addiction. She would look the other way. She would grant him all benefit of doubt. She would let him abuse her publicly on those rare occasions when he was so driven. She did so out of compassion for the sad, insecure man she knew existed underneath the bravado. In doing so, however, she gave him an additional unbearable burden—the guilt of being forgiven for acts that did not deserve such quick absolution. They had allowed a demon into their love space.

9

THE
DARK ISLES

We must go, go, go away from here;
On the other side the world we're
overdue.

—*Rudyard Kipling*

On October 7, 1907, the newly painted and repaired *Snark*
pulled out of Hilo, the port on the large island of Hawaii,
toward the Marquesas Islands. Roscoe Eames and Bert Stolz
had returned to the States, both filled with angry stories they
gladly told anyone willing to listen.[1] Tochigi also left, preferring the islands to the sea. The crew now consisted of Herrmann de Visser, a young Dutch sailor; Yoshimatsu Nakata, an
eighteen-year-old using the valet job as a way to return to
Japan; and Wada, a Japanese chef bored with schooner life. For
sailing master Jack hired James Langhorne Warren, a paroled
murderer who had been pardoned earlier by the governor of
Oregon after Jack interceded on his behalf. With much seago-
ing experience behind him, Warren promised to be efficient

and competent. Martin Johnson remained on, in charge of the engine, general repair work, and photo developing.

The passage to Tahiti from Hawaii was described by sailors as one of great difficulty, requiring sailors to traverse both the northeast and southeast trade winds. The passage to the Marquesas, eight hundred miles to the northeast of Tahiti, was thought to be almost impossible because of unfavorable wind conditions. Indeed, none of the sailing records listed a single instance of anyone accomplishing the feat. Undeterred by the word "impossible," Jack's plan was to run the boat eastward as far as possible so as to run down the islands to the lee. It was only two thousand miles, he calculated. What he did not calculate was that in crossing the Variables, an area of unpredictable winds, the boat would not be sailing in a straight line: two thousands miles became in fact four.

Early on the plan seemed a good one. The crew recuperated quickly from initial seasickness and proved to be hard working and cooperative. Now completely involved in his novel of the sailor-turned-writer, *Martin Eden* (then titled *Success*), Jack looked "a happy, blue eyed sailor" to his wife. So much had she written about their travels, that by now she was splitting her manuscript into two separate books, one on Hawaii, the other on the South Seas. Away from the distractions of civilization, the couple slipped into its comfortable habits of work, cards, reading aloud, and lovemaking. Charmian's headaches and insomnia disappeared.

They felt less secure as they discovered yet other weaknesses of the feisty ketch. When setting the topsail one day, they found it did not fit and understood why Roscoe had been so quick to call it down on the previous leg of the journey. The engine, which had supposedly undergone total overhaul during the five-month break in Hawaii, mostly sputtered, and Martin verified it needed further work. Worse, they found that the massive oak beams were really of an inferior wood and did not run full length as they were supposed to. Yet somehow the *Snark* bobbled along over the impossible route, and all aboard praised its responsiveness.

Though the crew was usually dauntless, fear did grip them at times. Charmian captured the feeling well one day:

Death is farthest from one's thoughts these pleasant, busy days of semi-calm, when there is just breeze enough to slip us along slowly over the smoothly rolling flood. We are complete in our little working-world; the domestic machinery cogs along much the same as in a land-home. There is little danger of anyone falling overboard unless he is attacked by vertigo, and we are in a live world in which death, I say, does not occur to our minds. But when, after such days, and placid evenings spent in the starlight with music and singing and poesy, one is startled into consciousness at midnight by being let down suddenly against the bunk-rail, and the further sensation of going over, endlessly, endlessly—then death is the first flashing thought. It might not be so to one in the open, on deck; but a closed forward stateroom, in a small yacht, is a trap. It may mean death by drowning, or what is worse, *sharks.* [2]

Within moments of writing this passage, she rushed to the deck to see that they were in the midst of some awful blackness caused by a gale that was arising with a ferocity never before imagined. She rushed to join the crew in its efforts to save the vessel, and "as death receded into dim distance," listened quietly while Warren emotionally praised the craft's behavior. Jack would later re-create the storm in his story "The Heathen."

The honeymoon did not last. In mid-November, without reason, Jack purposely shook her from her hard-claimed slumber. She wondered "when I'll get hardened. There's only one way—to love him less." Another night he bluntly avoided her goodnight kiss, and she spent the evening on deck alone, crying. The next morning he made up with her, and within hours they were laughing and playing cards. Even when his dark moods appeared so unpredictably, and they did intermittently throughout their marriage, their joint work never faltered. Personal grievances were not allowed to fester enough to interfere with the progress of manuscripts and other business.

Jack seemed to act as though he could not stand intimacy for extended periods. Eventually he had to test Charmian, usually with a cruel comment or physical rejection. She would be torn by conflicting emotions of anger, self-pity, and compassion for the hurt he must feel to treat her so badly. Her response would be to withdraw. Within a short time, as in these cases, he would apologize.

They did, after all, live very entangled lives, and it is a wonder that they had so few difficulties. Very likely their playful competitiveness provided an alternative way to express negative feelings. Yet these games could also spark discontent. Was it coincidence that one of Jack's moods came right after several weeks of Charmian beating him consistently at cribbage? They kept detailed records—when running out of paper on the *Snark* they used endpapers from their books to note the accounts of who owed whom. Similarly, on land, the boxing and fencing allowed them to express any brewing resentments.

Overall good spirits were the rule. Charmian gave much credit to Jack:

> Jack has the delightful characteristic of always wanting to share everything in which he is interested—his amusements, his books, or the thing he is studying. He explains to me his advancing steps in navigation; he reads aloud to me; he wants me to feel the tug of the fish on the line; and he draws all of us together to reread, aloud, some book he knows will give pleasure. Sunday afternoon, having done more than his usual "stint" of writing the previous day, he took a holiday and read Conrad's *Typhoon* aloud, to the delight of the sailormen. And so, a unity of good spirit is preserved aboard, because one man is fond of sharing knowledge, the acquirement of which is the business of life.[3]

This passage tells as much about Charmian's curiosity and openness as it does about Jack's.

Among the others aboard, Charmian was honored as "one of the boys." She claimed no exemptions from her share of the work and brooked no pretense or euphemisms around her. Yet she also remembered she was a woman, and thought of the women of her New England family, who had watched their husbands go off on ships, waited for them for years at a time, only to find some swift disaster eventually leaving them widowed, stranded, desolate. "It seems odd that I, born and reared in the opposite corner of the Union, should be out adventuring to strange lands myself with a man who loves to sail the sea. How much closer I shall ever be to those women of my father's family."[4]

Cards, poetry, and Conrad aside, the crew's good humor was sorely tested. They had to contend daily with being blinded by the brassy glare of the sun, with sunburn, with keeping clothes and supplies from rotting in the constant salty dampness, with just keeping clean while surrounded by grease. Weevils and beetles infested the food stores, and a variety of resident tropical bugs enjoyed the nooks and moist corners of the cabins. The lack of opportunity for vigorous physical exercise particularly disheartened Charmian, who found target practice with her rifle and gun an inadequate substitute. Eventually one person snapped—Warren would strike out in rage at Wada and Herrmann for the most minor oversights.

Then one day the worst possible calamity that could befall an ocean vessel took place. In a sudden squall, during the hoisting of the spinnaker boom, the faucet on the port bow water tank was turned on and not discovered until the next morning. Upon checking the other tanks, the crew found they had miscalculated their supplies and were seriously low. They were in the suffocating heat of the doldrums, with little prospect of storm to save them and only a quart of water per day available for each. The fuel ran so low that their dinners consisted of tinned food, cold. Just when they began to face the reality of death, a squall appeared, a brief one, but enough to fill the sails with the life-giving liquid.

Eight weeks out bonitas, gooneys, and a variety of small birds began to follow the boat. The crew took bets on who would spot land first. Charmian fantasized "fields of cabbages and onions, potatoes, cauliflowers and luscious tomatoes . . . taro patches and fabulous banana- and cocoanut- and breadfruit-groves." Captain Warren lusted for a chicken coop, while Martin longed for a meal of one dozen eggs. Jack tried to get shoes on feet that had gone unshod for two months. On December 6, 1907, early in the morning, Captain Warren won the bet, spotting Ua Huka's volcanic form shimmering in the sunrise radiance.

*   *   *   *

Having achieved the impossible, the *Snark* continued on toward the island of Nuku Hiva with its valley of Typee, which had been immortalized by Herman Melville. A French colony, the Marquesan population had dropped in recent decades from 50,000 to 5,000 as a result of the introduction of European diseases against which they had no immunity. Even today off the tourist track, the islands then were primarily visited by artists. Both Melville and Robert Louis Stevenson had lived there, and Paul Gauguin had died on the isle of Hiva Oa just a few years before, in 1903.

The couple adapted easily to the languid life of the islands. Charmian unhappily donned a dress and shoes to go ashore, only to find to her pleasure that the sole white women in the area were a boarding-house proprietor, her daughter, a French teacher, and a few nuns. None cared about proper attire. They rented a native cottage, which came with a caretaker who was constantly attended by her hog. (Charmian quipped, "She fondles it as if it were a beloved dog—although I could not help wondering if her affections were not slightly gustatory in nature.")[5] Like many older Marquesans, the woman bore ancient tattoo markings on her face and hands, giving her a lace-covered appearance. The men wore skimpy loincloths, the women variations on the Mother Hubbard dress.

While a cheerful and friendly lot, the islanders were not sturdy. In spite of chronic lung ailments, young and old, male and female, smoked continually. The population was so lacking in robustness that traders often had difficulty finding enough able men to unload their small cargoes.

While physically depleted, the Marquesans had lost little of their spiritual wealth. Charmian and Jack were invited to a feast commemorating the first anniversary of one man's mother's death. While fourteen coconut-fattened hogs roasted in the ground amid hot stones, a group of chanting dancers bore what appeared to be human bodies on tall bamboo poles. The grisly forms proved to be pigs wrapped in leaves, intended to mimic the booty of ancestors. The feast ended with an orgy of hula dancing. To reciprocate, the Londons brought their "Victor" out the next night, providing a concert of Sousa, Chopin, the Marseillaise, and opera arias to which the natives danced.

From a distance the Londons looked over the Taipi (Typee) valley and found it as Melville had described it, down to the exact location of footpaths and waterfalls. "It is when one walks

Jack was an earnest,
well-behaved boy who
preferred books and boats to
play. *(Estate of Irving
Shepard)*

Jack was twenty before he
learned that John London was
not his real father. *(Estate of
Irving Shepard)*

Flora London shirked no demeaning
work to see Jack fed, but was unable to
express her love. *(Estate of Irving
Shepard)*

This portrait exposes the Jack friends admired—boyish, open, gentle, and generous. *(Estate of Irving Shepard)*

Carrie Sterling was a melancholy woman who wanted a businessman, not a poet, for a husband. *(Estate of Irving Shepard)*

Jack and Bess Maddern did not believe in love, but based their marriage on scientific principles to breed "sturdy Saxons." Joan and Becky were the result. *(Estate of Irving Shepard)*

Charmian's father, Captain Willard Kittredge, could do little to please his troubled wife. *(Estate of Irving Shepard)*

Charmian's mother, Daisy Wiley Kittredge, had a poetic temperament that was not suited to Western frontier life. *(Estate of Irving Shepard)*

Even as a teenager, Charmian showed an appreciation for fine fabrics and a distinct style. *(Estate of Irving Shepard)*

Charmian and Jack spent two sleepless days and nights following the progress of the great fire after the 1906 earthquake. *(Estate of Irving Shepard)*

For fun, Charmian would mount the ropes of this mast of the Dirigo and read a book from the top. *(Estate of Irving Shepard)*

Macmillan printers found this photograph of Charmian at a Solomon Islands market offensive. (Note the pistol and holster at her side.) *(Estate of Irving Shepard)*

The Snark, Jack's ''inconceivable and monstrous'' boat, proved a sturdy vessel. *(Estate of Irving Shepard)*

The motley crew of the Snark included Captain Warren (far left), a paroled murderer, and Martin Johnson (next to Jack), a Kansas farmboy who had never been on the ocean. *(Estate of Irving Shepard)*

A leper woman on Molokai taught Charmian to make leis. *(Estate of Irving Shepard)*

When the Snark voyage ended, Martin Johnson married Osa Leighty, a woman like Charmian, who joined him in filming exotic places. *(Estate of Irving Shepard)*

Holding a baby pig, Jack shows the pride and happiness he felt in his Beauty Ranch. He ran the place according to principles of organic farming. (*Estate of Irving Shepard*)

Charmian felt honored to have a career as Jack's assistant. (*Estate of Irving Shepard*)

Though a diligent worker, Jack valued playfulness. *(Estate of Irving Shepard)*

Charmian used a flirtation with Australian concert pianist Laurie Smith to interfere with Jack's preoccupation with his business. *(Estate of Irving Shepard)*

Charmian's sleeping porch expressed her preference for simple, natural decor. *(Estate of Irving Shepard)*

During the final months in Hawaii, Charmian carried Jack emotionally as well. Here are the well-muscled legs that Jack admired so much. *(Estate of Irving Shepard)*

The copra plantation in Penduffryn was the site of marijuana parties, which Charmian never mentioned in her published accounts. *(Estate of Irving Shepard)*

The Roamer was the
Londons' winter home on
the Sacramento delta.
(Estate of Irving Shepard)

The Wolf House was a
large lodge, not a mansion.
(Estate of Irving Shepard)

Jack's hunting was limited to ducks on the Sacramento delta. *(Estate of Irving Shepard)*

The Crowd hoped Jack would leave Charmian for drama critic Blanche Partington. *(Bancroft Library)*

In 1913, houseguest Allan Dunn stole Jack's pajamas. The prank inspired this cartoon. *(Estate of Irving Shepard)*

Daughters Becky and Joan had very different childhood memories of their father, but agreed about their love for him. *(Estate of Irving Shepard)*

Like a sailor, Jack had a tight, well-organized work space. *(Bancroft Library)*

Charmian with her notorious cross saddle and shocking split riding skirt. *(Estate of Irving Shepard)*

The modest farm cottage with his and hers sleeping porches. *(Estate of Irving Shepard)*

Jack took greatest pride in his Beauty Ranch. *(Bancroft Library)*

Jack atop Sonoma Mountain, overlooking the Valley of the Moon. *(Estate of Irving Shepard)*

George Sterling, Jimmy Hopper, Harry Leon Wilson, and Jack at the summer encampment of the Bohemian Club in 1915, when it really did consist of Bohemians. *(Bancroft Library)*

A publicity shot taken in Los Angeles for movie contract talks; the Londons never owned an automobile. *(Estate of Irving Shepard)*

In 1914, Charmian and Jack took a steamer to Mexico to cover the revolution. Jack gained weight because of his failing health brought on by kidney disease. *(Estate of Irving Shepard)*

Several days before his death, Jack briefly exposed his suffering. *(Estate of Irving Shepard)*

The mystery of who set fire to Wolf House has never been solved.
(Estate of Irving Shepard)

Jack's grave is covered by a boulder that was too large to be used for
Wolf House. *(Estate of Irving Shepard)*

in the old paths and comes close to Typee that the change hurts," for a curse had clearly befallen the place.[6] Unkempt grass houses perched upon ruins of decayed affluence. The inhabitants were wretched, sick with leprosy, elephantiasis, lameness, blindness, and consumption. Where once two thousand persons lived, now only several dozen remained. In nearby Hoouni Valley they met a wealthier, if not healthier group, for some women proudly showed off their symbol of Polynesian success, the sewing machine. Repulsed by the hip bulges of her riding breeches, the women avoided Charmian; she put them away for the rest of the journey.

Jack went off one day to return with calabashes, tapa cloths, shirts made of human hair, and for George, a wizened clitoris. Charmian did not welcome the artifacts without guilt, feeling sorry that the people were placing "the last of their relics into the hands of the interlopers."[7]

From their experiences, both concluded the local whites were wrong to claim the natives were licentious, displaying little love and no gratitude. Instead, they agreed with Melville, who fifty years earlier had found the Marquesans modest, proud, and friendly. If they practiced polyandry, it was simply an institution of old standing and high repute. The Londons wondered how odd they must have appeared in return, "in our kimonos as we trail over the landscape bareheaded under a pongee parasol, our bare feet thrust into Japanese sandals."[8] One conclusion was certain: the intrusion of whites had destroyed a rich and thriving culture.

* * * *

Tahiti was the next stop. A rare bout of homesickness for California weather pestered Charmian, and she soon had her wish fulfilled. The three months of mail awaiting them reported dire financial difficulty—there was only sixty-six dollars in the bank. The country was in the midst of a minor financial panic, which had led to a drop in both the magazine market and book sales. Worse, Netta had been selling Jack's works at giveaway prices. The always accommodating George Brett of Macmillan wired money for a round-trip steamer passage to San Francisco, which the pair took in early January. Just before departing, Jack told Charmian that, when studying the wrinkled hand of an old woman, he had imagined her hand would grow that way, and he would love it more than ever.

Predictably, the one week in Oakland spoiled all romance. Most time was spent with the Crowd, which meant the usual rounds of drinking and smoking that overstimulated Jack and alienated Charmian. They may have been gossiping about her again, for she felt him distrusting her. "I'm paying for my lifelong experience with liars! Too bad." Another day, "One of my few crosses, and a bad one. Some day I'll put it to him." But she would not confront him. Courageous and assertive in physical confrontations, Charmian kowtowed in emotional ones.

The brief visit also included a meeting with his girls, who had not seen him in nine months. Joan London later recalled how he showed up with the Sterlings and took them out to a restaurant. She never forgot how each time Jack and George ordered a round of dry martinis, they ordered glasses of lemonade for the youngsters; by the end of the afternoon, her place setting was cluttered with untouched drinks. Despite this odd reunion, "the loom of our relationship was rethreaded." She was pleased when he included a vaudeville show that featured Sophie Tucker, Alice Lloyd, and other popular performers.

On the return trip to Tahiti, though ill with flu and neuralgia, Jack ignored his work and spent his time at the poker table. Charmian often spent the time crying, sometimes wondering if she loved him anymore. "I think Jack is sick sometimes, mentally, or he wouldn't do as he does."

He made up with her in Tahiti, bringing her pearls one morning and announcing he would rather have her than all the wealth of Morgan and Rockefeller. It was true in a way—however bad his money situation, he could not resist spending yet more on those he loved, as well as on strangers who sought his beneficence.

Tahiti witnessed the last signs of their active participation in socialism. Charmian went through a pile of political volumes, including friend Austin Lewis's *Rise of the American Proletariat.* Their main companion, Ernest Darling, was a "nature man" who had deserted California for the relaxing climes, yet flew a red flag over his hut and continued to "deliver the message." Writing to her "Dear Comrades" in *Wilshire's,* Charmian described the problems of locating a place for Jack to give his "Revolution" speech. It finally was delivered at the Folies Bergere, a bar, in spite of the chief of police's harassment, even during the lecture. With pride she concluded, "By last mail we see that the *Iron Heel* [now published by Macmillan] is disturbing the capitalist press considerably, which is good news, of course. . . . Yours for the Revolution."[9]

They stayed in Tahiti for two months so Jack could concentrate on his writing. Fidelity became a conspicuous topic of discussion. One day he told her he had never cheated on her during the marriage (a claim he repeated to the disbelieving George Sterling and Mary Austin several years later).[10] Then he had dreams of her being unfaithful to him, followed by those of her being harmed, of a shark getting her hand. Had he cheated? Was this some unconscious expression of guilt? He confessed one day that she had come to mean more to him than even his children. Finishing *Martin Eden,* the story of the successful writer who commits suicide, he declared Martin's problem was not having a woman like Charmian to love.

With that novel sent off to Brett, they set sail again, this time for Raiatéa and Bora-Bora of the Society Islands chain. A runaway seaman replaced Herrmann, who had quit after being hit one time too many by Warren. Martin left behind at least one pregnant native woman.

A young couple, Tehei and Bihaura, took Jack and Charmian under their care and introduced them to their island culture. Charmian found a repeat of the sad fate of the Marquesans: "careless government . . . its sinned-against people." No longer did these Polynesians play the sports and games of the previous generations—no more archers, fleet racers, agile boxers, strong swimmers. Not even a cockfight. Any fishing or farming was done to meet immediate food needs, not for economic and social exchange. The natives' favorite word was *ariana,* meaning "tomorrow or the next day or maybe not then."

Tehei and Bihaura's charm made up for the sad decay. He cooked, "an excellent custom in Polynesia that carries no onus with it." They took the Londons to the local churches and met the local queen of Bora-Bora and her husband, both in tatters and disfigured by elephantiasis, yet cordial and unembarrassed by their appearance. Jack and Charmian were distressed to learn that many gifts to these peoples indebted the recipients. Thus, repeated refusals of presents from the natives went unheeded, for the gifts were placed on the planks of the *Snark*, which grew cluttered with bananas, coconuts, papayas, yams, oranges, protesting chickens, and one suckling pig. Deeply touched by the warmth of the people, they returned to their room one evening in tears, Jack exclaiming, "Wouldn't it be an awful thing stupidly to *hurt* them in any way?" The Anglo-Saxon overlord withered away in his mind. Charmian thought how "it gives new lights upon cannibalism as practiced on white sea captains who requited love and courtesy like this with deception and abuses worse than death."

The tragic theme continued in American Samoa, where Charmian felt special sympathy for the Manuans, many afflicted with blindness or hunchback, others missing hands from accidents while dynamiting fish. Lack of rain and the presence of sharks in shallow waters hampered the Manuans from attaining their high standards of cleanliness, and they were humiliated by this condition. They enjoyed several banquets as guests of King Olosenda, who asked Jack to see if the Americans would send a Manuan boy to law school, in order to educate the elders in the American system. A photograph of Teddy Roosevelt, portending change, smiled down on the proceedings.

*　　*　　*　　*

The Londons were both familiar with Joseph Conrad's "Heart of Darkness," the frightful tale of a trip down an African river to a compound overseen by a mad white trader. The South Seas trip was beginning to take on all the characteristics of that fictional journey, even more as they moved into the lands of the Melanesians. The increasing rawness and savagery of the cultures invaded the psyches of the crew. "Well for our peace of mind that we knew them to be friendly, for the bushy-headed, negroid-featured staring-black-eyed savages were not reassuring on the face of it."[11] The natives responded with grins, waves, and shouts as Charmian and Jack made their way toward the quaint, incongruous English village of Suva, in the Fiji Islands. There the hotel offered four-poster beds, candlelit rooms, and meals of fresh vegetables, beef, and rare cheeses. The town itself was so sophisticated that the great singers of the time—Nellie Melba, Carreno, Blanche Arral—included it in their regular tours.

Suva proved a fitting place for a last meal before a series of trials and adventures, for now they entered authentic cannibal country, under the direction of Jack, who had finally fired the obstreperous Warren. Anchoring at Point Resolution in the New Hebrides, they sensed immediately a wildness to the land. The local missionary assured them that no white man had been killed on the shore for thirty years, though five miles inland natives were still eating each other. Charmian knew differently from her reading, having learned that the history of these islands was marked with a special ferocity toward intruders, the list of slaughtered missionaries and seamen a long one. Noting this particular missionary's parishioners were Polynesian, not Melanesian, she doubted his accuracy even more.

Undaunted, they made treks onto the island. The native style of decoration repulsed them at first. Virtually naked, the tribes people pierced and stretched their earlobes to carry pins, shells, doorknobs, and other objects of interest, and liked to hang shards of English porcelain plates from their necks.

As the first white woman to be seen by many local natives, Charmian was an odd curiosity in their eyes. At the first village they approached, the women had been placed behind a kind of grill, from behind which they pointed and giggled continually at this funny creature. Ordered by the men not to photograph any females, Charmian snapped forbidden pictures nonetheless by turning her body toward the local volcano and exclaiming with feigned excitement, all the while holding her camera toward the unsuspecting women.

Throughout their forays Charmian took special interest in the position of women. In Santa Ana of the Solomon Islands chain, she observed:

> The straggling oblong houses have very low sides and long-eaved roofs. Doors do not extend to the ground, but are reached across a waist-high, roofed platform resting on logs. There are no windows whatever, and the interiors are dark and smelly. Children squat and squabble on the

platforms, while shy women lurk in the shadows behind.
. . . [The women] are beasts of burden, carry loads, and
do heavy work, while the men do the jamboree.[12]

(The jamboree was dancing to the music of instruments similar
to jew's harps.)

As he was led away to the sacred canoe houses, where no
female foot was permitted, Jack teased Charmian for being of
such inferior clay that she could not follow him. Follow she did,
stealthily, until some grunts of displeasure behind her warned
she had been discovered. Later Jack described to her the scene.
One hut contained obscene figures atop king posts, a canoe,
and a dangling package containing the remains of chiefs; the
other had what he hoped was a pig being smoked for later use.
On the next island, the chief would not shake Charmian's hand
because it was taboo for him to touch "the lesser animals."

Jack observed such occurrences with light humor. "Not for
nothing have I journeyed all the way around to the Solomons.
At last I have seen Charmian's proud spirit humbled and her
emperious queendom of femininity dragged into the dust."[13]
He joked at the prospect of her returning to civilization with
bowed head, walking a yard behind him.

Yet there was more. At a village on Langa Langa the natives,
who had been hospitable throughout the visit, suddenly set a
large tree trunk before a bridge to block their crossing. Following an extensive exchange of pidgin English, they learned that
all except "Mary," the lingua franca for woman, could cross.
"Ah, how my chest expanded. At last my manhood was vindicated. In truth I belonged to the lordly sex. Charmian
traipsed along at our heels, but we were MEN, and we could
go right over that bridge while she would have to go around
by whale-boat."[14]

These episodes gave the couple the opportunity to reaffirm
their commitment to sexual equality. They found the treatment
of women in these villages more strange than a nose pierced
with a pencil or a piece of macaroni. It is doubtful many other
white men landing on these shores saw as Jack did or would
ridicule the patriarchy and his place in it.

Yet, however curious the customs of these tribes, the Londons seldom slipped into their old stereotypical ways of think-

ing either. Having been raised with the prejudices of the period, Jack and Charmian never lost all their clichéd preconceptions—witness the happy-go-lucky plantation workers in Hawaii. Nonetheless, the thrust of their commentary was sympathetic to the island cultures and critical of the behavior of the colonizers. The "white man's burden" took on ever more tragic dimensions as they viewed it firsthand.

Piercing the heart of the Solomons, the Londons faced real and immediate threats on their lives. This was copra-plantation and slave-trading territory, where white heads hanging behind a chieftain's chair were of highest value as a display of strength. In preparation, they brought on deck every possible weapon, from bottle, coconut shell, and match box to Mausers, Colt pistols, and Smith and Wesson revolvers. Charmian now kept a Colt perched on her hip and carried a .22 automatic when exploring the inlands. Since the white traders had little use or respect for women, she found it useful to establish her status by casually popping off some difficult target. Given her exceptional marksmanship, the local bird population decreased significantly during her stay, and the men kept their mouths shut.

At Penduffryn they tried to rest a while on a plantation run by two Englishmen, Tom Harding and George Darbishire. Even Charmian was uneasy, being "in the queerest situation, in a big house with a retinue of servants culled from the cannibal tribes." Caution required that no natives other than house staff step on the porches, let alone enter the buildings. Her bedroom had a rack of loaded rifles, and she was ordered to keep her revolver ready to shoot day and night. Harding quizzed them hard about the trustworthiness of the *Snark* crew, for several schooners had been cut out and burned, their masters slaughtered, by mutinous natives. (A popular form of murder involved tribes signing up for plantation work, boarding the boat, and then hacking off the traders' heads.)

Inspired by these surroundings and the gruff men running the plantations, London started what is arguably his worst novel, *Adventure.* Possibly conceived as another tribute to Charmian's strong character, he built the story around Joan Lackland, a shipwrecked pistol-packing heroine who convinces a despotic plantation owner that her more benign, paternalistic attitude toward native workers is more economically sensible than his antagonistic one. Though spurning marriage and spouting feminist slogans throughout, ultimately Joan settles down with the brutish lout who has been her nemesis, though there is a hint she does so partly out of recognition that her chances of survival in that dark world are greater with him. The love story has all the verisimilitude of Charmian marrying the crude and repressed Harding. Very likely London married the two characters off at the end because the morals of magazine readers required a conventional resolution.

When the work was published, the reviewers, who of course had never been close to the South Seas, criticized the story for inaccuracies. They simply rejected the idea that jungles filled with head-hunting tribes existed, that copra plantations were run so ruthlessly. As some modern readers do today, they misread the plot as a support for the system of injustice. In fact, London understood that the copra plantation was even more hideous than the American form of slavery had been. Men were rounded up, kidnapped from their families, kept in all-male compounds of nameless horrors, and cleverly encouraged through drink and frustration to strike at one another rather than at their captors. Untreated disease exterminated them with the regularity of more planned genocide found in slavery institutions elsewhere.

London struck hard at the nobility of the white supremacist view in other South Sea tales. "Yah! Yah! Yah!" told, from a native point of view, how the natives, a fierce and proud people, had been brought to utter submission under a single white tyrant. "White man are hell," explains the old storyteller, who relates a tale of dynamite tossed from ships to slaughter the tribesmen, of gunfire massacres in the villages, of infecting several natives with smallpox and then sending them home. "The Terrible Solomons" is more direct. In order to spend a long time there, the white man

> . . . must have the hall-mark of the inevitable white man stamped upon his soul. . . . He must have a certain grand carelessness of odds, a certain colossal self-satisfaction, and a racial egotism that convinces him that one white is better than a thousand niggers every day in the week . . . Oh, and one other thing—the white man who wishes

to be inevitable, must . . . also fail to be too long on imagination. He must not understand too well the instincts, customs, and mental processes of the blacks, the yellows, and the browns; for it is not in such fashion that the white race has tramped its royal road around the world.

The irony continues as the story relates how a group of such unseemly types trick another. The narrator of "The Inevitable White Man" is one such himself, who describes the brutality of another of the breed, appropriately named Saxtorph.

Given the chance to play at being "inevitable white men," Charmian and Jack rejected the role. During a trip on the blackbirder *Minota,* the ship crashed against a reef and soon found itself encircled by tribespeople in canoes hoping to get booty from the wreck. Although the first impulse was to pull out rifles, the crew soon set about saving the craft. Jack went out in a small boat with tobacco in hopes of bribing the threatening mob. Eventually a whaler appeared, "white man to the rescue of white man the world over," Charmian noted, but she gave the credit too glibly. The fact is they could have used gunfire to chase off the predators, but they did not. Given the history of the Solomons, this was not a typical response for whites under similar circumstances.

Charmian described another threatening incident when the captain of the *Minota* invited them to go into the mangrove swamps to dynamite fish for supper:

> Bristling with rifles, every man of us (!) with a pistol in his belt, we approached to within less than thirty feet of a fallen tree outjutting from that soundless, moveless wall of mangroves, reversed the boat, and the charge was tossed into the water. And simultaneously with the explosion, like screen pictures on a prepared scene, there appeared a score of stark naked cannibals, armed to the eyebrows with every fighting device known to savage man, while one, who had leaped to the end of the fallen tree, held his rifles on us. . . . Absolute silence, absolute immobility, save for shifting eyeballs. . . . Then the savage on the fallen limb slowly, slowly lowered his barrel and his eyes fell as he smiled sheepishly.

The captain then invited the natives to share in the white-bellied litter of floating fish. Throughout this tense scene could be heard floating over the lagoon the tune of "Just Because You Made Those Goo-Goo Eyes" from the record player of the German mate.

Their activity in the Solomons is all the more remarkable for the state of their health. Every *Snark* crew member was in pain or disabled all the time. The slightest skin abrasion, say from scratching an insect bite, resulted in spreading, oozing ulcerations that healed only very slowly with continual applications of corrosive sublimate, a mercury salt. In addition to suffering frequent blinding headaches, they showed the initial signs of malaria with its accompanying fits of fever, chills, and delirium. The least fit member was Jack, who suffered his usual dental problems (and visited dentists on every island that had one) and of late was passing blood in his feces. The most fit member was Charmian, who had only one ulceration on an ankle and a mild attack of malaria. She became Jack's nursemaid, to the point of administering regular enemas in hopes of relieving his intestinal pains and infection.

In spite of illness, danger, and overwork, the crew managed to have its humorous times as well. One episode, never reproduced in the public version of Charmian's diaries, aptly illustrates the playfulness that grew from the camaraderie of their isolated and difficult fate. In mid-July of 1908, Bernays, a trader they had befriended, brought out some hashish. The group decided that each night one crew member would be given an especially large dose of the drug. The first night they took Bernays's stupored body, painted it green and red, laid it out in state on a platform, surrounded it with skulls, flowers, and candles and held a funeral ceremony complete with dirges, misereres, howls, and wails. Several nights later they dressed Darbishire in red garters and pantalettes. When Charmian went out the next morning, she found him on his bier, still rouged and begartered, satisfying his fearsome appetite with a pile of doughnuts. Wada and Nakata walked past impassively, as though the sight were a daily occurrence.

Of course, Charmian did not smoke. When Jack's turn came, he became ill ("as he always had with the drug," she noted in her diary) and was put right to bed without foolishness. The next day she marked, "Mate the lover, but very dull and crusty from hasheesh." He made up for it several days later with "an orgy of love on embroidered rug on the floor." "Aren't you ashamed of yourself," he teased.

Sailing from the Solomons toward Java, Charmian fantasized:

> What a pity that so wonderful a space of great islands so rich in promise, would be so variously unhealthful. But never mind—such things are beaten out slowly—the day will come when, along with the wondrous savannahs on Guadalcanal, all these lands will be brought under scientific cultivation and control, the striped mosquito that is the author of so much suffering and disability shall be destroyed, there shall be no devastating ulcer-poisoning and filthy flies to carry it to flesh that is no longer unantisepticised—a time when the islands will lie blossoming under the light of applied knowledge, and disease and unnecessary death shall be no more.[15]

Many of her dreams did come true in subsequent decades, and she would have been pleased to see their effects upon the native populations. Death, however, returned as the land was devastated by war. As an old woman, Charmian would receive representatives from the American navy who wished to use the *Snark*'s charts and logs for use in planning an assault on the Japanese.

Nerves exhausted, Wada had fled the boat following the wreck of the *Minota*. They had accidentally given away the last of their flour and left their remaining supply of sublimate ashore. Tehei suffered blackwater fever, usually fatal, and having survived, "lost his wits altogether." A little terrier they had collected on the journey fell down the cabin companionway and was lame. What forced the change in plans, though, were Jack's new ailments: a swelling of his hands, chilblains, excessive skin peeling, and odd thickenings in his nails. Finding nothing in his medical references to account for the symptoms, he worried about leprosy.

By late October 1908 Jack joked that the book he expected to name *Around the World with Two Gasoline Engines and a Wife*

should now be called *Around the World in the Hospital Ship Snark.*
He had decided to go to Sydney for an operation on his bowels,
then spend several months traveling and recuperating in Australia and Tasmania. He decided to leave the *Snark* behind in
Java until he was ready to travel again, so ordered steamer
tickets to Sydney for Charmian, Nakata, Martin, and himself.
Weary of playing nurse to all the ailing men, which meant
picking up many of their duties on the boat, Charmian looked
forward to the break, but even more to the continuation of the
voyage. "When we return from Australia, all mended and fresh
for a new start, we shall go aboard the *Snark* and immediately
fill away to the west—always west, and north of west, and south
of west, and round world 'round until we are bound at last
around Cape Horn to San Francisco Bay."

Yet even throughout all the tribulations of the South Seas
traverse, the couple had worked without break. Jack wrote
George Brett that he now had on hand: *Lost Face,* a fifty-two-
thousand word collection of Klondike stories; *Revolution and
Other Essays,* forty-five thousand words; *When God Laughs,* forty-
two thousand words of miscellaneous short stories; *Tropic Tales*
(later *South Sea Tales*), with fifty-three thousand words of short
stories; his *Snark* book, eighty-one thousand words of articles
on the voyage; plus thirty thousand words of Hawaiian stories
and twenty thousand words of the novel *Adventure.* [16] In addition to typing all these manuscripts, Charmian had her own two
books, which, given her more descriptive prose, ran to over
three hundred thousand words. She had also taken boxes of
photographs to document their activities.

The purpose of this impressive productivity was simply to
produce money to finance their dreams. Since *The Pacific
Monthly* had bought the serial rights to *Martin Eden* for seven
thousand dollars, they carried with them in their manuscript
boxes a veritable gold mine. No wonder that, when threatened
with attack in the Solomons, Charmian had stolen overboard
with their precious trunk of papers.

They were now, by most of their readers' standards, quite
wealthy. On October 21, 1907, while they drifted in the warm,
soft winds toward Tahiti, a panic hit Wall Street. The consequent hard times and unemployment continued throughout
1908. A well-educated and experienced bookkeeper would be

happy to bring home twelve dollars a week to his family, and a common laborer such as Jack had been would be delighted with much less. Yet the first president of the Intercollegiate Socialist Society showed no interest in the fate of labor at home. Adventures in the South Seas had tempered all desire for adventure in politics and left Jack feeling even more confident of his ability to run his life his way without need of anyone save Charmian—and the ever present Oriental valet.

10

SONOMA
EDEN

A delicate odor is borne on the wings
of the morning breeze,
The odor of deep wet grass, and of
brown new-furrowed earth,
The birds are singing for joy of the
Spring's glad birth.

—*Oscar Wilde*

Charmian collapsed during the final days in the Solomons. Her skin was so ulcerated that she hid in her bedroom where she could rest naked soaking in a tub of water throughout the day. She had uncontrollable crying spells, a release of emotion frightening to one usually so restrained. "Work is a bugbear—my beloved work. I have to whip myself to the typewriter."[1] Whip herself she did, such that by the time they completed the stormy crossing from Java to Sydney on November 14, 1908, the newspapers found her "a white-faced, fairhaired, nervously alert little woman." The doctors who diagnosed Jack's bowel ailment as a fistula urged her to rest her "neurotic heart," but she would not comply.

On November 30 Jack went on the operating table, while

Charmian waited outside writing letters furiously. The operation a fine success, he now faced the trying regime that follows bowel surgery: a week without any food or nourishing liquids, a much longer period of discomfort. Malarial fever struck Charmian so badly that the nurses set up a bed next to his, where she spent hours "jabbering at white heat."

Though Jack's intestines were healing, the rest of him was not. He was in even worse emotional straits than she, given to fits and shakes the doctors could not diagnose. Worse, the medical specialists did not realize that his thickening nails and peeling skin were symptoms of advanced pellagra, and their ignorance fed his anxieties. Charmian was heartbroken in accepting his decision to quit the adventure. She could have spent the rest of her life at sea and felt little elation at the prospect of returning to civilization.

A writing assignment sped Jack's need to recuperate. He had been asked to cover the upcoming Johnson-Burns fight to be held in Sydney. Jack Johnson, a superb black fighter, was on his way to winning a series of heavyweight bouts with white contenders. Jack had accepted the contract on condition that Charmian be allowed to accompany him, not a simple request in a country like Australia.

As Charmian observed early in her visit, this puritanical land was not advanced in its treatment of women. The sexes were separated on the beaches, and a man who kissed his wife good-bye at the railway station was arrested for "disorderly and riotous conduct." She wrote their friends:

> Women's work here is relegated to the Woman's Page, or some column entitled "Mainly About Women." The interviews are mostly not illuminating. Space seems to be curtailed, and the reporters cram questions and answers into inadequate columns. The interests of men and women seem to be widely separated. There doesn't seem to be much companionship or unity of purpose. And the women vote, too [unlike women in the United States at that time]. But they go their way and the men go theirs.[2]

The men also determined where the women could go, and they could certainly *not* go to a fight.

As the big day approached Jack went to see local bouts in the evenings, Charmian accompanying him to observe crowd reaction to her presence. She received no response beyond curious stares; not a word appeared in the newspapers. She also went with him to the training sites, and she wondered how a short fellow like Tommy Burns could beat a giant like Johnson. "He is a fine-looking negro. . . . he looks like an imperturbable Sphinx; and when he tilts his head back and smiles, his head is like a bas-relief."

The night of the fight, Charmian was more apprehensive, aware the men were quick to "hoo-hoo" anything they disapproved. Though she could have gone wearing a male disguise, as other women did, she refused to compromise herself. If she met with no hisses, the papers did make big play of her presence. "Well, good or bad, this is what I get for marrying a man who likes a comrade for a wife, and a wife who is interested in the things he loves." As for the fight, she found Johnson's victory a walkover and was angry at the rudeness of the Australians toward him. "No matter how bad we all wanted the white man to win, on general principles, the white man *didn't* win, and the black man did, and shouldn't be hissed for his color."

While the Sydney men commiserated in the pubs, Charmian was at the typewriter, helping Jack prepare his thousand-word cable to the *New York Herald,* the first writing he had done in several weeks. "He never rests unless he is ill," she had once noted. Actually, when ill he read his medical library, marked the appropriate places, dug through his sizable medical case, and pulled out the fitting treatment, one of the many pharmaceuticals of the day. He had proved an effective therapist on the *Snark,* even pulling teeth when necessary. It was he who pushed the new malaria cure, quinine, on doubting crew members. He was especially proud of convincing Charmian, "raised a vegetarian and sanitarian," to take the drug, unaware that she had thrown it overboard out of distrust of any medicine.

Her intuition about quinine was wrong, but she was right regarding the other pills. Many drugs of the day were not safe. At the hospital in Sydney, Jack was given opium as a painkiller even though its addictive qualities were well known. When his health did not improve fully, he doctored himself with Salvarsan, the new miracle cure for syphilis that was in fact a toxic arsenic compound that had serious side effects on the kidneys and urinary tract. As Jack's physical ailments increased in subsequent years, he looked to the opium derivatives he had learned about in Sydney to bring relief. In his day, he was thought to be acting very sensibly; today, of course, it is known that he was inviting his own destruction.

New Year's 1910 was the first for which Charmian had little good news for her diary. Friends criticized them for risking their lives. Charmian came under special attack for "tagging along" with him. She reprimanded their correspondents:

> I feel it will be a long time before Jack and I feel that we have had "enough" of the things that mean seeing life and new things to keep us from atrophy. We love it all, personally—not for the mere reason of wanting experience, but because we LOVE experience. . . . Jack daily grows to a realization that I am actually more grieved at the turn things have taken, than he is. It's pretty nearly equal, but if there's any difference in intensity of regret, it's mine.[3]

One rare cause for laughter was a news clipping from the States announcing, "Jack London denies that he has been eaten by cannibals. Anyhow, it's very questionable if Mr. London looks good to anybody unless it be Mrs. London."

Mail from home carried two interesting stories. Netta and Roscoe were getting divorced—he already had made plans to marry a young French teacher who had camped at Wake Robin the previous summer. The second news was of Bess London's engagement to Charles Milner. "I wish to cremate my memory of Jack London and have a home with children," she told a reporter.[4] She was not to succeed. She notified Jack of her engagement while also requesting more financial assistance from him, adding she would not marry unless he met her terms. In a scathing letter, Jack called her bluff, saying he did not care if she ever married, even though it meant continued financial expense on his part.[5] She never did remarry—within a year she was telling reporters that "the man has not been born yet that I would wed."[6]

When Jack's nervous ailment failed to heal, he decided they

should rest in Tasmania before trying the return home. Always looking for ways to save costs, he signed a contract to provide weekly articles for an Australian paper, the pay to include travel expenses. In the quiet of the resort hotel, Charmian soon regained the strength to ride horses and play piano, and soon adjusted to the new order of things, making endless plans for the future on the ranch. She rejoiced that the card games and playful pillow fights had returned to their life. "But everything pales before the fact that Jack is not well," she sorrowed, neither physically nor emotionally. It was after all solely his inability to continue, his illnesses, that had terminated the journey. That fact must have been an ignominious pill for him to swallow.

The remainder of the *Snark* crew was not having an easy time. Jack had turned the boat over to one Captain Reed, who ran it like a navy ship. A cautious man, he so protracted the crossing from Java to Australia that the men ran out of almost all provisions and spent their last days surviving on weevil-infested hardtack, spoiled beans, and tea. When the boat lumbered into port in March, Jack and Charmian ferried out daily to remove their belongings and pack up for the sad eastward return journey. The boat itself was sold for a tenth its cost to a group of Englishmen, and the Londons would never see the *Snark* again. Hermann de Visser left for Pago Pago, Tehei to Raiatéa. Martin decided to continue working his way around the world and eventually with wife Osa became a celebrity as he toured with shows of their documentary adventure films. Nakata gave up his dream of returning to Japan and asked to stay on as their servant.

In late March the couple applied for passage on the *Tymeric*, a cargo steamer headed for South America. The company's policy matched that of the Melanesians—no "Mary" was allowed aboard. It relented for Charmian only because of Jack's fame. Their five-week crossing of the Pacific did not settle their nerves as they had anticipated. From Quito in Ecuador they rode a train slowly northward, stopping along the way to explore local events and customs. In New Orleans they paid a large bond so Nakata could enter the country with them. Following a brief visit to the Grand Canyon, they reached Glen Ellen in mid-July of 1910.

The country the Londons found in 1910 was not very different from the one they had left in 1907. True, the economy had undergone upheavals, not only as a result of the panic, but from Theodore Roosevelt's trust-busting activity. That policy had caused dissension within the Republican party between progressives and conservatives, which seemingly had ended when Roosevelt's handpicked successor, William Howard Taft, had been elected President. But Taft soon reneged on his promises to progressives to improve working conditions and surrounded himself with conservative advisers. This double cross raised the ire of labor leaders and social activists, who renewed their commitments to working people's rights as well as their fighting among themselves as to the best way to achieve their ends.

The popular culture, however, had remained the same. Puritanical morals were prominent in everyday affairs. When Richard Strauss's opera *Salome* opened in 1907 at the Metropolitan Opera, it was discontinued by such directors as J. P. Morgan and August Belmont for its "revolting" and "degrading" dance of the seven veils. The new entertainment, motion pictures, was censored with the organization of the Society for the Prevention of Vice. Respectable ladies still wore layers of clothing, adorned their heads with feather-plumed hats, and were considered "fast" if they wore the new shirtwaists with lace inserts. The length of one's hair remained a measure of femininity (which put Charmian, with her waist-length locks, in good stead). While the ladies complied with these demands, some showed signs of rebellion by smoking cigarettes and speaking out about such topics as suffrage and prohibition. London would be quick to discern his readers' new interests and reinforce their beliefs.

Jack and Charmian returned to the Bay Area to find San Francisco risen from its ashes, with more automobiles and telephone wires adorning the streets, but little else relevant to them had changed. The cities held little interest anyway, except as a place to frolic with friends and check the latest in theater or music. Bound to the ranch, they were determined to make of it as much of an adventure as their Pacific journey.

Netta had overseen changes on the property during their absence. An imposing stone barn capped with red Spanish tile now housed their collection of South Seas curios as well as the horses and buggies. She had also purchased an adjoining spread that doubled their holdings. The stock of colts, calves, chickens, doves, and pigeons multiplied with biblical regularity.

In other regards Netta was an expensive annoyance. Deciding to renovate Wake Robin, her own property, she and lover Edward Payne took the money from Jack's account. "I know you will enjoy the conveniences of the house and God knows it will be sweet to have a *family* again. I am a poor woman to live without *children.*"[7] Later she reported that she would pay off part of the "loan" by taking money from Charmian's Berkeley rentals and putting it in Jack's account, "because she, dear child, remembers that I gave her my last three-hundred dollars to buy her a piano and typewriter." (Those purchases had been made when Charmian was a young teenager.) As for the remainder of the debt, she hoped Jack could make enough by renting out part of Wake Robin to cover the repairs. Never subtle in her manipulation, Netta asked to be included under their roof and suggested that Jack save money by putting his mother "in a cheap house." Her machinations went for naught: Jack and Charmian moved into Wake Robin and sent Netta and Edward to live on the part of their holdings known as the Fish Ranch, reasonably close but far enough away to prevent easy drop-in visits.

During his recuperation in Australia, Jack had reacquainted himself with the state of socialism in the United States, which was splintering over tactical disagreements, and began to distance himself further from the formal organization. As he explained to William Walling, Anna Strunsky's husband, he believed to affiliate with the American Federation of Labor as some recommended would be suicidal, as would any compromise. For proof he pointed to Australia's vigorous socialist movement, which had faltered as a result of a similar alignment. "I shall always stand for keeping the socialist party rigidly revolutionary," he insisted, aware he had much less company than several years earlier.[8]

London had lost little of his idealism about socialism. Soon after returning to Glen Ellen he heard a minister give a sermon condemning the hero of *Martin Eden* as a man who failed be-

cause of lack of faith in God. That was not his fictional character's problem, responded Jack—it was Martin's lack of faith in
man: "I retain my belief in the mobility and excellence of the
human. I believe that spiritual sweetness and unselfishness will
conquer the gross gluttony of today. And last of all, my faith
is in the working class. As some Frenchman has said, 'The
stairway of time is ever echoing with the wooden shoe going
up, and the polished boot descending.' "9 Unfortunately, Jack
failed to see that it was he that now wore the polished boot, that
his present relationship to working men was as their employer.

What inspired him now was the productivity of his land,
which had been managed during his absence under the capable
supervision of Werner Wiget. This discovery gave Jack a new
outlet for his revolutionary fervor. Indeed, from this point he
came to see himself as a rancher first, one who happened to sell
his writings as a way of capitalizing his agricultural dream.

His new philosophy found expression in plans for a new
novel, *Burning Daylight,* the story of the transformation of a
highly successful businessman to a rancher. Hero Elam Har-
nish is nicknamed Burning Daylight for his mastery of the
rigors of the Yukon wilderness and his success in the gold
fields. When he moves south to the Bay Area to test his skills
in business, he finds civilization to be more savage than the
cruel demands of nature. Just as Martin Eden found the bourgeois to be mediocre and hypocritical, Daylight finds the capitalists to be soulless and immoral. Unlike Eden, who, disgusted
by the world of success to which he had aspired, commits
suicide, Daylight adapts and becomes a manipulative businessman, as well as a lonely, egotistical alcoholic.

His secretary Dede Mason introduces him to another set of
values. Dede is a twin of Charmian when Jack met her: a well-
read typist who rides her horse alone in the Piedmont hills and
finds delight in the simpler pleasures of life. Daylight's admiration for Dede makes clear Jack's admiration of Charmian:

> He decided from the way she carried it, that she deemed
> her body a thing to be proud of, to be cared for as a
> beautiful and valued possession. . . . Two other immediate
> things about her struck him. First, there were the golden
> spots in her eyes. . . . And then she was so natural. He had

been prepared to find her a most difficult young woman to get acquainted with. Yet here it was proving so simple. . . . Her joys were in little things, and she seemed always singing. Even in sterner things it was the same. When she rode Bob and fought with that magnificent brute for mastery, the qualities of an eagle were uppermost in her.[10]

Even the decor of Charmian's rooms in Berkeley match Dede's: bare floors, wolf and coyote skins lying about, the crouched Venus on a piano, an oak dressing table, a broad couch piled high with cushions, used as a bed.

London also included his unconventional view of women as companions to challenge his readers' conventional beliefs. Where Daylight had previously seen women as either harpies or wives and mothers, he now conceives of woman as "comrade and playfellow and joyfellow."

The rest of the plot does not follow the real-life relationship so clearly. Dede resists Daylight, saying she cannot marry a man possessed by his money. One day he discovers the Valley of the Moon and, on the crest of Sonoma Mountain, finds spiritual inspiration, a redemption from the "sordidness, meanness, and viciousness that filled the dirty pool of city existence." Renouncing his fortune and alcohol, Daylight wins Dede's heart and moves her to a ranch like the Londons' own in Glen Ellen.

As for Daylight, he learns "he had been afraid of love all his life only in the end to come to find it the greatest thing in the world." The book was thus a remarkable reaffirmation of Jack's love for Charmian and his optimism about their life in the country. It was also a philosophical expression of his agreement with Luther Burbank that environment was crucial in shaping the excellent physical specimen, that by avoiding the treacheries of urban life he could avoid his troublesome addictive habits. As Daylight proclaims to his love:

I know what I want, and I'm going to get it. I want you and the open air. I want to get my foot off the paving-stones and my ear away from the telephone. I want a little ranch-house in one of the prettiest bits of country God ever made, and I want to do the chores around that ranch-

house—milk cows, and chop wood, and curry horses, and
plough the ground, and all the rest of it; and I want you
there in the ranch-house with me.[11]

It was the Edenic dream, but as anyone familiar with Genesis
knows, Adam's plowing of the ground was his punishment
following banishment from the Garden. And London was not
exempt from the sins of Adam.

If Jack found new enthusiasms, Charmian felt that her world
was closing in on her. She returned to more of the same—
editing, typing, note-taking—in the more social surroundings
of their home. Where she had been Jack's sole confidante and
companion for over two years, she now shared him with admirers and friends who streamed onto the property with or without invitation.

So often did visitors arrive that the couple distributed an
instruction card to acquaint new guests with their schedules:

Our work here is something as follows: We rise early, and
work in the forenoon. Therefore, we do not see our guests
until afternoons or evenings. You may breakfast from 7 till
9, and then we will all get together for dinner at 12:30.
You will find this is a good place to work, if you have work
to do. Or, if you prefer to play, there are horses, saddles
and rigs. In the summer we have a swimming pool. We
have not yet built a house of our own, and are living in a
small house adjoining the ranch. So our friends are put in
little cabins nearby, to sleep.

Their hospitality was legendary. A typical reaction was that
of George Wharton James, famous lecturer and California
pitchman who found the food plain, the intellectual fare rich,
the music from the piano and Victrola entertaining: "His home
is as near to perfection as I have ever seen a home and his
comradeship with his wife is something to be seen. It does not
require any intelligence to discover the secret of his immense
capacity for work. He is living in an artistic atmosphere, every
element of which is congenial."[12] Sculptor Finn Froelich found
Jack and friends "playing like children, playing tricks," with
Jack as the leader, laughing even louder when the joke was on
him.

Jack flourished amid the company of many associates. He captivated his guests as he had captivated the crew of the *Snark*. Froelich's observations were matched by others over the years:

> I never saw a man in all my life with more magnetism, beautiful magnetism. If a preacher could have the love in his make up, and the life, God, this whole world would go religious. When he talked he was marvelous. His hair was bushy, and he wore an eyeshade, and his eyes were big, and his mouth was just as sensitive and full of expression, and the words came out of him just rippling. It was something inside of him, his brain just ran 60 miles a minute, you couldn't follow him. He talked better than he wrote.[13]

When Froelich first arrived, he noted how Jack always talked about Charmian, that he was "crazy about her."

Corroborating Jack's admiration, Charmian "was the queen, the general, the first rank." When she was in her normal good spirits, as one neighbor recalled, "Charmian always talked a lot, but she was a tonic, she spurred people on to want to read or think about something. She seemed well-informed, well-read. Always knew where to find things in books. A bright little woman holding her own."[14] She joined in the frolics with the rest and added her own talents in leading musicales and directing horseback trips.

But she was also responsible for reining in activities when they got out of hand, for ensuring Jack had his time to work, for ensuring that the tricks did not become too malicious. As such, she was not always viewed favorably by those who wanted total license in their behavior on the ranch.

However gracious Charmian could be, she was by temperament more solitary, preferring select and intense ties and sharing them only with Blanche Partington, whose job prevented her from frequent or lengthy stays on the ranch. Used to the more quiet life of the *Snark,* the crush of the Crowd's chatter and drinking overwhelmed her. When Jack invited Cloudesley and his family for a month's visit, she cried to herself, "Will we ever be alone? Where is the quiet of the country? The long days of horseback in the hills?"

Increasingly agitated, she developed paranoid fears. Late

summer is fire season in that dry country, and she fanatically noted each new blaze in the valley, rode out to watch it, study it, and worry whether the wind would whisk the embers over to consume their property. She grew certain Jack was in danger from some unknown force. "Love him so, that the very thought of him harmed makes my blood run cold." The crying spells returned, forcing her to use excessive powder and rouge at dinner.

One day, after a thoughtless outburst, she determined with her usual steely will to sit quietly in public from that point. Wishing to hide her condition from Jack for fear it would disturb his fresh-won enthusiasms for life, she spiraled deeper into depression. Each additional act of passivity or social accommodation further masked her ability to confront her sadness and acknowledge the validity of her grief. "My mind's gone. No *hope* in anything. Just a dull, dread vista of doing things with no purpose. This is not I! I must lie up and find myself." Members of the Crowd misinterpreted her sullenness for rejection, finding in her behavior proof of what they thought all along, that she was a troublesome woman.

By fall she was confessing to Blanche, "marriage is sweet, but far better bachelor-girlhood all your life than a half-way marriage. I look around me at the half-way marriages, and know in my inmost soul that rather than be married that way, I'd a thousand times prefer my old work and my two little rooms and my independence." In October she advised Blanche to be less generous toward others. "Yes, we [women] do like to hog the giving, and it must be bad for us personally. Don't let those around you take much for granted."[15] Still she refused to confront Jack, to admit her growing anger over his current preoccupations.

If Jack seemed better adjusted because of ranch life, he provided sufficient clues, unnoticed by all, that the coping was merely an act. He demanded constant company, as if to make up for the two years on the *Snark.* One evening, when George Sterling arrived drunk and made a scene with a female guest, Jack actually threw him off the property. Another night, when a woman persisted in her side of an argument, he threw beer in her face.

In October Jack organized a yachting trip up the Sacramento

delta. Since by this point Charmian's poor condition was evident even to him, he told her she could not go along. The first night away he sent her a rushed and rambling letter, urging her to go to Burke's Sanitarium, a health resort, and join them on the river when she felt strong enough. He also bought her a new automatic rifle as a going-away present. When George and Carrie arrived at the dock, they discovered Jack had loaded up plenty of whiskey and beer, but very little food.[16]

Charmian could not relax—it had been on a similar cruise that Jack had started his affair with Blanche. There followed dreams of earthquake, eerie landscapes of desolation, of Jack's leaving her. "Don't know who I am—neither maid, wife, nor widow!" Finally she acceded to others' urging and left for Burke's. "Am growing *terribly* restless for Mate. His going was a disaster so great that I was numbed—like an earthquake. Now I am wakening to a great sense of loss."

In thinking Jack was withdrawing from her, that she was losing him, she was very wrong. Ten days after his departure, he begged to visit her briefly. She refused, feeling unready to face yet another farewell. Then he admitted he had not been well lately either, that he was unable to write. Thus, when he arrived at the ranch in early November, the reunion was similar to that spring day in 1905 when they had drawn together out of mutual sadness. "I think I can help him: so comforting to feel him next to me again." Sick with a cold, and injured from an accident on the boat, Jack stayed in bed for many days, Charmian beside him, recovering as well. For the first time since their return from their voyage, they were alone.

Only Netta remained a problem. Miffed that she must move to the upper acres of the ranch, she worked herself into a fine hysteria, even slugging Edward at one point. Jack's comment to Charmian regarding Netta must have raised some fears concerning her own recent behavior: "There is, I fear me, no managing her mental processes. Possibly, as you suggest, she has lost her head over the number of lovers she has had just now. I do hate to hear of her going off her base that way with Edward. Insanity, even temporary, is not nice to contemplate in those we love."[17]

As Charmian's mental state improved, her physical condition worsened. Her periods became irregular and frequent, occurring every two weeks or less; her chronic headaches and neuralgia pounded for days. She bloated up, cramped, and could not wear corsets anymore. "Maybe it's indigestion," she thought in late December.

In fact, at thirty-eight years of age Charmian was pregnant for the first time. Hopeful of a male heir for his growing spread, Jack was boyishly gleeful. They decided upon the names, Mate for a boy, and Joy (the translation of the Greek Charmian) for a girl.

Free of visitors, they continued the private rituals of work and pleasure Charmian preferred. She filled her diary with wonder over the changes in her body. "This is a Red Letter Day, in one sense; it's the most uncomfortable one I ever spent in my life. Baby not still for one minute." Following a day of fainting spells, she commented, "I want to be a woman again, not an incubator."

The idyll ended in March 1910 when they went down to Carmel to join the Crowd. Though they kept to themselves during the day to work, there were enough frenetic dinners for Charmian to repeat the old refrain, "I am tired—tired of people: deadly tired of seeing 'em drunk." If that trip had any compensations, it was in Carrie Sterling's solicitude. Carrie came by to give Charmian rubdowns and massages, and perhaps to talk about her marriage, which was collapsing under the strain of George's repeated and public infidelities.

Once home, a most eminent guest appeared. Charmian found Emma Goldman, now one of the most notorious women in the country, "not remarkable intellectually, but a good, wholesome, loveable woman—though many may not guess it." Emma in turn found her witty, very intelligent, and spirited— too spirited, she feared, for a pregnant woman. Charmian approved less of Emma's companion and lover Ben Reitman, a man inclined toward such misogynistic remarks as "Rape is assault with intent to please."

Jack reveled in the company of these political activists, not only for the opportunity to debate their ideas, but to practice his full array of practical jokes. One of his tricks on new guests involved assigning them to a cabin in which the bed had been hooked up on ropes that led under the floor. Late at night Jack would go under, pull the ropes to shake the bed, and yell

"Earthquake, earthquake!" His tailor-made joke for Reitman was a little red book placed on his dinner plate. Entitled *Four Weeks, A Loud Book,* upon opening the volume exploded in Reitman's face. Jack laughed hard at this proof that anarchists were "such soft people when it comes to actual violence—when they try it, they make a mess of it, because they're dreamers."[18]

Jack's own agrarian dream burst with possibilities on May 14, 1910, when he took the deed to the Kohler and Frohling property, an old vineyard. The seven hundred acres connected his four smaller parcels, and provided miles of frontage along three creeks, forest, and a magnificent slope of mountain. He must have felt the contentment of Burning Daylight, "to watch the procession of the days and seasons from the farm-house perched on the canon-lip; and to shelter in the big room where blazed the logs in the fireplace he had built, while outside the world shuddered and struggled in the storm-clasp of a south-easter."[19] A child, an heir, was all he needed to complete the vision.

As the delivery date approached, Charmian consulted widely as to the best doctors and hospital, settling upon Fabiola Hospital in Oakland. This was the first time in her life she was putting herself in a doctor's hands, and she had not been an easy person to convince. Other preparations were also made. Her fine needlework produced an extensive layette for the baby. Bursting with pride, Jack spent an entire royalty check to give her the Steinway grand piano she had always wanted. He could not really afford that lush present, however, and was forced to accept Hearst's contract to cover the upcoming Jack Johnson–Jim Jeffries fight, which was scheduled on Charmian's due date. She told him to take the offer, that the baby would come with or without him. "Just think—I'm going to be a mother! I wonder if it's the sweetest thing in the world— sweeter than wifehood—if only tangled up with and supplementing wifehood."

On June 19, around 1:30 in the morning, her time came. Jack lay on the bed beside her during her labor. "Helped me, breathed with me, until I could stand no more, and made no headway, so they gave me ether, and took my baby from me. And I came to and heard her cry and saw the top of her little head, and then she went to the nursery. We named her Joy."

Jack told her about the baby, her fair skin and gray eyes, and reassured her, "Boy or girl, it doesn't matter—so long as it's Charmian's!"

The placenta did not deliver properly, so within hours she was returned to the operating table. She was unconscious from the anesthesia for many hours after that.

On the twenty-first, Jack and Eliza came into the room, one on each side of the bed, and told her she would never see the baby again. Though perfectly healthy, in the course of the difficult delivery, the doctor had broken its spinal cord. The child lived only thirty-eight hours. What they did not add was that Charmian herself was in danger of dying. Unaware of this fact, she insisted he go off and cover the practice camps preceding the fight. After he had left the room, she looked in the mirror and, upon seeing her bloodless face, realized the seriousness of her condition.

Although her child was dead, Charmian had to remain in the obstetrics ward to recover. "More babies are being born. I learn their voices—some loud and strident, others soft and cooing, conciliatory, caressing—I love to hear them and still must not think." She could see only one visitor a day, for a few minutes. One day she wrote an entry in her diary that was to be repeated in similar form throughout the years of her long life. "And my Joy-Baby would have been a week-old today."

True to her character, as soon as her strength began to return, she started to work on responses to the many condolence messages. The most poignant:

I thought we loved each other to the fullest, but this fight for our baby has doubled every cord that binds us. It is many times over the pain and loss. "How many patients in the Maternity Cottage?" I asked my nurse yesterday. "Nine mothers and eight babies," she replied. *I* am the ninth mother. But how much better that my arms never nested her, seeing she was to go so soon. She is more a child of the imagination, and must always remain so; but, more tangible than this, are the sweet months of carrying her, when I was so well and happy among the hills, during long trips with Jack, days upon days, and dreaming of the nursery to be. I am a mother—I bore a child—but there is not a child. It puzzles me in the twilight of these long summer days.[20]

When Jack returned from covering the fight, she told him there would be another baby, and they both hoped it would be a girl, to name Joy.

The night Jack had learned the baby (and possibly Charmian) would die, he went to visit with reporter friend Joseph Noel, and then to an Oakland bar. When the bouncer in that smoky setting saw Jack head for the men's room, he mistook the book under Jack's arm for venereal disease posters and ordered him to leave. Puzzled and confused, Jack challenged the bouncer to force him to leave. A scuffle resulted, and the police were called. Noel met Jack at the night court, where Judge George Samuels decided the fracas had been a private argument and threw the case out of court. Jack was furious that his attacker, a man of "odious reputation," had not been prosecuted. Soon enough he found a possible reason: Samuels himself owned the bar and was the bouncer's employer.

The incident was blown out of proportion by the press. Headlines read "Classic Features of the Pen-Wielder Marred by Black Eye and Conflict Scars."[21] Years later Joseph Noel wrote Charmian that he knew Jack had been wronged, that the writer had not been drunk before or after the encounter. (And by then Noel had many grievances against Jack, so his testimony rings especially true.)

London's complete innocence in the matter may explain some of his subsequent behavior. Furious, he composed a strident letter to the judge, with copies for seven local newspapers, in which he threatened, "Someday, somehow, somewhere, I am going to get you."[22] Worse, he referred to Samuels as a "sheeny shoe peddlar" in private conversations. Like many others of his time, he was ambivalent toward Jews. Though he did not avoid Jewish acquaintances—witness his affection for Anna Strunsky—when a Jew crossed him, he slipped readily into anti-Semitic talk. Consequently, while he may have been on the right side of justice, his rash reactions brought him little sympathy, save from Charmian, who seemed if anything to welcome the brouhaha as a distraction from her grief.

Charmian took her first steps a full month following the

delivery. Shuffling over to her locker for a bathrobe, she found the dress that had briefly adorned Joy. Sadly, it had been placed there by a thoughtless attendant.

She went to recuperate at the home of friends in Oakland and there rejoiced over Jack's daily notes, most filled with loving phrases and humorous gossip. Understandably, by the time she returned to the ranch, she felt "as if the bottom has fallen out of things. Wonder if I *am* daffy." She mourned quietly, solitarily, fearful no more children would come at her age.

As often happens with grief, the break came in the course of a small, familiar act. She mounted a horse for the first time in a year, roamed the woods long enough to catch a severe poison oak rash, and returned with new hopes about her life. Even the arrival of Netta for a short stay did not dampen her improving spirits. Now in her sixties, Netta had finally agreed to marry longtime lover Edward Payne. Jack paid for the cost of the wedding, and Charmian contentedly observed, "preparing for the other honeymoon in midst of my own."

By now their romance was being treated as public legend in the press. *Progressive Woman* featured Charmian as "the companion-wife who has figured largely in London's romances." A syndicated news story on literary lives singled Charmian and Jack out as one of the few successful marriages involving a writer. *Woman's Home Companion* captioned her photograph, "To be the wife of Jack London is to be the heroine of many a charming story."[23]

They ended the year with a long trip on the *Roamer*, filling their evenings with future hopes: another child, more travel. Jack continued to smoke; Charmian complained about it less. Jack drank too much at times; Charmian announced "it's Prohibition ticket for me." On their wedding anniversary she accounted, "Joy's fifth month birthday, and our fifth anniversary. Five years gone by, and we *are*."

II

TO TILL
THE SOIL

Sweet as a wind-lute's airy strains
Your gentle muse has learned to sing,
And California's boundless plains
Prolong the soft notes echoing.

—*Dayelle Wiley Kittredge*

Their hopes for parenthood destroyed, the Londons found a ready substitute, one seemingly indestructible, free from accident or human error: a home to fulfill their personal dreams. Although Charmian was blamed as the source of Jack's materialistic striving, he was the likely initiator of these plans —recall how, as a boy, he had been entranced by Washington Irving's stories of the Alhambra, that complex and mysterious castle in Spain. London conceived a building of similar mystery and complexity and soon set dozens of men to building it.

The Wolf House, as it came to be known, has struck many observers as baronial, aristocratic, mimicking the grandness of a mind and ego that could conceive the Alhambra. True, it was to be immense, to rise imposingly from the knoll that overlooked the valley below. But a second glance at the plans hints at deeper motives, values more profound than mere self-aggrandizement. It was the embodiment of a concept formed in 1907, following the San Francisco earthquake, which found public expression in his essay "The House Beautiful."[1]

"An honest house tells the truth about itself," he intoned. That meant honest builders. He had seen the new seven-million-dollar city hall become worth thirty cents after twenty-eight seconds of shaking, the result of inferior materials and workmanship. On his own property, he discovered of his new barn: "The man who was a liar made beautiful stone walls. I used to stand alongside them and love them. I caressed their massive strength with my hands. I thought about them before I went to sleep. They were lies." The earthquake uncovered the core of the walls to be hollow, filled with clay, loose dirt, gravel, air, and kindling. "A thing must be true or it is not beautiful, any more than a painted wanton is beautiful."

The second guiding principle was his belief that "construction and decoration must be one." Temperamentally opposed to waste, he worshiped utility, arguing further that utility and beauty should be unified. He deplored his house at 490 27th Street in Oakland, where his mother now lived and he maintained the upper floor as a pied-à-terre for himself and Charmian. "No drunken rowdy nor political enemy can insult me more deeply as that house does." The reason—the bas-relief ionic capitals at the corners, purely for decoration. Design for utility, on the other hand, had a beauty and strength that transcended the function of the item.

London's views echoed those of many during the Progressive era. In addition to seeking improvements in working conditions, social reformers became supporters of the Arts and Crafts movement, an aesthetic based on use and quality rather than on Victorian gaudiness and quantity. A home designed with these principles in mind, some argued, enabled its dwellers to defeat the values fostered by city life—materialism, wastefulness, dishonesty.

A further correlate of this movement was the reunion with nature. The influence of Theodore Roosevelt, who called for a revival of the "strenuous life," and impassioned naturalists such as John Burroughs and John Muir stirred a craving among urbanites for fresh air and vigorous outdoor activity. One result was the rise of college athletics, the boy scouts, and family camping. In California, with its temperate climate, the craftsman's bungalow style became popular for its unadorned lines, windows open to nature, and sleeping porches. More fortunate Californians, like Jack and the Carmel crowd, were able to go one step further by actually moving to the country.

London's particulars of his own house beautiful, which he expected then to be seven to ten years away, illustrated his application of these principles. More important than a grand staircase would be "a body that sings." Hence, as with the *Snark,* the most expensive space in the house would be the bathroom, "even if we are compelled to build it first and live in a tent until we get more money to go on with the rest." No delight would be lacking in its planning. The materials would be selected to make the room easy to clean and keep tidy, for "why should a servant toil unduly that my body may be clean?"

Indeed, the entire house was planned to make its maintenance as effortless as possible. London apologized for his need for servants, making clear he hoped for "the golden future of the world, when there will be no servants—naught but the service of love." In the meantime, practicality and necessity forced him to accept the division of labor, "but such acceptance does not justify me in lack of consideration for them." He wanted his workers to have as good a bath and as many comforts as his own, along with afternoons free every day "for swimming or hammocking."

Worse than servitude, he argued, was the policy of spic-and-span cleanliness. He remarked on his observation in Korea that the wealthy all wore white to show superiority in cleanliness. The result was hard on the women and coolies made to do the cleaning, and made dirty by the labor. Consequently, he would have hardwood floors without polish, no rugs to collect dirt— much like the decor Charmian had created during her single years. Pretension and display had little place in this setting.

According to his belief in utility, the house would open up to the outdoors through screened bedrooms (a most popular health practice in California at the time) and include extra-large windows to let in sunshine. Fireplaces would abound to warm chilly fog-laden morns.

Drawn up under Jack's close supervision by noted architect Albert Farr, the house was to be built of local products: redwood, deep chocolate–maroon volcanic rock, blue slate, boulders, and concrete. It would be U-shaped around a large pond (fifteen by thirty feet) filled with mountain stream water and stocked with black bass. The foundation was to be earthquakeproof, its concrete slab strong enough to support a skyscraper. The roof would use the familiar California Spanish tiles, colored specially to harmonize with the maroon of the rock and provide a fireproof cover. Rough tree trunks were to shape the lines of the porte cochere, and rough-hewn redwood logs would serve as exposed rafters.

The interior, similarly rustic, suggested a hunting lodge. The most secluded wing would include Jack's workroom, nineteen by forty feet, with a library of the same size directly underneath. The base of the U held the great living room, eighteen by fifty-eight feet, extending over two stories high, with redwood balconies extending from the second floor. An immense fireplace was to provide a more cheerful touch to this medieval space, along with a music alcove designed to hold Charmian's Steinway. Underneath in the basement was a Stag Room, planned for gaming tables and male banter, adjoined by a smaller room for gun storage and trophy display. (Jack's animal trophies were for the most part purchased, not shot by himself.)

The third wing contained the guest rooms and Charmian's apartments, Jack's bedroom above hers, all with open-air sleeping porches. Significantly, there was no nursery, although one unidentified room on Charmian's floor drawn in the plans would have served well as one.

Finally, throughout the house would be the latest in modern conveniences—hot water, a heating system, electric lighting, a refrigerating room, a vacuum-cleaning plant, and laundry—all arranged for efficient use by servants. Additionally, the food-preparation area would include store rooms, a root cellar, and a wine cellar.

Further proof that this was a house planned for work and comfort, not show, can be seen in the cottage built in 1911. This small white clapboard home was attached to an old stone winery building, which served as the kitchen and dining wing.

Save for the bathroom, which was crude and basic, as was fit for what was to be a temporary dwelling, the remainder of the home had all the elements of Jack's house beautiful. He and Charmian had separate sleeping porches on either side of the entryway. The main living area was decorated with simple custom-made furniture, South Sea artifacts, and Charmian's reproductions of classic Greek sculptures. There were no plush upholsteries or silks, nothing that could not hold up to ranch life. Rather, the brown-toned tapa cloth drapes and table dressings, the displays of dried wild plants, wedded the interior to the outdoors. The cottage was utilitarian, even spartan, an honest pronouncement of its owners' values.

If Wolf House was conceived on a grand scale, it must be remembered that its majestic size was required. Much of the Londons' immense library and boxes of notes were scattered among the barns. Too, Jack in particular believed a house was nothing without laughter, that it was to be shared freely with friends and acquaintances. Given these considerations, it was not too large, but had been planned with careful thought for its functions, not its impression on others.

The house would require a lengthy construction time, dependent as it was on Jack's unpredictable earnings and the unusual methods of building. In accordance with his belief in avoiding waste, the redwood would come from ranch holdings, from natural prunings of the forest. The rock was to be used exactly as blasted from nearby quarries, not cut to fit. The boulders and cobblestones were to be gathered from the ranch fields, where in that volcanic country they seemingly sprouted overnight. These unconventional techniques demanded the most experienced builders, and Jack found them in local immigrant Italian craftsmen.

Recalling well the sad fate of the *Snark,* almost ruined by poor construction management and the greed of suppliers, Jack chose a superbly qualified overseer for the project, his sister Eliza. Now separated from her aged husband, she felt undaunted loyalty for her younger brother. Though some found her cool and forbidding, she was a woman of quiet warmth, quick to perform the small kindness that showed her deep understanding of the recipient. For example, she often used her artful hand with the needle to make dresses for Charmian. A shrewd and pragmatic person, she saw that Wolf House would rise exactly as designed, as an honest house built by honest labor.

*   *   *   *

Jack's ranch plans began to mature in other ways during 1910–11. Neighbors and friends alike thought his dream of revitalizing the worn-out soil of the mountain a foolish one. After all, the six bankrupt ranches he now owned represented in fact a total of eighteen farmers who had "lost their money, broken their hearts, lost their land."[2] London's scheme was to adapt practices he had seen in Japan and Korea, as well as read of in books about China. From these sources he conceived an ecological model of farming, one aimed at self-sufficiency and preservation of the soil. This approach called for farming without commercial fertilizer, and rebuilding the soil with green manures, nitrogen-gathering cover crops, animal manures, the rotation of crops, and careful systems of tillage and drainage. London argued that the Asians, who had forty centuries of success using these methods, were clearly using wiser methods than the accepted farming practices of the United States, a mere upstart in agricultural history.

Essentially a city-bred man, Jack was of course considered an upstart as well. He saw no limitation in his urban past, determined that by studying agricultural practices and consulting with the leading experts of the time, he could not only make up for his lack of experience but actually surpass the production of California farmers whose families had been working their plots for several generations.

His ignorance then was striking. Take the simple matter of buying a good cow. Frustrated in this search he wrote to the editor of the *Pacific Rural Press,* "A wail of woe! Where under the sun can I buy a thoroughbred Jersey cow? I have answered advertisements in your columns, and all the offerings I get in reply to my letters are Bulls, Bulls, Bulls. I haven't learned the art of milking a bull. What I want is a thoroughbred Jersey cow. Can you give me any clew [sic] for the obtaining of same?"[3] He would eventually find his Jersey milk herd, along with Angora goats, pigs, and his favorite horses, the massive shires. But he did not just buy any animal. From the beginning, perhaps influenced by his friend Luther Burbank, he sought the best of breed and developed an active breeding program of his own that was to win him medals at the state fairs.

Aware that a working ranch requires years of capital for building fences, pens, and barns, buying tools and equipment, Jack searched for a crop that could bring in the money needed to establish the concern. It should be easy to plant and tend, inexpensive to maintain, and provide a certain profit within a short time. After much study he hit upon eucalyptus.[4]

To look in some detail at Jack's involvement with eucalyptus provides a telling case study of his approach to the ranch—how he made decisions and how he used his name to achieve his agricultural dream. This close examination will also settle an old score with regard to London's talents as a rancher. Namely, it will show that to evaluate him as most other biographers do, on the basis of current knowledge of the tree, belittles Jack's ability, for it ignores the beliefs about the tree commonly held in 1910. One finds then that he acted sensibly, not thoughtlessly.

To understand the purported value of the tree in 1910, it helps to know what happened to the California forests as a result of settlement. When masses of hopeful settlers reached California, they saw a land of limitless resources. Needing food, they cleared the valleys of trees, often through the expedient method of burning. Needing meat, wool, and leather, they let sheep and cattle graze on surviving shoots. Needing firewood, they cut down the oaks and madronas on the hillsides.[5] While at first they lived in tent cities and small shelters, as the Bay Area and Sacramento valley were settled, their need for timber products grew. Lumber was used for building houses, barns, shops, sidewalks, carriages, wagons, sleds, farm implements, mining implements, weirs, sluices, mine shafts, piers, and ships.

As early as 1849, some neighborhoods had been stripped clean. Missionary William Taylor, finding that firewood was selling for forty dollars a cord in San Francisco, told how a sandy meadow had replaced the thick covers of evergreen scrub oaks that had once covered the hills behind his home. By 1860, magazines were running articles on solutions for the fuel crisis and predicting timber famines for the near future. In

1869, the president of the state's Board of Agriculture reported that at least one-third of all accessible timber of value had already been consumed or destroyed.

Of course, the timber was becoming increasingly inaccessible as lumbermen moved further north and west into the higher elevations of mountain ranges, requiring costly, often dangerous systems for cutting and transporting the wood to the cities. The city dweller had to pay a high price for civilizing warmth.

In fact, California's problem was part of a national one. Arbor Day was first declared and celebrated in Nebraska in 1872, and a national Timber Culture Act passed in 1873 required homesteaders to set part of their land grants aside for trees. But this new patriotic movement had a special impact in California, which had the smallest area of tree-covered land in the United States in 1875, according to Department of Agriculture statistics—only 4 percent of the land was covered with timber.

The state itself recognized the growing problem. In 1870 the California State Agricultural Society offered a premium of fifty dollars to be awarded to the best timber plantings that winter. It was at this point that the blue-green eucalyptus began to cover fields in large numbers. Planters relied on the claims of French botanists that the tree had great medicinal powers, including the ability to purify the air and eliminate malaria. The species *globulus* grew well in a variety of soils, took only seven years to mature, and important for Californians, tolerated drought periods well. Ellwood Cooper, a retired diplomat who did much to spread the tree's popularity, wrote of his plantation near Santa Barbara, "I have growing about 50,000 trees. The oldest were transplanted three years ago. A tree three years and two months from the seed, transplanted two years and ten months ago is nine and one-half inches in diameter and forty feet and six inches high."

Others preached the values of the wood beyond the fuel it provided. Its tea was a tonic that would cleanse the system. Smoking its leaves would cure bronchial disorders. Planting it around buildings would prevent cholera epidemics. Formed into shingles, it would give fire resistance to roofs. No less eminent a body than the Central and Southern Pacific Railroads decided to plant the aromatic giants along its tracks to provide a constant timber supply for roadbed repairs, as well as to absorb malarial poisons along the lines. The eucalyptus was, according to the best scientific sources, a miracle tree.

The first boom in commercial eucalyptus plantings died away with the century. The reasons are not clear but may well have been tied to the economic depression of the 1890s. With the return to prosperity at the turn of the century, a second boom began. This one, supported by Jack London and other ranchers throughout the state, closely resembled the first.

Jack probably first began reading about eucalyptus upon returning from the *Snark* voyage in the fall of 1909. Most likely he was initially spurred by some of the advertisements in *Sunset* in 1909, in which companies sold shares in plantations for "a ten year investment that combines ABSOLUTE SECURITY, ABSOLUTE CERTAINTY, ABSOLUTE HONESTY." Doubtless Jack thought an even safer investment would be to have ownership of one's own plantation. Thus, on January 7, 1910, he ordered fifteen thousand *E. tereticornis* from the nursery of W. A. T. Stratton.[6] On the fourteenth, he sent another letter, indicating his intention to pull out vineyards and eventually plant one hundred thousand trees. (Jack pulled the vines because grapes were bringing less than they cost to grow at the time; also, he predicted correctly that the Prohibition ticket would one day achieve success.)

As with all his plans, Jack included a search for expert advice. His ranch file on eucalyptus grew fat with pamphlets from such sources.[7] These included bulletins from the California Department of Forestry ("Yield from Eucalyptus Plantations in California") and the Forestry Society of California ("Eucalyptus Commercially Considered"). Characteristically, Jack underlined passages and made brief marginal notes throughout the pages. The claims of these references repeated those of the earlier boom: eucalyptus was the perfect choice for California and would find many markets. Claims for the wood's value went far beyond furniture making—"Circassian walnut," as it was called, could be used in construction, particularly for pilings and posts.

Pleased with the first shipment, he ordered fifteen thousand more. The investment itself was so small that one can understand why he was quick to jump in. Ten thousand trees cost him only one hundred dollars, a meager sum compared to his other expenses at the time. Even figuring in the labor, which ran $1.75 a day per man, the cost remained low, certainly under five hundred dollars.[8]

In late 1910 Jack sought advice on the San José blue gum. He was looking for a "quick-growing and beautiful eucalyptus" to line the half-mile driveway. He made similar plantings in the winter of 1911–12. There is no further record of his work with eucalyptus until 1914 when, according to a newspaper report, London added five thousand more trees to the ranch.[9] All told, then, before his death he planted about eighty thousand trees.

Jack's correspondence with others at this time suggests he was planting much more extensively. In fact, he was playing with the facts for other purposes. Even a slight familiarity with Jack's letters reveals that many of them overstate his commitments in an effort to gain sympathy from others, particularly in matters of money. These letters were sent to all kinds of people: strangers asking for money; his first wife, Bess; magazine and book publishers. Because Jack sent these letters so often, they developed a life of their own—the same sad tale, repeated again and again, developed small exaggerations that in time sprouted larger ones. For example, when he wanted a large advance on *John Barleycorn* from the Century company, he explained, "You see, I am running an expensive ranch—said ranch being expensive because of the fact that I am investing heavily in it. I am planting eucalyptus trees, and at present moment have a hundred thousand trees in. . . . This makes a rather tidy wage-list when, for months at a time, there are fifty men on the pay roll."[10]

Jack may even have believed these statements. Although he was a master record keeper, he failed in all his business dealings to keep clear and organized records of their progress, a fault that was to cripple his efforts more than once. He was not lacking in desire or ingenuity in his schemes—he did lack time. Furthermore, his temperament was mercurial, that of an impatient learner, who catches the basics and then moves on in boredom as soon as the important qualifying details demand attention.

Some biographers suggest that London simply followed the

craze of the second boom, along with the other fools. That
these investors were not unwise, given the scientific literature
of the period, should now be evident. Furthermore, the facts
suggest that, if anything, London played a role in starting the
craze. Not only did he plant before the major forestry bulletins
appeared, he used the scheme in his publicity for his writings.
For example, in an interview on June 12, 1910 with the *New
York Herald,* which was serializing *Burning Daylight,* London told
how he had just set out fifteen thousand trees of the "hardy
Australian variety."

Soon after this interview appeared, John J. Welch, president
of the American Corporation for Investors, asked London for
an endorsement for the company's Eucalyptus Timber Corporation.[11] Welch offered London a five-acre tract of trees for half
price. London turned down the land, yet signed his name to a
letter created by the company. It was no less lacking in hyperbole:

> It has been my privilege to visit almost every country on
> the globe and to see and study the people of this old earth
> in almost every phase and condition. . . . When Dede
> Mason suggests to Burning Daylight the idea of planting
> Eucalyptus trees in California, she but foretells the begin-
> ning of what is destined to be one of the greatest and most
> profitable industries in this country—the commercial cul-
> ture of the Eucalyptus tree.

London went on to praise the company for its use of "modern
forestry methods" and warned against "wild and unauthorized
claims" being made by others. But he really had no basis for
judging it. The company happily used London's encouraging
remarks in a fancy brochure, "Jack London and Eucalyptus."
Thus, as we find so often in London's life, his celebrity was
used to market a product or concept.

The second eucalyptus boom had some aspects of a craze—
one brochure was titled "Do You Want a Permanent Home on
Easy Street?" However, London's interest was spurred by the
scientific support, which he read critically. Where one forestry
document asserted the fire-retardant qualities of the wood,
London put a question mark in the margin. This notation is

typical of the inquisitiveness he brought to all his activities. Had he discussed this characteristic of the wood with those he consulted at the University of California at Davis, they would have reassured him that the tree was indeed a good fire protectant. Today we know the tragic misrepresentation of that claim, for the oils in the limbs and leaves carpet the surrounding ground with a highly flammable fuel that worries hill dwellers during the dry season.

Anyone visiting California today can see the results of the eucalyptus boom—the trees are everywhere, at times in old groves, more frequently as wind breaks or boundary markers between properties. The trees are so much a part of the landscape that conservationists debate whether they deserve to be preserved, or whether they should be torn out as non-native specimens. Their presence is puzzling: if eucalyptus has so many uses in construction, animal feed, and pharmaceuticals, why were they not harvested? The reason is that only a few of the dozens of available varieties of eucalyptus were planted in California. The most popular of these, the blue gum, makes poor lumber and is difficult to process for other uses. Once this became known, the tree was written off as a nuisance, when in fact some of the other varieties could have been profitable.

Jack died before he could explore the relative utility of his crop, which contained three varieties of the tree. As with his other ranch endeavors, he experimented—in this case by having a cabinetmaker work up several pieces of furniture for his home. Given his bent for agricultural innovation, it is not tenable to conclude that he would have walked away from the crop as others were to do, and write it off as a loss. Had Jack lived longer, California agriculture may have taken some different directions, not only with particular regard to eucalyptus, but more broadly by concentrating on his use of organic methods and an ecological model.

*　　*　　*　　*

Joyful over his life on the ranch, London conceived a story even stronger than *Burning Daylight* to laud the paradise of Sonoma country life. He called it the *Valley of the Moon* in honor of the land he found so bountiful. In the first section of the story Saxon and Billy Roberts, a young working-class couple in

Oakland, grow disenchanted with urban life. Though devoted union activists, they become dismayed by the increasing violence and seeming futility of the labor struggle. With wonder, Saxon realizes, "Oakland is just a place to start from." The two abandon their past, sell their hard-earned household goods, and take to the road in search of a place where they can have a farm and raise their children in peace and health. It was to become a book that many Americans, troubled by the rapid growth of cities and smoky factories overrunning the landscape, would identify with.

As a writer who borrowed extensively from personal knowledge in his sketches, London thought it necessary to retrace the one part of the Robertses' route he himself had never taken, a journey through northern California and neighboring towns along the Oregon border. To add to the verisimilitude of the plot, he and Charmian (with Nakata of course) would travel in a four-horse rig and camp most of the way. They chose this mode of transportation not only to re-create the story, but because it reflected their preference in travel. They never owned an automobile nor showed an interest in having one. They preferred the leisurely ride, a slow cargo freighter to a fast tourist steamer, a horse to a gas engine. Although modern in most respects, they remained contentedly in the nineteenth century with regard to modes of travel.

Not only friends, but even Charmian thought he was daft to try a four-horse rig, for as he explained in a whimsical essay on the trip in *Sunset:* "What I knew about horses, much less about breaking them, was just about as much as any sailor knows."[12] She argued for a simple span with one horse, which she could drive as well, but eventually agreed with his choice, provided there be a trial period. By the time the trip began, she could handle the four-horse rig as well as he.

London's detailed account of this breaking-in time hints to the untutored reader the enormous difficulty of managing a four-horse team. There was the problem of the horses' personalities. For example, Milda was a "manger-glutton," who, no matter how far from home, bolted at precisely six o'clock and took the most direct route to the stable, road or no, while Outlaw, true to her name, kicked and jumped and bit her teammate on the nape. Learning to hold four reins in the left hand and control with the whip in the right meant that Charmian and Nakata were smacked as often as the horses were in the early trials.

The journey began with a meander through what is now Marin County: Point Reyes with its wild beaches, dunes, and rolling hills; Mill Valley, nestled on the back of camel-humped Mount Tamalpais; Olema, surrounded by lush wildlife-filled meadows. They then continued northward, through Sonoma County to the Russian River, which they traced toward the ocean, then along the coast to Oregon, returning through the Cascades and central valley of California. Only mornings were devoted to the hard driving so that the remainder of the days could be spent at work or fishing for their evening meal. Happy to be on an adventure again, however mild when compared to their previous one, Charmian felt better than she had in many months.

Actually, they were seldom far from people, even in the sparsely populated redwood forests, for small lumber camps dotted the inland roads, and fishing villages lined the calmer sections of the coast. Some towns were large enough to include hotels, where they could sleep on a soft bed; opera houses, where Jack could give one of his standard talks on socialism; and newspapers, which could publicize the couple's activities. One paper pictured Charmian with a Baden-Powell hat, a cravat, and a purse dangling off her belt. She said that she did no housework but rather worked and played with Jack. She also discussed her *Snark* manuscripts and her hope for their publication.

Their life on the road was thus not much different from ranch life. Mail was forwarded along to post offices along the route, so that correspondence, always voluminous, continued to claim their attention. Since Jack had an assignment to write articles about northern California, Charmian prepared notes on her impressions for his use. Her one clear writing strength was in lyrical description of landscape and setting, the very type of writing he found most difficult.

Charmian actively assisted Jack in writing his fiction, providing masses of detail to flesh out his skeletal plots, but nowhere is her hand more evident than in *Valley of the Moon*. Jack consulted her frequently about the details of Saxon's character.

What were her feelings as a young woman in love? What did her embroidery and decorative work look like? How did she receive sex education? What happened during the consultation with a doctor who whispered the illegal secrets of birth control in her ear? With the help of Charmian, Jack was able to delineate his most sensitive and realistic female character, providing a revealing glimpse of the activities of such young women in the cities of that time. So pleased was he with Charmian's help that one day, while reviewing her latest notes, he told her she might become a writer, could she gain the patience.

Jack further showed proof of his continual, ever growing love for his wife at this time when he rewrote his will. Since his return from the *Snark* adventure, Bess had been using her control of the children as leverage in her financial dealings with Jack. Following the death of Joy, Jack longed to see his daughters more frequently and approached Bess with two plans: one was to move them to a nearby house he would build for them in Glen Ellen; the other was to let the girls stay with him during every other vacation, on the ranch. Bess refused both.

Bess's sole reason for rejecting both plans was Charmian: she could not bear to have the girls in her presence. Bess's hostility toward Charmian not only frustrated Jack's attempts at maintaining a steady relationship with his daughters, but affected Joan's mind-set in particular. Joan's only memory of Charmian together with Jack was in 1905, when she went to visit him in the hospital following his hemorrhoidal surgery. Both Flora and Bess began to fuss, and Joan soon figured out the reason: "A strange woman was sitting in a dark corner near the bed, staring at us. She did not speak, nor did Daddy introduce us to her, but her eyes did not leave us until the disconcerting visit was over." More poignant was her reflection on what Jack's remarriage meant for her: "How difficult it must have been, I think, for that little girl who was I to have competed, year after year, with an unknown rival who for long was nameless, and for even longer faceless." Bess not only kept Charmian's name from the girls, but did not inform them of her pregnancy until the baby was born. Hearing the news of Joy's birth, Joan was fiercely resentful, then glad when she learned the baby had died.

With so much rancor on Bess's part, Jack responded in kind.

Early in 1911 he attacked her furiously, calling her "a mere jealous, sexually-offended, unmotherly, peasant-minded female." He pointed out that he was not making as much money as he had in the past, yet his bills for the care of "Grandma, Jennie, Johnnie, doctor bills, houses, taxes, life insurance, etc., and all in addition to you and Joan and Bess" plus the expenses of laborers, wages, horses, wagons, harnesses, plows, and maintenance had left him thousands of dollars in debt. "I can live on $20 a month," he asserted. "Do you think this is for Charmian? She could do the same."

Knowing Bess was teaching the girls to hate Charmian, he added:

> Do you think Charmian wants to alienate my children from you? Please don't forget that no woman is particularly enthusiastic about taking any hand in raising another woman's children. Yet Charmian is noble, Charmian has no peasant mind, and Charmian is willing to meet me and go any distance with me in this matter. . . . Another thing you must not forget, is: That over half my work is done by Charmian. That for every dollar that you receive from me, Charmian has earned over 50 cents of it; that every piece of bread or butter or chunk of meat that you put in your mouth, Charmian has paid more than half of the same. And yet you are willing to eat this bread and butter and meat, and ask for more, and at the same time deny me any acquaintance with my children.[13]

Jack then sealed his feelings with the third (and final) will written since his marriage to Charmian.

Composed in 1906 and 1909, his previous wills contained elaborate formulas for the division of property, monies, and literary rights among Bess and his daughters, Eliza, Flora, Jenny Prentiss, and Charmian. Tired of Bess's manipulation of the children for revenge, he now drafted a brief direct request: Charmian was to inherit essentially everything. His daughters were to receive a small monthly allowance, with all else to come from "the kindness of Charmian," who was "to personally house and manage" them as well. Eliza, Flora, and Jenny Prentiss were granted small regular incomes from the estate. Bess was granted five dollars, plus the use of the home he had built for her.

Upon his death, the pittance left his first family in the will was expected to be fattened by the insurance policies required by the divorce decree. In that matter a shadow passed over his life. When one of his policies came up for renewal, the company canceled, citing Jack's poor health as the reason. Charmian and Jack were puzzled. True, he had been more prone to colds and infection since the South Sea illnesses, but he had proven his strength and stamina through the physically arduous four-horse drive. What they did not know was that some of his minor symptoms signified serious problems. He suffered chronic flare-ups of sties, a common side effect of opium use. He began to notice joint pain and swelling, the start of the general deterioration brought on by his poorly functioning kidneys. The lovers failed to see that Jack at thirty-five had a much older body than Charmian did at forty.

PART III
FROM WILDERNESS TO REDEMPTION

So well it were to love, to love,
And cheat of any laughter
The fate beneath us and above,
The dark before and after.

William Ernest Henley
Nuptial Sleep

12

CONFESSION

The Tipple's Aboard, and the night is
    young,
The door's ajar and the Barrel is
    sprung,
I am singing the best song ever was
    sung,
And it has a rousing chorus.

—*Hilaire Belloc*

During 1910–11 neither London's pace as a writer nor his popularity with the public slackened. He published thirty-seven stories and articles in the leading magazines, especially the *Saturday Evening Post* and *Cosmopolitan*. Six novels and story collections appeared, two of which were also serialized. In spite of his frequent cries of indebtedness, he was now the highest-paid author in the United States, earning around one thousand dollars per story and publishing everything he submitted.

London's obsessive work style was the counterbalance for his more destructive addictions, smoking and drinking. These behaviors harmed not only his weakened body, but his relationships with others.

To call London an alcoholic draws criticism from some scholars, who point to both his enormous productivity as a writer, farmer, and businessman, and his ability to go for periods at a time without drinking at all.[1] The term also rankles some because, too often, biographers have pressed the issue so much that London has been characterized incorrectly as a drunk, hence not a figure for admiration. London sympathizers fear the image of the man clasping the bottle is somehow more lasting than that of the man steering a small boat through a storm, rousing a crowd to support the rights of the working man, writing a mythic story of nature's ultimate power, or riding on horseback to check a hay harvest. And given the uneasy and equivocal way drinking is treated in our society, their wariness is probably correct.

Yet there is no denying that Jack London drank a lot during certain periods of his life, and one can track these cycles in his own autobiographical essays and in Charmian's diary entries. Various reports of those who knew him generally agree with the concise summation of fellow journalist Oliver Madox Hueffer:

> Among the apocryphal legends attached to his name, and founded very possibly on his own statements, was that of his almost superhuman drunkenness. That at one time or another he drank too much I can believe—certainly in all the time of our acquaintance he never showed any sign of it. He was by no means a teetotaler; but I never saw him drunk. Nor did he ever boast of his drinking prowess in my presence.[2]

If he was not a drunk and could abstain, then was he an alcoholic? The answer may be beside the point.

Whether Jack London was an alcoholic in the technical sense mattered little to those closest to him. From their points of view, his behavior was clearly affected by his drinking in a way that made their lives more difficult. Family therapists today would agree that even if Jack was not fully addicted, his actions provoked patterns in his relationships with others that are typical in families of alcoholics. Research indicates that alcoholism more resembles a disease, in that its course is outside the drinker's control, than a self-willed act of moral turpitude. Moreover, a good number of alcoholics function well at work; their intimate relationships suffer the greatest disruption.

One example of the consequences of Jack's drinking can be seen during February 1911, at the height of his struggle to gain more visitation with the girls. One day he provoked an incident at Bess's house that resulted in a tremendous argument years later when Joan and Becky were adults. Reflecting on her child-hood, Joan told how Jack seemed to want to make up for the long absence caused by the *Snark* trip.[3] He sent dozens of books, provided dance and piano lessons, kept every promise of a telephone call or visit. Unfortunately, she added, he some-times showed up drunk; on one particularly besotted day he threw Becky through the living room window.

Becky was dumbstruck by this charge. She said Jack never drank before arriving nor in their presence, and that her mem-ory was substantiated by others she spoke with after his death. As for the window episode, she explained:

Daddy, Mother, Joan, and I were in the sitting room. . . . What had started it, I don't know, but Mother and Daddy were very angry and saying terrible things to each other. Joan had gone over to stand beside Mother. I was sitting on the floor beside Daddy. Suddenly Daddy said, "You know I wouldn't hurt either of my daughters. They trust me to take care of them. Don't you Joan?" And Joan said, "Well, I don't know." Daddy turned to me and said, "If I told you to put out your hands in mine and I would throw you through the window (which was closed) would you believe me?" I said, "Yes, Daddy, and I know you wouldn't hurt me. I trust you." . . . He was so angry I'm sure he didn't know what he was doing. He picked me up from the floor and swung me toward the window. One foot crashed through, there was a loud noise and he pulled me back instantly. He was contrite and after exami-nation thought it was just a slight cut. He carried me across the street to the hospital.[4]

It is the type of horror story many a family has in its book of secrets, with a plot particularly familiar to families with an alcoholic parent. The children take sides according to temperament. Joan, serious and righteous like her mother, moves to be her protector when the argument develops. Becky, a playful, spunky girl who often felt stifled by her stern mother and older sister, aligns with her father. Both parents have heaped abuse on the two girls by arguing frightfully in front of them. Jack finds himself unwittingly harming his baby daughter. Bess and Joan now have more reason to harass him, and he is left with a burden of guilt of the worst kind.

Significantly, Becky did not recall what the argument was about. She said she remembered clearly what happened to her because it was "something that didn't happen to a little girl every day." This claim rings true. What less satisfies is her certainty he had never drunk before seeing them, for often children of alcoholics are not wise to the signs, even when the behavior is outlandish.

Given Jack's animosity toward Bess and Charmian's records of his drinking in her diary, it is reasonable to suspect he would not appear at Bess's door without some fortification. So one is inclined to find some truth in both girls' stories, that on this day at least, he imbibed beforehand and that, in self-defense during the fight with Bess, pushed too far.

The real victim in the event turned out to be Joan. She was traumatized by what she had seen, and even when her mother assured her that Jack had not meant to hurt Becky, refused to believe her. She saw the clay feet in the idol she had made of her father, and in a real sense felt the meaning of the divorce for the first time. She still adored her father but was more wary of his intentions.

The kind of drinker who was aware of his consumption, if not the consequences of such, Jack sought to compensate for loss of control in one area of his life with firm control in others. Hence the continued devotion to a rigid work schedule, now complicated by the additional self-imposed goal of creating a model ranch. As if these two careers were not enough, he was also considering various business ventures, including motion pictures.

A thoughtful man who regularly included himself as a topic of scrutiny, London examined closely his relationship to the bottle, and as a result composed an extraordinary autobiographical document, *John Barleycorn*. It was a smash with the public after it appeared in 1913, and played a large role in accelerating the drive toward prohibition. But while the confession contributed to others' sobriety, it did not inspire the same result in the confessor.

As the first chapter opens, Jack has returned from voting for the woman's suffrage amendment. Charmian expresses surprise at his vote, knowing that as a youth he had been opposed to feminism and only recently accepted it as "an inevitable social phenomenon." He explains in return, "When women get the ballot, they will vote for prohibition. It is the wives, and sisters, and mothers, and they only, who will drive the nails into the coffin of John Barleycorn." (London's belief that women would be the moral saviors of society was so prevalent that the major financial resources against suffrage came from the liquor industry.)

Charmian suggests he should set down his own acquaintance with John Barleycorn. "The memoirs of an alcoholic," he replies. Significantly, she corrects, "No, alcoholic memoirs. You have shown yourself no alcoholic, no dipsomaniac, but merely an habitual drinker." This little exchange superbly encapsulates the dynamic of the drinker and spouse: disavowal. At most, the imbiber has a "little difficulty" or "delicate condition," which even he may acknowledge in those terms, and the spouse reinforces his belief by refusing to accept its severity. To do so is to admit to the accompanying grievances—the injustices, embarrassments, broken promises, and hostility—endured during drinking episodes.

This psychology must seem odd to people who have not lived among intimates with an addiction problem. Why should the wife collaborate by minimizing the case? Typically the spouse has needs that dovetail with the alcoholic's, a low self-esteem that drives her to look up to her husband for reassurance. Often she is isolated from others and lacks independent proof of her worth. When, like Charmian, she received little love as a child, the ardent attention from the man fills an enormous void, and she feels safe for the first time in her life. As the alcoholism develops, then, she grows fearful of losing what security she has gained, and learns to make do, to pretend everything is fine, and in the process loses even more her sense of self-worth. Charmian swallowed her anger at the mistreatment she received, allowing herself only a line or two of honest feeling in her diaries.

By 1911, however, the honeymoon was over, and she began to speak out. We know today from studies of alcoholism and the family that her response was of a common type, and one certain to fail. She began to bargain with Jack, to use reason and downright wheedling to convince him to change his behavior. She should have known it would not work, any more than it had with his quitting cigarettes. Still, given Jack's great emphasis on logic, it must have made sense to her. In November of that year she convinced him to agree to limit his drinking to three drinks a day, in turn for which she would have another baby. It was not so crass an offer as it appears on the surface: she understandably feared bearing another child, both for the child's sake and her own. He grabbed at the idea, and she observed afterward that he became more demonstrative with her in public. The agreement healed her period of mourning —she took the baby clothes and furniture out of the barn with expectant hope instead of sadness.

London told George Sterling of his pledge, who in apologizing for being a fool during a recent party at the ranch, added, "Wished next morning, that I'd been under your 'three drink' regime." Alcohol was a frequent theme in the correspondence, even acting as a means of a subtle competition between the two. George often listed the number of days he was on his current wagon: "No drink for 58 days!" or "No booze till we meet again." During one period of abstention he felt "like a mountain lion in a butcher shop." Another time he apologized, "I always have to be sick or soused when I'm at your place! You never see me at par."[5] George's preoccupation with abstention during these months may have been brought on by his desire to appease Carrie, who in spite of his efforts decided to divorce him when his latest love affair proved too public a scandal.

Though both men were frank about their problem, George with his Catholic background was more attuned to the effects of his behavior on others and suffered guilt for the harm he had done. Jack was more self-deceiving in this regard and saw drinking as a personal problem, one that harmed his writing and his physical health. Where George felt humiliation and shame for his behavior, Jack felt frustration over a hint he was not in full control of his actions. Certainly he was not much aware of how his behavior at times hurt those he loved.

* * * *

As it turned out, Charmian's delight with Jack's sobriety pledge was premature. They had made arrangements to sail on the final trip of the *Dirigo,* one of the noted steel-hulled sailing ships of A. Sewall and Company, around Cape Horn. With the Panama Canal nearing completion, it was a journey few again would experience. The true adventurer of the two, Charmian was hungry to be out on the ocean and alone with Jack, away from the social scene on the ranch. What she did not consider was that they would have to stop in New York City and settle business affairs before meeting the ship in Baltimore.

On the train ride across the country, Charmian was most content, describing the passage to be like a honeymoon. Suffrage was strong in Jack's mind then. In Denver, he said he supported the woman's vote because it would "tear up the social structure and root it out, but the structure will be better in the end, just as you improve a house when you remodel it."[6] He alerted friends in New York that he would be ready to give his public stamp of approval to the movement.

Upon reaching the east coast, Jack changed his vow, promising Charmian he would stop drinking for good following one last fling. It was the kind of backsliding common to alcoholics, one that would only secure a further breakdown of his own crumbling self-esteem. When he came in very drunk following a lunch with the *Cosmopolitan* editor the following day, she refused to join him and a friend for dinner. Instead, she completed her application to sail on the *Dirigo* (another ship allergic to women) in expectation that its approval would soon get them out on the healing seas.

The following days were a confusing swirl of activities for both of them. Much of the time Charmian was alone, working in the apartment and waiting to hear from Jack, venturing out to a concert, or visiting with one of her many friends there, including Emma Goldman and Arnold Genthe. Some nights Jack did not return at all. Several times while dining out with a friend, Charmian would run into Jack and his buddies at the same restaurant.

Some of the socializing was of course connected to work. The major magazine publishers were in New York, and London had to apply his charm to tempt more money from them. Also, he was unhappy with Macmillan over its "careless staff," which had lost precious films and prints from the *Snark* trip and was withholding proofs. This meant a search for a new book publisher.[7] In addition, he was organizing a partnership with Joseph Noel, who had moved to New York, and George Sterling, starting up the Millergraph Company, which would manufacture new lithographing equipment invented by F. R. Miller.

Nevertheless, much of Jack's bustle was purely social. His companions included a strange array of people, among them composer Victor Herbert, popular portrait painter John Butler Yeats, writer Adolphe Roberts, and editor Henry Gallup Payne, along with lesser-known others. One of the unknowns was nicknamed the Blasphemer; another, the Great Lover. Joseph Noel later recalled how tired and anxious Charmian seemed during this trip and how clearly she disliked the talk of many of these men.[8]

Another story hints at the men's decadent style. One evening Noel asked Charmian how the Great Lover was doing. "He's dead," she responded. Naturally doubting her, he pressed for more information. Charmian explained that the man had gone to visit a married woman, only to be surprised by the sounds of the husband's early entry. To avoid detection he jumped out of the bedroom window, forgetting that it was four stories up. Indeed, the man was dead.

This shifting group of cronies was joined by women much of the time, and Charmian could not ignore Jack's wandering eye. The story he gave the press was a different one. In interviews he claimed to find city women unattractive, his main reason being they did not treat other women well. He also condemned the city as a "wild maelstrom with which Rome in its wildest days could not compare." He observed that making an impression and pretense mattered more than being a good person. The city women, with their possessiveness and carping at men, disgusted him. It was a good act, playing to his audience of conservative middle-class readers.[9]

Very likely he was not disgusted by one city woman. His interviews were all with one reporter, Sophie Irene Loeb, the only woman during this time of carousing who was frequently in Jack's company. Thirty-five and divorced, Sophie was embarking on a new stage of her life that would bring her renown for her unflagging and successful efforts in support of most of the welfare legislation in New York state. Then, in early 1912, she was already a popular feature writer with the *Evening World*, using her position to publicize the need for child welfare improvements, school lunches, education for immigrants, economic support for single parents, and other social causes. Before her death at fifty-two, she would be known in Europe as well as in the States as "America's Greatest Mother" for her indefatigable efforts on behalf of children. Such a bright and self-motivated woman must have appealed greatly to Jack, and her resemblance to Anna Strunsky could only attract him more.

Though there is no hard evidence that they ever had an affair, something was brewing between the two. Jack sent George a letter and asked him to burn it afterward, which he did.[10] Charmian knew that he visited Sophie's apartment—presumably with others in tow—and that he spoke often with Sophie on the phone.

Charmian was particularly on edge when he chose to go to Boston alone and failed to communicate with her during the trip. Upon his return Jack's familiar pattern of remorse and reconciliation appeared. He explained his silence had been caused by despondency over his failure to strike a contract with Houghton Mifflin. He took her to hear Enrico Caruso sing. Jack "nearly died of bliss," she wrote Blanche, and "sank his head on my shoulder, much to the delight of a very young girl on his left."[11] (Always careful to portray him as the attentive lover, she did not tell Blanche of his previous cruel behavior.) In a most unusual break from schedules they spent the entire next day in bed making love. He started taking her out with him, including a dinner with Carmel friend Mary Austin and the great feminist Charlotte Perkins Gilman. They made social calls at the home of writer Ella Wheeler Wilcox, a favorite of theirs, and that of Anna Strunsky, now living on an estate on Long Island. They even dined together with Sophie Loeb.

Charmian did not respond to Jack's renewed attention as she had following similar past imbroglios. She continued to doubt and question his motives. "Mate the lover, but I am so hurt, I can't rise." She had cause to be mistrustful, for he suddenly reverted to his old behavior. When one day Emma Goldman appeared at the door with a bouquet of lilies of the valley, Charmian accepted her invitation that they go off alone together for several days.

By early February she felt consumed by nightmares. The *Dirigo* management continued to resist her pleas for passage. Even misogynist Noel, a frequent companion of the two, had some sympathy for her situation. Of a subway ride he observed:

Jack had been out all night, and while most men would have been tired, he was on edge for some fresh adventure. Anyone could see it. Charmian was emotionally upset. Anyone could see that, too. . . . That day Jack was trigger-tempered. Brushing her words away with something like a sneer, he told Charmian with unmistakable emphasis that he would keep his house in order, that it would be one-sided, that he would have all the say, and she knew what she could do about it if she didn't like it. Charmian's face went a rusty gray.[12]

Noel came away feeling sorry for Charmian; she seemed to be aging rapidly under the demands of Jack's overpowering energy. He also admired her, deciding her smooth management of the household and her willingness to go on adventures "eased the strain on Jack," indeed kept him from dying earlier in his life.

As February wound down, Jack swung back again, taking Charmian to lunch and buying her a fox fur. She made one last try to get permission to join the *Dirigo* by writing directly to the captain. He swiftly agreed to accept her, and on February 15 she found the packing seventeen boxes of clothes and supplies to be a sweet labor.

Baltimore—a few days in the charming port city promised a time for recuperation. In a revealing act of self-abasement, Jack went to the barber and had his head shaved, just as it had been shaved in the Erie Penitentiary. Dumbstruck, Charmian refused to be seen with him. For comfort, she bought a fox terrier pup, Possum, the first of a long line of dogs in her life.

The familiar dance continued. Jack swore to forgo all alcohol, to prove for good he was not an alcoholic. She bought him a stocking cap and accompanied him in public once more. She made excuses for him, noted his poor health—from the cold Baltimore winds, she thought. More likely it was from withdrawal from his drug, along with his growing chronic ailments. They once again covered themselves with a blanket of pretense and denial.

*　*　*　*

Jack's head-shaving was an extraordinary admission to himself and Charmian of the destruction he had brought upon them. *John Barleycorn* is remarkable because it was equivalent to shaving his head for the entire nation to see. It was really an attempt at therapy, a confession of guilt with hope for absolution. Doubtless he thought that by describing the problem with brutal frankness and analyzing its course, he could control it. And to a point he did a magnificent job of ferreting out some of the reasons for his addiction.

An astute amateur sociologist, London understood that his early childhood experiences were significant in producing his habit. Indeed the first two-thirds of the book concern his childhood and youth. He correctly notes the relationship between alcohol and definitions of masculinity among the working class, the pecking order of the saloon, the role of alcohol as a diversion from hard physical work and economic oppression. He is candid about his own insecurities: "I drank because the men I was with drank, and because my nature was such that I could not permit myself to be less of a man than other men at their favorite pastime." He is graphic in his descriptions of various times the drug was a factor in his almost dying.

London emphasizes throughout that he dislikes the taste of liquor, that the roar of the crowd drew him to imbibe. He is also convinced that he was never a true alcoholic because he could abstain whenever he was away from male social settings. As we know today, such situational drinking is a more insidious form of alcoholism, because the drinker wrongly believes he is in control. He is not a twenty-four-hour lush, penniless and helpless. Because this kind of alcoholic, like Jack, is so competent in other areas of his life, he has many preoccupations to keep him from dealing with his illness.

London explores how the nature of drinking in the middle class was different, how it brought him more objectivity. He discusses the time around 1904–5, what he called his Long Sickness, when his separation from both Bess and Charmian left him wandering the streets with George, the result being mornings too hung over to work. During this time, he recounts, he came to confront what he dubbed the "White Logic."[13] This is the soul sickness brought on by alcohol, whereby the drunkard knows "standing up on two legs swaying . . . he is compounded of meat and wine and sparkle, of sun-mote and word-dust, a frail mechanism made to run for a span, to be tinkered at by doctors of divinity and doctors of physic, and to be flung into the scrapheap at the end." He sees through all illusions. "God is bad, truth is a cheat, and life is a joke." He feels a puppet of chance, that the old values engendered by wife and children are worthless, that only suicide offers hope.

London argues he was saved from submitting to the White Logic by two causes: socialism and Charmian, "a rare soul, or a fool, who never bored me and who was always a source of new and unending surprise and delight." She could not, however, keep him from drinking: "I could not spend all my hours in her company. Nor would it have been fair, nor wise, to compel her to spend all her hours in my company. Besides, I had written a string of successful books, and society demands some portion of the recreative hours of a fellow who writes books. How to face the social intercourse with the glamour gone? John Barleycorn!"[14] Thus he depended on the cocktail to carry him through the hours with friends and hangers-on. While Charmian helped him once again to appreciate the little pleasures of life—a Turkish bath, a horseback ride, an evening of theater —he used drink to pitch his happiness higher. He learned to pace his drinks, to spread them out and never drink while writing.

The *Snark* voyage proved a release for, as long as they were at sea, all he imbibed was muscatel. On shore, the pressures of writing, doctoring illnesses, overseeing boat repairs, and arranging his befuddled finances all pressed him toward the bottle. John Barleycorn gave "strength. It is a real strength. But it is manufactured out of sources of strength, and it must ultimately be paid for." As a youth, whiskey had enabled him to pass coal on a steamer for eight days straight; as an adult it fueled his role as "an overworked business and professional man." Once in Australia he began drinking heavily, increasing his intake when the demands of the growing ranch became great.

London elaborates the price in detail: the sleepless nights, the "jingle" that occurs during the day when the alcohol rubs the tender edge of nerves. Because his system never had a chance to work off the alcohol,

> I awoke with mouth parched and dry, with a slight heaviness of head, and with a mild nervous palpitation in the stomach. In fact I did not feel good. I was suffering from the morning sickness of the steady, heavy drinker. What I needed was a pick-me-up, a bracer. Trust John Barleycorn once he has broken down a man's defenses! . . . I achieved a condition in which my body was never free from alcohol.[15]

Although he made a rule never to drink until the work was done, he found he could not write without a drink first.

Eventually the White Logic appeared, speaking to him as if a spirit. He explains that to describe this visitor is as difficult as explaining the time and space distortions caused by hashish. It places a debt on the mind, extracting a toll worse than that already depleting the body. It brings pessimism and cynicism where there should be meaning and celebration of life. "Alcohol tells truth, but its truth is not normal. What is normal is beautiful. What is healthful tends toward life." Instead, the White Logic teaches "the antithesis of life, cruel and bleak as interstellar space, pulseless and frozen as absolute zero."

As the book draws to a close, London reflects on his deteriorating body, with its many missing teeth, crippled thumbs, bloated stomach, aching joints:

> I am aware that within this disintegrating body which has been dying since I was born I carry a skeleton; that under the rind of flesh which is called my face is a bony, noseless death's head. All of which does not shudder me. To be afraid is to be healthy. Fear of death makes for life. But the

curse of the White Logic is that it does not make one afraid. The world-sickness of the White Logic makes one grin jocosely into the face of the Noseless One and to sneer at all the phantasmagoria of living.[16]

Working around his ranch, he reflects on its origins as part of the Rancho Petaluma, the generations of men who took the land and turned it into vineyards. The White Logic replies that their striving was based on a lie. He points to bookshelves, the mausoleum of the thoughts of men, as "phantasms of hope."

London then tricks the White Logic with a twist of its own reasoning. The White Logic would have all life disguised as hedonism, but if the ghost has been true to this point, then hedonism itself is a lie. With that realization he conquers the pessimism and sings to himself, "The clown's the thing, the clown."

London ends by repeating his argument that he was not a true alcoholic—witness his five months of sobriety on the trip around the Horn. He refuses to reform, to give up the glass in hand, although he feels certain he can control the number of glasses. His hope in writing the book is not for himself, but for the "normal, healthy boys, now being born." He urges women's suffrage and prohibition: "The women know. They have paid an incalculable price of sweat and tears from man's use of alcohol."

This remarkable confession is rich with both the realities and rationalizations of the alcoholic. The tales of his youthful encounters with near-death shock with their bluntness. The delineation of the powerful social pressure for drinking in all-male settings remains valid today. The prideful periods of sobriety are common among drinkers, faulty proof they remain in control. The White Logic, his poetic expression of the twisted psychology of the drinker, reverberates powerfully along with its companion image of the Noseless One.

The book is also characteristic of alcoholics in its total self-centeredness. Despite passing reference to the sufferings of women, London ignores the consequences of his drinking on those around him. It destroys *his* body and mind; it is *his* problem, not others'. Since only he suffers, only he is to have a say in management of his problem. Hence he denies how drink encouraged him to pick fights with friends, to insult Charmian in public, perhaps even to injure his daughter's leg.

It is the nature of addiction to feed egocentricity. What nonaddicts (especially the righteous ones) fail to appreciate is the tremendous internal dialogue that surrounds the addiction. There is the obsessiveness of the addiction: that the person is thinking of the drug all the time, so much so that objectivity becomes lost. That London omitted mentioning his harm to others does not mean he was unaware of it; on the contrary, these unmentioned acts likely formed the major motivation for writing *John Barleycorn*. London was astute in emphasizing his youthful adventures—his adult reactions were too seamy for middle-class tastes. The audience of 1913 was not ready for the wrenching tales of drunkenness that appeared fifty years later. To get his thesis accepted, he had to portray his adult behavior as that of the congenial, clowning drunk, not the cruel, hostile behavior of fact.

London also failed to see how the deprivations of his early childhood fine-tuned him for addiction. Without that initial sense of insecurity and self-doubt engendered by Flora, he might have been able to resist the pressures of the all-male world. Proving his masculinity would not have been so important an issue had John London been a more competent model. But London did not blame either parent for his behavior. He preferred to see his trouble as caused by social learning in the saloons and perpetuated by the poison of the drug upon his will. He was of course correct in his position, his error being one of omission.

It is interesting to consider what would have happened to London had Alcoholics Anonymous been available to him.[17] Certainly he would have given it serious thought, for his curiosity and interest in the newest psychology would have led him to learn about this process of cure. The basis for change in that philosophy is the recognition that the will cannot effect the cure, that the addict must defer to powers beyond himself in order to loosen the pull of the drug. But the philosophy London adopted at that point in his life venerated the will. Several years later, when it was too late, he would find a book that tempted him to explore beyond his will, to submit to a grander view of the universe.

What stands out in London's experiences with alcohol are not the episodes of cruelty that did occur, but his courage, his ability to continue pursuing his dreams and achieving, day in and day out. He was recalled by many as "the most honest of men," and nowhere does that show more poignantly than in his memoir of drink. He was not proud of that part of his life, but he was not too proud to share it with others in hopes they might find redemption. Indeed, today it is passed among recovering alcoholics for its fearless account of a story they share.

*　*　*　*

The cruise of the *Dirigo* certainly bolstered Jack's belief he could take or leave John Barleycorn.[18] That Captain Omar Chapman was a teetotaler secured his determination for the five-month voyage. Also, by the time he stepped on the stately four-master he had already endured the worst side effects of drying out.

Officially the London trio were also crew members: Jack a fourth mate at $175, Charmian a stewardess at $75, and Nakata a cabin boy, actually a nonexistent position on the vessel. Their cabins were well appointed and close to the captain's. Though the sail around the Horn was dangerous, Captain Chapman's experience eased any doubts. Since this was his final trip before retirement in Seattle, he had special reason for its success.

Within several days of sailing, Charmian broke out in a strange skin rash and felt weak and anemic. Jack's recent outrageous behavior continued to nag her. "He doesn't realize how worn out I am. Men are so strange. I actually believe he has forgotten the past two months, or that he never realized what they were meaning to me. He called me Kid-Woman [a favorite nickname] today, and it almost hurt." She soon responded to his pressing affections, for after all, work was waiting—the manuscript of the *Valley of the Moon.*

Charmian kept a second, more detailed diary of this trip with hopes of turning it into a book. Five months at sea on a sturdy vessel with a competent crew does not make for a fascinating plot. But for the couple it was an important time of healing, a return to simple pleasures. She recorded over fifty books they read together, often aloud. Their tastes remained wide ranging and unconventional for the time, including obscure histories, Oscar Wilde, Strindberg plays, a biography of Nietzsche. Evening card games grew feverish as they invited other ship's officers to join round-robin tournaments.

Three weeks out, the captain studied Charmian's doleful appearance and ordered an inspection of her stateroom, which uncovered the cause of her ailments, bedbugs. She slept in the chart room while hers was disinfected and painted. After several days she felt well enough to don boxing gloves for the first of many matches during the journey. The crew gathered around for each performance, "grinning the tops of their heads nearly off." At other times the couple took their rifles up to the poop deck to shoot at objects in the water far below. Always the collector, Charmian saw to it that Jack caught her bird specimens along the way, including a splendid albatross with a wing spread of over ten feet. (Nakata counted taxidermy among his duties.)

Their subtle competitiveness soon took a more dangerous form:

> After boxing, to my own surprise, with Jack looking on almost skeptically and a bit cautiously for me, I scale the mizzenmast per shrouds, of course, to its top, and thence grin down superciliously at my lord and master, who declares he is too busy to follow. But with the glare of battle in his big sailor-blue, deep sea eyes, he licks the stuffing of me in three games of cribbage.[19]

Several days later Jack took her challenge and crawled up behind her. Although several short climbs almost nauseated her, she was determined to finish the main climb, a full ninety feet above the swaying, dipping deck. This time she asked Jack to lead so she could have a safety rope attached to her. Clambering up "as carefully as any cat on a shark hazard," she threw the rope down upon reaching the tiny platform. With their usual nonchalance, she pulled out a bit of embroidery, he a book, and sat there for several hours, chatting and reading aloud to one another. Later that evening Jack confessed he did not like the descent, which required going under and over the rigging. From then on she ascended alone.

One day Charmian was inspired to write a short story, a sea tale entitled "The Wheel," and worked secretly on it. When she showed it to Jack, he reassured her that it was not amateurish and deserved her full attention. More a sketch than a story, it aptly described the feel and sounds of a large sailing ship and displayed an ear for the sailors' dialect. Yet the plot was flimsy, concerning a trick several sailors played on one another. The story was sold eventually, but in later life Charmian ignored it and explicitly asked others not to mention it when they prepared biographical articles about her. She was later proud to earn money from it, but saw no comparison with Jack's work.

As Jack recognized, she was most powerful in her lyrical descriptive passages, such as this one from her unpublished *Dirigo* notes:

> A sharp squall comes up about 8 P.M. Strange sight—from through the half-door at the end of the corridor to the main deck, we see the great ship "sending" along, ourselves with it, under shortened sail; wind humming and thrumming in the rigging, long deck shining—wet in dim moonlight, ghostly, unbelievable picture in which we two find ourselves, arms around and muted. The only human thing visible the solitary figure of an officer on the fairytale fore-and-aft bridge. The skeleton masts with their small rags of sail add to the ghostly, impossible thing that this voyage, long-dreamed, means to us.[20]

Storms increased as they neared the Horn. Penguins filled the water to mock welcome to the dangerous passage. Snow fell, obscuring the rocky reefs. Adding to their anxiety, blood poisoning in a bruised finger sent Charmian to the captain's big brass bed, where Jack rubbed her back to ease her to sleep.

Nearing the treacherous waters, nightmares of dogs giving birth to humans and of panthers biting through her foot haunted Charmian. She attributed the threats to the mysterious change in the journey: "Strange, unearthly noises around ship—animals of sea groan and make slubbering, slithering noises, perhaps seals, but no guessing; penguins cry in the dark. And before blackness came, we could see the great albatrosses wheeling and diving above the inky tide." The first sight of land in two months proffered not relief at the safety of a nearby shore, but increased terror, with its graveyard of skeleton hulls that had crashed upon the rocks.

As the endless storms deluged the ship for several weeks, Charmian took to her room whenever she noted fear or terror in the practiced seamen's eyes. There she would type or embroider to distract herself. Her needlework led her to meditate on how "our values are so false. A man who paints pictures or designs houses is an equal—nay, superior—a man or a woman who creates gowns or hats is beneath social notice. And a creature who creates beautiful, practical things carries the world on his or her shoulders—by damn!"

Romance thrived in such a setting. In late May Charmian declared to her diary, "I am planning to make Mate a great gift tomorrow. It will take him unawares." She offered her bargain again.

> Ripe and willing and desirous I laid myself in my husband's arms and told him, if he was strong and willing and ready, we would "send" for another baby. He ready? and strong? and willing? He wasted no time either at this timely time. And so I, Charmian Kittredge, the same old girl, deliberately went after a child to replace the child that appeared and that left so great a lonely desire in me.

She became pregnant, indeed may well already have been so, for her diary noted other signs of such.

The trip ended in tragedy for the crew. Captain Chapman was obviously very ill. Having lost weight and energy steadily during the voyage, he could no longer hold any food in his stomach. Charmian, suspecting cancer, used her memories of her father's dying to prepare special foods and comfort the man. When they docked in Seattle on July 26, he had to be carried from the ship on a stretcher, and died two weeks later.

Once ashore, greeted by Martin Johnson and his new wife Osa, the couple went out to celebrate the end of the voyage. Jack stuck to his promised limit of three drinks. Charmian noted fastidiously in her diary he had maintained "148 days of abstinence," and he sent the same proud news to George.

Once they returned home, the Crowd flocked to the ranch.

Charmian was grateful to go to Oakland to see her doctor there. His news was not good. He informed her that unrepaired lacerations from her previous botched delivery could threaten the fetus. The next day she started spotting and went right to bed on the doctor's advice. The crisis passed.

Several days later Jack called from the ranch and asked to join her. She refused, assuring him she was well. As soon as she hung up the phone she realized she was beginning to miscarry. "Another hope lost."

13

ILLUSIONS
DASHED

The music had the heat of blood,
A passion no words can reach;
We sat together, and understood
Our heart's own speech.

—*Arthur Symons*

The loss of a second child brought not grief but bitterness and anger. In a classic understatement Charmian wrote, "One can't lose two children through one doctor's ignorance, or carelessness, or fear, or whatever it was without feeling feelings." Ordered to rest in bed for several days, she took solace in the tender nursing of Eliza and her Wiley relatives. Jack was strangely silent, unhappy as she was in acknowledging that this had been her last chance for a child. She would soon turn forty-one and must wait several months for a minor operation before any possibility of impregnation. On August 24 he sent her two books, whose inscriptions were flat in light of his earlier claims of love:

These, too, are our isles, and seas, and peoples, and we have lived with them, you and I, in the tales they have lived. [*The House of Pride*]

We have sailed these turquoise seas together, together lifted these palm-fronded isles out of the sea's depths; and together known these perishing sons of the sun. We know! We know! [*A Son of the Sun*]

Perhaps inspired by the growing manuscript of *John Barleycorn,* Jack made special efforts to stop drinking. He ordered Nakata to line his desk in the mornings with thermoses of cool drinks—water, vegetable juice, grape juice—which Jack would empty during his several hours of writing. It was a wise move, most likely an unconscious one, to protect his body from the toxins of his failing kidneys. The success of his efforts for many months is demonstrated in Charmian's diaries, which no longer made cryptic references to her "trial."

While she returned from the hospital to find a more sober mate, she also discovered a more frenetic one, who was more than ever determined to surround himself with crowds of cronies and interesting guests. Charmian knew few of the visitors and disliked in particular those who drank too much, who insulted or even pawed her and other women guests in their expressions of male bravado. As one guest observed of this time:

I was surprised to see all the different people there, from the lowest sailor to the millionaire types, artists, delightful artists, then the "Road Town" man, who was planning to make a house from S.F. to New York. I had never seen a collection of people like that in my life. . . . Some of them staying with them smelt bad, they hardly ever took a bath, so Jack built a little house for them out in the woods. But they all ate at the same table. . . . Princess Ula Humphrey, who had been in a Sultan's harem, she was an actress. Some old maids sent by churches to find out about Jack London. Then some beautiful woman that I felt could simply have eaten him up.[1]

Such a collection would challenge the talents of the most gracious and skillful hostess, and there was no way Charmian

could satisfy everyone's expectations of her. Certainly her
being a teetotaler did not help her reputation among the syba-
rites. Still, during this period she determined for Jack's sake to
put up a good front and save her mourning for private. Only
her closest friends knew at what cost she presented a cheerful,
hospitable face.

Feigning goodwill paid off. Several of the visitors took to
Charmian. One admirer was John Barrymore, of the acting
family, who appreciated Charmian's flair for the dramatic in
dress and music. Like other performers, he saw a kindred soul
in her, as well as one totally lacking the great prejudice against
stage actors so common in those days. Two young men, both
in their twenties, also distracted her from the loss of the child.
One was Allan Dunn, a handsome English-born bon vivant and
aspiring writer. The couple had met Dunn just before the sailing of the *Snark*, when he interviewed them for a story for *Sunset*
magazine.[2] Within days of Dunn's arrival appeared Laurie
Godfrey Smith, who quickly swept Charmian away from everyone else on the ranch.

Smith was an aspiring concert pianist, an Australian bursting
with the raw physicality of that country. No one in Charmian's
long life would ever match her so closely in temperament and
interests. Smith in turn seemed entranced to find a woman who
would play virtuoso music on the piano, dash a horse recklessly
through fields, and swim like an Amazon. They filled their days
with each other's company: practicing piano together, singing
duets, talking endlessly while she drove them about the hills in
a carriage.

Her diary gushed with excitement: "Laurie plays beautifully,
and he's a *man*, before he's a musician—an all-around man
. . . Laurie is splendid rider, and likes his horse too. He's crazy
over new horses. . . . I'm acquiring an accent from Laurie." She
also noted Jack's accompanying them on rides, but his presence was not the source of her pleasure these days.

Throughout the fall Jack was too busy to notice his wife's
infatuation. By now he considered writing simply a way to make
money, admitted frankly that his most recent book of stories,
Smoke Bellew, was strictly hack to put bread on the tables of four
households and feed the pigs. A lucrative contract with *Cosmopolitan* promised steady serialization income provided he grind
out novels at an unstinting pace. He was also exploring various

business ventures in addition to the Millergraph process: a grape juice company to exploit the expected furor over the forthcoming prohibition book, mining stocks, and that most promising of all new industries, the movies.

The ranch was a different matter, more deeply satisfying to him than his other income propositions. It became his spiritual font, the center of his values, the purpose for his other frenzied activities. He had taken fully to heart the vision, expressed in his agrarian fiction, of the land as the closest earthly version of Eden. Like Burning Daylight, he

> who had played the game in its biggest and most fantastic aspects, found that here, on the slopes of Sonoma Mountain, it was still the same old game. Man had still work to perform, forces to combat, obstacles to overcome. . . . Achievement was no less achievement, while the process of it seemed more rational and received the sanction of his reason. . . . His life was eminently wholesome and natural.[3]

His vision grew as he educated himself through study of agricultural manuals and scientific tomes. He conceived of a system of ranching that today would be praised for its ecological wisdom. "I adopted the policy of taking nothing off the ranch," he told one farm magazine reporter. "I raised stuff and fed it to the stock. I got the first manure spreader ever seen [here] and so put the fertilizer back on the land before its strength had leaked out."[4]

But then it was thought folly to terrace the fields on the hillside, to build a covered manure pit, and to erect a circular piggery that saved considerable man-hours in feeding the animals. Local farmers and the press made his innovations the butt of many jokes, yet he went on his independent and creative way. He could at the least point to awards won at the state fair for his stock breeding, which was influenced by his friendship with Luther Burbank, as well as the wise advise of experts at the University of California at Davis.

The ranch was now a massive project, with dozens of workmen in the fields, the barns, and on the Wolf House site. London had them erect the first concrete silo in California, dam a stream for irrigation and fire protection (as well as fishing and water play), rotate three crops in his fields enriched by the addition of both manures and nitrogen-rich cover crops, and follow exacting schedules for the care of the beehives, ducks, pigeons, geese, chickens, pigs, cows, bulls, and horses. He was proud of his self-sufficiency, bragging that only cement came up the long road from the valley below. He had his own blacksmith's shop, machinery to crush rock or mix mortar, draft animals to haul heavy burdens. He was prouder of this spread of land than anything he had done in his life.

By now London too was at the height of his celebrity. Having written stories of adventure with love interests obedient to the morals of the day, he retained his middle-class readership. Having written books and stories of social conscience in a style that appealed to working people, he was a folk hero to many in that class. The result was a daily pile of pleas for assistance. In response to one from an old socialist comrade, he explained with little hyperbole how he averaged one hundred gold-mine propositions a year, one hundred perpetual motion machines, three hundred manuscripts that hopeful writers expected him to edit, endless applications from men who wanted to leave in his care "their mothers, wives, children, grandparents, etc., while they pursue their own favorite phantoms," men by the score who wanted to die on his ranch from whatever fatal illness they suffered, and over three hundred propositions a year "to take care of people, furnish college educations to orphan boys, endow old ladies' homes with libraries, muck-rake the powers that be from one end of the world to the other, and contribute to every bazaar that was ever got up by a Ladies' Aid society."[5]

He left out another class of requests, from advertisers asking for the use of his name in testimonials. These he often accepted, with the result that readers frequently found his face and signature attached to a blurb for this breath mint or that suit. This clever cooperation with advertisers shows further his understanding of the media, how to use it to his best advantage. Had he lived in contemporary times he would have made use of talk shows, posters, children's games and cartoons, and any other device that would put his name before the public. He was never ashamed of marketing himself, indeed thought those who were above such acts only hurt themselves and the public, which enjoys such displays.

Most celebrities ignore charitable appeals, turn them over to a clerical service, or send out a standard form letter. From mixed motives of deep generosity and personal insecurity, Jack could not accept any of these options. The public had chosen to write him, after all, and as a socialist who had seen tough times, he believed the majority of these pleas were deserving, not attempts to take advantage. Thus, he read this mail thoroughly and selected cases for benefit, whether sending money, reading the manuscript, accepting a paroled man to work on the ranch, giving a job to an ex-convict, letting an ailing one die in a spot of beauty. To others he sent brief, kind replies, in some cases explaining why he was not wealthy.

In a few instances, the response invited friendship. One recipient was Ralph Kasper, a devoted socialist and wholesale cigarette salesman living in Chicago.[6] Jack traded opinions with him, shipped off books he thought Kasper should read, and in return was gifted with cartons of Sanos, Oxfords, Imperiales, and "explosive smokes" for tricking guests. Kasper got Jack's permission to print up copies of "Revolution" and similar socialist pamphlets for distribution and was fired from his job when his boss learned of his proselytizing. As will be evident later, Kasper proved a helpful contact once the movie business was underway.

Another beneficiary was Louis Hamburg, a fifteen-year-old San Francisco newsboy who wrote that he had read all of Jack's works and wanted to know if he could meet him in person. Charmed by the youth's naive enthusiasm, Jack had him up for a visit, and over subsequent months shaped the boy's reading. London told him to "live in the real world, not the world of illusion" and inspired him to attend socialist debates in the city. Charmian also took the boy to heart and sent motherly notes. He grew to idolize her, claiming "You are a woman above all women, and as I wrote long ago, a MATE for men to be proud of, to hold and fight for."[7]

It was easier now for Jack to take care of requests for help because he had bought a dictaphone, which allowed him to press records at any hour of the day for Charmian's later transcription. Consequently they saw less of each other, and she had less input into his various plans. He consulted with her briefly each morning to provide his latest manuscript pages and give his orders for research notes. When that meeting was over, he would call in Eliza to review the Wolf House construction and ranch management.

Though busier than at any point in their marriage, Jack was in good spirits. If anything, Charmian's friendships with the attractive young male guests made her more appealing to him. One evening she sang to Laurie's accompaniment, moving Jack to write her the following:

> I am still filled with the joy of your voice that was mine last night when you sang. Sometimes, more than any clearly wrought concept of you, there are fibersounds in your throat that tell me all the lovableness of you, and that I love as madly as I have always loved all the rest of you.[8]

She found the message "a love letter that made me move all day in a dream."

A week later Charmian went to Oakland for correction of the vaginal injuries remaining from her first delivery. Laurie accompanied her and joined her at the opera and theater beforehand. Jack appeared at the surgery to hold her hand while the anesthesia took effect. While going to sleep she still worked, for he wanted her to talk aloud so he could file her experiences away for use in a book. To her surprise he sent her violets in addition to the reading matter she more expected of him. His letters were teasing and playful, cajoling her to recuperate quickly and return to him. "To hell with telling you how much I miss you any more. If you don't hustle along I'll do some real flirting."[9] But she also received flowers from Laurie, who spent hours at her bedside reading aloud.

Jack wrote gossipy news he knew would cheer her, such as notes about the horses. When he informed her that her story "The Wheel" had been sold to both British and American magazines, she was pleased to learn her earnings exactly matched the hospital bill, allowing her with pride to pay her way for once. When she inquired whether he was jealous of her writing success, he answered, "Heavens! Artistic jealousy! There might be did I worship my work. As it is, for your sake, for *our* sake, I'd give anything to see you eclipse me."[10] When she pouted over the continued presence of the "intellectual hobos" who shared room and board with them, he corrected her, saying that the ranch was *his* problem and adding that what Eliza, Netta, and Wiget "have lost for me in cash is a thousand times more than the price of the few meals and beds I've given my bums. I've not much heart-throb left for my fellow human beings. Should I cut this wee bit out too?"

At the conclusion of her month's hospital stay, Charmian relished Jack's news that he had invited Laurie to join them on their annual winter cruise up the Sacramento delta. Laurie was the only person ever taken on one of these trips, which the couple had always cherished for the privacy they offered, the opportunity to renew and celebrate their intimacy. From her window Charmian searched San Francisco Bay with binoculars for the approaching *Roamer,* and found Jack "sweet and tender with his little sick wife." The next day, however, she was just as charmed when Laurie arrived to play piano for her while she packed for the journey.

The couple broke another ritual on this sailing as well: Jack announced he would do no writing; hence, Charmian would have no work either. Accompanied by Nakata and a Japanese chef, the three explored the delta in a carefree mood. They returned to Oakland in time for Christmas, which was spent visiting relatives. On the next day Charmian and a favorite cousin went to a local restaurant only to discover themselves facing a table with Jack, Bess, and the girls. Charmian was greatly upset by the sight and went to dinner and a play afterward alone with Laurie.

* * * *

Charmian completed typing *John Barleycorn* as 1913 rang in, and true to its superstitious-laden component, the year was most unlucky. It began with small crises, one after another, leaving little room for rebound. Young Irving Shepard, Eliza's only child, suffered a severe electric shock and was in bed many weeks. When Laurie left in early January for Australia, Charmian agreed with Jack's comment that "it was as if someone had died" and found herself unable to touch the piano. She took up the habit of sleeping down the hill at Wake Robin, perhaps to help Eliza in her nursing chores. Next they learned of the death of a Hawaiian acquaintance, who surprised Charmian by leaving some jewels to her. Later in the year a fine brood mare was found shot dead in a ravine.

In spite of these events, or perhaps because of them, the couple drew together in mutual comfort. To pay for his ranch dreams, Jack had mortgaged everything he could, including Charmian's own property, her "insurance policy." She trusted him, believed that whatever the risks he would find a way. What mattered to her most was not any worldly consideration, but that they be together, that he attain his agricultural vision. Consequently she joined him on ranch business, shopped with him for pheasant cockerel and hens, shire stallions, Jersey cows, and pigs. By mid-February, however, he was growing somewhat fanatical about his plans, pressing Eliza and Wiget hard, and had less time to spend with Charmian.

She found new diversion on February 27 when Allan Dunn once again came to visit. As with Laurie, she took Allan out riding and sang with him, sat by him as he painted landscapes, took long walks in the fields with him. Other guests were on the ranch, so they were not often alone, and Jack at times joined the two. By March 3, she noted, "Allan and I ride to Sonoma Mountain & have a glorious time watching the fog clear & crowd in again. Lovely, rainless weather—booful, but bad for ranch. Trees blossoming and flowers. Having a lovely experience." Very likely no actual infidelity occurred, for later in life Charmian made references to the time when she found it necessary to "raise the spectre of adultery" on her part to call Jack's own bluff on the issue. Many times she had stifled anger at dinner while listening to her husband support the case for free love. Monogamy, he claimed, was a necessary element in marriage, although for the "higher classes," meaning himself of course, divorce was permissable in the event one partner fell in love with someone else. Too, during some intimate conversation Jack had confessed breaking his vow to her just once in an overnight fling. Allan Dunn gave Charmian an opportunity to throw that news back in Jack's face.

On March 10 Charmian drove Dunn to the train and returned to "cuddle up father." They discussed her infatuation, and he proclaimed, "I am the proudest man in the world; I found that I have a heart." Charmian slept well that night. The next day she puffed up with pride, "Feel very much of a battle ground. But what men. I can't help pouting out my chest. But I am heartbroken over Mate Man's suffering. Just the same— he has learned about women from me." Clearly her daring to follow temptation not only sent a shock through Jack, who loved her "to death" for days afterward, even on the living room floor, but made Charmian more sympathetic for the feelings he had been holding back in his determination to play scientific and rational farmer.

The ranch had a steady flow of guests in April, Allan among them, but he was just one among many during these "Great days—full of beauty, of interest, of situation, Blue-eyed men." His effect had been intense and brief—just two weeks—and it was over.

Charmian's next mention of him in her diary was a mysterious "AD in papers" on June 24. The story was sensational. Allan Dunn, "well-known to literary and club set of the area," had admitted to robbing jewels from a noted hostess. He explained he had been unlucky of late in selling his stories and tried to tide himself over by stealing the jewelry during a weekend party and pawning it under the name of Elbert Hubbard (the noted printer and furniture designer from New York). His victim reported, "I don't think it was kleptomania. I think it was just a plain case of robbery."[11] The article itemized the recovered stolen items, which included a pair of Jack London's silk pajamas, which would have been easy to slip from Jack's sleeping porch. No charges were pressed, however, and Dunn fled to New York City, where some time later George Sterling found him posing with another hanger-on from the Crowd as husband and wife.

*　　*　　*　　*

On March 14, the day after Charmian called Jack's bluff, he wrote to an editor with a "splendid motif for a novel":

Three characters only—a mighty trio in a mighty situation, in a magnificently beautiful environment. Each of the three is good; each of the three is big. It will be a winner. It is all sex from start to finish—in which no sexual adventure is actually achieved or comes within a million miles of being achieved, and in which, nevertheless, is all the guts of sex, coupled with strength. Oh, my three are not puling weaklings and moralists. They are cultured, modern, and at the same time profoundly primitive.[12]

This marriage of Nietzsche and Havelock Ellis became *Little Lady of the Big House,* one of London's most curious and hotly debated works. Some critics call it his very worst book and others place it among his best. Evaluation of its artistic merit aside, it has deservedly spurred much speculation about London's intimate life.

The leading character of the book is Dick Forrest, manager extraordinaire of a quarter-million-acre ranch in the Sierra foothills. Now forty, "clear-eyed, calm-hearted, hearty-pulsed, man-strong," flashbacks tell how Forrest came to this place. His wealthy father had required him to be exposed to the poor, to know the seamier side of life, so that he grew up "a reared aristocrat and a grammar-school trained diplomat." By embracing all social classes, Forrest is classless, free from the strictures of any stratum.

Forrest demonstrates his independence when, orphaned in his teenage years, he flouts his guardian's urging and takes to the road. On one trek he watches a close friend die under the wheels of a train (as London himself had witnessed), thus learning "the mischance of life and fate, the universe hostile to man." From this point he commits himself to the philosophy that illusion must be discounted, for reality never lies. Returning home, he hires the best minds as consultants for his business. Following a decade of youthful fun as a "lusty, husky fool," he settles into marriage with a woman from a family of wealth and breeding. Their "Big House" is a massive Spanish-style hacienda and compound.

The story opens with Dick in his workroom, decorated like Jack's sleeping porch, arranged for total efficiency, complete with weather instruments, special lighting, books, a dictaphone, and thermoses. A Chinese servant enters and picks up a lacy boudoir cap, evidence of an earlier sexual encounter. Dick climbs a hidden stairwell to his library, just as Jack hoped to do in Wolf House. Through various incidents London paints a portrait of the cold-blooded American male, superb at managing objects, animals, and workers, yet out of touch with his feelings and insensitive to the possibility of genuine intimacy. He lives amid fecundity of his own making—abundant crops and the finest farm stock. Yet curiously he himself is sterile. In spite of his frequent chants to Paula, his wife—"I am Eros. I stamp among the hills . . ."—she remains childless.

Paula too is presented as not quite fully mature and fecund. When she enters for her assigned few minutes on his morning schedule, she calls herself his "Lady Boy" and other such paradoxical terms of maturity-immaturity similar to those the Londons applied to themselves. As he talks with her, he keeps his finger marking a spot in a book, glances at the clock to speed her off. She departs full of resentment, he unaware that "her voice was a trifle, just the merest trifle, subdued."

Later Dick announces to Paula and her sisters, who live with them, that Evan Graham, an explorer friend, is coming to visit. Evan, a tall blond gray-eyed man like Dick, is more graceful, less formidable. Graham's first sight of Paula is from the swimming tank, where he comes upon "a woman as white as the white silken slip of a bathing suit that molded to her form like a marble-carven veiling of drapery." She is crashing through the pool on the back of a horse, "her slim arms twined in yards of half-drowned stallion mane, her white round knees slopped on the sleek, wet, satin pads of the great horse's straining muscles." His response to this erotic posing is an odd mixture of imagery: to him Paula resembles a woman, a Dresden china figure, a midget, a tiny fairy, a boy, a pagan, a Maxfield Parrish reminiscence. Dick identifies her as his wife, a creature who has proved utterly fearless even under gunfire. Echoing a statement Jack once made to Charmian, he says, "Sometimes it seems to me that I don't know her at all, and that nobody knows her, and that she doesn't know herself." Their motto, he adds, is "Damn the expense when the fun is selling."

Evan becomes intrigued by the little lady. To him, she evinces naturalness and joy with her uncorseted manner, but more than that, pride "in every muscle, nerve, and quiver of her." He learns she plays piano "like a man" and is equally proficient at stock breeding and embroidery. Dick often brags about her—how she defeated insomnia, how she outsavages her stallions, how she can do anything she sets her mind to, not as he does, through careful plan and self-education, but with a "witchlike, irrational way." Evan observes, however, that Dick is cruel to Paula in subtle ways, makes her the butt of irrational jokes in public and brushes off her affectionate gestures. He senses her restlessness. One night she admits that the only rival she has had in their years of marriage is the ranch. Then, while Evan and Paula sing together one evening, each senses a madness drawing them together. Dick, nearby gambling at cards, fails to see the change.

Paula grows more outspoken in her criticism of Dick, attacking his preoccupation with efficiency and rationality. She responds to Evan's advances, shows him affection so openly that Dick finally realizes what is happening. Still, trapped by his rational ideology that he accept fate, he does nothing. Paula tells Evan that she loves both men and cannot choose between them. Alone, she wonders why Dick is not acting to solve things as he had always in the past. Meanwhile she cherishes the attention from both, though "almost with a touch of cruelty," for she knows at heart that Dick suffers behind his stoical front. "Deep down she was conscious of her own recklessness and madness, and of an end to it all that could not but be dreadful to some one of them or all of them." She decides to play the scenario out, come what may. She feels fully alive for the first time in her life—understandably so, for it is the first time she has taken control, rather than allowing another to make a major decision.

Dick's continued boorishness drives Paula closer to Evan's tenderness and humanity. Tortured by the circumstance, Dick one day admits to Paula that he has been unfaithful, then demands fidelity from her. He urges her to choose, saying he will give her a divorce. After leaving the room, she turns to go back and say more, but from the secret passageway overhears him on the phone coolly arranging a business deal. "There he was, with his love-world crashing around him, calmly considering dams." What she does not know is he has decided just as calmly to commit suicide through a feigned hunting accident.

The next morning from her bedroom Paula calls Dick at his office. "Red Cloud, I think I love you best. I have made up my mind now, once and for all." A shot rings out in the compound, and both men rush to find Paula dying. She tells Dick that she loves him best and is sorry there were no babies; she looks lovingly at Evan. While she loses consciousness the two men sing and chant to her. Then she dies, "Sleepy, boo'ful sleepy."

Little Lady upset readers in London's day for its gushing sexual imagery ("erotomania" cried a leading reviewer), its close portrayal of the tempting pull of adultery. Modern critics, on the other hand, deride its Victorian coyness and sentimentality, its unrealistic characters. Both were correct—it was too sexy for readers in 1915, when it appeared, and not sexy enough for readers beyond the sexually free twenties. But focusing on the sexual element of the story misses its main point.

Certainly *Little Lady* is as much a confessional as *John Barleycorn.* It was (with *The Iron Heel*) Jack and Charmian's favorite of his novels, for it expressed for all to see the detailed dynamics of a situation that almost destroyed their marriage. They were both proud they had not let the relationship die, that they had both after ten years learned about one another anew and strengthened their bond as a result.

It is understandable why modern critics consider it an awful book. The use of baby talk between the lovers repulses late-twentieth-century readers, yet it is an accurate depiction of how people spoke intimately to one another then. It was part of Charmian and Jack's own love language and can be found in other writers' stories of the day. Also, London is so determined to show why Paula (Charmian) is a fantastic person that he overwrites his descriptive passages. It is a tone poem of love for the woman who stood by him through the Long Sickness, the trials of the South Seas, the White Logic, and more. Beleaguered by his failing health, angry over problems in his business dealings, furious with Bess over her refusal to share the children, he found he needed Charmian more than he had acknowledged prior to the temptations of Laurie and Allan.

The book also upsets modern male critics because it cuts to the quick of masculine values, digs at their worth, and questions the purity of the Arcadian dream, the strive for perfection. London shows that relentless male achievement, even in the idyllic setting of agrarian reform, is not alone the answer to a man's needs. If he retains the traditional male values of

American society, those premised upon efficiency, show of strength, emotional repression, he cannot develop fully as a human being.

Woman cannot save man simply by virtue of being female, for she is ultimately trapped by society's dismissal of her self. Though Paula had more options and resources than most women in society of her time, she had not been allowed responsibility for herself and could not handle the decision to choose maturely between the two men. Dick has used her as he would a fine breeder stock animal, except she was ironically childless. How appropriate that Paula's bedroom should be in a tower, for she was the trapped princess incarnate. It is a damning indictment of sex roles, too damning for many readers to admit.

Several critics have preoccupied themselves with the conclusion of the book, claiming it was evidence Jack had an unconscious wish to kill Charmian. This is true only in that passions of love release those of violence, and much fiction enacts those most tabooed fantasies lovers feel at times for the loved one. But this type of comment distorts the feelings expressed by the married couple in the book: Dick is planning to kill himself over losing Paula, and Paula does kill herself rather than lose both men. Yet no one has suggested that Jack was thinking of killing himself rather than lose Charmian.

The odd ending of the book most likely resulted because London simply did not know what else to do. Like his other triangle plots (of which he had many), he exposed weakness on the part of one of the men, which should have allowed Paula an easy decision. But in identifying so strongly with Dick, London could not allow the most logical conclusion, that Paula go off with Evan. Anyway, that had not happened in real life. As Charmian wrote Blanche during the writing of the manuscript, "Jack is reluctantly killing off his perfectly good and sweet and nice little heroine in his current novel—but it's got to be done, because she loved 'em both and couldn't choose either."[13]

The uneasy resolution of the novel reflected a problem remaining in the real-life relationship. Laurie Smith and Allan Dunn had alerted Jack to a part of himself he had cut off in his determination to conquer the earth, the darker feminine side. Both men were the Mate-Comrade types he had praised to

Charmian, the men who combined male and female in their psyches. Like Dick Forrest, Jack had come to emphasize the masculine side of his nature, and depended upon Paula/Charmian to fill in the vacant feminine side. Her threat of adultery forced him to reevaluate his behavior, and he began to change his thinking to reintegrate the feminine into his self-concept. In a real way, on March 13, the day Charmian confronted Jack, he underwent a conversion experience.

But in his relationship with her, he was unable to relinquish easily his desired view of her as both a child and a woman. Indeed, more than ever afterward, he referred to her as his "Kid Woman," the "girl who never grew up." What he did not understand was that the choice was out of his hands. On March 13 Charmian came into her own as well and saw the reality of the sad, failing man beside her. She was woman enough to see the importance of playing to his fantasy needs.

* * * *

That important symbol of their union, Wolf House, neared completion. Jack teased one reporter that he had "canned the Louis Quinze stuff and the blue room and pink room ideas and built this for beauty, comfort, and a workshop." Artist Finn Froelich was kept busy sculpting and carving furniture for the new home. Charmian often visited the site, letting its powerful mass quiet her worries about finances and the dubious likelihood of getting pregnant again.

On August 21, the day before the planned move, they rode down to the site one last time to wonder over their hopes fulfilled, their sacrifices repaid. Back at the tiny cottage, Jack presented Charmian with a copy of *John Barleycorn* with the inscription, "You know. You have helped me bury the Long Sickness and the White Logic."

That hot and stifling night a young girl in Glen Ellen went outside to sit on the porch in hopes of catching a cooling breeze. As she sat, she fixed her attention upon a glow off in the distant dark, a light shimmering like a star, gradually brightening. Suddenly she realized it was not a star but a fire. Calling to her mother, she realized the fire was on Jack London's property: Wolf House was burning down! Eliza too happened to look out the window, spotted the fire, and sensed an empty hopelessness.

Even today in the dry months of that valley, farmers and country folk fear blaze. August in this land means that five months have passed since rain, the dry brush and eucalyptus sheddings waiting like ready victims for the flames. Though water might be trickling through nearby creekbeds, the sharp gullies and ravines of the mountainside obstruct its easy use to douse flames. At midnight Eliza unhappily knocked on the sleeping porch windows to rouse Jack and Charmian. They saddled horses for the quick mile ride downhill. "And our Wolf House is destroyed. Mate and I are cheerful enough until we get back, at about 5 A.M. Mate breaks down completely."

The fire could have been the result of spontaneous combustion. Workmen were varnishing the woodwork in recent days, leaving cans of combustible liquids and rags on the site. The foreman, Forni, had been careful each evening to gather any loose rags but had been distracted that night and forgot to do so. The next day Jack and Charmian brought him up for dinner to reassure him. "He's almost crazy. 'My child! My child!' he cried before the burning house." The fire continued to burn for several days until the surrounding redwoods Jack had soaked stilled the spitting embers.

Cleaning up the ruins, a workman came across a candle in an air passage of the house. Other evidence of arson was found. As Charmian explained to Anna Strunsky:

Our fire, a most ghastly reality, dear Anna, and a true press report, for once, *has* crippled us, as you suggest. We lost nearly $50,000 net, Jack tells me. But more than any financial loss is the deep hurt that we felt over the wanton destruction of so much beauty. . . . the deepest hurt lies in the indisputable fact that it was set afire by some enemy. Isn't that awful? Who it could be we have no idea.[14]

They never learned the culprit.

Despite Jack's chest pains and Charmian's heart palpitations, the couple maintained their usual schedule. September was state fair time, which meant two weeks in Sacramento during which they studied livestock competitions to prepare their future entries. Jack allowed no break in his writing and soon completed *The Mutiny of the Elsinore,* a melodramatic sea story inspired by the *Dirigo* voyage. Their lovemaking increased. Charmian recommended to a sympathy-note writer, "In the meantime, love each other; never be indifferent to a caress, never fail to appreciate each moment of loving. Every kiss we take or give leaves us less of life to live."

14

WORLD
WEARY

I did what I could. But it was all of no use
—of no use!

—*Ouida*

As if the threat of adultery and the loss of Wolf House had not been enough tragedy, Jack suffered other losses in 1913 as well. He instigated a major break with his daughters. Since early 1911, when Bess had fought his hopes for more visitation, Joan had noted a gradual change in his attitude toward her. As the correspondent for the family, she was responsible for relating news and making requests for funds. Consequently, she took the brunt of Jack's growing hatred of Bess. One day, without warning, he canceled her piano lessons. Another day, when he learned she had been baptized as an Episcopalian and was in a confirmation class, he bullied Bess into transferring the girls' religious affiliation to the Unitarian Church. With more money going out for the ranch and Wolf

House than coming in, he became fussy about small expenses.

The final blowup began because of Joan's consideration of a career in the theater. Greasepaint ran through the veins of many Madderns, and Joan wanted to join her aunts and uncles on the stage. Perhaps recalling how her own family had stifled her same dream, Bess supported her eldest daughter. Jack was displeased and invited Joan to stay with him on the ranch for a while during a vacation, possibly to have more sway in her career plans.

Had Wolf House not burned, the conflict may have been resolved more easily. As it happened, Bess did not tell Joan about the fire. Astonished at receiving no word of sympathy from his daughter, Jack wrote her: "My home, as yet unoccupied, burns down—and I receive no word from you. When you were sick I came to see you. I gave you flowers and canary birds. Now I am sick—and you are silent. My home—one of my dreams—is destroyed. You have no word to say."[1] These were tough words to send a twelve-year-old girl, but they were mild compared to what followed. Subsequent letters grew confusing and cruel.

Bess and Jack were equally responsible for forcing Joan into an irresolvable conflict. By now she was aware that her mother's obstinacy regarding visitation was unreasonable, a way of punishing Jack that was punishing the girls as well. Yet, as Jack's diatribes against Bess increased, Joan "was shocked into realizing for the first time how much I loved her, and a fierce loyalty to her kindled a resentment of his unjustice and unkindness that distressed me."[2]

Finally, in early October he met with Bess and Joan to discuss the matter. Even then Joan was hopeful "that somehow Mother and Daddy would compose their differences and be friends again, that Daddy would say he was sorry for his unkind words about Mother, that Mother would finally see that no harm would come of my visit to the ranch." Jack showed up unsmiling and stern; Bess was tense and silent through much of the discussion. To Joan's surprise, Jack quoted at length from the Bible and referred often to Christ. Joan pleaded with them "to grow up a little more," but she realized the situation was being ruled by the presence of an invisible force, Charmian, "and Mother and Daddy were adversaries, not parents seeking only the happiness of the daughter they both loved."

Afterward Joan wrote her father that she would not visit him on the ranch until she was older and pleaded with him to appreciate her dilemma. Although his subsequent letters were less frequent and remote in tone, she thought the crisis had passed, that he was just taking time to readjust to her refusal. Then, on February 24, 1914, he sent a brutal notice effectively divorcing himself from his first family. "When I grow tired or disinterested in anything, I experience a disgust which settles for me the thing forever. I turn the page down there and then." He wrote of having warned Bess that her denying him the opportunity to see the girls would result in such disgust, and that he had reached that point. He made clear he would help Joan materially, and wished "to see you marry for love when you grow up. That way lies the best and sweetest of human happiness." But as for her everyday activities, he had no concern. Toward the end he grew even more mean-spirited:

> Unless I accidentally meet you on the street, I doubt if I shall ever see you again. If you should be dying, and should ask for me at your bedside, I should surely come; on the other hand, if I were dying I should not care to have you at my side. A ruined colt is a ruined colt, and I do not like ruined colts. . . . I realize that a colt is ruined by poor training, even though the colt never so realizes.[3]

He did not see her for more than two years. By then, Joan, more wise than either parent, had through persistent letters won back his interest. But he was a very different man then, in the final stages of his fatal illness, his passion spent. Only a hint of their previous relationship returned.

Joan and Bess were handy scapegoats for all the failures in London's recent life. Joan herself realized this years later when she considered the bad news Bess had kept from her, and she empathized with the frequent blows her father had suffered on the ranch. She forgave him, preferring to remember his more noble dreams, his spirit of endurance through adversity.

*   *   *   *

One area the adult left-wing Joan London explicitly ignored in her story of her father's life was his involvement with the movies. His interest had been piqued in late 1911 when he received an intriguing request from stage actor Sydney Ayres. Ayres had just signed on with Selig Polyscope and wondered if Jack would let him make *The Sea Wolf* into a motion picture. Jack thought it was a fine idea and that Ayres himself had the perfect physique to carry off the lead. They met on the ranch to discuss the matter, and Ayres went off to Chicago to sell his plan to Selig management. Not understanding the slower pace of business decisions, which depend on group negotiation, Jack grew impatient. When he arrived in New York prior to the *Dirigo* voyage, he wrote Eliza, "Let Sydney Ayres and his motion picture proposition go to hell," for he had found a woman who was going to serve as his agent and sell his stories to movie companies.[4]

Apparently nothing resulted from his New York contact, for late in 1912 London was in touch once again with Ayres, who was now under contract with Balboa Amusement Company in Los Angeles. Balboa was one of many independents competing against the monopoly Motion Pictures Patent Company, an alliance of major producers with the Edison Manufacturing Company. In holding patents to motion picture film, cameras, and projectors, the MPPC threatened outside producers by confiscating bootleg equipment and pressing lawsuits. Despite these threats, shrewd independent owners like the Horkheimer brothers of Balboa accepted the risks for a chance at quick fortune. Indeed, the spying, chicanery, and sometime brutality were accepted as normal business. Such an opportunity to test his wits was irresistible to London, a man prideful of his mental agility.

His initial attraction to the business was money. Jack and Charmian recognized that movies would only add to their publicity machinery. Longtime manipulators of the press and magazines, they understood how any mention, foul or fair, could help the marketing of their products, be they books or social ideology. On January 13, 1913, Charmian mused in her diary, "Maybe we'll have a company working on a stage on the ranch next summer."

On February 26 Jack assigned the movie rights for his novels to Ayres, who used them to advance his case with Balboa. On April 26 Jack and Charmian took the steamer to Los Angeles, a city they despised, to settle details. An amended contract

provided that Ayres was to produce four films by July 1, one
of which must be ready for exhibition by August 15. Thereafter
Ayres was to produce four films a month for an average of six
months of the year.

The time frame, ludicrous by today's standards, was typical
then. Nickelodeons changed features daily, forcing the producers to create one- and two-reel films within a single week to
meet the demand. With an accumulation of over 170 fictional
works in print, London had no worry of meeting his side of the
contract.

Spring 1913 seemed a promising time for both independents, such as Balboa, and famous writers. The Edison Company had recently lost a patent suit against independent
William Fox in federal court. Then the public acclaimed the
nine-reeler *Quo Vadis* in New York on April 21—even though
the admission price was an astronomical one dollar. Independents grew convinced that, contrary to MPPC claims, Americans would sit still for more than five or ten minutes in a
darkened theater.

Important too for Jack was news that American Film had paid
Roy McCardell thirty thousand dollars for the story "The Diamond in the Sky." Before this, most writers earned fifty to five
hundred dollars a story for film rights, and no novelist had ever
received more than one thousand dollars. Ayres told London
that the one-third interest he held in the Balboa productions
would bring in a steady income of five hundred dollars a week,
that the first movie to be shot, "Just Meat," should bring in at
least thirty-five thousand dollars.[5]

Clearly Balboa and London were well placed to profit from
a new epoch in movie making, one in which audiences sat in
comfortable and commodious theaters to watch lengthy plots
unfold. They were also both ripe for exploitation.

Ayres was as naive and self-interested in the bargain as Jack.
He wanted to become a director and hoped his rights to the
London material would win him that role at Balboa. His letters
to Jack belied his ignorance of business. While he spoke often
of his efforts to produce the "works of quality" Jack's novels
deserved, he erred at the same time in discrediting the Horkheimer management. For example, he observed how the company was spending excessive amounts of money in the

construction of studio sets he claimed were unnecessary. It was not a way to keep London's confidence.

Nevertheless, Jack seemed generally pleased with the progress and expressed few doubts. Indeed, he approved the filming of a scenario based on *The Sea Wolf* and urged Ayres to go ahead. He kept close track of the progress of the films and had strong opinions on their use. Thus, he wrote screenwriter Charles Menges that his recent "*John Barleycorn* should not be used in moving pictures until it has made an ascertained strike as a book." His plan was to wait for interest to grow "not only with the Prohibitionists, but, as you say, with the suffragists."[6]

In late June, Jack began to receive other information. With the July deadline approaching, H. N. Horkheimer wrote to negotiate an extension of the contract. He advised Jack that twelve to thirteen thousand dollars had already been invested in getting the pictures together and just a bit more time would ensure their completion. He also bad-mouthed Ayres, calling him a "lovely personality" hampered by a lack of business experience. His direction was "just as good as the average director, but not the genius Jack London's works call for."[7]

Jack did not know about the chaos at Balboa. They had hired one of the best cinematographers of the day, but he was slowed down by having to learn to use the new Bell & Howell camera provided him. Cash-flow problems prevented steady and well-planned production. Even without this knowledge, Jack grew suspicious. Fond of Ayres, he wired Horkheimer on June 30: "Come up and see me. I don't see where Ayres is hurt if he gets his percentage without doing any Director's work. Come up and drive brass tacks with me to a brasstack conclusion. Telegraph when coming so I can meet you at train. Bring wife if you can."[8] Encouraged by this response, Horkheimer responded that Jack's was "the best telegram I ever received in my life. You won't regret sticking to me in this proposition."[9]

Unfortunately, on July 6, as the men sat down to discuss the matter, Jack developed abdominal pains and was rushed to Merritt Hospital in Oakland for an appendectomy. The Horkheimers accompanied Charmian on the trip. She noted in her diary that the contract had been void as of July 1, indicating the Londons felt they had the upper hand in the negotiations.

The next day Horkheimer wired that Ayres wanted to sell his

rights to William Selig, a producer affiliated with the MPPC. Meanwhile, having learned that Horkheimer had been dealing behind his back, Ayres contacted Jack, who was determined to resolve the situation. He warned Horkheimer to "discontinue any work on my stories" until all three men could review the matter following Jack's operation.[10]

Unknown to both Ayres and Horkheimer, another suitor had entered the picture. An employee of Balboa, Hobart Bosworth had been sent to San Francisco to arrange the rental of a boat for use in *The Sea Wolf.* Instead, he contacted London, trying to convince him to reassign the movie rights to a company he was forming.

Bosworth had attractive credentials. Like Jack, he had gone to sea:

> A great many experiences of the rough life we had shared. I had been a prize fighter and slung wheat sacks and shoveled coal in San Francisco, a city Jack loved as I did, with its peculiar charm which leaves all of us old boys with deep yearnings of nostalgia. Jack once said that he had only one experience of rough living I had not shared. He laughed, his eyes twinkling—I had never been to jail, though God knows, I probably deserved it more than he![11]

In this reminiscence Bosworth was being modest. Like Jack he was by this time a successful artist, a landscape painter and then an actor. His energy, curiosity, and drive fit London's model of the ideal man. He also had the backing of Frank Garbutt, an astute and perceptive Los Angeles capitalist made wealthy from successful real-estate and oil dealings.

Bosworth and Garbutt had another quality Ayres and Horkheimer lacked: Anglo-Saxon blood. (In her later discussion of this time, Charmian referred to "the wily but ingratiating Hebrew, Mr. Porchclimber.")

As soon as Jack was well enough to travel, he and Charmian went down to Los Angeles, where Ayres, Horkheimer, and Bosworth waited, each certain he was about to acquire London's literary gold mine. Jack and Charmian allowed themselves to be wooed, first by the Horkheimers, then by Ayres, who took them to the Selig production lot, finally by Bosworth, who showed them some of the many movies he had performed in. Certain they had found better producers for the films, on July 26 the Londons signed a contract with Bosworth and Garbutt.

During July, while the secret negotiations were underway, Bosworth had remained at Balboa, which was still working on the London films. Three had been completed: *The Sea Wolf, A Piece of Steak,* and *To Kill a Man.* Several employees later claimed he used this time to convince several Balboa workers to join his new company, which was not difficult given their problems getting paid by Horkheimer. Another employee claimed that Bosworth unsuccessfully pressured him to quit printing copies of the London films and suggested an "accidental" destruction of the negative for *A Piece of Steak* through creative tampering with the electricity.

Once the contract was signed, Bosworth rushed to complete his version of *The Sea Wolf.* As a way of adding authenticity to the stories, each was to begin with footage of London himself. On August 14 Bosworth shot scenes on the ranch of Jack with his favorite shire stallions, Neudad Hillside and Maid. The next day Jack and Charmian watched Bosworth play Wolf Larsen on a boat in Sausalito Harbor. Movie-struck, Charmian rushed off to see *Quo Vadis* and urged Bosworth to hire one of her nieces.

Days later, while the Londons were mourning over the ashes of Wolf House, a messenger brought news of a lawsuit charging Jack with violating his contract with Horkheimer, and Bosworth with chicanery at Balboa. It was also argued that any novel serialized in a magazine was public property because no copyright notice had accompanied it. This attack inspired Jack to defend writers' rights. Informing George Brett of the "pirate raid" on his material, he asked for assistance: "It seems to me that the present situation is as big as the whole writing and publishing game in the United States. Prompt action is needed, and prompt assurance that you are joining in the big fight."[12] Jack also called on the Authors League of America, which he had helped form, to lobby for changes in the copyright law (which they eventually did with success).

Meanwhile Garbutt oversaw most of the defense of the case. When it was clear Horkheimer intended to market his versions

of the stories, Garbutt recommended "an end run" by notify-
ing the theaters that only Bosworth films were legitimate. This
strategy had little effect, for the exhibitors, a ragtag group,
were mostly interested in obtaining cheap reels to fill their
projectors, rather than in the niceties of literary rights assignments. Three months later Garbutt's men were still jostling
with Horkheimer's men in various cities over the exhibition of
The Sea Wolf.

More curiously, Garbutt's dealings with Horkheimer shifted
from tough negotiation to a virtual accession to Balboa's demands. In December he advised Jack to pay Balboa five thousand dollars to eliminate their "inferior product" from the
market. Horkheimer then demanded ten thousand dollars plus
the right to sell the films under different titles.

The case was finally settled in federal court, where Jack came
out the loser. Garbutt was made trustee of the Balboa films and
charged to sell them for exhibition under new names, with all
proceeds to go to Balboa. Garbutt was to receive no fee for his
services and was to sell to any purchasers Balboa found. Neither party received damages, and each had to pay its own legal
costs. (By now poor Sydney Ayres had made a hapless move to
the American Film Company in Santa Barbara, where, six
months after the collapse of his plans, he began to wonder if
Jack had not been partly to blame for his loss. Ayres was too
nice or too innocent to follow up with a lawsuit on his own
behalf.)

As if this suit were not enough, London discovered other
raiders. He sued Biograph for stealing the story "Just Meat"
and titling the movie *For Love of Gold.* This case went on for
several years before London, who won the case originally, lost
it in the U.S. Second Circuit Court of Appeals in 1916. His
other battle was waged in England, where another sea adventure falsely linked to him was being distributed at the same
time as Bosworth's version of *The Sea Wolf.*[13] Garbutt did his
best to stifle the bastard version.

If there was one promising note, it was the reception of
Bosworth's portrayal of Wolf Larsen. The film promised to
outshine the competition because of its quality. The public and
critics raved, and it looked as though the Londons could count
on receiving some money to pay off the old Wolf House bills

and start over. Beaten by Balboa (though he never admitted it), Jack nevertheless readied himself to enjoy the returns from the Bosworth film. As writers in the movie business have been discovering since its inception, being paid for film rights was much less predictable than collecting a royalty check from a publisher. Consequently, throughout 1914 Jack wrote pleading poverty in an effort to encourage Garbutt to send him some of the profits—to no avail. Although his contract with Garbutt specified he was to receive the first five thousand dollars of any profits from the films, all he was seeing were legal bills.

London displayed a rare patience and obsequiousness toward Garbutt, who had an uncanny ability to hold him off. One of Garbutt's tactics was to enrapture London with the publicity angles for the various films. For example, when *John Barleycorn* was ready for distribution, Garbutt recommended: "In connection with your presidential campaign [a publicity stunt of London's to stir up temperance support for his prohibition book], this ought to make pretty good dope. Possibly you can come through with a burst of virtuous indignation which may add fuel to the flames."[14] Later, when censor Maud Murray Miller of Columbus, Ohio, ordered the crucial scene of children drinking cut, Garbutt hired New York press agents to arouse the Women's Christian Temperance Union and prohibitionist ministers around the country to protest: "Impress upon all parties the mistake in weakening the lesson by eliminating the telling parts. The censors will be too broad-minded to be offended if handled diplomatically."[15] An astute publicist himself, London must have appreciated Garbutt's clever manipulation of social groups to sell tickets at the box office.

Interspersed with news of these public relations ploys were Garbutt's claims of insolvency. On March 19, he stated, "Our sales are one-fourth the outgo, but may be increasing." On June 6, there was still no money, and *The Sea Wolf* negative had been destroyed in a fire. On July 24 trouble arose with *John Barleycorn* when the head censor in Philadelphia, in the pay of the breweries according to Garbutt, railed against the film. On September 11, *Martin Eden* was "not going well." Two days later unnamed exhibitors from the east complained London's movies lacked plot. On September 14, London still had received no money, and the MPPC was threatening to sue the company over the use of patented cameras. By November, the latest films were doing poorly, with the Chicago censors now threatening to delete boxing scenes from *The Valley of the Moon*. Garbutt also hinted that the accounts of William Hodkinson, the main distributor, were problematic. By December, Garbutt advised, "The weather has been very bad here—so that we have had photographic troubles aplenty."

In late January 1915, a year and a half after signing the contract, Garbutt finally sent a check to Jack. During the year London received a total of ninety-three hundred dollars, well below his expectations of fifty thousand dollars per film. That March London wrote that he had seen only half of the movies himself and had not only failed to make money on the deals, but because of copyright battles had paid eight thousand dollars out of his own pocket to cover legal costs.

It is tempting to conclude Garbutt had been highly successful at playing the game known as "hide the money," which is still prevalent in the movie industry today. Though their agreement specified he was to send London financial accounts on the fifteenth of every month, he released none. Only after considerable badgering from London did he send money, and then only as an advance against royalties.

Garbutt's claim that the eight films were financial losers is dubious.[16] Garbutt had been willing to buy out Horkheimer to protect his investment and kept close watch over the marketing and distribution of the films. His public relations schemes must have had some impact, and his product, featuring Bosworth, a recognizable name if not a star, was praised in the press. The Londons' personal scrapbooks were filled with news clippings on the films, and letters from friend Ralph Kasper in Chicago hinted at the extent of Garbutt's marketing and its success. Kasper wrote that *John Barleycorn* was being widely advertised both in newspapers and through posters placed in all the elevated train stations. *The Sea Wolf,* which played at the Ziegfield Picture Playhouse, was announced via a "thoroughly attention-getting and compelling" two-color electric sign. Charmian informed Kasper that the same movie ran two weeks at the million-dollar Strand Theatre on Broadway in New York City, where it "broke all records."[17]

Other facts belie Garbutt's claim of financial ruin. The dis-

tributer he discredited, William Hodkinson, was a major in-
novator in movie exhibition who introduced managerial order
and planning to his segment of the chaotic movie industry.
Hodkinson was respected for behaving responsibly in his business dealings. Hardly a fly-by-night dealer, he was the founder
of Paramount, and in starting that group had signed Bosworth/
Garbutt, along with Morosco of the famed theater chain to a
twenty-five year agreement. Paramount took the lead in intro-
ducing multireel films with runs of more than one day. Its
phenomenal success in reshaping viewing habits forced others
to follow. The movies ceased to be "a cheap show for cheap
people."

On the other hand, Garbutt was not totally guilty in the
matter. Some of his criticisms of the later movies, such as the
public's dislike of the endings, and of exhibitor cancellations,
ring true. Moreover, a commitment to the feature film was
premature from the exhibitors' point of view. It would be a
scant year later when these important figures in the business
warmed to longer screenings. History played its hand as well
—by late 1914 the war in Europe, where London's name had
been a popular draw, kept people out of the theaters. Also, in
the United States, London's adventure tales were suddenly
feeling old-fashioned to a public that finally made the adjust-
ment to an urban society.

In February of 1915 Garbutt reported that Bosworth was
unhappy with the reception of the latest film and was seeking
another affiliation. When Bosworth did move to Universal,
Garbutt said the actor's work had not been "of the class that
is demanded of our program." He advised Jack to sell his rights
to Universal, so long as Garbutt received some profit from the
deal, and said he would pretend to balk over the sale so Universal would up the ante.

By May the relationship between Garbutt and London had
deteriorated to short letters. Fleeced, London was grateful to
walk away with a letter from Garbutt granting him the right to
create scenarios "without prejudice to contract." The wily
businessman went on to become a major behind-the-scenes
operator in the motion picture business, so trusted that when
scandals involving Fatty Arbuckle and others threatened the
industry itself, feuding company heads asked him to oversee

the public relations campaign on their behalf. He managed that task just as smoothly as he had manipulated Balboa, Jack London, and Bosworth.

Several years after Jack's death, Charmian and Bosworth became business partners. One day, when he felt she was ready to hear the bad news, he explained to her how Garbutt had essentially robbed both of them of several hundred thousand dollars through his scheming. By then she saw no point in prosecuting but used this knowledge to bargain hard in future movie dealings, and did so successfully.

* * * *

London's movie lawsuits were further complicated by an act of generosity made years earlier. Before departing on the *Snark,* he had given Joseph Noel dramatic rights to *The Sea Wolf.* To simplify his court cases, he asked Noel to return the rights to him. Noel objected, and claimed exorbitant payments were owed him for what had initially been a gift from Jack. Noel's argument was that his dramatic rights included motion picture display, and he should be recompensed accordingly for the loss.

By early January 1914, Jack had decided he had no choice but to go to New York and deal with Noel and his lawyers on other court cases in person. Charmian was dazed. There was scarcely money for Jack's transit, so she had to stay behind, fearful of the pressures New York would impose on his fragile spirit. After saying good-bye to Jack at the train station, she was embarrassed to find herself penniless, and had to borrow cab fare from Martin and Osa Johnson, who had also come for the farewell. Returning to their flat in Flora's house in Oakland, she took solace in the theater to fill the time between telegrams and letters.

On January 26, Flora called Charmian at a friend's house to read a telegram that had just arrived from "Amy": "London is spending all his time with a woman who lives at the Vancourtland Hotel on 49th Street." Charmian was "startled but not scared of course," relayed the story by wire to Jack, and went off to see a performance of *Kismet.* For years Jack and Charmian had been besieged by husbands and boy friends of women who had been seduced by one or another Jack London imposter.

Enterprising female con artists had even impersonated Charmian to gain the comfortable hospitality of the unsuspecting rich. In a time when travel was slow and newspaper illustrations seldom provided accurate portrayals of their subjects, it was easy for the crafty, dramatically gifted to exploit the innocent. Charmian may have convinced herself this was another such episode.

Jack answered that the telegram had been a malicious joke, saying he had discussed the incident with the manager of the Vancourtland. He closed the letter by pronouncing his desire to die "with my head on your breast, your arms about me, my arms around you."

A later letter compared her to a thoroughbred, which no man may ride "without tenseness and irritation along with the corresponding joy that is aroused by the very tenseness and irritation. . . . You are my one and only woman, and my feelings and heart I need not repeat. You will remember the last months from Allan's time and know what my feelings and heart are."[18]

Although Jack's responses calmed any concerns Charmian may have had about a strange woman in the hotel, his behavior was not above reproach. One night he went out with theater manager Frederick McCloy to Harlem. Afterward his party asked the leading lady and several show girls to join them for dinner at a café. Later, five of the group decided to enjoy the high life downtown and sped southward in a taxi. At 83rd Street the cab in front of them collided with a limousine, and to avoid the wreck their own cab overturned. Describing the event to Charmian the next day, he wrote, "Our taxi flew to pieces as if it had been exploded by a bomb. As usual, I was under the whole pile. Four other persons were mixed with me, mostly on top of me. And broken glass! I lay and spit it out of my mouth for a very long time—everybody still piled on me."[19] Amidst the crowd of police and spectators, Jack and his party escaped from reporters into another cab and sped again southward. Subsequent news stories failed to identify the famous victim and his friends.

The interesting question is whether Jack was seeing Sophie Loeb during this visit. Though no evidence for such meetings exists, later correspondence with her, preceding another planned trip to New York, hints that the relationship had not been forgotten by either.

Jack's various business dealings did not conclude well. He was given to snap decisions and dispute. Patience had never been his strong suit, and its absence brought heavy financial losses as well as the alienation of the lawyers he had hired to fight his battles.[20]

During Jack's absence George Brett visited the ranch to work out a contract with Charmian for her two *Snark* books. She was surprised to hear he wanted the final manuscript of the first within a few months. When Jack returned he hired Jack Byrne, the widower of his sister Ida, to take over some of the clerical work, primarily dealing with the ranch. Though dismayed at first by the intrusion on her territory, Charmian became grateful for the free time to work on her own books.

Her work was soon interrupted by the call of war. Several months earlier Hearst had offered Jack a lucrative salary to cover the Mexican revolution when it came to a head. In 1911 London announced his pleasure in identifying with the "chicken thieves and outlaws" who were trying to overthrow President Porfirio Díaz and his clique of wealthy landowners. As was his usual practice, he also wrote a fictional piece to express his political beliefs in a fashion that would be attractive and palatable to middle-class readers. The *Saturday Evening Post* published "The Mexican," the story of Felipe Rivera, a zealous young revolutionary dedicated to buying weapons for the revolution against the Diaz dictatorship.

By the time Hearst contacted him in the fall of 1913, however, Jack was not concerned with revolution. He had never been a solitary comrade; cut off from his socialist friends in the East Bay, he had retained little of his youthful fervor. By this time his socialism had been twisted into a kind of agrarian paternalism: his ranch would become a model community of healthy, educated workers and their children. Since the workers could not help themselves, he would use his munificence and magnanimity to create for them the best possible world. Because that grand social experiment would take much money, Jack wired Hearst he would go—only if accompanied by Charmian and Nakata. Hearst agreed, but then the two had a falling out over the salary.

Meanwhile, Americans with extensive holdings were anxious to see the country put its bully hand into the civil conflict south of the border. They took advantage of already existing anti-Mexican sentiments to portray Pancho Villa and Emiliano Zapata as wild men in order to strengthen the hand of the more malleable Venustiano Carranza. American oil interests also worked to support the defeat of the British favorite, Victoriano Huerta. In late March 1914, General Huerta's officers arrested a young officer from an American naval squadron that was stationed offshore. When Huerta failed to apologize for the incident, President Woodrow Wilson authorized the seizure of the customs house in Veracruz, an invasion that resulted in four deaths. The U.S. Army soon followed, with General Frederick Funston leading four regiments to occupy the city. Needless to say, their presence added to rather than reduced the dangers to American residents there, who found themselves the targets of attack from Mexican citizens on all sides of the conflict.

Just before the invasion of Veracruz, in anticipation of major activity, the editor of *Collier's* wired Jack to leave immediately for Mexico, which he did, along with Charmian and Nakata. In Galveston they happened to meet the head of the Gulf Steamship Line, who offered them free passage on his ships any time and helped to expedite Charmian's admission into the war-ravaged country. One would hardly think the couple was preparing to enter a combat area, for they spent their days in wait for passage shopping at fine stores. Now in the early stages of menopause, Charmian was secretly joyful over the false belief she was pregnant. Their delay turned out to be caused by the War Department's false accusation that Jack had written "The Good Soldier," a propaganda pamphlet urging young men not to sign up for the army. Thanks to the intervention of his major journalistic competitor, the dashing Richard Harding Davis, he was allowed to go ahead on a transport ship and managed to obtain the unheard-of permission for Charmian to follow soon afterward on a destroyer. Instead, she chose a fruit boat bearing a Norwegian flag, bring with her letters from many army wives to their husbands in the war area.

At this point they seemed to enter a stage for the theater of the absurd. Jack did go on brief expeditions into combat areas, several times to help bring out refugees from behind the lines, once on a sortie to find a sniper's machine gun. But the real reporting was being done by younger men, such as revolutionary John Reed, who rode with the peasants and lived in their camps. Most of the time Jack and Charmian joined other reporters in the general atmosphere of celebration in the town, where their ready American dollars were welcomed to feed the war-torn economy. Charmian and the few officers' wives that had been allowed into the area behaved as though on holiday, strolling about the parks and cathedrals, buying exquisite laces, designing dresses to be made up by the meticulous (and inexpensive) seamstresses. She had developed an eye for opals, and Jack always made sure she had enough money on her to buy some on her many shopping trips.

Charmian also went on journalistic assignments for him, took notes, and explained what she had seen. For example, while he was on a ship for several days, she remained behind to cover a local provost court. Jack then used her notes to prepare an essay on the court system, written as if he had been the observer. She accompanied him on more gruesome expeditions, such as that to a hospital ship, where they watched amputations.

London's articles reflected the shift in political sympathies that accompanied his becoming a large landowner and employer. Seduced by the untapped wealth of the oil fields, he foresaw a new Yukon for the United States, believed our country had a duty to "police, organize and manage Mexico" to protect its resources for our use.[21] Many of the freedom fighters, he argued, were simply bandits and outlaws, previously powerless men who now hid behind the barrels of their guns to murder, rape, and rob without mercy or principle. Today's historians acknowledge that some revolutionary activity was indeed an outlaw banditry on fellow peasants.[22] But London's charges were one-sided. His strongest attack was upon the mestizos, the half-breeds who possessed "all the vices of their various comingled bloods and none of their virtues."

The radical press winced in disbelief at his imperialist and racist announcements. Socialist John Kenneth Turner charged that London had actually been paid by oil interests to write a brief in their behalf. Even the *Nation,* a more moderate voice, wondered how the "eminent apostle of the red revolution should audibly be licking his chops over millions of gold dollars wrested from its rightful owner, the Mexican peon."[23] Reflecting on this period of his life, his daughter Joan argued bribery was unnecessary: "His was a more tragic sellout, for he had been subsidized, bought body and soul, by the kind of life he had thought he wanted, and it was destroying him."[24]

To say success corrupted him, however, seems an oversimplification of this apparent break with socialism. True, he busied himself with the movies and other business ventures in hopes of making a large return, but his goal was not idle consumption, but capital for his ranch experiments. As he explained to a reporter for *Western Comrade,* "To me my cattle are more interesting than my profession. I feel that I have done my part. Socialism has cost me hundreds of thousands of dollars. When the time comes I'm going to stay right on my ranch at Glen Ellen and let the revolution go to blazes. That's the way I feel now. I suppose when the time comes I'll let my emotions get the best of my intellect and I'll come down from the mountain top and join the fray."

In light of the tragedies of recent years, Jack's bitterness and desire to hide on the mountain is understandable. The socialists, even his friends, overlooked these and tended to see his life as a series of successes. Emma Goldman jibed him for living in his "Dreamland" while she fought on the barricades, and even hinted that Charmian was perhaps responsible for the loss of Joy, because she was so physically active during the pregnancy. Never a realist about everyday life, George did not understand the fervor Jack held for his farming, nor the tremendous organizational and financial burden it represented. If Jack's comrades and friends were feeling resentful toward him, it was not all his doing—they were faulting him because he was unable to be the Jack they wanted.

The photographs of Jack taken during the Mexican revolution hint at another source of weariness. For the first time a significant edema is apparent—a sign of serious weakening of his kidneys. As with previous adventures, Jack's body gave out and forced an early return to New Orleans. Amebic dysentery almost killed him. Characteristically, Charmian rose to the occasion, turning the hotel room into a hospital room, sending

Nakata for a hot plate and kitchen tools so she could cook rice water in the room to nourish him. Unable to sleep at all, Jack was a difficult patient. Still, she controlled everything, kept his other reporter chums from disturbing him, and patiently sat with him day and night to attend to his needs. She noted the drugs he took did not work well, a sign Jack had developed higher levels of tolerance after years of self-medication. She kept her solitary vigil aware of her own narrowing waistline, a mocking reminder that her hopes once again had proved fantasies.

15

THE
SOUL
EMERGES

Along the silent way, time's shadow
  fell,
And years covertly touched with ashes
  white,
Spring came but wan to blossoms
  fading gray.

—*Margaret S. Cobb*

Tragedies often force a conversion experience, a new definition of one's relationship to the world. The loss of two
children, Wolf House, financial investments, and full health
broke Jack's defenses, opening his mind to possibilities he had
previously mocked or dismissed as lunacy. Defeated by matter,
he shed his materialism and began a quest into the spiritual
realm. For London, this search was not so much religious as
psychological.

Both *John Barleycorn* and *Little Lady of the Big House* hinted at
the changes. The drinker examines his self-destructiveness, his
weakness built on false pride. Dick Forrest discovers the scientific approach to life has deceived him, for it considers and
values only those objects amenable to easy measurement. A

successful rancher and businessman, he has nonetheless failed to master his own soul. Paula's death will force him to integrate into his own personality those characteristics he had denied— intuition, playfulness, love.

But the book that most marked London's change of thought was written in the months following the destruction of Wolf House. He called it *The Star Rover.* Its theme was a far cry from the superreal naturalism of his earlier writings—it concerned reincarnation and transmigration.

Signs of fascination with the spiritual realm had crept into some of London's previous work. His various stories of Alaskan, Polynesian, and South Sea tribal cultures often emphasized and praised their mystical and intuitive ways, their respect for the environment, as superior to the white man's use of science and force to control nature. He believed magic and superstition were false terms used to ridicule a real power present among native peoples.

The most direct predecessor to *The Star Rover* was a novel completed in 1906, *Before Adam,* the story of a Pleistocene tribe's hopeless struggle against the superior Fire People. He designed the story within a frame, the dream life of a contemporary narrator: "In my dreams I never saw *anything* of which I had knowledge in my waking life. My dream life and my waking life were lives apart, with not one thing in common save myself. I was the connecting link that somehow lived both lives. . . . It was not till I was a young man, at college, that I got any clew [sic] to the significance of my dreams, and to the cause of them."[1] Based on the professor's explanation of racial memory, the narrator concludes that a separate and distinct personality takes over during the night, and that this personality's memories possess a different fund of experiences than that of the waking mind.

London used a similar frame idea for *Star Rover* but shifted his interpretation of the events from a materialistic to a spiritual base. This time the narrator, Darrell Standing, is a lifer at San Quentin frequently tortured by being laced in a straitjacket, a canvas cocoon actually in use at the time. Another prisoner, Ed Morrell, convinces Standing that it is possible to endure the days of suffering by training the mind to leave the body. Morrell claims that in this transcendent state he has left San Quentin to visit his sleeping mother and haunts from his past.

Standing attempts the technique and finds himself traveling not in contemporary time but into the past. He experiences his previous lives as a swashbuckling count in France, as a boy at the notorious Mountain Meadows massacre where Mormon settlers murdered a wagon train of hungry travelers, as an Elizabethan sailor shipwrecked in Korea, as a Danish free-slave of the Romans serving in the militia of Pilate at the time of Christ's death, and as an American sailor shipwrecked on a desolate island alone for eight years in the early 1800s.

When London finished the book and sent it to Roland Phillips, editor of *Cosmopolitan,* he sold it on two themes. One was his knowledge of actual prison conditions, described to him by ex-convicts he had befriended. The other was:

> . . . the tricks I have played with philosophy, exposing the power of mind over matter, and making it good accessible stuff to the Christian Science folks, and for all the New Thought folks, and the millions who are interested in such subjects in the United States today. While this is pseudo-scientific and pseudo-philosophic, nevertheless it will make it most palatable to most of the rest of the folk who will read it.[2]

London was correct in recognizing the appeal of the work to the many middle-class readers fascinated with spiritualism. He was not being totally honest with Phillips, however, in playing down this material as pseudo-scientific. The truth is that London himself was considering these ideas seriously.

While Jack had been an unrelenting materialist in his twenties, by the time he married Charmian he had moderated his position. For the most part the shift was made to recognize the existence of an undefinable power known as love. As he and Charmian shared one tragedy after another, he clung to their relationship as his main ballast, and more frequently mentioned the redeeming value of love between man and woman in his letters and writings. Three of the main stories in *Star Rover* center on love, and in a late chapter his paean to love gushes over the pages:

Sometimes I think that the story of man is the story of the love of woman. This memory of all my past that I write now is the memory of my love of woman. Ever, in the ten thousand lives and guises, I loved her. I love her now. My sleep is fraught with her; my waking fancies, no matter whence they start, lead me always to her. There is no escaping her, that eternal, splendid, ever-resplendent woman.[3]

It is woman "who works magic in our dreams and in our veins," who tempts men to fight and conquer and create. It is a reaffirmation of the vision of love and womanhood the Londons had been reading of in nineteenth-century Romantic literature for many years and had come to adopt as true for them.

The more significant and dominating argument of *Star Rover*, however, is its claim that the spirit is real and outlives matter. Because it is so contradictory to most of London's previous thought, it is easy to think he was in fact just playing to a particular audience. This conclusion ignores London's practice of always using his writings as *his* soapbox, shaping the material to make it more congenial to his middle-class readers. He never championed a position with which he disagreed just for the sake of selling a book. Indeed, he was fearless about pushing unpopular material, such as his revolutionary essays, in spite of the effects criticism would have on the sale of his other works. When putting pen to paper, he kept his integrity.

London's growing attention to metaphysics was probably inspired by two sources: normal personality changes at midlife and the experiences of people close to him. His more recent writings reflect what psychologists discovered later—that in the late thirties men in our society shift from external exploration to internal examination, to investigation of life's meaning. Truths are questioned, assumptions overturned. London's self-doubt was of course assisted by significant losses, indications that all was not well in his ties to the universe.

Yet more direct and mundane influences affected him. Much of his youthful discrediting of spiritualism had been bound up in his twisted feelings toward his mother. He blamed her Indian guide's poor advice, not his father's weakness, for the family's poor financial state. He even gave this experience to a doubting prisoner in *Star Rover,* Jake Oppenheimer. Always doubtful of Standing's claims of traveling to other times, Oppenheimer tells how his mother "never came across with any goods" after consulting the spirits. London then mocks this view, one he had held for many years, by having Standing observe how Oppenheimer "was an earth-man in his devotion to the irrefragable fact, and his logic was admirable but frosty."[4] Throughout the book Oppenheimer is discredited for being a man of no faith.

By 1913, however, Jack was acquainted with three people who had known experiences similar to those described in *Star Rover.* He was quite familiar with Charmian's "beatitudes," her uninduced trances in which she participated in events from many eras and cultures. Not given to analysis, Charmian simply accepted these incidents matter-of-factly as a personal trait that made her different from others. She enjoyed the "visits," shared them with Jack, who like her did not try to interpret them within some epistemological framework. They just were.

London also knew that Eliza had special abilities, which would be called extrasensory today, and she did not discount one such vision of Charmian's that included her. When both women were elderly, Charmian awoke one night in a Paris hotel room to find Eliza ablaze in light, walking toward her. The next day she called California and learned that Eliza, unknown to Charmian, was ill and had almost died at the very time of the vision. The powers of these two women awed him at times, and their casual acceptance of their unusual knowledge must have swayed him. They laughed with him at the seance machinations of Flora, Netta, and the flocks of others who had been duped by the planchette and its automatic writing, thus lending credibility to their particular wisdom, separate as it was from the fads of the time.

Furthermore, he knew that Luther Burbank, the plant wizard, deserved that name because much of his activity in the laboratory was described by assistants as being uncanny, stemming from some sixth sense more precise and adept than scientific principles. Burbank's mysticism centered upon his hands, which he used not only to "read" plants, but to heal others. It is not surprising, then, that Darrell Standing's occupation was that of "an agriculturalist, a desk-tied professor, a laboratory slave, interested only in soil," a man who was successful through his use of instinct, not science. Just as Burbank could sense a plant's future growth chart by touch, Standing could read a cow's butterfat production by eye.

London's new beliefs are evident in his repetition of philosophical arguments throughout the book, to the point where they intrude upon the story and eventually spoil his attempt. He seems almost to be trying to convince himself, an earlier self, of previous error; then, toward the end, he celebrates his revised position, glorying in its rightness. He is so successful that he undercuts the force of his antiprison abuse argument, for the reader becomes so accepting of the transmigratory adventures that the real-life torture of the jacket recedes. And when Standing goes to the gallows at the conclusion, the reader feels little loss, convinced that Standing will appear again in the future in another form. The certainty of his reincarnation not only diminishes the injustice of his prison life, but makes his capital punishment a release. Thus, the book's metaphysics negates its social propaganda.

Although London repeats three themes throughout *Star Rover,* he was not fully committed to all equally.

One theme was that of racial memory—"I am all of my past, as every protagonist of the Mendelian law must agree." As a Darwinian, he was attracted to this idea, and in many of his writings intimated the effects of past memories on his characters, particularly the intrusion of the primitive on the modern mind.

As for the theme of transmigration, he had an open mind. He was versed in stories from Eastern cultures of yogis being able to separate mind from body, and he must have wondered about Charmian's stories, whose rich sensual images conveyed a reality hard to deny.

He was less a supporter of reincarnation. Indeed, in *Star Rover* he muddled the idea within his discussion of racial memories.

While it is wrong to say London subscribed to all the ideas in this curious novel, it is clear he was affirming the existence of the spirit, of phenomena beyond the immediate reach of our limited ways of knowing. He also wistfully hoped that Standing's discoveries might indeed be true, that his own death would not be final, like a squashed mosquito. He wanted faith.

He may have hoped at one point to find an answer in Christianity. One portion of *Star Rover,* which he called his "Christ Story," was his favorite. The notion of doing a book on Jesus had been on his mind for some years, but this one section of one novel was his only expression of that goal.[5] Although Jack had received no religious education in his family, he was exposed to the Bible at an early age, for it was often the only book a pioneer would carry across the country. He had not objected to his daughters' being reared in a religion and had during some visits to the East Bay attended Congregationalist services with Charmian. Overall, his attitude toward Christianity was shaped by Nietzsche, leading to a respect for the principles of Christ and a ridicule of his hypocritical followers. ("For me to believe in their redeemer," suggested Nietzsche, "Christians would need to sing better songs and look more redeemed.") Thus, attacks of the California prison system in *Star Rover* were accompanied by reminders that these odious practices were born of Christian society.

London's preoccupation with Jesus during this period suggests serious consideration on his part, not just the milking of history for a plot. Recall that he urged his daughter to study Christ as a model for adulthood. His re-creation of Christ's last days is wonderfully rich in its portrayal of Biblical times, depicting the conflict among the various Jewish sects and Romans so realistically that one hears the crowds taunt Pilate, sees the dust from the donkey's feet, and hears the whip crack on Christ's back. Yet the story also has the mark of London's unconventional mind, for the lead character, Radnar Lodbrog, a Roman soldier of Danish birth, admires Pilate and wonders at the craziness of the Jews, their obsession with finding the correct religious position.

He also portrays Christ as a nonbeliever would then, a strange leader of fishermen, a "king of the beggars and his fellow beggars," who enjoys wine and "the company of nameless women." As for his being the Son of David, Lodbrog's lover advises him, "It is absurd. Nobody at Nazareth believes it. You see, his whole family, including his married sisters, lives there and [he] is known to all of them. They are simple folk, mere common people." When Lodbrog's lover and Pilate's wife change their mind and accept Jesus as the Messiah, Lodbrog laughs about the "charmer of women." His conversion soon follows, when the Roman soldiers cloak Jesus and mock him as King of the Jews: "And I, looking on, learned the charm of Jesus. Despite the cruel mockery of his situation, he was regal. . . . It was his own quiet that went into me. I was soothed and satisfied, and was without bewilderment. This thing had to be. All was well. The serenity of Jesus in the heart of the tumult and pain became my serenity."[6] Encouraged by his lover to use his militia to free Jesus, Lodbrog refuses, saying to do so would be to interfere with the truth of the Messianic prophecy. "Am I greater than the gods that I may thwart the will of the gods?"

London's "Christ Story" was less about Christ than about others' conversions. It is a story of faith, as is the subsequent tale, in which a shipwrecked American sailor has faith in himself to sustain a good life all alone on a tiny outcrop of rocks. London did not convert to Christianity as a result of his search, but he did open his mind to a system of belief that incorporates more than facts and figures. He would find his faith in a few months, with the appearance of a book, the translation of a work on dreams by a Swiss psychologist.

* * * *

As Jack turned inward and grew more meditative, Charmian moved out into the world. Her conversion had come during her flirtations with Laurie and Allan, when she recognized her power to attract others and hurt Jack. Wisely, she stepped back before acting on her feelings, accepting Jack's apology and request for forgiveness for taking her for granted. Nonetheless, she felt invigorated by the experience, even proud of herself, and did not want to lose that heady feeling of acting according to her own needs. She was no longer going to bite her tongue and behave like the proper lady when Jack or others misbehaved. As it happened, Jack did not misbehave, indeed showed every sign of being a contented husband, preferring his wife's company to any others.

Upon returning from Mexico, she put her own work first, the completion of the *Snark* manuscripts. She was anxious for adventure and hoped news of World War I would mean another joint war correspondence trek with Jack. She was also obsessed with pregnancy, noted every deviation from her bodily patterns, went several times to her doctor in expectation he would say she was with child. Meanwhile, Jack was writing *Little Lady,* and both would cry as they read various passages aloud from it.

While they sealed their loyalty to one another, they found their ties with others weakening. The most significant shift was in their relationship with Netta. Even after marrying Jack, Charmian continued to be bound to her aunt, to share almost every imaginable intimacy with her. Throughout the entire *Snark* voyage, Netta was the only one to receive personal letters from Charmian, some running several dozen pages. Clearly Netta expected to be told everything about her niece and to be allowed to comment on her and Jack's behavior. Jack's attachment to Netta remained strong as well—until he realized how poorly she was managing his business affairs. Nonetheless, he continued to contribute toward Netta's living expenses.

Once the couple moved away from Netta's vicinity, she grew irksome, angry over being cast out of Jack's limelight. As Charmian began to believe in her own self-worth, she started to question Netta's behavior and motives. She turned more to other Wiley relatives, who must have supported her growing criticism, for she felt free to pass on disparaging comments about her aunt. It was these relatives who nursed her following her hospital stays, who solaced her following tragedy, and who gave her a sense of family membership she had never known as a child. They were solid, upright, successful middle-class folk who appreciated Charmian for herself, and unlike Netta were not influenced by the fact that their relative happened to be married to one of the most famous men in the United States.

In the summer of 1914, Netta started on a rampage that was to continue for two years. She learned that Jack had put a mortgage on Charmian's Berkeley property, as he had done with all his properties in his attempt to settle the financial losses from the Wolf House disaster. Netta bluntly stated that this move was inexcusable. Using self-serving logic, she drew a lengthy picture of Charmian's responsibilities to her. Simplified, the argument went: Charmian's several inheritances during her teenage years almost broke up Netta's marriage because Roscoe wanted the money to be put toward Charmian's support, in other words, to feather his nest indirectly. Netta had intervened and made sure the money was invested in the Berkeley properties. Charmian had sold one to fund her trip to Europe, had later built a house on the other. With regard to the latter, Netta raved, "She was *never* to risk that property. I had saved it at the expense of my blood and muscle, and she had no more right to ever let it go out of her hands or jeopardize it in any way."[7] The agreement was that, upon Charmian's marriage, she would inform her husband of this arrangement. Meanwhile, Charmian was to use the rental profits from the property to pay Netta monthly support as well as additional bills. Concluding, Netta averred, "I *have confidence* that the dear child, *in her heart,* sees the ethical right of such course toward me." She also accused Jack of being a wastrel for ignoring her in her old age.

Now forty-three, Charmian was hardly likely to take well to being called a "dear child" and with Jack was furious at Netta's interference. The fact is that not only had she met her obligation, unsavory though it was, but Jack had contributed to Netta's upkeep as well. Jack responded that it was he, not Charmian, who paid the insurance, taxes, and other expenses on the Berkeley property, that, while he had lost ten thousand dollars already that year, he had not neglected to support his relatives.

This was not the only matter Netta complained about. She and Edward wanted Jack to rebuild pipes they had previously removed to improve their water supply. He was not about to satisfy a problem they had brought upon themselves.[8] His response was to them a challenge to warfare. That each felt it necessary to convey their positions in writing, instead of visiting the other's nearby home or placing a phone call, indicates how alienated the two couples had become.

The Londons' ties with the members of the Crowd were also shifting during this time. Now divorced from George, Carrie grew closer to Charmian and visited her on the ranch, where one night they had a gay time together "ragging" to the phonograph. George had moved to New York, where he drifted between Sag Harbor, his family's original home town, and New York City. He was lost without Carrie, did not even take up with other women (though he may have taken up with young men),[9] and seemed to be performing an act of penance for his poor behavior toward his wife. His luck with publishers ebbed and flowed, and he still gave accounts of his latest efforts to stop drinking. His sweet and generous side continued to bloom, as he took in Bowery bums and cooked omelets for them.

Other members of the Crowd had left the area as well. Mary Austin was moving toward what became her eventual resettlement in the southwest, which she extolled so well in her later books. Arnold Genthe was in New York City, along with Joseph Noel (who was driving Jack and George crazy with his confusing and contradictory claims about the progress of the Millergraph company). Jimmy Hopper had bought the Sterling house in Carmel from Carrie but was no longer part of Jack's circle of friends. These days Charmian and Jack were more likely to entertain other wealthy ranchers and socialites living in the valley than bohemians. More to the point, the bohemians no longer were—they had grown up and were dealing with their respective successes and failures.

During the fall of 1914, when the couple took their annual *Roamer* cruise of the Sacramento delta, Jack developed a puzzling and persistent rash that failed to respond to doctoring. On their return in early December, he went down alone to Los Angeles to force money on the movie deal from Garbutt. Rebuffed, he returned saddened, and told Charmian there was no likelihood they could rebuild Wolf House. They sought solace again on the *Roamer,* where she helped him compose "The Acorn Planter," a play he hoped would be accepted for production at the next Bohemian Grove outing. Determined to distract Jack from his growing disabilities, she forced playfulness —snowball fights in the Sierras, a renewal of the boxing matches—despite her own problems with chronic neuralgia of the neck. She would be his "little Kid" if doing so would ease his dark moods, and it usually did.

Jack's physical ailments were likely as much a result of his self-medication as the underlying kidney disease. While on the *Roamer* holiday, he received a medicine kit from his doctor containing relaxants like aconite and belladonna, along with painkillers such as heroin, morphine, and opium, all legal drugs at that time. Although prescriptions were required for these medications, he had no trouble getting new supplies, and taught himself to make up injections, using his medical books as guides for dosages. He took rightful pride in the reduction of his alcohol consumption, neglecting to see his new addiction to drugs. Of course, the notion of such addiction was little acknowledged by anyone then, and he and his doctors likely believed they were following a wise course.

His deterioration was not lost on Charmian, who began to note his symptoms with the regularity she used to display in recording cribbage scores. She could not ignore that his body was now large and puffy, not from overeating but from the buildup of fluids. Months later, in spite of a relatively quiet life carefully orchestrated by her, he showed little improvement. In February 1915 he suffered a severe foot inflammation, which he diagnosed as rheumatism. It was probably gout. He spent several days bedridden on Charmian's sleeping porch, where he read to her between sleeping spells. "Happiest period we have spent here in years," she noted, "No crowd, lots of work, happy spirits. A load off my hands to have a secretary."[10]

*   *   *   *

When Jack felt well enough to travel, the pair attended the 1915 World Exposition in San Francisco, then boarded the *Matsonia* for Hawaii. Fearful of the consequences of several lawsuits relating to the movies and his other business ventures, Jack had transferred most of his property to Charmian's name and thought it would be prudent to leave the mainland while the cases chugged through the various courts. She welcomed the warm and healing climate.

The islands were not what they expected. Commenting on Charmian's writings about this period, Hawaiian historian Ruth Tabrah praised her as an "astute observer" who understood that "Hawaii was indeed a paradise . . . but only for the well-to-do," a paradoxical land where a few wealthy cosmopolitans and military elite ignored the growing power of the Polynesian and Oriental working class.[11]

It was not just the social schisms that upset the couple. Honolulu showed sad surprises. The sands in front of their beloved Seaside Hotel had washed away, leaving an uninviting coral hummock whose knife-sharp projections prevented enjoyment of the water's shallows. A forbidding seawall buttressed the hotel lawns; in place of its charming tent houses now stood the Outrigger Club, with its bath houses, lanais, and dance pavilion. The only recognizable landmark was the date palm that once cornered their cottage, now locally dubbed the "Jack London Palm" in remembrance of their earlier visit. "And all this meant Ford, Ford, Ford!" complained Charmian. Their young surfing teacher's public relations schemes had been eminently successful, to their dismay.

Exploring the city, she found only growth and change. Areas once devoted to marshlands and duck ponds now were dotted with landscaped bungalows. Military fortifications cut off entry to Diamond Head's rosy cradle. Residences slithered into the valleys, past the midlands of Kapiolani Park, up the ridges of the vernal heights. The automobile had made the island smaller, the trip around the perimeter now taken easily in one day.

Charmian found it strange to drive over roads they had once traversed by carriage or on horseback. Hearing that Kilauea was erupting, they rushed to the Big Island. Then they joined the meanderings and celebrations of a congressional junket that had come on a so-called fact-finding trip. Returning to Molokai, they were pleased to learn the population had dropped from one thousand to six hundred over the past eight years, thanks to new treatments that meant most of the afflicted need no longer be isolated.

In a teasing letter, George Sterling wrote, "I suppose you're having a great time. I can see the day coming when you and Charmian get a submarine and escape your friends entirely." He was right—they would have done so given the chance.

One day Jack told Charmian of a vision he had experienced while lying on a California beach long before he met her. His arms over his face, he heard above the splashing of the surf the voices of a man and a woman. For a long time he could not locate the source of the sounds. Then he saw a couple coming slowly from the water, talking cozily "as unconcerned and comfortable as if sitting in chairs or on the sand." He grew sad, wondering if he would ever find a woman "with whom I could go out to sea, without boat or life-preserver, hours in the water holding long comradely talks on everything under the sun, with no more awareness of the means of locomotion than of talking."[12]

This story helps explain why they took some rather frightful chances with the ocean during this vacation. In particular Charmian counted two incidents throughout her life as proof of their valuing courage as the most important virtue after love and loyalty.

The first episode began one heavy-surfed day when Jack asked Charmian to follow him into deep water. Outrigger Club members warned them it was hardly a day for surfing, but he rebutted they were going out to swim, not surf. Now experienced in handling heavy breakers, they were confident of their abilities to handle the water. Getting beyond the shallows through an almost impassable mass of seaweed to face the stupendous crashing waves itself was a struggle. Charmian heeded Jack's instructions to "keep flat, keep *flat*" and pushed past the surfline into the calmer, deeper waters. From there, after a half-hour's steady swimming, they seemed no closer to shore. Were it not for the appearance of several Outrigger members on surfboards, they might have perished.

On another day, in deep water, Jack was seized by a cramp in his foot, "from which he suffered at night, a painful and increasing symptom of breakdown in his ankles." She turned him onto his back and treaded water while massaging his leg. Again, a passing surfer came to the rescue. They lay Jack on the board and worked on him until he felt able to swim ashore on his own. Charmian wrote about this incident to Anna Strunsky:

> If we had the least panic, the cramp would have been augmented as likely as not, and we might have both drowned. We took it as a mere incident; because we knew its gravity we comported ourselves as if it were all in the day's work, or play. And we went out the next day, wiser than ever before, knowing that each knew how to handle a like situation—with little fear of it.[13]

Charmian's interpretation of these events is telling. She explained she had implicit faith in Jack's judgment (which in truth had never failed her in the past):

But that a small, sensitive female of the species should
follow him in the water where experienced members of
the Outrigger failed to go, and that she should not lose
her head in his disablement, from his angle surpassed
intellectual achievement, because it called for spiritual
courage. "I'd rather see my woman to be able to do what
she did, than to have her write the greatest book ever
published or unpublished," tersely summed up his philosophy of values.

She trusted him completely, but he did not seem worthy of her
trust in these circumstances. It was foolhardy to place them
both in life-threatening situations, a reckless move he would
not have taken in the past.

Eventually Charmian realized that Jack's behavior had undergone a change, that he was more tense and argumentative
than she had ever known. Always a man who enjoyed debate
and controversy, previously he could stop arguing before he
had pushed a point too far. Now he seemed more driven and
determined in his verbal parrying and uncharacteristically held
grudges against others. Similarly, she noticed how Jack often
made excuses not to join daytime social activities, preferring to
stay in to read or even sleep. She was not very concerned,
however, because he continued his writing, completing two
new novels about dogs (*Jerry of the Islands* and *Michael, Brother
of Jerry*), which when published would stimulate the formation
of animal welfare clubs and protective legislation both in the
United States and Europe.[14]

Following five months of rest, they returned to Glen Ellen,
with a new valet. Nakata had fallen in love during the visit to
Hawaii and decided to marry and become a dentist. His departure was a great loss for them. Jack had once observed to
daughter Joan that he was much closer to Nakata than to her
because he had shared so much of his life with his servant.
Nakata also missed them, and always had only good words to
say about his life with the Londons.

Jack faced a new lawsuit, this time surrounding the Jack
London Grape Juice company. "I go into the cleanest sort of
business, to make the best nonalcoholic drink known, and I get
it in the neck, *pronto*—just like that."[15]

Upon returning to Glen Ellen, Charmian developed anxiety attacks and heart palpitations, which ended when her first book appeared in print. Anna Strunksy's first book, *Pere Lachaise,* was also about to appear, and Charmian responded, "We are wildly happy about it. Widely as our books differ (I hate to think how widely in thought and executions, dear Anna) I think it is just sweetly wonderful that you and I, Anna and Charmian, so long bound by dear ties, should each have a book published in the same year."[16] She need not have held such fears about *The Log of the Snark*—it was a most creditable book.

Macmillan distributed this 487-page journal of the South Seas portion of the voyage in October 1915. Critics responded favorably, praising it as equal to Jack's earlier volume about the journey, *The Cruise of the Snark.* More than one reviewer apologized for approaching the book with prejudice, believing her story would be mediocre or simply a rehash of Jack's material. One observed, "She writes with charm, she shows keen observation and an abounding interest in the human side of the experiences she met with, and she knows how to enliven her pages with humor and anecdote." Another mentioned that "... being a sociable sort of woman, she had no trouble getting into the palaces, the homes, and somewhat into the lives of the people. Being naturally curious, the author took special interest in the women, in their customs and habits, their religion, morals, and social standards. Few writers have gone into these features as thoroughly and as carefully as Mrs. London." Reviewers agreed that her future books were worth anticipating. Only one cynical New York critic looked askance, suggesting that some of the scenes reminded him "of the not so pretty pictures of one of those Gilbert and Sullivan islanders, in being just a bit pot-bellied."[17]

The majority of the critics were correct. *The Log of the Snark* is an intimate book, both touching and amusing in anecdote, filled with splendid passages of description. Modern readers might find some passages sentimental or quaintly naive, but the voice was modern for its day. London scholars have virtually ignored the work in a manner suggesting not that they have discounted it so much as simply failed to read it. In that regard they have been no different from other followers of famous men, quick to dismiss or ignore the words of the women who were intimate with them. In doing so they have neglected the major detailed document of Jack's day-to-day character.

Fortunately, Charmian did not have to deal with the rushed judgment of modern critics and, buoyed by the good notices, sat down to complete an accompanying volume on the Hawaiian segment of the voyage.

The couple decided to return to Hawaii in December for Jack's health. Before departing, they spent Thanksgiving Day with Harry Houdini and his wife Bess. In a rare entry of special praise, Charmian wrote, "Charming Houdini. I shall never forget him." The four got along well and agreed to try for future meetings, little dreaming that, three years later, frequent meetings would occur between only two of the participants, Charmian and the magician.

The year 1916 rang in with promise. Jack had just completed *Hearts of Three,* a book based on a movie script composed by *Perils of Pauline* writer Charles Goddard. The twenty-five thousand dollars he received from this deal, part of a movie contract with Hearst, settled most of his debts. The mortgages were lifted, and with them, financial worries gone for the first time in their marriage. Eliza divorced her recalcitrant husband. Netta was out of their life temporarily. Joan and Becky were back in Jack's good graces. The ranch was thriving under Eliza's careful management.

Despite the tragedies of recent years, despite his failing vigor, Jack London was able to write a stranger who inquired on the value of life:

> . . . after having come through all of the game of life, and of youth, at my present mature age of thirty-nine years I am firmly and solemnly convinced that the game is worth the candle. I have had a very fortunate life, I have been luckier than many hundreds of millions of men in my generation have been lucky, and, while I have suffered much, I have lived much, seen much, and felt much that has been denied to the average man. Yes, indeed, the game is worth the candle. As a proof of it, my friends all tell me I am getting stout. That, in itself, is the advertisement of spiritual victory.[18]

16
REDEMPTION

My wages taken and in my heart
Some late lark singing,
Let me be gathered in the quiet west,
The sundown splendid and serene,
Death!

—*William Ernest Henley*

How different this couple must have appeared now to friends on the islands. Both were overweight: Jack from his illness and consequent lack of exercise, Charmian from a slight middle-age softness that seemed much more on her tiny frame. He teased her, calling her "Fatty," but she did not look plump once fitted in her clinging wool tank suits, which she knew showed off the strong, supple legs he adored. Though he was thirty-nine, she forty-five, he was the older-looking of the two. He was tired, he was dying from kidney failure, and he consciously chose to live out these days away from the pressures of publishers, creditors, or ranch hands.

Accepting this last respite with grace, he seldom drank, save for a "near beer." His daily schedule was simplified: morning for writing, afternoon for rest, evening for playing bridge.

Charmian seemed revived from the previous years' trials. Perhaps it was the success of her book, perhaps it was resignation to her motherless state, perhaps it was a subconscious response to Jack's deterioration. She showed a new self-confidence, her happy public face matching her contented feelings about herself.

The visit began auspiciously. On New Year's Day they attended a reception for Queen Liliuokalani, who received guests in the Throne Room for the first time since her overthrow over twenty years before. Accepted members of the military scene, Jack and Charmian also attended a ball in the armory, dinner at the country club, and finished off with a night of wild fun at Heinie's restaurant. Jack did not drink at all throughout the evening, which ended with a storm. Charmian recorded only beauty: "Rain it did, and bountifully, a tepid torrent of liquid jewels in the many-colored lights of the city streets, which kept no Pierrot nor Pierette indoors. The very gutters ran colored streams, what of the showers of confetti."

During most of the seven-month stay they rented a small house on Kalia Road near the Halekulani Hotel. There they entertained as on the ranch, only more lavishly and more often. They filled a round table seating twelve almost nightly, with Charmian keeping records of seating plans and menus. It was as though she were the primary host, unlike the situation at the ranch, where Jack's preferences reigned, where men's rougher sociability sometimes overran women's gentle manners.

Their hospitality was possible because, through his writing, Jack was magically defeating their debts. For a brief period they lived the charmed lives of the well-to-do, off to polo matches, automobile races, horse races at Kapiolani Park, military reviews, historical pageants, surfing and swimming contests. Jack even relinquished his work schedule to accompany Charmian, whose popularity pleased him.

An introduction to Mary Low, a member of the eminent Parker clan, roused London's growing interest in spiritual issues. A woman of extraordinary knowledge of local history, Low captivated Jack with island lore and tales. She so delighted the couple that they invited her to accompany them on a six-week tour of the major ranches and ruins. Her folklore inspired

Jack to return to writing short stories, a genre he had abandoned several years earlier out of deference to the larger earnings available from novels. He had written about the islands before, but now a fresh spirit inspired him. His earlier credos —social Darwinism, materialism—had crumbled, and unhappy with developments in the labor movement, he seriously questioned staying in the Socialist party.

Filling the void was the young science of psychology, with its speculations about the unconscious. The impact of this revolutionary idea on London is clear in his final writings, which glow with rich, evocative symbolism and haunting story lines. Following five years of producing mostly potboilers, he turned again to the creation of serious fiction. He began by studying the master, Sigmund Freud, but it was the renegade Carl Jung who most captured London's soul. The influence of these men was so great that his artistic work, which reflects his primary activity at the time, centers on ruthless self-analysis.

Jack first became familiar with the work of Freud when he received a copy of *Selected Papers on Hysteria* in 1912. In 1916 he added the recently translated *Three Contributions to the Theory of Sex,* and Edwin Holt's commentary *The Freudian Wish and Its Place in Ethics.* That he studied these books carefully is evident by their frequent markings and side notes. The most important book in his library, however, was Jung's *Psychology of the Unconscious,* and he told Charmian upon reading it that he felt he was "standing on the edge of a world so new, so wonderful, that I am almost afraid to look into it."

Of London's final works, only one shows the clear influence of Freud. Like the other autobiographical works based on his relationship with Charmian, "On the Makaloa Mat" suffers serious structural faults but provides insights into Jack's changing viewpoint.[1]

The story opens with Ida and Lee Barton crossing a Hawaiian beach past gaping onlookers. "Dowager, matron, or maid, conserving their soft-fat muscles or protecting their hothouse complexions in the shade of the how-tree arbor, felt the immediate challenge of her." The unidentified narrator intrudes with a Freudian explanation that the women's condemnation of Ida's bathing suit is only a substitute for their envy of her beauty. Then he waxes ecstatic for paragraphs over Ida's legs, referring to them variously as boy's legs or women's legs, high-lights "the arc of the front line of the upper leg," "the knee that is a knee," and so on. These lavish descriptions derive from an earlier unpublished sketch London wrote about Charmian, "Her Body."

Lee and Ida laugh at the gossip and dive into the ocean, swimming far out beyond the diving platform and flat surf into the treacherous Kanaka. In disbelief an outrigger captain studies them through his glasses, certain he is to witness a tragedy. The couple dodge and ride the waves so skillfully that they seem to prove the narrator's contention they are genuinely superwoman and superman. As popular visitors to the islands, they are feted by local society at lunches, dinners, luaus and poi suppers, swims, and dances. During these events Lee prefers the company of a once-lively group "who had settled down somewhat of sedateness, who roistered less, and who played bridge much and went to baseball often."

Enter Sonny Grandison, a Hawaiian-born, Harvard-trained scientist, a handsome millionaire widower. The three appear coincidentally at many social events, at which Ida gradually gravitates toward Sonny:

> About Sonny's state of mind and heart, Lee had no doubts. It was patent enough for the world to read. But how about Ida, his own dozen years' wife of a glorious love match? He knew that woman, ever the mysterious sex, was capable any time of unguessed mystery. . . . Lee Barton was not happy. A dozen years of utmost and post-nuptial possession of his wife had proved to him, so far as he was concerned, that she was his one woman in the world, and that the woman was unborn, much less un-glimpsed, who could for a moment compete with her in his heart, his soul, and his brain. Impossible of existence was the woman who could lure him away from her, much less overbid her in the myriad, continued satisfactions she rendered him.

In response to these threats and confusions, Lee replaces his fruit juices with whiskey, bullies up the poker limits, and drives carelessly over the Pali Road. Ida seems too eager to have him play cards while she goes off alone socially. She carries on merrily, carelessly, while he keeps tormenting accounts in his mind: one column of her loving acts, one of her unclassifiable expressions, the third of her gestures toward Sonny.

One night, unseen, he comes upon Ida and Sonny in an embrace. Returning home later, he finds her combing her hair as if nothing had happened. Struggling with sleep, he takes the opium he has on hand for nighttime cramps.

Still under the influence of the drug, the next day in the Kanaka surf, Lee feigns leg cramps to tempt her close to him, then leads her into a maddening, death-threatening game. Deliberately he moves his leg to cause and intensify real cramping. Sinking into the water, he grabs "as a drowning man might try to climb out on an oar and sink her down under him." She goes under, swallows water, loses her cap, and comes up blinded by her hair. He shoves her away: "The drug still worked in his brain, so that he could play-act cruelly while at the same time he appraised and appreciated her stress of control and will that showed in her drawn face, and the terror of death in her eyes, with beyond and behind it, in her eyes and through her eyes, the something more of a spirit of courage and higher thought and resolution." Ida persists in counseling him to relax, slacken out, stay with the pain till it passes.

Urged by "the poppy juice" he decides to perform the "acid test," doubles up, and pulls her under with him:

And then he would put her down again, going from bad to worse in his ill-treatment of her; making her swallow pints of salt water, secure in knowledge it would not definitely hurt her. . . . Although she struggled and tore herself from his grips, in the times he permitted her freedom she did not attempt to swim away from him, but, with fading strength and reeling consciousness, invariably came to him to try to save him.

Convinced of her loyalty, with the cramps dissolving, he quits the game.

While floating back to shore, Ida confesses that she feared she would lose Lee. That evening she admits that Sonny had fallen for her but that she too bore guilt in having encouraged him. The night before she had rejected his overtures but allowed him one kiss as a maternal gesture. Lee says he has a story to tell her in five years, if she will wait. Ida sighs that she can wait fifty.

This curious and maudlin tale is an obvious retelling of real-life events for dramatic purposes. The triad theme repeats Charmian's ranch romances. The couple's brazen surf adventure mirrors that of 1915. That Ida enjoys a flourishing social life while Lee sits at the card tables matches Charmian's diary notes from the period. The other women's envy of Ida was an important fantasy in Jack's perceptions of Charmian, but may have been based in fact, for her careful health habits left her looking more vivacious and youthful than her contemporaries. He cleverly combined these diverse feelings and perceptions into a classic, albeit perverse, story of jealousy and envy.

Limited by ill health to a sedentary life, Lee envies Ida's greater mobility. The fictional Charmian is eight years younger than her husband, as the real Charmian may well have seemed to Jack at that time. Moreover, she has managed in spite of twelve years of marriage to maintain an air of mystery so ineluctable that other women could not hold his attention for long. Yet she might dare to accept the overtures of another man and therefore deserves to have her loyalty cruelly tested.

Was the flirtation in the plot based on truth? Nothing in Charmian's diaries hints at the possibility—Jack was at the center of her thought and actions. It is true she was a popular dance partner, a valued conversationalist who held the center stage he had once enjoyed. Certainly he felt threatened by her recent independence, her casual willingness to leave him behind while she went to parties alone.

For Charmian, going on with her own life was, in reality, not so easy to do. Other than completing his thousand words a day, she observed:

> . . . there was scant exertion in his habit of life in the palm-furnished, breezy bungalow of wide spaces, and the deep gardens of hibiscus and lilies. Too little exertion. Too seldom was the blue-butterfly kimono changed for swimming suit or riding togs; too often, from the water, I cast solicitous eyes back to the hammock, where, out of the blue-figured robe, a too white arm waved to show that

he was watching me put to use the strokes in which he had
coached me. "Oh, yes—no—yes—no, I think I'll hang
here and read," he would waver between two impulsions.
Or, "No thank you, I'll read instead—all this stuff I want
to catch up on. I'm glad you asked me, though," half-
wistfully, "—you forgot yesterday and went in alone."
Forgot, no! Never once did I forget. I was avoiding all
approach to the "nagging" we still never permitted in our
family of two.[2]

Aware of his suffering, she put on a brave face and went to
parties alone, for to do otherwise would be to concern him
about the seriousness of his condition. It was an awful choice
that she knew would make her look frivolous and vain in retro-
spect, but she rightly understood it to be the most loving
choice under the circumstances. She would retain his dignity
at all costs to herself.

Adding to their anguish is the likelihood Jack was no longer
very potent sexually. While the evidence is circumstantial, it
remains forceful. The high blood pressure and kidney problems afflicting him could well have interfered with his ability to
achieve or maintain an erection. Two years earlier Jack read in
a medical journal about an experiment performed by G. Frank
Lydston, a noted physician who had taken the testes of a suicide victim and implanted them in his own scrotal sac. Later he
removed sections to study the implant's viability, reporting
favorable results. Jack wrote, "I think the biggest thing in many
a year is your implantation of sex organs. I shall not begin to
tell you how wild I am to hear of your further progress."[3] By
that time Charmian was reporting only scattered instances of
lovemaking in her diary, even during times of greatest intimacy.

Though during the 1915 Hawaiian visit Charmian noted
days of "love fest" and "lolly," similar comments disappeared
in 1916. On one day in February she wrote "Mate, the big
lover," but the entry was followed by an erasure of the words
"in the strange circumstances." Something of major importance was passing between them at this time, for they spent
afternoons at Chaplin movies and many hours in conversation.
Following a moonlight swim one evening, she recorded, "Oh,

those dreams of magic nights. I shall never feel that I have not loved them when I had them." By May Jack was teaching her a "new philosophy of love." Was it perhaps based on less sexuality?

The most striking feature of "On the Makaloa Mat" remains Lee's desperate game in the water, which was a metaphor for Jack's actions toward Charmian throughout his final months. Now ravaged with illness, led astray by "the opium lie," confused and tempted by the new psychology, he "went to startling lengths in the risky game of 'playing with souls.' " He resurrected old curiosities in his friends' behaviors, experimenting on them with his own brand of psychoanalysis. Most people were found wanting in his eyes, and Charmian feared that in finding his associates deficient, Jack's alienation would increase to the point where his will to live would break down. The roughest games were reserved for himself and Charmian:

> The test of my endurance was severe, for Jack required so greatly of me in the capacities of wife, lover, friend, even confessor, for he withheld nothing—nothing, I repeat—of what he was passing through; and my responsibility, it may be guessed, was almost more than I could bear. . . . No matter how strange he seemed at times, nor how isolate, I learned I must stand by, night and day, for his instant heed.[4]

He broke out in sudden tirades, and she soon realized that it was better to stick with him, all night if need be, in argument than to withdraw and leave him festering. Just as suddenly he would quit fighting, smile, and fall asleep on her. Wakening penitently, he would say something like, "Bear with me, Mate —you're all that I've got." She vowed that she would.

At first "too close to it all to see the full drift of his fall," by summer she could not deny the signs. Sadly she realized that his unwillingness to exercise was caused by weakness, not lack of will. When they dined, even with company, he ate hardly any food, distracting others with a flow of witty conversation. When she prodded him to eat, he told her not to worry, assuring her that he ate a large breakfast while she slept. He did not tell her what she also knew, that he was vomiting his meals within a half-hour of completion.

One morning Jack awoke in crippling pain and roused her to call a doctor. The physician diagnosed a kidney stone and urged Jack to eliminate heavy proteins from his diet in favor of fruits and vegetables. He also made it clear to Charmian that Jack was seriously ill and would die soon unless he changed his habits. In fact, by then it is unlikely any change would have lengthened his life greatly.

In spite of Jack's agonies and brusque restlessness, Charmian's diary abounded with signs of renewed warmth and commitment. "The most wonderful of love days with Mate, founded on the very most wonderful philosophy. Verily, I am loving." One day Jack told her he could refuse her nothing, that he would murder for her if need be. In light of all this evidence, it is ironic that friends and biographers would later claim Jack had fallen in love with another woman in Hawaii, even decided to leave Charmian so he could have another chance for a son. The original source of this story was George Sterling, who passed the word to others after Jack's death.[5] Yet nothing, however slight, in the London-Sterling correspondence hints at this possibility, just as no other evidence of it from the period exists. The truth is, if Jack did manage a secret love affair during this time, he would have been like Lee Barton, a superman.

* * * *

Jung's influence upon Jack was complicated by his preoccupation with death, externalized through a fascination with war. The battles in Europe disheartened him, especially America's failure to join on behalf of the nations beleaguered by Germany. When he learned of the execution of British nurse Edith Clavell, something in him snapped, observed Charmian, and he grew furious over the stupidity and brutality of "the Hun." She would come upon him speechless in wonder over the monstrous images of German propaganda. He heaped scorn on "the Mad Dog of Europe," with its paranoic, insane view of the world.

Yet he also saw the war as a means of cleansing humanity, in that it forced people "to return from the cheap and easy lies

of illusion." When asked whom he supported for president, he
said there was no one who would:

> brilliantly guide the United States down from her fat,
> helpless, lonely, unhonorable, profit-seeking way to the
> shambles to which her shameless unpreparedness is lead-
> ing her. . . . We are become the fat man of the nations,
> whom no nation loves. My choice for President is Theo-
> dore Roosevelt, whom nobody in this fat land will vote for
> because he exalts honor and manhood over the cowardice
> and peace lovingness of the worshipers of fat.[6]

The revolutionary remained: he had little pride in a country in
which thirty-five thousand died every year because of accidents
on the job, and ten times that many suffered dismemberment
and disability. That such a country, rich in material goods,
would fail to stand by the most basic moral principle of helping
one's neighbor sickened him. That many socialists led the
cause of pacifism added to his disgust, for he saw them as
cooperating with the capitalist enemy.

   This position was at odds with the majority membership of
the Socialist party, who in September 1915 had endorsed a
manifesto condemning the war as the result of imperialism,
commercial rivalries, lack of democracy, powerful armament
interests, and a jingo press, all ready to send workers to death
to make the industrialists rich. Jack had for several years been
unhappy with the party's tendency toward a soft reformism run
by politicians rather than a tough revolutionary movement
guided by workers. Eugene Debs was one of the few leaders
who agreed with him that the party was being subverted by
bourgeois ideals, yet neither of these two icons of the movement were given much attention.

   In March 1916 Jack felt impelled to take the unhappy step
of resigning from the party. (He included Charmian in the
resignation, but she reinstated herself after his death and was
for decades one of two registered socialists in the town of Glen
Ellen.) The party responded with a nasty rebuke, picking not
only at him but the "peaceable membership in Glen Ellen." It
was an unfair blow, and London was correct to lament, "They
deny I ever struck a blow or did anything for the Cause, at the

same time affirming that all the time they knew me for what I was—a Dreamer."[7]

His reading included many books on war. George Crile's study *A Mechanistic View of War and Peace* fascinated him for its analysis of human behavior: the reasons for singing while marching, the effects on the body of waiting under fire, how people face death. Such study led to plans for a new novel, *How Men Die,* which would give the subjective accounts of five different men as they faced their final withdrawal from the world and shed their illusions.

That London himself was relentless in his own search for inner truth in the face of death is evident in his Jungian stories. One could spend an entire book exploring his self-analysis through these tales, so only an outline of the process can be included here, with examinations of the two most powerful stories, "The Red One" and "The Water Baby."

Once during a conversation George Sterling wondered what would happen if a meteor or extraterrestrial object landed on a South Sea island. The image stuck with Jack, but it was not until these terrible days that he converted the image into his greatest work of science fiction, "The Red One." The plot concerns Bassett, a wreck of a naturalist, a devotee of Darwin, during his final months of life in the Solomon Islands. He has just lost two fingers and nearly his scalp in an ambush but has saved himself with his shotgun.

During subsequent wanderings he encounters one horrible scene after another, such as a young woman, her bones crushed, suspended by one arm in the heat of the sun. One day, when Basset is near death, a ghastly looking woman with a pig's tail shoved through the hole of one earlobe appears and nurses him. In time he realizes she is fattening him for supper and is spared only when an inquisitive tribesman, exploring Bassett's unfamiliar rifle, shoots the head off of a fellow native.

Throughout his wanderings Bassett has been provoked to discover the source of a strange sound, like sobbing and babbling. He learns it is from the Red One and that many of the tribal slaughters are sacrifices to this deity. Bassett tries unsuccessfully to obtain a description of the being or find anyone willing to take him to see it. He knows in time he will be slain, that his head will join those others hanging in the curing hut.

For the cause of science, he marries Balatta, the ugly woman, and after enduring her "pig-like gurgly noises of delight" during lovemaking, takes her down to the stream for a thorough scrubbing. Eventually he convinces her to violate the taboos and lead him to the Red One. There he finds a pearllike sphere, glowing red and iridescent, in a crater, surrounded by the scattered bones of sacrifices. He laughs over the irony "of this wonderful messenger, winged with intelligence across space, to fall into a bushman stronghold and be worshipped by ape-like, man-eating and head hunting savages. It was as if . . . the Sermon on the Mount had been preached in a roaring bedlam of lunatics." Later, weakened by illness, he meditates on the meaning of what he has seen, concluding that this proof of an intelligence from somewhere else speaks to a unifying force in the universe. He celebrates his membership, feeling "his soul go forth in kinship with that august company, that multitude whose gaze was forever upon the arras of infinity."

Realizing he is to die, he asks to be taken to the Red One, where he hears "the voice of God . . . the interfusings and intermating transfusings of matter and force." In the instant of his beheading, he senses the "impending marvel of the rending of walls before the unimaginable."

This story repeats London's frequent criticism of the ultra-rational, manipulative man, with one exception. While in his previous writings such men died because of prideful arrogance in the face of vanquishing nature or lost a woman to a more integrated and androgynous male, in "The Red One" the calculating hero completes the passage to wholeness as much through his mating with the ghastly Balatta as through his merging with the Red One. It is London's pronouncement of both faith and hope, his claim that the universe is not all chaos and chance, however grotesque the appearance.

"The Water Baby" further supports the notion that Jack experienced a major psychic integration during his final days. Its narrator John Lakana—"London" in Hawaiian—finds himself with a hangover in the fishing boat of an elderly Polynesian, Kohokumu. The fisherman talks of his religion, of his belief that "when I am really old, I shall be reported as drowned in the sea. . . . In truth, I shall have returned to the arms of my mother, there to rest under the heart of her breast until the second birth of me, when I shall emerge into the sun a flashing youth of splendor like Maui himself when he was young." Lakana patronizes the old man, finding the stories queer and quaint in light of Western science.

Kohokumu challenges Lakana, asking, "How do you know but what you are old Maui himself asleep and dreaming that you are John Lakana talking with me in a canoe?" Perhaps all life is a dream, he suggests, perhaps our own dreams are reality.

Then Kohokumu relates the story of the Water Baby, Keikawai, a boy born with knowledge of the language of fishes. His king wanted lobsters, which could be had only from a lagoon infested with forty sharks. Keikawai tells the shark that he plans to dive for a lobster and that no harm shall befall him "because the shark with the shortest tail is my friend and will protect me." With that he throws a rock to another part of the lagoon, distracting the creatures, and dives down to grab a lobster.

When the sharks see the Water Baby has succeeded, they search to see who has the shortest tail, for that one must be a traitor. They then devour it. In the meantime, Water Baby takes more lobsters. This process continues until only two sharks are left in the lagoon. By then the fortieth shark, having eaten nineteen others, has a difficult time consuming the thirty-ninth, also with nineteen in its belly. The next morning the people find the last shark has burst.

As Lakana is about to express doubt about the truth of the story, Kohokumu says he can show him the lagoon with the thirty-nine rocks the Water Baby threw to distract the sharks. "You can count them any day for yourself."

As with "The Red One," this story lends itself to extensive interpretation of the symbolism. The first half of the tale concerns death and rebirth imagery, with the Great Mother of the sea as the source of new vitality. The old London, made wise by his readings of Jung, respected this source of renewal, but the real physical London was exhausted and doubtful, hung over from grasping too much of life.

To emphasize his point, the wise voice tells of the forty sharks destroying themselves through insecurity and greed, just as London's impulses had warred within him for forty years. The Water Baby, wise to the ways of these unruly animals, as a man undergoing analysis would become, outtricks them. Through his intervention these destructive creatures consume one another, leaving the lagoon safe and the natives secure.

In later years, when reflecting on these discoveries, Charmian said that Jack found through self-analysis that he was not merely a series of reactions to stimuli, but to a certain extent a self-creating and self-determining being. It may seem odd that a man so active and assertive in the world would not have already reached that conclusion, but he had been driven in his ceaseless quests more by unconscious impulse than by conscious self-expression. This knowledge was to him, she said, "like a dazzling light" beyond comprehension, hinted at only in his final stories. Confronting the cycle of death and rebirth rich in the Jungian literature, "Jack *chose* death, or shall we say another form of re-birth. . . . He went like the conqueror, not the vanquished. He went with the illumined smile of one who has chosen well."

*   *   *   *

In early July the couple returned once more to Glen Ellen. After Eliza saw Jack, she remarked to a friend that "our Jack has not come back to us." He went off to the Bohemian Club Hi-Jinks and returned depressed that his play *The Acorn Planter* had been rejected for presentation.

If London can be said to have chosen death, it was through his simple refusal to moderate those habits that were shortening his life. He would eat the duck and drink the whiskey and drive hard through the hours, extracting all he could from life. Who can judge the pain he suffered? Who has the right to fault his choice? Eliza and Charmian, both toughly facing the inevitable outcome, watched in rare helplessness. Worsening their situation was his new cantankerous nature, brought on by both the disease and the drugs.

He inflicted his poor mood upon Joan once again. His oldest child had grown weary of having to make special requests for every need—carfare, school books, tickets to a show, summer coats, a school pin—and gathered her courage to ask him over lunch simply to increase her and her sister's allowances accordingly, to take into account their greater needs as teenagers. His response shocked her:

He was furiously angry, and although I immediately withdrew my proposal, he insisted upon discussing it further. "Discussing" is scarcely the right word for what followed: accusations, upbraidings, erection of straw dummies that were instantly demolished, self-justification that sank finally into self-pity. Whatever I tried to say was cruelly twisted into its opposite intention.

When the tirade ended, he asked Joan to send him some figures, and he would make up his mind. She and Becky accompanied him in tense silence to the Orpheum, where he was meeting Charmian and some friends for the show. He gave them perfunctory kisses, moved toward the lobby, and turned to gaze at them before continuing on. Joan had an impulse to run and fling her arms about him, but his unsmiling face inhibited her. He turned and went inside. Jack's daughters were never to see him again.

In September Eliza accompanied the couple to the state fair in Sacramento, where Jack exhibited many of his livestock and garnered many honors. While there, the "rheumatism" in his left foot flared up so seriously he could not attend the competitions. Consequently, Eliza took over the showings with her usual deftness, while Charmian nursed Jack in the hotel room, diverted him with cards and games, invited callers in. She left the room only three times that week, in each case to buy books.

The fair over, it was clear Jack would have to be driven back "by machine," so Charmian arranged to have a doctor accompany them. During the ride the couple argued as to what turn to take along a strange road. Though his sense of direction had been faultless in the past, it turned out her way was, atypically, the right one. She interpreted this incident as a bad omen.

Twilight spread slowly over their lives. Jack decided to go to New York to arrange new publishing contracts, as his five-year commitment to *Cosmopolitan* was drawing to a close. Increasingly aware of her need to establish her own source of support, and perhaps hoping she could dissuade him from the trip, Charmian refused to join him. She insisted she be free to finish her book on Hawaii, which she found to be "pretty rotten, but I'm beginning to get interested and see new possibilities."

Jack insisted he would go anyway, which disappointed her.

Here an odd letter shows up in the files, from Sophie Loeb. Written to "My Dear Wolf," it asks if he would be interested in covering the upcoming World Series for her paper, the *Evening Star*. Though most of the letter mixes cordiality with business, and includes a description of her dancing with a judge she had gone to interview, it ends:

> I saw a star last night—a new star—like no other yet discovered. I will give you three guesses as to what I have named it.
>
> As ever,
> Star[8]

The reference likely is to Robert Browning's poem "My Star," in which he uses the image of the star to show how the soul of the loved one reveals itself fully to the sympathetic insight of the lover alone. That Jack informed Sophie of his expected arrival, that she would close with such an intimate remark, adds to the evidence that she was indeed his paramour during his visits to New York City, a relationship limited to that place only. A dedicated career woman who never remarried following an acrimonious divorce, Loeb would not make demands on Jack in exchange for intimacy. Thus, he could enjoy her company with no fear and little guilt, for she was certainly no threat to his marriage.

When asked if Jack had another woman on his mind at this time, Finn Froelich, who was on the ranch during Jack's final days, later reported that Jack "never once thought of leaving Charmian. He didn't have that in his head, that he wanted to leave her, and I think I would have known." Froelich did observe that Jack was "going down," that he lacked both the old gleam in his eye and the familiar laughter. Totally out of character, he made nasty comments about friends and grew suspicious of those who did appear on the ranch.[9]

October brought a string of troubles. First, his insurance company canceled his remaining policies, citing poor health as the reason. On October 22, the sudden and unexpected death of Jack's favorite prize-winning shire stallion, Neudad Hillside, struck him hard.

Next, Jack got into a dispute with George that set the latter reeling. George had not been doing well in recent years—his writing was not selling (and he borrowed money from Jack several times to survive); his loss of Carrie continued to distress him; and he was no longer able to abstain from drink. Also, aging terrified George, who held a romantic view that art and youth were synonymous. He was turning into a bitter, cynical, malicious man, more than a little envious of Jack's apparent successes.

In late October he asked to visit Jack, and bring a woman along. George did not appear, nor call to inform of his cancellation. Jack sent a forthright letter reminding George of the inconvenience he had caused both to Jack and his man who had gone to meet the train. Although it was a typical London reprimand—to the point, yet loving—George took undue offense and never responded.

That same month Jack tried to convince Bess to absolve him of his commitment here in exchange for a promise of an equivalent amount of money being set aside for the girls. She refused.

Then Netta and Edward Payne, along with other Glen Ellen residents, sued Jack for damming Graham Creek, a source of water on Sonoma Mountain. The impending trial forced Jack to postpone his New York trip.

Wanting to save her the embarrassment of attending proceedings at which she was being sued by her own relatives, Jack advised Charmian not to join him in court. Left alone at home to worry, she was most grateful when Blanche came on the scene and helped her sort out the baby layette she had always kept, to send to Nakata and his wife.

On November 10 Jack passed another kidney stone, yet insisted on attending the trial. On the fourteenth the court ruled against the injunction, though the decision did not add anything to prevent the plaintiffs from pressing their claims again. In generous spirits, Jack extended his hand to his accusers and invited them to a dinner on his ranch to heal the breach. Netta turned her back.

Several days later a filmmaker visited the ranch. His surviving pictures show Charmian galloping pertly across the fields and Jack at his piggery beaming with pride at the tiny piglets he holds in his hands. He appears gentle and innocent, though the knowing eye can read the signs of his illness in his distended stomach. While Charmian had not slept well for weeks and was plagued by her chronic neck spasms, she too forced a smiling front for posterity.

On November 18, a woman friend, Madame Von Ende, asked Jack if he would be executor for her will, to which he chirped, "Sure, put my name down." Two days later he urged Charmian to go riding with him so he could show her some prospective ranch additions. Exhausted by her own illness and worries, she refused. By now the toxemia had made him feverish and manic; he displayed uncontrollable excitement over new ideas for the ranch, which focused on new amenities for the workers and their families, including a school. He painted for her a worker's idyll, a community based on socialist and cooperative principles.

On the twenty-first, Jack joined Charmian in her room after eating. Subdued, he pointed lifelessly to a box of books he had set aside for the night's reading. "But you don't *have* to do it," she counseled. "You make all this work and overwork for yourself." She told him he would break soon if he did not ease up. "You are tired, almost tired to death. What shall we do? We can't go on this way."

He rose to go to his room, turned, and added mysteriously, "Thank God, you're not afraid of anything." That night, while walking around the grounds, she could see him asleep on the porch, his eyeshade still on, his head on his chest, and was grateful he was at rest. She awoke the next morning to find Eliza and valet Sekine at her side, both shaking her to say they had been unable to rouse Jack. Rushing to his side, she found him unconscious, breathing hard, showing plain symptoms of the increased poisoning he had suffered in recent weeks. They had attributed these more frequent vomiting spells to ptomaine and continued to do so. Believing that was the problem, she called several doctors and tried to get the comatose man to drink coffee.

Throughout the day they worked on him, both physically and psychologically. They yelled that the dam had broken, hoping the news would stir him from his coma. Whenever a sign of change appeared, Charmian would call, "Mate, Mate, come back." There was no hope—he was drowning in his own toxic fluids. It was a day of alternating hope and despair, "and the end, when he beat us out and went into the great dark with a smile—the smile he haunted to wear at the finish."

He had died on her couch, where only hours before he had said, "You're all I have left." She sat for hours by his sheeted form, "until every atom of understanding I possessed, I had reckoned with for all time with the hitherto unthinkable: that ultimate silence lay upon the lips of my man."

The next day she lay out his body in his favorite gray suit, similar to the one she had first seen him in seventeen years earlier. Passing by, she thought he looked much smaller in his cradlelike casket than she recalled him to be. She let the neighbors and workers view the body, though she knew he would not have thought much of such an exhibition.

The newspapers also had to be notified. Eliza first reported to the journalists that Jack had suffered from food poisoning and was responding to treatment. When he died, the papers reported erroneously that he had collapsed several hours after eating a hearty meal. The confusing and contradictory news reports provided fuel for Sterling and others who believed Jack had committed suicide. Although the verdict will always be out on that possibility, it is unlikely. The day he died he sent his daughters a note making an appointment to take them out before leaving for New York, and he showed no other signs of wanting to end his suffering by killing himself. It is possible, as historian Andrew Sinclair has concluded, that he sped his death unintentionally by taking too large a dose of narcotics that evening. Yet even without that assistance he would soon have died naturally from the kidney disease.

Awakening to the sounds of the death-wagon rattling up the hill, Charmian went to Jack's workroom, which Sekine had prepared that day as though Jack were to return. The valet entered to tell her he had slipped a note into Jack's pocket saying, "Your speech was silver, your silence is now golden." Charmian waited there while Jack's body was removed and taken down the hill, accompanied by Eliza. That day, the funeral day, "not my day, but the other's day," Jack was cremated in Oakland and a small memorial service was observed, against his express wishes. Charmian lied to the papers, saying she was too ill to attend. In fact, she deferred to Bess and Jack's daughters so there would be no complications from her appearing with them. Charmian was now responsible for that family, and she made this gesture as her first proof of good intentions toward them.

While she remained at home, relatives and friends gathered around to comfort her. Blanche and Carrie came for extended visits. (She told Carrie that after Jack's death, she slept well for the first time in weeks, a remark Carrie took as a sign of Charmian's lack of concern for him and spread as malicious gossip among the Crowd.) Charmian's uncle, Willard Growall, had been named co-executor of the estate with Eliza, and came to provide the wise counsel he would continue to offer over the years.

The obituaries reflected Jack's divisive character. Mainline newspapers such as the *New York Times* praised his contributions to American letters, but ignored his earlier important contributions to the socialist movement. The socialist journals, however, forgave his contrariness, which they attributed to his poor health, and instead emphasized his willingness to write in support of the cause at the expense of his popularity among middle-class readers, his never-failing generosity to fund drives, and his compassion for the working class and its struggles. His greatest pride, his ranch with its new model of farming, went ignored.

George Sterling and Ernest Matthews brought the urn with Jack's remains. He had asked that his ashes be spread over the ranch, but Charmian and Eliza agreed that they should be buried on a knoll near the Wolf House site in a spot adjoining the graves of the pioneer Greenlaw children who had once lived on the property. In light rain, Charmian carried the small vessel to the same wagon in which they had made the four-horse trip. With each step the urn seemed to get heavier, drawing her hands down to the earth, but she struggled to overcome her feelings, and placed it safely on the seat. She and others had wreathed it with Jack's favorite ferns and primroses, as well as some withered Hawaiian leis. Up on the hillside, ranch hands cemented the container in place to ensure that no ghoulish person would destroy the contents, and as a final guard, positioned over it a large red boulder from the ruins of

Wolf House. As she aptly observed, "This rugged monument, by his own wish, could never be a place for mourning, a spot to sadden his sweet and happy hillside."

The contents of the will, with its insult to Bess, embarrassed her, and she found his bequests to the other beneficiaries "trifling." She was determined to be more generous than he, though it would be most difficult now that she had to support the ranch and his many dependents without benefit of their major income source, his writing.

"I am possessed to *go on,*" she thought as she wandered over the ranch, admiring the piglets he had so recently fondled, taking notes on which heifers to buy. She expressed the source of a new-found vitality in a letter to Cloudesley Johns:

> Never have I been so possessed, nor so courageous. It seems as if Jack is in my brain. While, in the past thirteen years, I have been learning from Jack, my brain has been dependent upon his to some extent—to a great extent. But instead of my brain having been pressed too much, it seems now to be profitting, blossoming. Of course, I make no promises; but just now it seems to me that I am very much alive, very independent, while at the same time, possessed. I mean the word in the broadest way. I feel his vitality, that's all. Ah but Cloudesley, one's heart hurts so.[10]

The work of answering condolence letters, directing the ranch, arranging for Jack's posthumous publications, and providing for his children claimed her days and eased the mourning.

She took her solace in the past. Only weeks before he died, Jack had left her perhaps the most moving inscription of all:

> Dearest Mate,
>
> After it all, and it all, and it all, here we are, all in all, all in all.
>
> Sometimes I just want to get on top of Sonoma Mountain to shout to the world about you and me.
>
> Arms ever round and around.
>
> Mate Man

EPILOGUE

In a sense the nineteenth century concluded in 1916, the year of Jack London's death. Within months the United States would be preparing to enter the war in Europe, becoming fully involved when the army's Rainbow Division arrived in France in November 1917. Also in 1917 Congress passed the Prohibition Amendment, New York gave women the right to vote, and Jeannette Rankin became the first woman to join the U.S. House of Representatives. Jack would have been pleased with all these events.

He would have been less pleased with the country's response to labor leaders and socialists who continued their rebellions. London had never been a great supporter of war and wanted U.S. involvement in Europe only to support the moral principle of defending friends besieged by madness. He may have tempered his attitude toward the pacifists when Emma Goldman was jailed and eventually deported for her anticonscription work, and mourned those activists around the country who were beaten, illegally arrested, and in several cases lynched for their commitment to peace. The use of the military in 1919 to break the strike of U.S. Steel workers objecting to the twelve-hour work day might have stirred his return to writing social propaganda.

The war marked the true turn of the century, its presence transforming all areas of life, shaking loose old ideas, leaving room for new ones to rise quickly in their place. In 1920 the urban population in the United States surpassed the rural for the first time, thus producing a shift in dominant values. London's back-to-nature plots with romances built on courtly manners seemed old-fashioned and silly to city dwellers versed in Freud and Havelock Ellis. The adventurous woman smoked, bobbed her hair, and showed her legs. All frontiers seemingly gone, men were left to express their masculinity through sports and spectatorship rather than direct confrontations with nature. The strong man was defined less by his ability to control life than by his adaptation to the hard knocks fate brought.

Left to face these changes in society, Charmian was grateful Jack was not around to see the consequences, the sudden devaluation of his works in his beloved country. She had his legacy of debt—his role as provider for all households related to him—and of riches—his piles of published and unpublished material. Truly alone for the first time in her life, she also confronted the troublesome problem of finding her own purpose after years of deferring to others.

Defined by her relationship to Jack, she kept the cloak of his identity and took on as her major role during the next forty years the continuation of his intentions. She rightly understood this to mean the preservation of the ranch, his first love. When she encountered obstacles, she used his writings to provide the needed resources. For the rest of her life she traveled widely to publicize Jack London, wrote about him, gave countless interviews, bargained with Hollywood moguls to translate his works into movies, fought off less than scrupulous biographers. She was tireless in this work because it was so satisfying, a way of keeping "My Man" alive.

The success of her efforts is evident. Outside the United States, in Western and Eastern cultures, in developed and Third World nations, Jack London is among the best-known and most popular American writers. Within his home country, where he has been generally ignored until recently, his books are among the most worn on library shelves. Much of his continued influence is due to Charmian's ceaseless work to keep his name prominent, to encourage the translation of his work into every language.

Yet even more London succeeds because he speaks to the common people, those he hoped would one day find the confidence and will to better their lot. Those who study London soon find themselves filling scrapbooks with anecdotes of how this sweet and vital man affected so many people in different ways. Lenin, on his deathbed, requested that "Love of Life" be read aloud to him. A librarian on a trip to China discovered all fifteen of her guides knew of Jack London because he was one of the few Western writers permitted during the repressive Cultural Revolution. A coal miner's son in Wales was inspired by *The People of the Abyss* to become a labor organizer. A young woman stole into the state park at night to sleep by his grave, to honor the inspiration his words brought her. A printer distributed freely "The Heathen," a story of friendship between a white and a black man, as a way of reminding people to honor the best in themselves.

Part of what appeals to these readers is London's very imperfection, his self-mockery, his slips in writing, his struggle with alcohol. His characters exhibit the contradictions readers often feel within themselves. Sometimes they are fools who die for their foolishness, but more often they find within themselves unexpected founts of courage and ethical behavior. They are never boring. As these readers learn about London's life, they are encouraged that life can be lived in ways beyond their narrow imagination, although not free of tragedy.

The legacy of London is certainly in his best works, those that touch the hearts of working people, but it is also on the land he worked to preserve. Only very recently have Californians recognized his contribution to agriculture and set to restoring the ranch he hoped would be the start of a new social experiment. He took a worn-out mountainside and turned it into a productive farm through ecological practices that only recently have been acknowledged to be wise.

Yet it is hard to imagine he would have tried and accomplished so much without the influence of Charmian. Certainly there would have been no sailing to Pacific isles nor the redemption of the Valley of the Moon. There would have been another woman to be sure, but not likely one who could master his mercurial temperament so well, who could provide the strength he needed to find his direction. Certainly Charmian's life would have been duller and less useful without his invigorating pull.

In the end it appears their mating, their concept of a man-woman relationship, was one of their most revolutionary acts. Their words of equality—mate, comrade, brother, twin—were matched by their devotion and loyalty to the concept. That each strayed or became preoccupied with other matters in life is beside the point, for that is true of any relationship. What stands out is their refusal to surrender to other temptations, to allow those seductions to destroy their interdependence, which above all else was based on friendship. Their nineteenth-century romanticism supported their modern beliefs.

Widowed, Charmian became a much stronger person, no longer ready to submit to authority, as she had to Netta and at times to Jack in the earlier years. In 1917 she took out her favorite Waterhouse pen and noted, "The strangest New Year of my life, my first year of *widowhood*. Sometimes it all seems as if I'd known it was going to be this way, that it's just the natural course of events, and that it's all natural and right; then comes almost a *fear* that I'll be able to realize that I am to be alone, always; for *never* shall I be wedded wife of any man." She never was, for no one of the many who tried could replace the memory of Jack London. But as for the fear of such solitariness, it was a wisp that soon vanished as she explored the untapped woman inside herself.

Moreover, the partnership was not a mundane one, but spurred to push two individuals to their limits. As Charmian reflected later, "I think the difference between [others] and ourselves was that Jack and I knew what we wanted, and in unison overtook in spite of colossal odds from all sides; while the others simply had mistaken their desires. The secret of finding our rainbows' ends always, I am sure, lay first and last in our knowledge of what we wanted. The longest search never palled, because the search was an end in itself."[1] This knowledge left Charmian with an overwhelmingly positive memory of her life with Jack, where the struggles and tragedies were tempered by the nobility of the attempt, whether socialism, South Seas adventuring, the creation of moving fiction, or farming experimentation. Late in life visitors would be taken by her talking about Jack as if he were still alive, still bringing her happiness.

ACKNOWLEDGMENTS

It is my sad regret that Irving Shepard, who originally granted me access to Charmian's intimate papers, and his wife, Mildred, did not live to see this volume. I hope my work has met their trust. Their son Milo matched their extraordinary generosity and support. The Shepards promised me complete freedom of interpretation, and they scrupulously took care to see I retained complete control of the topic and its direction. In discussing my relationship to the London family with other biographers, I realize I have been blessed with an ideal situation, one I much appreciate.

In the course of my work I met literally dozens of people working on some aspect of London's life or collecting his works, all of whom provided me with some information or insight. Earle Labor, leading literary interpreter of London, welcomed this heretic sociologist into the fold and revealed many shortcuts. Russ and Winnie Kingman were always ready to provide checks on factual details and gave access to all materials in their Jack London Research Center. Sal Noto, a major collector and regional historian, provided constant encouragement and a meticulous reading of the various drafts. Andrew Sinclair, when writing his biography of Jack, not only discussed ways we could ensure distinct products, but informed me of major breakthroughs as he came upon them. These authorities did not agree with all I state here, yet supported my efforts wholeheartedly.

Among other London informants and scholars were Jack's daughter Becky London Fleming, Elsie Martinez (widow of Xavier), Tony Williams, Dennis Hensley, Robert Leitz, Susan Ward, Katherine Littell, Carolyn Willson Johnston, Richard Etulain, David Schlottman, and the late James Sisson. Peter Scarlet, Bill Forshay, Denise Langille Wolff, Ardath Lee, and Elizabeth Pomada provided helpful criticism on earlier versions of the manuscript. Nancy and Alan Jacobsen, Richard Bellamy, Gay Robbins, J.J. Wilson, Howard Becker, Suzanne Lipsett, and Jay Stewart were frequent cheerleaders. I apologize to those I may have overlooked in my recall of over ten years' work.

Matt Atkinson and Gregory Hayes, rangers at the Jack London State Historic Park, were quick to answer questions about the buildings and ranch itself. Glenn Burch, state historian, patiently sifted through hundreds of negatives with me. Ron and Susan Silverek capably printed most of the archival photographs from the London collection, which are now with the State Park offices in Santa Rosa, California. Because part of this material was unavailable at the time, the Jack London Research Center contributed additional prints. With the exception of those noted as coming from the Bancroft Library, all illustrations are published with permission of the State Parks and the estate of Irving Shepard.

Librarians are the mainstay of work such as this. Thus I thank the staff at the Henry E. Huntington Library, the Merrill Library at Utah State University, and the Bancroft Library, not only for their efficient service, but their initiative in mentioning material I might otherwise have overlooked. Reference to the primary London papers—unpublished letters, diaries, scrapbooks—is with the kind permission of the respective collections. Diane Price, then at Merrill Library, deserves singular recognition for her resourcefulness and ideas. Others at the Reuban Salazar Library at Sonoma State University, the University of California at Los Angeles, and the New York Public Library handled specific requests beyond my expectations.

The National Endowment for the Humanities provided two Summer Research Stipends and one Travel-to-Collections grant. I applaud their sticking with me on a lengthy project and not expecting immediate results. A sabbatical award from Sonoma State University freed time to prepare the final draft.

I benefited as well from the warmth and perception of my agent, Elizabeth Frost Knappmann, and the thoughtful editorial support provided by Toni Lopopolo and Robin Kessler at St. Martin's Press. Linda Venator brought an incisive and critical understanding to the final editing of the manuscript.

The book would never have happened were it not for the astute suggestion of a neighbor, Dana Garcia, who told me about the existence of Charmian.

My daughter, Kendra Stoll, a small child when I started the project, grew up with it and eventually became my able research assistant.

My husband, Michael Orton, did not realize what he was getting into when he married a writer—worse, a London fanatic. He handled my preoccupation with grace, accompanied me on research jaunts, and kept faith in the work when I had given up.

My special gratitude to Mary Brock, Baillie Kay, Linda Lipps, and Cathleen Stasz for being "ordinary" women like Charmian, women of compassion, strength, and loyalty. I lament that three other such women, Nan Becker, Barbara Rosenblum, and my mother, Mary Stasz, did not survive to celebrate the completion of the project with me.

NOTES

The epigraphs at the start of each part and chapter are generally taken from Charmian and Jack's favorite readings. Most of the poetry selections are from a group Charmian typed up for ready access on evenings when there was to be reading aloud. It is hoped these brief lines will remind the reader of the tone of thought held at the time, particularly with regard to love and romance.

Because the majority of readers are not expected to be academics, I have made neither many nor detailed references. I leave such precision to my scholarly publications. Those studying London already know the sources that back up the discussions of large parts of his life. Consequently, I have emphasized citations to material the lay scholar can readily access or that support interpretations at odds with previously accepted thought.

Although I have seen the London correspondence in the original, whenever possible I have cited the printed version from Hendricks and Shepard's *Letters from Jack London* to assist those who lack access to the special holdings. Similarly, because few, including scholars, have first editions of his works, I cite chapter locations rather than page numbers when quoting his writings. (His chapters are typically brief, and the quotation quickly located within.) Similarly, I have not made reference to Charmian's diaries, which underpin so much of the discussion. Researchers wishing the exact location of certain themes in the diaries are invited to write me.

The following abbreviations are used in the notes:

CKL   Charmian Kittredge London
JL   Jack London
BL   Bancroft Library, University of California-Berkeley
ML   Merrill Library, Utah State University
HEH   Henry E. Huntington Library

PROLOGUE

1. Novelist David Graham Phillips in a *Cosmopolitan* feature of the period, as quoted by Peter Gabriel Filene, *Him/Her/Self*, 73.
2. As quoted in Filene, *Him/Her/Self*, 71.
3. *Atchison* (Kansas) *Globe*, 4 November 1905.
4. *Buffalo Times*, 15 November 1905.
5. *Washington* (Iowa) *Democrat*, 29 November 1905.

CHAPTER 1

1. Daisy's letters to Netta are in HEH. Material here comes from those dated 22 October 1866, 30 October 1866, 5 December 1866, 11 December 1866.
2. Daisy Wiley to Netta Eames, 11 December 1866, HEH.
3. From the notebook, "Dayelle: A Leaf from My Life," Salt Lake City, 11 September 1867, HEH.
4. "Dayelle: A Leaf from My Life," 11 September 1868, Santa Clara Valley, San Buenaventura; 11 September 1869, Wilmington, California, HEH.
5. Notebook entry, 12 August 1872, HEH.
6. *Petaluma* (California) *Argus*, 24 February 1873.
7. *Petaluma* (California) *Argus*, 23 June 1873.
8. During the 1930s, Charmian was attempting an autobiographical story, "Charmette," and asked Netta to provide details on this time from her childhood. Netta's self-description is among these notes, u.d., HEH.
9. Notes to "Charmette." These were originally viewed at the Jack London ranch, and are now in HEH.

10. Netta Eames Payne Springer to CKL, u.d., HEH.

11. These letters are published in Kingman, *Pictorial Life of Jack London,* 1979, 18–21.

12. For a moving glimpse of this spunky and fascinating woman, exploring her roots as death approached, see Dale L. Walker, "Letters from Joan London."

13. Virginia Prentiss spoke to Jack's daughter Joan, who discussed these times in the unpublished "Jack London with His Daughters." This quote is from a version of her manuscript edited by Richard Etulain, Jack London Research Center, Glen Ellen.

14. Notes for "Jack Liverpool," ML.

15. Atherton's "Jack London in Boyhood Adventures."

16. This remark comes from Franklin Walker's rough notes for a biography of Jack, Jack London Research Center.

17. CKL, *Book of Jack London,* chap. 4.

18. "Jack Liverpool," ML.

19. "Jack Liverpool," ML.

CHAPTER 2

1. Mark Twain, *Roughing It* (New York: Harper and Brothers, 1899), 151.

2. CKL, *Book of Jack London,* 33.

3. This and subsequent first-person comments by Charmian are taken from her assorted autobiographical notes made during 1912 while on the voyage around Cape Horn on the *Dirigo.* She seems to have been considering a book on her relationship with Jack. These notes are in HEH.

4. Beth Baxter Wiley to CKL, 26 March, c. 1937.

5. Raine Edward Bennett, "The Intimate Jack London," *San Francisco Magazine,* March 1976.

6. CKL, "Cross-Saddle Riding," 28–29.

7. JL, *Valley of the Moon,* book 2, chap. 3.

8. CKL, autobiographical notes, HEH.

9. CKL, autobiographical notes, HEH.

10. Netta Eames to Emma L. Hume, 10 August 1899, BL.

11. JL, *John Barleycorn,* chap. 5.

12. JL, *John Barleycorn*, chap. 7.

13. JL, "How I Became a Socialist," originally printed in *The Comrade,* March 1903; reprinted in Foner, *Jack London: American Rebel,* pp. 362–65.

14. JL, *John Barleycorn*, chaps. 7–11, which discuss his view of oyster pirating and saloon life.

15. JL, *John Barleycorn*, chap. 10.

16. JL, *John Barleycorn*, chap. 7.

CHAPTER 3

1. The material in this chapter covers one of the most thoroughly studied periods of Jack London's life and relies most heavily on the careful scholarship in the biographies prepared by Joan London, Franklin Walker, Russ Kingman, and Carolyn Johnston, as listed in the bibliography.

2. As quoted in Kingman, *Pictorial History of Jack London,* 49.

3. For more details on this trek, see *The Palimpsest* (Iowa City, State Historical Society of Iowa, June 1971).

4. JL, "Pinched," *The Road.*

5. JL, "The Pen," *The Road.*

6. JL, "What Life Means to Me," *San Francisco Bulletin,* 2 December 1916.

7. Georgia Loring Bamford, *The Mystery of Jack London,* 18.

8. James Hopper, quoted by CKL, *Book of Jack London,* I, 211. She took these from notes Hopper made up on his impressions of London, now at BL.

9. JL, *Martin Eden*, chap. 24.

10. JL to Mabel Applegarth, 8 August 1897, as quoted in Kingman, *A Pictorial Life of Jack London,* 71.

11. Edward Morgan, quoted in Walker, *Jack London and the Klondike,* 111–12.

12. Atherton, "Jack London in Boyhood Adventure." Atherton describes the two boys' harassment of shopkeepers in Chinatown. In another incident, while out hiking, they push several large boulders down a hill and see one crash into a cottage below, from which appears a Chinese man. They were not concerned about the man's belongings.

13. Emil Jensen, quoted in Kingman, *A Pictorial Life of Jack London*, 79.

14. JL, "What Life Means to Me," *San Francisco Bulletin*, 2 December 1916.

CHAPTER 4

1. This is a description of Dede Mason, heroine of Jack's novel *Burning Daylight*, chap. 14.

2. JL to Mabel Applegarth, 28 February 1899, HEH.

3. JL to Cloudesley Johns, 3 October 1899, quoted in Hendricks and Shepard, *Letters from Jack London*, 60.

4. JL to Anna Strunsky, 21 January 1900, quoted in Hendricks and Shepard, *Letters from Jack London*, 84.

5. JL to Cloudesley Johns, 30 March 1899, quoted in Hendricks and Shepard, *Letters from Jack London*, 26.

6. JL to Cloudesley Johns, 5 July 1899, quoted in Hendricks and Shepard, *Letters from Jack London*, 44.

7. Austin Louis, quoted in Joan London, *Jack London and His Times*, 191.

8. JL, "The Question of the Maximum," *War of the Classes*.

9. Anna Strunsky, quoted in CKL, *Book of Jack London*, I:320.

10. JL to Anna Strunsky, 29 December, 1899, quoted in Hendricks and Shepard, *Letters from Jack London*, 78–79.

11. JL to Anna Strunsky, 13 February 1900, quoted in Hendricks and Shepard, *Letters from Jack London*, 92.

12. Netta Eames to Emma L. Hume, 18 June 1897, BL. Netta describes her vacation with Charmian and landscape painter Harry Culmer, during which Netta has difficulties withholding her true feelings while trying to appear respectable.

13. CKL, Prologue, *Book of Jack London*. Charmian describes their meeting in more detail here, one of the few sections of the book that seems uncensored in terms of her feelings and perceptions. Had the rest of the book contained the candor here, the biography would have been a much greater accomplishment in terms of both satisfying the reader's desire to know and stylistic craft.

14. JL to Cloudesley Johns, 10 March 1900, quoted in Hendricks and Shepard, *Letters from Jack London,* 100.

15. CKL, published under the authorship of Netta Eames, "Jack London," *Overland Monthly,* May 1900, 417–25.

16. Joan London, "Jack London with His Daughters"; this manuscript provides further detail on the relationship between Bess and Flora as well.

17. For further details see "Advice to Unknown Writers," reprinted in Dale Walker, *Jack London: No Mentor but Myself* (Port Washington, NY: Kennikat Press).

18. JL, *Daughter of the Snows,* 108–9.

CHAPTER 5

1. CKL to Netta Eames, 6 March 1919, ML.

2. Charmian's undated autobiographical notes allude to these situations with Minstrel and Dugan, as does O'Connor, *Jack London, A Biography,* 1964, 185. O'Connor says she was engaged to Minstrel in 1900, and adds that Netta forced a breakup with Dugan at an unspecified date. Consequently, it is impossible to tell which man, if either, was the cause of the rift between the two women.

3. JL, *San Francisco Examiner,* 18 July 1901.

4. *San Francisco Examiner* columnist Yorick, quoted in Joan London, *Jack London and His Times,* 235.

5. JL, quoted in Foner, *Jack London: American Rebel,* 45. Foner notes London "put up a good campaign," which is not indicated by either press notices or London's own records.

6. Yorick, *San Francisco Post,* 26 January 1901.

7. *Oakland Enquirer,* 16 March 1901.

8. *San Francisco Examiner,* 25 February 1902; *Oakland Enquirer,* 25 February 1902.

9. Elsie Whitaker Martinez, interview by Franklin Walker and Willa Klug Baum, BL, 123, 126.

10. Elsie Whitaker Martinez, interview by Franklin Walker and Willa Klug Baum, BL, 123, 126.

11. For further details on the various houses and Bess's reactions, see Joan London, "Jack London with His Daughters."

12. JL to Cloudesley Johns, 23 February 1902, quoted in Hendricks and Shepard, *Letters from Jack London,* 133.

13. Sterling has yet to be given his fair due by critics. The most careful and perceptive analysis of his relationship with London is Howard Lachtman, "Jack and George: Notes on a Literary Friendship." In the late 1930s, Cyril Clemmons hoped to write a biography of Sterling and wrote to many of his friends for information. These responses, often contradictory, are in the BL.

14. Anna Strunsky to CKL, 6 October 1905, HEH. Anna was writing Charmian as the latter was about to leave for the midwest to marry Jack.

15. London has always been described as detesting Bierce. His early letters to Cloudesley Johns show otherwise. For example, on 10 April 1899 he criticized Bierce's "total absence of sympathy," yet added he was "a great admirer of him, by the way, and never tire of his Sunday work in the *Examiner.*" See Hendricks and Shepard, *Letters from Jack London,* 25.

16. JL to Cloudesley Johns, 6 December 1901, quoted in Hendricks and Shepard, *Letters from Jack London,* 126.

17. JL to Anna Strunsky, 5 January 1902, quoted in Hendricks and Shepard, *Letters from Jack London,* 127.

18. JL to Anna Strunsky, 5 January 1902, quoted in Hendricks and Shepard, *Letters from Jack London,* 127.

19. Joseph Noel, 1940:148.

20. JL to Anna Strunsky, 22 March 1902, HEH.

21. JL to Anna Strunsky, 10 June 1902, HEH.

22. JL to Anna Strunsky, 7 July 1902, HEH.

23. Netta Eames to Emma Hume, 12 January 1902, BL.

24. JL to Anna Strunsky, 22 August 1902, HEH.

25. JL to Anna Strunsky, 29 September 1902, HEH.

26. JL to George Brett, 9 November 1902, quoted in Hendricks and Shepard, *Letters from Jack London,* 138.

27. JL to Anna Strunsky, 3 February 1903, HEH.

28. Elsie Whitaker Martinez, interview by Franklin Walker and Willa Klug Baum, BL, 126. Elsie was a teenager when this incident occurred, and an admirer of London.

29. JL, *The Call of the Wild,* chap. 3.

CHAPTER 6

1. JL to Cloudesley Johns, 27 January 1903, HEH.

2. JL to Carrie Sterling, 15 September 1905, quoted in Hendricks and Shepard, *Letters from Jack London,* 181.

3. JL to CKL, HEH. Charmian later marked this as being sent in June 1903.

4. In his correspondence to both Mabel and Anna can be found several letters in which London claims to be exposing his true self, when in fact he wallows in self-pity, as he does in letters throughout his life. His love letters to Charmian are uncannily self-analytical in comparison.

5. JL to CKL, c. June 1903, HEH.

6. JL to CKL, c. June 1903, HEH.

7. JL, "Her Body," unpublished sketch, HEH.

8. JL to Cloudesley Johns, 11 July 1903, quoted in Hendricks and Shepard, *Letters from Jack London,* 151–52.

9. JL to Carrie Sterling, 15 September 1905, quoted in Hendricks and Shepard, *Letters from Jack London,* 182–83. Also see Bess's first divorce complaint, which states that on July 12 she found a letter Jack claimed was from an old high school girl friend. Jack's biographers have preferred to ignore this evidence that Bess was not, as she claimed, led by him to believe everything was fine in the family. As in most marital breakups, both sides were duplicitous.

10. Edward Payne to JL and CKL, 3 August 1903, HEH.

11. JL to CKL, 1 September 1903, HEH.

12. JL to CKL, n.d., quoted in CKL, *The Book of Jack London,* II:82.

13. JL to CKL, 24 September 1903, HEH.

14. JL to CKL, 20 October 1903, HEH.

15. JL to CKL, 6 July 1904, HEH.

16. CKL to Blanche Partington, 8 March 1907, BL.

17. JL to CKL, 28 September 1904, HEH.

18. CKL to Blanche Partington, 8 March 1907, BL.

19. CKL to Blanche Partington, 14 March 1907, BL.

20. JL, "Planchette," *Moon Face,* 268–69.

21. CKL, *Book of Jack London,* II, 34.

CHAPTER 7

1. JL to George Sterling, 1 June 1905, quoted in Hendricks and Shepard, *Letters from Jack London*, 172–73.

2. Carrie Sterling's gossipy letters to Blanche Partington during this period are in the Bancroft Library.

3. Because London so often rewrote his personal history to fit his contemporary mood, London scholars have often been confused about when he was first exposed to a set of ideas. Though he had heard of Nietzsche well before 1904, he did not actually read him until then, when he used the philosopher as a comforter during this very trying time in his life. On 29 September 1904, he wrote Charmian he would soon turn her loose on *Genealogy of Morals*. Charmian records reading *Zarathustra* in the summer of 1905, noting it was "my comfort."

4. The best discussion of these books in terms of Jack's relationship to Nietzsche is in Johnston, *Jack London—An American Radical?*

5. These quotes are taken from typescripts of fragments of Jack's letters to Charmian from Korea during the spring of 1904, as found in the London Ranch papers. She probably typed these after his death.

6. The full text of the speech can be found in Foner, *Jack London: American Rebel*, 488–504, which contains many of Jack's best socialist writings.

7. CKL to Frederick Bamford, 7 August 1905, HEH.

8. This and similar clippings can be found in the London scrapbooks, HEH.

9. Much of the discussion of the honeymoon trip weaves material from Charmian's diary and her *Book of Jack London*, II.

10. Charmian refers to Jack's weak ankles and wrists in her assorted unpublished notes. Becky London told me of how the cab drivers in San Francisco were always happy to see her father coming because they knew they would get a lot of business.

11. JL to George Sterling, 28 May 1905, quoted in Hendricks and Shepard, *Letters from Jack London*, 172.

12. Plans for the craft and photographs of its construction can be found in *Nautical Quarterly*, Winter 1981, 57–75. Also included in this issue is Jack's essay "The Inconceivable and Monstrous," which appeared originally in *The Cruise of the Snark*,

and from which his quotes about boat building in this section are taken.

13. JL, "Story of an Eyewitness," *Collier's Weekly,* 5 May 1906.

14. This and similar quotes in this section about their relationship come from CKL, *Book of Jack London,* chap. 26, which discusses their first months together in Glen Ellen before the marriage, as well as autobiographical notes, undated, HEH.

15. *San Francisco Examiner,* 25 September 1906.

16. "Recollections of the Late Jack London," *Overland Monthly* 69 (1917): 433–34.

17. JL to Frederick Bamford, 15 May 1906, in Bamford, *The Mystery of Jack London,* 207.

18. Austin, *Earth Horizon,* 303.

19. Genthe, *As I Remember,* 75–76.

20. This quote is from the *Los Angeles Times,* 22 May 1910. Though written several years later, it typifies the impression the Crowd was making on the general public. For a more tempered view, see Buchanan, "Story of a Famous Fraternity," 65–83.

CHAPTER 8

1. CKL, *Log of the Snark,* 5.

2. CKL, *Log of the Snark,* 6.

3. CKL, *Log of the Snark,* 13.

4. CKL, *Log of the Snark,* 20.

5. See chap. 4, "Finding One's Way About," in *The Cruise of the Snark* for Jack's amusing discussion of this incident.

6. CKL, *Our Hawaii,* 37–38.

7. *Wilshire's,* November 1907.

8. CKL, *Our Hawaii,* 56–58.

9. Jack Kersdale's lover is also Polynesian, which could lead one to wonder if London is arguing against racial mixture. Nothing in the story leads to such a conclusion. Lucy Mukunui is presented as a stunning exemplar of womankind. Also, in "Aloha Oe," he explicitly supports racial mixing.

10. See, for example, "On the Makaloa Mat," in which the women protagonists are described in detail by their bloodlines and praised for their youth and vitality.

11. Luther Burbank, *Training of the Human Plant* (New York: Century, 1907), 4–5.

12. Burbank, *Training*, 9–10.

13. CKL, "From Mrs. Jack London," *Wilshire's*, November 1907. Another article in this issue identifies Charmian as one of several celebrity women who have become members of a new socialist organization, the Women's National Progressive League.

14. JL, *The Cruise of the Snark*, 67.

15. CKL, *Our Hawaii*, 75.

16. "A Royal Sport" and "Riding the South Sea Surf," *Woman's Home Companion*, October 1907.

17. Most of this discussion is based upon CKL, *Our Hawaii*, 117–48.

18. CKL, *Our Hawaii*, 136–37.

19. CKL, *Our Hawaii*, 141.

20. CKL, *Our Hawaii*, 126.

21. These articles and London's exchange of letters with Thurston occurred in the winter of 1909–10. See JL to Lorrin Thurston, 7 January 1910 and 1 February 1910, quoted in Hendricks and Shepard, *Letters from Jack London*, 295.

22. For more details on this part of the trip, see CKL, *Our Hawaii*, 154–79.

23. Charmian often discussed her work in her diaries.

24. JL to George Sterling, 25 July 1907, HEH.

25. JL to Frederick Bamford, 14 June 1906, in Loring, *The Mystery of Jack London*.

26. CKL to Netta Eames, 25 July 1907, HEH.

CHAPTER 9

1. See correspondence in HEH from Netta Eames and George Sterling to Jack around this time for evidence here. Always the great peacemaker, George unsuccessfully begged Jack to forgive Bert. When Netta complained about Roscoe's treatment, Jack sent her a lengthy list of the man's failings on the trip.

2. CKL, *Log of the Snark*, 38.

3. CKL, *Log of the Snark*, 80.

4. CKL, *Log of the Snark,* 68.

5. CKL, *Log of the Snark,* 100.

6. CKL, *Log of the Snark,* 122.

7. CKL, *Log of the Snark,* 136.

8. CKL, *Log of the Snark,* 145.

9. CKL, *Wilshire's,* June 1908.

10. Mary Austin to CKL, 4 April 1927, HEH.

11. CKL, *Log of the Snark,* 307.

12. CKL, *Log of the Snark,* 355–56.

13. JL, *Cruise of the Snark,* 230.

14. JL, *Cruise of the Snark,* 231.

15. CKL, *Log of the Snark,* 437.

16. JL to George Brett, 25 October 1908, quoted in Hendricks and Shepard, *Letters from Jack London,* 260–61.

CHAPTER 10

1. This and other quotes concerning the final stage of the *Snark* voyage come from an unpublished, typed version of the journal Charmian prepared as a long round-robin letter for friends. The heading is "Mt. Royal Hotel, Brown's River, Kingston Reach, Tasmania, January 22, 1909," but provides a day-by-day account from 4 October 1908 up to the end of that year, along with some notes on earlier experiences in the Solomons. This material was viewed at the Jack London Ranch and is now at HEH.

2. CKL, unpublished notes, 26 November 1908, HEH.

3. CKL, unpublished *Snark* journal and round-robin letter sent from Australia, HEH.

4. *Oakland Tribune,* 22 April 1909.

5. JL to Bess London, 27 October 1908, quoted in Hendricks and Shepard, *Letters from Jack London,* 267–71.

6. *Oakland Tribune,* 25 June 1910.

7. Netta Eames to JL, 21 February 1909, ML.

8. JL to William English Walling, 30 November 1909, quoted in Hendricks and Shepard, *Letters from Jack London,* 289–90.

9. JL to Rev. Charles Brown, 5 June 1910, quoted in Hendricks and Shepard, *Letters from Jack London,* 306–8. London sent a copy of this letter to *The Workingman's Paper* to prove he had not abandoned socialism.

10. JL, *Burning Daylight,* chap. 15.

11. JL, *Burning Daylight,* chap. 22.

12. George Wharton James, "A Study of Jack London in his Prime," *Overland Monthly* 69(1917): 361.

13. Finn Froelich, interview by Irving Stone, UCLA.

14. Mrs. Robert Hill, interview by Irving Stone, UCLA.

15. For more about this difficult time, see letters from CKL to Blanche Partington, 26 August 1909, 3 September 1909, 1 October 1909, BL.

16. For George's view of this trip, see James Henry, *Give a Man a Boat He Can Sail,* 1980.

17. JL to CKL, n.d., Stone collection, UCLA.

18. CKL, *Book of Jack London,* 2:184.

19. JL, *Burning Daylight,* chap. 26.

20. CKL to "Fannie," 1 July 1910, HEH. Charmian corresponded with at least three different Fannies; the specific woman here is unknown.

21. *Oakland Tribune,* 22 June 1910.

22. JL to Judge George Samuels, 29 July 1910, quoted in Hendricks and Shepard, *Letters from Jack London,* 314–15.

23. These and similar articles can be found in the Jack London scrapbooks, HEH.

CHAPTER 11

1. JL, *Revolution and Other Essays.*

2. JL, quoted in Haughey and Johnson, 1985: 13.

3. JL to editor, *Pacific Rural Press,* 1 October 1911, HEH.

4. For a more extensive discussion of how later biographers misrepresented London on this issue, along with more specifics on the scientific issues in eucalyptus silviculture, see Stasz, "Jack London and Eucalyptus."

5. The historical references in this section are discussed in more detail in Gayle M. Groenendaal, "Eucalyptus Helped Solve

a Timber Problem: 1853–1880," *Proceedings of a Workshop on Eucalyptus in California, June 14–16, 1983, Sacramento, California,* General Technical Report PSW-69, Richard B. Standiford and Thomas F. Ledig, technical coordinators (Berkeley, CA: Pacific Southwest Forest and Range Experiment Station, Forest Service, U.S. Department of Agriculture), 1–8.

6. The subsequent discussion is based on letters from JL to W. A. T. Stratton between 7 January 1910 (misdated 7 January 1909) and 22 May 1911, HEH.

7. The eucalyptus material is found among the files of ranch papers in the London collection, HEH.

8. Using a very low estimate of twenty trees planted per hour, the cost of labor comes out to only $164. If the land were already cleared, the planting would go more quickly during the rainy season, when the ground can be worked easily. The labor would be more expensive if acreage needed clearing. Even so, the expense was not a great one compared to the cost of livestock. For example, a pair of serviceable work mares, and Jack was to have more than a dozen, ran from $550 to $700. See correspondence, JL and Ernest Matthews, who served as an agent to buy horses for London during 1911, HEH. These letters again show that London was not fully knowledgeable about a product before purchasing it during the early ranch years.

9. "Jack London Plants More Eucalyptus Trees," *Santa Rosa Press Democrat,* 8 April 1914. It is possible London changed suppliers or that later correspondence with Stratton is missing. This seems unlikely, as he also fails to mention eucalyptus planting in later letters to people he kept well informed about his ranch activities, such as George Brett of Macmillan.

10. JL to William Ellsworth, 7 September 1912, quoted in Hendricks and Shepard, *Letters from Jack London,* 363.

11. John J. Welch to JL, 29 July 1910, 3 August 1910; JL to Welch, 12 August 1910, 7 December 1910, HEH. The American Corporation for Investors brochure is also at HEH.

12. JL, "Navigating Four Horses North of the Bay," *Sunset,* November 1911.

13. JL to Bess Maddern, 8 January 1911, quoted in Hendricks and Shepard, *Letters from Jack London,* 329–31.

CHAPTER 12

1. No point drew more extensive and impassioned criticism from London experts reading the draft of this book than my discussions of alcohol. Indeed, the pressure of these individuals has been so strong that in the earliest versions of the book I accepted their stand that London did not have a drinking problem. Upon investigating the evidence, notably Charmian's diaries and firsthand accounts from his friends, I believe their objections are no longer credible.

2. Oliver Madox Hueffer, "Jack London: A Personal Sketch," *The Living Age*, 13 January 1917, 124.

3. This episode is described in detail in Joan London, "Jack London with His Daughters."

4. Becky London, quoted in Kingman, *Pictorial Life of Jack London*, 228.

5. George Sterling to JL, 27 February 1911, 14 December 1911, 17 December 1911, 6 September 1912, HEH.

6. *New York Call*, 31 December 1911.

7. JL to George Brett, 26 October 1911, quoted in Hendricks and Shepard, *Letters from Jack London*, 355.

8. Joseph Noel, chap. 21. Noel's recollections of London have often been attacked because he was angry and hurt after the collapse of the Millergraph company. Although his book does suffer from a "get-him-now-that-he's-dead" tone, it remains the only first-person account of this period in New York and is validated by comments in Charmian's diaries.

9. *New York Evening World*, 6 January 1912, 10 January 1912.

10. George Sterling to JL, 13 February 1912, BL.

11. CKL to Blanche Partington, 20 January 1912, BL.

12. Joseph Noel, 220–21.

13. London describes the White Logic in detail in *John Barleycorn*, chap. 35.

14. JL, *John Barleycorn*, chap. 29.

15. JL, *John Barleycorn*, chap. 34.

16. JL, *John Barleycorn*, chap. 36.

17. *John Barleycorn* is recommended to AA members today as a valuable resource, further indication of the perspicacity of London's analysis.

18. This section is based on Charmian's typed journal of the *Dirigo*, available at HEH. A much-abridged version of this appears in CKL, "Diary of *Dirigo.*" Charmian long intended to prepare a book with this material but was never successful in producing a finished draft.

19. CKL, *Dirigo* journal, 10 April 1912, HEH.

20. CKL, *Dirigo* journal, 30 April 1912, HEH.

CHAPTER 13

1. Finn Froelich, interview by Irving Stone, UCLA.

2. Allan Dunn, "The Sailing of the Snark," *Sunset,* May 1907, 3–9.

3. JL, *Burning Daylight,* chap. 35.

4. Unidentified article quoted at length in CKL, *Book of Jack London* 2:273–74.

5. JL to Fred Berry, 26 June 1913, quoted in Hendricks and Shepard, *Letters from Jack London,* 388–89.

6. The Kasper correspondence is split between BL, which contains Charmian London's letters, and HEH, which has the letters between Jack and Kasper.

7. This comment is from Hamburg's condolence letter to CKL after Jack's death, 11 December 1916, HEH.

8. JL to CKL, inscription in *Smoke Bellew.*

9. JL to CKL, 17 November 1912, ML.

10. JL to CKL, 19 November 1912, ML.

11. *San Francisco Call,* 25 June 1913.

12. JL to Roland Phillips, 14 March 1913, quoted in Hendricks and Shepard, *Letters from Jack London,* 374–75.

13. CKL to Blanche Partington, 4 December 1914, BL.

14. CKL to Anna Strunsky, 14 November 1913, ML.

CHAPTER 14

1. JL to Joan London, 24 August 1913, quoted in Hendricks and Shepard, *Letters from Jack London,* 394.

2. See conclusion of Joan London's "Jack London with His Daughters."

3. JL to Joan London, 24 February 1914, quoted in Hendricks and Shepard, *Letters from Jack London,* 414–17.

4. JL to Eliza Shepard, 22 February 1912, quoted in Hendricks and Shepard, *Letters from Jack London,* 362.

5. Sydney Ayres to JL, 10 January 1913, HEH.

6. JL to Charles Menges, 6 June 1913, quoted in Hendricks and Shepard, *Letters from Jack London,* 386–87.

7. H. N. Horkheimer to JL, 6 June 1913, HEH.

8. JL to H. N. Horkheimer, 30 June 1913, HEH.

9. H. N. Horkheimer to JL, 1 July 1913, HEH.

10. JL to H. N. Horkheimer, 7 July 1913, HEH.

11. Hobart Bosworth, "My Jack London," *Mark Twain Quarterly,* Fall/Winter 1949, 3.

12. JL to George Brett, 7 October 1913, quoted in Hendricks and Shepard, *Letters from Jack London,* 403–4.

13. See, for example, Frank Garbutt to JL, 23 September 1914, HEH.

14. Frank Garbutt to JL, 2 March 1914, HEH.

15. Frank Garbutt to Edwin K. Gordon, 19 July 1914, HEH.

16. The movies were based upon *The Sea Wolf, John Barleycorn, The Valley of the Moon, Martin Eden,* "An Odyssey of the North," *Burning Daylight* in two separate parts, and *Smoke Bellew.*

17. Ralph Kasper to CKL, 6 April 1914, 14 July 1914, 13 September 1914, 2 April 1915, BL.

18. JL to CKL, c. 30 January 1914, ML.

19. JL to CKL, 29 January 1914, ML.

20. See the correspondence between Jack and lawyer Arthur Train (HEH) during this time for an obvious example of London's inability to think his side through clearly. He so harangues Train, who is apparently doing a competent job, that the lawyer finally withdraws from the case.

21. London's articles include "The Red Game of War," *Collier's Weekly,* 16 May 1914; "Mexico's Armies and Ours," *Collier's Weekly,* 30 May 1914; "Trouble Makers of Mexico," *Collier's Weekly,* 13 June 1914; "Our Adventures in Tampico," *Collier's Weekly,* 27 June 1914.

22. Michael Killian, "Villa Rides and Fights," *Chicago Tribune,* 10 March 1987.

23. As quoted in Foner, 118.
24. As quoted in Foner, 118.
25. As quoted in Foner, 119.

CHAPTER 15

1. JL, *Before Adam,* chap. 1.
2. JL to Roland Phillips, 26 March 1914, quoted in Hendricks and Shepard, *Letters from Jack London,* 418.
3. JL, *Star Rover,* chap. 21.
4. JL, *Star Rover,* chap. 14.
5. London collected many books on Christian history and marked them up. Mary Magdalene particularly interested him, and he had originally planned to give her a large role in his "Christ Story," but she plays none in *The Star Rover.*
6. JL, *Star Rover,* chap. 17.
7. Netta Eames Payne Springer to JL, 11 July 1914, HEH.
8. JL to Netta Eames Payne Springer, 8 July 1914, 12 July 1914, HEH.
9. George's letters from Sag Harbor refer to young male hangers-on. Friends of George contacted in the late 1930s by Cyril Clemmens also intimated he was bisexual.
10. This quote is evidence to dispute other biographers' claims that Charmian was angry when Byrne was brought on, because it was Jack's way of cutting Charmian off. Quite the opposite was occurring. Jack wanted to give Charmian the assistance she deserved. Byrne handled only the most perfunctory correspondence, while Charmian continued to handle Jack's manuscripts and important letters, and was his only assistant during the long absences from the ranch.
11. Ruth Tabrah, *Hawaii: A Bicentennial History* (New York: Norton, 1980), 133.
12. CKL, *Our Hawaii,* 292.
13. CKL to Anna Strunsky, n.d., HEH.
14. Both books have been discounted as mere dog stories by critics. For a contrary view, see Tony Williams, *"Jerry of the Islands* and *Michael, Brother of Jerry," Jack London Newsletter* 17 (1984): 28–60. Williams shows how these works reiterate themes found

throughout London's opus: the oppression of workers, initiation through trial, the edenic escape to Sonoma, and others. One change is London's recognition that oppression affects the elderly and animals as it does workers.

15. CKL, *Book of Jack London*, 2:317.

16. CKL to Anna Strunsky, 18 May 1915, ML.

17. Charmian saved her reviews in her scrapbooks, Hendricks and Shepard, *Letters from Jack London*, 460–61.

18. JL to Elthelda Hesser, 21 September 1916, Hendricks and Shepard, Letters from Jack London, 460–61.

CHAPTER 16

1. The story is found in the collection of short stories with the same title.

2. CKL, *Our Hawaii: Islands and Islanders*, 338.

3. JL to G. Frank Lydston, 26 March 1914, quoted in Hendricks and Shepard, *Letters from Jack London*, 419.

4. CKL, *Book of Jack London*, 2:325.

5. George mentioned this possibility in a letter to Margaret Cobb, 5 September 1923, HEH. See also Noel, *Footloose in Arcadia*, 271–73, who says George told him the woman was English, and Jack had known her a long time. One day on the Jack London Ranch I came across a packet of dining charts Charmian used to record her guests during the final Hawaiian trip. These showed no pattern suggesting a particular woman, and from her diaries, it is hard to believe Jack was going off without her knowledge. There is none of the suspicious pattern recorded during the New York stay preceding the *Dirigo* voyage.

    All evidence suggests that George's rumor was either a misunderstanding or a malicious, neurotic expression. He remained on affectionate terms with Charmian after Jack's death while spreading the rumor. In 1918, she learned of his gossip and grew cool. However, she hired him to help her edit *The Book of Jack London* because she knew he needed the money, and did not let on she was aware of his bad-mouthing. After George died, Charmian published a fond and perceptive analysis of his character, in effect forgiving him for his unseemly side, because he could not help himself. See CKL, "George Sterling—As I Knew Him," *Overland Monthly and Out West Magazine*, March 1927, 1–7.

6. CKL, *Book of Jack London*, 2:348.

7. For Jack's resignation letter, a segment of the party's response, and this personal reflection by Jack, see Foner, *Jack London: American Rebel*, 123–28.

8. Sophie Irene Loeb to JL, 25 September 1906, HEH. Following Jack's death, Charmian visited Loeb in New York and learned that more had been going on during the visits than she had realized at the time. It could have been then that Loeb confessed the affair.

9. Finn Froelich, interview by Irving Stone, UCLA. It is interesting in light of this interview that Stone claims in his book that Jack was trying to find a woman who would give him a son. This charge makes even less sense given that in the mass of both private and public statements made by Jack London, an interest in children is virtually absent. The adults in his novels are not parents. Jack's desire to have children was revealed only during the brief time of Bess's first pregnancy and Charmian's pregnancies. He showed none of the mania for male progeny some biographers claim.

10. CKL to Cloudesley Johns, 22 December 1916, HEH.

EPILOGUE

1. CKL, Autobiographical Notes, HEH.

SELECT BIBLIOGRAPHY

1. WORKS BY CHARMIAN KITTREDGE LONDON

The Log of the Snark. New York: Macmillan, 1915. (British editions published by Mills and Boon are entitled *Jack London in the Southern Seas, Voyaging in Wild Seas,* and *A Woman Among the Head Hunters.*)

Our Hawaii. New York: Macmillan, 1917. (British edition published by Mills and Boon is entitled *Jack London and Hawaii.*)

The Book of Jack London, 2 vols. New York: Century, 1921. (British edition published by Mills and Boon is entitled *Jack London.*)

Our Hawaii: Islands and Islanders. New York: Macmillan, 1922. (Also referred to as *Our Hawaii, Revised Edition,* which is a misnomer, as the majority of material is new. British edition published by Mills and Boon is entitled *The New Hawaii.*)

"Diary of *Dirigo.*" In *The Sewall Ships of Steel,* Ed., Mark W. Hennessy, Augusta, ME: Kennebac Journal Press, 1937: 582–600.

"Jack London Afloat." *Sunset,* 1903: 190–91.

"Cross-Saddle Riding for Women." *Out West* 21 (1904): 27–37.

2. BOOKS BY JACK LONDON

The Son of the Wolf. Boston: Houghton Mifflin, 1900.

The God of His Fathers. New York: McClure, Phillips, 1901.

Children of the Frost. New York: Macmillan, 1902.

The Cruise of the Dazzler. New York: Century, 1902.

A Daughter of the Snows. Philadelphia: J. B. Lippincott, 1902.

The Kempton-Wace Letters (with Anna Strunsky). New York: Macmillan, 1903.

The Call of the Wild. New York: Macmillan, 1903.

The People of the Abyss. New York: Macmillan, 1903.

The Faith of Men. New York: Macmillan, 1904.

The Sea Wolf. New York: Macmillan, 1904.

War of the Classes. New York: Macmillan, 1905.

The Game. New York: Macmillan, 1905.

Tales of the Fish Patrol. New York: Macmillan, 1905.

Moon-Face and Other Stories. New York: Macmillan, 1906.

White Fang. New York: Macmillan, 1906.

Before Adam. New York: Macmillan, 1907.

Love of Life and Other Stories. New York: Macmillan, 1907.

The Iron Heel. New York: Macmillan, 1908.

Martin Eden. New York: Macmillan, 1909.

Lost Face. New York: Macmillan, 1910.
Revolution and Other Essays. New York: Macmillan, 1910.
Burning Daylight. New York: Macmillan, 1910.
When God Laughs and Other Stories. New York: Macmillan, 1911.
South Sea Tales. New York: Macmillan, 1911.
The House of Pride and Other Stories. New York: Macmillan, 1912.
A Son of the Sun. Garden City, NY: Doubleday, Page, 1912.
Smoke Bellew. New York: Century, 1912.
The Night-Born. New York: Century, 1913.
The Abysmal Brute. New York: Century, 1913.
John Barleycorn. New York: Century, 1913.
The Valley of the Moon. New York: Macmillan, 1913.
The Strength of the Strong. New York: Macmillan, 1914.
The Mutiny of the Elsinore. New York: Macmillan, 1914.
The Scarlet Plague. New York: Macmillan, 1915.
The Star Rover. New York: Macmillan, 1915.
The Little Lady of the Big House. New York: Macmillan, 1916.
The Turtles of Tasman. New York: Macmillan, 1916.
The Human Drift. New York: Macmillan, 1917.
Jerry of the Islands. New York: Macmillan, 1917.
Michael Brother of Jerry. New York: Macmillan, 1917.
The Red One. New York: Macmillan, 1918.
On the Makaloa Mat. New York: Macmillan, 1919.
Hearts of Three. New York: Macmillan, 1920.
Dutch Courage and Other Stories. New York: Macmillan, 1922.

3. WORKS ON JACK AND CHARMIAN LONDON

Atherton, Frank. "Jack London in Boyhood Adventures." Unpublished. Rohnert Park, CA: Reuben Salazar Library, Sonoma State University, n.d.
Bamford, Georgia Loring. *The Mystery of Jack London.* Oakland, CA: Piedmont Press, 1931.
Bosworth, Hobart. "My Jack London." *Mark Twain Quarterly* 5 (1943): 2–5, 24.
Day, A. Grove. *Jack London in the South Seas.* New York: Four Winds Press, 1971.
Etulain, Richard W. *Jack London on the Road.* Logan, UT: Utah State University Press, 1979.
Foner, Philip S. *Jack London: American Rebel.* New York: Citadel Press, 1947.
Haughey, Homer L. and Connie Kale Johnson. *Jack London Ranch Album.* Stockton, CA: Heritage Publishing, 1985.
———. *Jack London Homes Album.* Stockton, CA: Heritage Publishing, 1987.
Hendricks, King, and Irving Shepard. *Letters from Jack London.* New York: Odyssey Press, 1965.
Johnson, Martin. *Through the South Seas with Jack London.* New York: Dodd, Mead, 1913.
Johnston, Carolyn. *Jack London—An American Radical?* Westport, CT: Greenwood Press, 1984.
Kingman, Russ. *A Pictorial Life of Jack London.* New York: Crown, 1979.
Labor, Earle. *Jack London.* New York: Twayne, 1974.
Lachtman, Howard. "Jack and George: Notes on a Literary Friendship." *Pacific Historian* 22(1978): 27–42.
London, Joan. *Jack London and His Times.* Garden City, NY: Doubleday, 1939.

———. "Jack London with His Daughters." Unpublished. Glen Ellen, CA: Jack London Research Center, n.d.

McClintock, James I. *White Logic: Jack London's Short Stories.* Cedar Springs, MI: Wolf House Books, 1976.

Martin, Stoddard. *California Writers: Jack London, John Steinbeck, the Tough Guys.* New York: St. Martin's Press, 1983.

O'Connor, Richard. *Jack London: A Biography.* Boston: Little, Brown, 1964.

Shivers, Alfred S. "Jack London: Not a Suicide." *Dalhousie Review* 49 (1969): 43–57.

Sinclair, Andrew. *Jack: A Biography of Jack London.* New York: Harper and Row, 1977.

Stasz, Clarice. "Androgeny in the Novels of Jack London." *Western American Literature* 11(1976): 212–33.

———. "Charmian London as a Writer." *Jack London Newsletter* 11(1978): 20–28.

———. "Jack London and Eucalyptus: Not a Folly." *Jack London Newsletter,* in press.

———. "The Social Construction of Biography: The Case of Jack London." *Modern Fiction Studies* 22(1976): 51–71.

Stone, Irving. *Sailor on Horseback.* Boston: Houghton Mifflin, 1938.

Walker, Dale. "Letters from Joan London." *Pacific Historian* 22(1978): 12–26.

Walker, Dale, and James E. Sisson, III. *The Fiction of Jack London.* El Paso, TX: Texas Western Press, 1972.

Walker, Franklin. *Jack London and the Klondike.* San Marino, CA: Huntington Library, 1966.

Watson, Charles N., Jr. *The Novels of Jack London: A Reappraisal.* Madison, WI: University of Wisconsin, 1983.

4. BOOKS AND ARTICLES ON THE TIMES

Austin, Mary. *Earth Horizon.* New York: Houghton Mifflin, 1932.

Bagwell, Beth. *Oakland: The Story of a City.* Novato: Presidio, 1982.

Benediktsson, Thomas Einar. "The Life of George Sterling." Unpublished Ph.D. dissertation, University of Washington, 1974.

Buchanan, Agnes Foster. "The Story of a Famous Fraternity of Writers and Artists." *Pacific Monthly* 17 (1907): 65–83.

de Ford, Miriam Allen. *They Were San Franciscans.* Caldwell, ID: Caxton Printers, 1941.

Degler, Carl. *At Odds: Women and the Family from the American Revolution to the Present.* New York: Oxford University Press, 1980.

Dubbert, Joe I. *A Man's Place: Masculinity in Transition.* Englewood Cliffs, NJ: Prentice-Hall, 1979.

Filene, Peter Gabriel. *Him/Her/Self.* New York: New American Library, 1974.

Genthe, Arnold. *As I Remember.* New York: John Day, 1941.

Goldman, Emma. *Living My Life.* New York: Knopf, 1931.

Henry, George. *Give a Man a Boat He Can Sail.* Detroit: Harlo, 1980.

Lewis, Oscar. *Bay Window Bohemia.* Garden City, NY: Doubleday, 1956.

Mood, Fulmer. "An Astrologer from Down East." *New England Quarterly* 5 (1932): 769–99.

Noel, Joseph. *Footloose in Arcadia.* New York: Carrick and Evans, 1940.

Sochen, June. *Herstory.* New York: Alfred, 1974.

Starr, Kevin. *Americans and the California Dream.* New York: Oxford University Press, 1973.

Sullivan, Mark. *Our Times: The United States 1900–1925,* 3 vols. New York: Charles Scribner's Sons, 1927.

Walker, Franklin. *San Francisco's Literary Frontier.* New York: Knopf, 1939.

———. *The Seacoast of Bohemia.* Santa Barbara, CA: Peregrine Smith, 1973.

5. WORKS ON FAMILY DYNAMICS

Black, Claudia. *It Will Never Happen to Me.* Denver: Medical Administration Company, 1981.

Bowlby, John. *Loss.* New York: Basic Books, 1980.

Miller, Alice. *The Drama of the Gifted Child.* New York: Harper and Row, 1981.

Norwood, Robin. *Women Who Love Too Much.* Los Angeles: Tarcher, 1985.

Peck, M. Scott. *People of the Lie.* New York: Simon and Schuster, 1983.

———. *The Road Less Travelled.* New York: Simon and Schuster, 1984.

Satir, Virginia. *Peoplemaking.* Palo Alto, CA: Science and Behavior Books, 1972.

Whitfield, Charles L. *Healing the Child Within.* Baltimore, MD: The Resource Group, 1986.

INDEX